Nanobiotechnology

AI and IoT Applications and Emerging Implications

Dr. Alok Kumar Srivastav
Dr. Priyanka Das

Apress®

Nanobiotechnology: AI and IoT Applications and Emerging Implications

Dr. Alok Kumar Srivastav
Department of Health Science
University of the People
Pasadena, California, USA

Dr. Priyanka Das
Department of Health Science
University of the People
Pasadena, California, USA

ISBN-13 (pbk): 979-8-8688-1774-8
https://doi.org/10.1007/979-8-8688-1775-5

ISBN-13 (electronic): 979-8-8688-1775-5

Copyright © 2025 by Dr. Alok Kumar Srivastav, Dr. Priyanka Das

This work is subject to copyright. All rights are reserved by the Publisher, whether the whole or part of the material is concerned, specifically the rights of translation, reprinting, reuse of illustrations, recitation, broadcasting, reproduction on microfilms or in any other physical way, and transmission or information storage and retrieval, electronic adaptation, computer software, or by similar or dissimilar methodology now known or hereafter developed.

Trademarked names, logos, and images may appear in this book. Rather than use a trademark symbol with every occurrence of a trademarked name, logo, or image we use the names, logos, and images only in an editorial fashion and to the benefit of the trademark owner, with no intention of infringement of the trademark.

The use in this publication of trade names, trademarks, service marks, and similar terms, even if they are not identified as such, is not to be taken as an expression of opinion as to whether or not they are subject to proprietary rights.

While the advice and information in this book are believed to be true and accurate at the date of publication, neither the authors nor the editors nor the publisher can accept any legal responsibility for any errors or omissions that may be made. The publisher makes no warranty, express or implied, with respect to the material contained herein.

Managing Director, Apress Media LLC: Welmoed Spahr
Acquisitions Editor: Spandana Chatterjee
Editorial Assistant: Gryffin Winkler

Cover designed by eStudioCalamar

Cover image designed by Freepik (www.freepik.com)

Distributed to the book trade worldwide by Springer Science+Business Media New York, 1 New York Plaza, New York, NY 10004. Phone 1-800-SPRINGER, fax (201) 348-4505, e-mail orders-ny@springer-sbm.com, or visit www.springeronline.com. Apress Media, LLC is a Delaware LLC and the sole member (owner) is Springer Science + Business Media Finance Inc (SSBM Finance Inc). SSBM Finance Inc is a **Delaware** corporation.

For information on translations, please e-mail booktranslations@springernature.com; for reprint, paperback, or audio rights, please e-mail bookpermissions@springernature.com.

Apress titles may be purchased in bulk for academic, corporate, or promotional use. eBook versions and licenses are also available for most titles. For more information, reference our Print and eBook Bulk Sales web page at http://www.apress.com/bulk-sales.

Any source code or other supplementary material referenced by the author in this book is available to readers on GitHub. For more detailed information, please visit https://www.apress.com/gp/services/source-code.

If disposing of this product, please recycle the paper

To my family and friends, whose unwavering support and encouragement have been my guiding light throughout this journey. Your belief in me has been the foundation upon which this work stands.

To my students, whose curiosity and enthusiasm inspire every page I write.

And to those who seek to understand the world through both science and faith, may this book contribute to your journey of discovery and wonder.

—Dr. Alok Kumar Srivastav

Table of Contents

About the Authors xix

About the Technical Reviewer xxi

Acknowledgments xxiii

Introduction xxv

Chapter 1: Introduction to Nanobiotechnology 1

1.1 Historical Background of Nanotechnology 1

1.2 Evolution of Nanobiotechnology 3

1.3 Core Concepts and Terminology 5

1.4 Key Application Areas 8

    Medical Applications 8

    Agricultural Applications 9

    Environmental Applications 9

    Industrial Bioprocessing 11

1.5 Emerging Trends and Prospects 11

1.6 Role of AI and IoT in Nanobiotechnology 15

1.7 Summary 18

Chapter 2: Nanomaterials and Their Properties 21

2.1 Types of Nanomaterials 21

    Dimensionality-Based Classification 22

    Composition-Based Classification 23

    Morphology-Based Classification 24

2.2 Physical and Chemical Properties 25

    Surface Effects and Surface-to-Volume Ratio 25

    Quantum Confinement Effects 26

TABLE OF CONTENTS

    Mechanical Properties 27
    Thermal Properties 28
    Chemical Properties 28

  2.3 Application-Based Classification 30
    Energy Applications 31
    Characterization and Standardization Challenges 31
    Safety and Environmental Challenges 32
    Regulatory and Commercialization Challenges 34
    Integration Challenges 35

  2.4 AI and IoT in Nanomaterials Analysis 37
    AI-Driven Nanomaterial Discovery and Design 37
    IoT Integration in Nanomaterial Synthesis and Characterization 38
    High-Throughput Experimentation and Automation 40
    Advanced Analytics for Nanomaterial Characterization 41
    Future Directions and Challenges 44

  2.5 Summary 46

Chapter 3: Cellular Nanostructures and Biomolecular Motors 47

  3.1 Overview of Cellular Nanostructures 47
  3.2 Functions of Biomolecular Motors 50
  3.3 Nanopores and Uses 53
  3.4 Bio-inspired Structures 56
  3.5 Technological Significance 60
  3.6 Summary 62

Chapter 4: Nanomaterial Synthesis 65

  4.1 Introduction 65
  4.2 Physical Synthesis Techniques 66
    Mechanical Milling and Ball Milling 66
    Laser Ablation 67
    Physical Vapor Deposition (PVD) 67
    Inert Gas Condensation 69

4.3 Chemical Synthesis Methods 69
Sol-Gel Processing 69
Chemical Precipitation and Co-precipitation 70
Hydrothermal and Solvothermal Synthesis 70
Chemical Vapor Deposition (CVD) 70
4.4 Biological Synthesis Approaches 71
Microorganism-Mediated Synthesis 71
Plant-Mediated Synthesis 72
Biomolecule-Assisted Synthesis 72
4.5 Hybrid Nanocomposites 73
4.6 Advanced Synthesis Technologies 73
Microfluidic and Continuous Flow Synthesis 73
Electrospinning and Electrospraying 74
Atomic and Molecular Layer Deposition 74
3D Printing at the Nanoscale 74
4.7 Summary 74

Chapter 5: Characterization of Nanomaterials 77
5.1 Introduction 77
5.2 Optical Techniques 78
Introduction to Optical Characterization 78
UV-Visible Spectroscopy 79
Photoluminescence Spectroscopy 80
Surface-Enhanced Raman Spectroscopy (SERS) 80
Optical Microscopy Techniques 81
5.3 X-ray Diffraction 82
Principles of X-ray Diffraction 82
Powder X-ray Diffraction 83
Small-Angle X-ray Scattering (SAXS) 84
Grazing Incidence X-ray Diffraction (GIXRD) 84

TABLE OF CONTENTS

    5.4 Electron Microscopy 86
        Transmission Electron Microscopy (TEM) 86
        Scanning Electron Microscopy (SEM) 87
        Scanning Transmission Electron Microscopy (STEM) 88
        Environmental and In Situ Electron Microscopy 88
    5.5 Size and Surface Analysis 90
        Dynamic Light Scattering (DLS) 90
        Zeta Potential Analysis 91
        Brunauer-Emmett-Teller (BET) Surface Area Analysis 92
        Atomic Force Microscopy (AFM) 93
    5.6 Method Comparison 96
        Complementary Nature of Characterization Techniques 96
        Selection Criteria for Characterization Methods 98
        Multi-technique Characterization Strategies 98
        Limitations and Challenges in Nanomaterial Characterization 99
        Future Directions in Nanomaterial Characterization 100
    5.7 Summary 101

Chapter 6: Thin Films and Colloidal Nanostructures 103
    6.1 Introduction to Thin Films 103
    6.2 Synthesis and Characterization 105
        Synthesis Methods for Thin Films 105
        Synthesis of Colloidal Nanostructures 106
        Characterization Techniques 107
    6.3 Colloidal Structure Dynamics 109
    6.4 Applications in Medicine and Electronics 113
        Medical Applications 114
        Diagnostic Applications 114
        Therapeutic Applications 115
        Electronic Applications 116
        Semiconductor Devices 116

Energy Applications 118

Display Technologies 119

6.5 Future Trends 120

Advanced Manufacturing Techniques 120

Novel Material Systems 121

Sustainability Considerations 122

Convergence with Other Technologies 123

Emerging Application Areas 124

Ethical and Regulatory Considerations 124

6.6 AI and IoT in Applications 126

AI-Enhanced Materials Discovery and Optimization 126

IoT Integration with Nanomaterial-Based Sensors 127

Edge Computing and In-Sensor Processing 128

Digital Twins and Predictive Modeling 129

Challenges and Opportunities 130

6.7 Summary 131

Chapter 7: Self-Assembly and Nanovesicles 133

7.1 Fundamentals of Self-Assembly 133

7.2 Nanovesicles and Mechanisms 136

7.3 Types: Nanospheres and Nanocapsules 139

7.4 Characterization Methods 142

7.5 Applications in Biotechnology 145

7.6 Summary 149

Chapter 8: Nanoparticles for Drug Delivery 151

8.1 Nanoparticles in Therapeutics 151

Introduction to Therapeutic Nanoparticles 151

Types of Therapeutic Nanoparticles 152

Clinical Applications and Current Market Status 152

TABLE OF CONTENTS

8.2 Optimization of Properties 153
- Physical Properties Optimization 153
- Chemical Surface Modifications 153
- Targeting Strategies 154

8.3 Cellular Entry Strategies 155
- Mechanisms of Cellular Uptake 155
- Endosomal Escape Strategies 156
- Intracellular Trafficking and Subcellular Targeting 156

8.4 Anatomical Permeability 157
- Blood-Brain Barrier Penetration 157
- Tumor Penetration Dynamics 157
- Epithelial and Endothelial Barriers 158

8.5 Future Prospects 159
- Emerging Delivery Platforms 159
- Personalized Nanomedicine Approaches 159

8.6 AI and IoT Integration 160
- AI-Guided Nanoparticle Design 160
- Smart Nanotherapeutic Systems 160
- IoT-Connected Nanomedicine Platforms 161

8.7 Summary 162

Chapter 9: Nanoparticles in Diagnostics and Imaging 163

9.1 Introduction 163

9.2 Theranostic Technologies 164
- Multifunctional Nanoparticle Platforms 164
- Clinical Translation Challenges 165

9.3 Stimuli-Responsive Systems 166
- Types of Responsive Mechanisms 166

9.4 Cancer Therapeutics 168
- Nanoparticles in Cancer Detection 168
- Therapeutic Applications 169
- Future Directions 170

9.5 Biosensor Devices 171
    Nanomaterial-Enhanced Biosensing 172

9.6 Innovative Imaging Approaches 175
    Multimodal Imaging Nanoparticles 175
    Advanced Contrast Enhancement Strategies 176
    Molecular and Cellular Imaging 176

9.7 AI and IoT in Diagnostics 178
    AI-Enhanced Nanodiagnostics 178
    IoT-Connected Diagnostic Systems 178
    Integrated Diagnostic Ecosystems 179

9.8 Summary 180

Chapter 10: Nanobiocatalysts and Their Applications 183

10.1 Concept of Nanobiocatalysis 183

10.2 Development Strategies 185
    Immobilization Techniques 185
    Material Selection Considerations 187
    Fabrication Approaches 187
    Design Optimization 188

10.3 Role in Drug Production 189
    Applications in Pharmaceutical Synthesis 189
    Industrial Benefits 191

10.4 Use of Nanoscaffolds 192
    Types of Nanoscaffolds 192
    Design Principles for Nanoscaffolds 193
    Enzyme-Nanoscaffold Interactions 195
    Advanced Nanoscaffold Systems 196

10.5 Future Insights 197
    Emerging Materials and Architectures 197
    Advances in Enzyme Engineering for Nanobiocatalysis 198
    Nanobiocatalysis in Emerging Applications 199
    Technological Challenges and Solutions 200

TABLE OF CONTENTS

10.6 AI and IoT Optimization 201
    AI-Driven Nanobiocatalyst Design 201
    IoT Integration for Process Monitoring and Control 202
    Cloud-Based Data Analytics for Nanobiocatalysis 203
    Intelligent Optimization Strategies 204
    Implementation Challenges and Solutions 205
10.7 Summary 206

Chapter 11: Environmental and Health Impacts of Nanomaterials 209

11.1 Environmental Fate 209
    Introduction to Environmental Fate 209
    Transport Mechanisms in Different Environmental Media 210
    Transformation Processes and Persistence 211
11.2 Toxicity Basics 212
    Fundamental Principles of Nanotoxicology 212
    Biological Interactions at the Nanoscale 213
    Dose Metrics and Exposure Considerations 214
11.3 Assessment Models 216
    Predictive Toxicology Approaches 216
    In Vitro and In Vivo Model Systems 217
    Risk Assessment Frameworks 218
11.4 Lifecycle Studies 220
    Cradle-to-Grave Analysis Approaches 220
    Release Scenarios and Exposure Pathways 221
    Environmental and Economic Impact Metrics 222
11.5 Containment Measures 224
    Engineering Controls for Manufacturing Environments 224
    Product Design for Minimized Release 225
    Waste Management Strategies 226
11.6 AI and IoT for Monitoring 228
    Sensor Technologies for Nanomaterial Detection 228
    Integration with Artificial Intelligence Systems 229

    Real-Time Monitoring Networks 230

    Practical Applications and Case Studies 233

  11.7 Summary 234

Chapter 12: Ecotoxicology and Lifecycle Assessment 237

  12.1 Introduction to Ecotoxicology 237

  12.2 Testing Models and Assays 240

    Standardized Testing Frameworks 240

    Challenges in Nanomaterial Testing 241

    Emerging Testing Approaches 242

    Tiered Testing Approaches 242

  12.3 Environmental Interaction 243

    Environmental Release and Transport 243

    Ecosystem-Specific Behaviors and Impacts 245

    Ecological Risk Assessment Considerations 247

    Analytical Challenges and Solutions 248

  12.4 Lifecycle Methods 249

    Fundamentals of Lifecycle Assessment for Nanomaterials 249

    Challenges in Nanomaterial LCA 250

    Methodological Approaches and Adaptations 251

    Uncertainty of LCA for Nanomaterials 251

    Case Examples and Comparative Studies 252

    Integrating LCA with Risk Assessment 254

    Future Directions in Nanomaterial LCA 255

  12.5 Regulatory Overview 255

    Current Regulatory Frameworks 256

    Challenges in Regulatory Implementation 258

    Emerging Regulatory Approaches 260

    Stakeholder Perspectives and Influence 261

    Future Regulatory Directions 262

TABLE OF CONTENTS

12.6 AI and IoT in Ecotoxicology 263
  AI Applications in Nanoecotoxicology 263
  IoT Systems for Environmental Monitoring 265
  Integrated Data Ecosystems 266
  Practical Applications and Case Studies 267
  Challenges and Limitations 269
  Future Directions 270
12.7 Summary 271

Chapter 13: Nanomaterials in Catalysis 273
13.1 Basics of Nanocatalysis 273
13.2 Nanobiocatalyst Development 278
13.3 Drug Synthesis Applications 281
13.4 Catalytic Role of Nanoscaffolds 285
13.5 Trends in Nanocatalysis 289
13.6 AI and IoT Integration 294
13.7 Summary 301

Chapter 14: Nanotechnology in Medicine 303
14.1 Scope of Nanomedicine 303
14.2 Peptide/DNA Nanoparticles 304
14.3 Lipid-Based Delivery Systems 306
14.4 Inorganic Medical Applications 306
14.5 Future Outlook 308
14.6 AI and IoT in Personalized Medicine 309
14.7 Summary 310

Chapter 15: Nanotechnology in Food Science 313
15.1 Introduction 313
15.2 Nanotechnology in Processing and Packaging 314
15.3 Pathogen Detection 315
15.4 Food Safety Innovations 317

15.5 Future of Food Nanotechnology 318

15.6 Industry Challenges 319

15.7 AI and IoT in Food Safety 320

15.8 Summary 323

Chapter 16: Nanotechnology in Water Remediation 325

16.1 Introduction 325

16.2 Techniques for Water Treatment 326

16.3 Nanopurification Technologies 326

    Nanoadsorbents 326

    Nanomembranes 327

    Photocatalytic Nanomaterials 327

16.4 Innovative Solutions 328

    Biomimetic Approaches 328

    Multifunctional Nanomaterials 328

    Nanotechnology-Enhanced Biological Treatment 328

16.5 Environmental Considerations 328

    Nanomaterial Toxicity 328

    Lifecycle Assessment 329

    Regulatory Frameworks 329

16.6 Industry Prospects 329

    Market Growth 329

    Cost-Effectiveness Analysis 330

    Scaling Challenges 330

16.7 AI and IoT for Water Monitoring 330

    Smart Nanosensors 330

    Predictive Analytics 331

    Remote Management Systems 331

16.8 Summary 332

TABLE OF CONTENTS

Chapter 17: MEMS and NEMS Based on Nanomaterials 333
17.1 Introduction to MEMS/NEMS 333
17.2 Role of Nanomaterials 334
17.3 Medical and Engineering Applications 335
17.4 Challenges and Opportunities 336
17.5 Trends in Technology 337
17.6 AI and IoT in MEMS/NEMS 338
17.7 Summary 339

Chapter 18: Safety and Regulation of Nanomaterials 341
18.1 Safety in Nanomaterial Use 341
18.2 Regulatory Structures 342
18.3 Testing Standardization 344
18.4 Ethical Framework 345
18.5 Industrial Safety Trends 346
18.6 AI and IoT in Regulatory Systems 348
18.7 Summary 349

Chapter 19: Genotoxicity and Cytotoxicity of Nanomaterials 351
19.1 Genotoxic Mechanisms 351
19.2 Cytotoxic Evaluation 352
19.3 Advancements in Testing 353
19.4 Health Risk Implications 354
19.5 Mitigation Approaches 355
19.6 AI and IoT in Risk Assessment 356
19.7 Summary 357

Chapter 20: Future of Nanobiotechnology 359
20.1 Emerging Technologies 359
20.2 Interdisciplinary Integration 360
20.3 Ethical Reflections 361
20.4 Societal Influence 362

20.5 Future Landscape 363

20.6 AI and IoT for Innovation 364

20.7 Summary 366

Bibliography 367

Further Reading 387

Index 395

About the Authors

Dr. Alok Kumar Srivastav is an accomplished Assistant Professor in the Department of Health Science at the University of the People, Pasadena, California, USA. His academic background includes a Ph.D., M.Tech, and M.Sc. in Bio-Technology; a Post-Doctoral Fellowship (Research) in Bio-Technology from Lincoln University College, Malaysia; and an MBA in Human Resource Management. He is a distinguished academic and researcher, recognized internationally for his contributions to education and research. In 2022, he was honored with the "International Pride of Educationist Award" at AIT, Thailand, for his pioneering contributions to advancing education in the digital era. In 2024, he received the prestigious "Innovative Academic Researcher Award" at HULT, France/UK, acknowledging his exceptional creativity, innovation, and impact in academic research. Most recently, in 2025, he was further recognized with the "Innovative Professional Achievement Award" in Sydney, Australia, for his impactful interdisciplinary innovations that have advanced professional excellence.

Dr. Priyanka Das serves as an Assistant Professor in the Department of Health Science at the prestigious University of the People in Pasadena, California, USA. She holds a Ph.D., M.Tech, and M.Sc. in Biotechnology along with an MBA in Human Resource Management. Prior to her current position, she was a Post-Doctoral Fellowship (Research) in Biotechnology at Lincoln University College, Malaysia. Dr. Priyanka Das is a dedicated scholar, contributing significantly to the field of Biotechnology.

About the Technical Reviewer

Sultana Begum is a semiconductor product management expert and AI technology enthusiast with over 12+ years of experience at Intel and Accenture. She is a quantum computing enthusiast with a deep understanding of quantum mechanics and physics principles of qubits and quantum dots. She is the lead author of the book *Competitive Semiconductor Product Management.* Sultana held critical roles in technical product marketing and hardware and software product management to gain a broad and deep-rooted expertise in the semiconductor technology industry. With deep technical expertise and a keen eye for strategic thinking, her expertise spreads widely across semiconductor design development to define and execute a competitive AI product strategy, with hands-on experience in launching multiple software and hardware products.

Sultana holds both bachelor's and master's degrees in electronics, an MBA in product management, and Stanford LEAD Executive Management Education from Stanford University.

Acknowledgments

Writing a book is a journey that often involves the support, encouragement, and contributions of many individuals and organizations. As we present this work, *Nanobiotechnology: AI and IoT Applications and Emerging Implications,* we would like to express our heartfelt gratitude to those who have made this endeavor possible.

First and foremost, we extend our sincere appreciation to our families for their unwavering support, patience, and understanding throughout the writing process. Your encouragement has been a constant source of motivation. We are deeply thankful to our colleagues and mentors whose guidance and expertise have enriched this book. Your insights have shaped our understanding of nano-biotechnology, particularly AI and IoT applications and emerging implications. We would like to acknowledge the contributions of the research institutions and libraries that provided access to valuable resources, making our research more comprehensive and thorough. Our gratitude goes to the reviewers and experts in the field who provided valuable feedback and constructive criticism, helping us refine the content and ensure its accuracy.

We extend our thanks to the publishing team, editors, and designers who have worked diligently to transform our manuscript into a published book. Last but not least, we are grateful to our readers, students, and fellow researchers who find value in this book. Your interest and engagement in the subject of nano-biotechnology drive our commitment to promoting sustainable practices and environmental stewardship.

This book would not have been possible without the collective effort and support of these individuals and institutions. We humbly acknowledge your contributions and express our deepest appreciation.

Dr. Alok Kumar Srivastav
Dr. Priyanka Das

Introduction

In the rapidly evolving world of science and technology, *Nanobiotechnology: AI and IoT Applications and Emerging Implications* offers a timely and comprehensive overview of one of the most transformative interdisciplinary fields. Nanotechnology, at the frontier of science and engineering, has revolutionized our ability to understand and manipulate matter at the molecular and atomic levels. When merged with biotechnology, it gives rise to nano-biotechnology—an innovative domain unlocking unprecedented opportunities to develop novel materials, devices, and systems. These advancements have far-reaching applications in medicine, environmental science, food technology, and more. This book not only explores the scientific foundations of nano-biotechnology but also emphasizes the growing integration of artificial intelligence (AI) and the Internet of Things (IoT), two transformative technologies that are reshaping research, innovation, and application across sectors. By combining these dynamic fields, the book provides readers with a holistic understanding of current developments and emerging implications that will define the future of nano-biotechnology.

This book is designed for researchers, graduate students, professionals, and enthusiasts in nanoscience, biotechnology, biomedical engineering, and related disciplines. This volume offers a structured journey through the fundamental concepts, materials, methods, and applications of nano-biotechnology. Each chapter delves into critical areas ranging from the synthesis and characterization of nanomaterials to their applications in drug delivery, diagnostics, environmental remediation, and catalysis. Importantly, the book also emphasizes the emerging role of AI and IoT technologies in optimizing nano-biotechnological processes, enhancing precision, automation, and real-time monitoring.

The book is organized into twenty detailed chapters, beginning with an introduction to nano-biotechnology that traces its historical roots, foundational concepts, and future potential. It progresses through the types, properties, synthesis, and characterization of nanomaterials, offering detailed insights into materials like quantum dots, metal nanoparticles, and polymeric systems.

INTRODUCTION

Midway, the focus shifts to biological applications, including cellular nanostructures, biomolecular motors, drug delivery systems, diagnostic tools, nanobiocatalysis, and their interactions with human health and the environment. Special emphasis is placed on AI and IoT integration across all domains, highlighting their roles in classification, monitoring, synthesis optimization, toxicity assessment, personalized medicine, environmental remediation, and real-time data analysis.

Chapters on ecotoxicology, safety, regulation, and ethical considerations provide a holistic view of the implications of these technologies, addressing concerns crucial to sustainable and responsible innovation. The final chapters explore nanotechnology's applications in food science, water remediation, MEMS/NEMS, and catalysis, culminating in a forward-looking discussion on future trends and interdisciplinary collaborations.

Throughout the book, readers will find dedicated sections discussing the integration of AI and IoT, underscoring their pivotal role in driving innovation and addressing challenges in nano-biotechnology. By bridging these domains, the book offers a unique perspective on how data-driven technologies and connected systems can accelerate discoveries and foster sustainable applications.

We hope this volume will serve as a valuable resource for advancing knowledge, sparking curiosity, and inspiring future innovations in nano-biotechnology. Whether you are a student beginning your journey or an expert seeking to broaden your understanding, this book strives to provide the insights and tools necessary to navigate and contribute to this exciting field.

> Enjoy the journey ahead—may these pages spark discovery, innovation, and a passion for the future of nanobiotechnology.

CHAPTER 1

Introduction to Nanobiotechnology

This chapter introduces the rapidly evolving field of nano-biotechnology, examining its historical origins and tracing its development into a distinct interdisciplinary domain. Beginning with foundational concepts and terminology, the chapter explores the convergence of nanotechnology with biological sciences, explaining key application areas including medicine, agriculture, environmental remediation, and industrial bioprocessing. The chapter further investigates emerging trends and future prospects, with particular attention to the integration of artificial intelligence and Internet of Things technologies with nano-biotechnological systems. Through comprehensive analysis of current research directions and technological capabilities, this chapter provides a framework for understanding how nanoscale manipulation of biological systems is revolutionizing our approach to global challenges in healthcare, food security, and environmental sustainability.

1.1 Historical Background of Nanotechnology

The conceptual origins of nanotechnology can be traced back to physicist Richard Feynman's visionary 1959 lecture titled "There's Plenty of Room at the Bottom," where he proposed manipulating individual atoms as a new frontier of scientific exploration. However, the formal birth of nanotechnology as a recognized field did not occur until the 1980s, when instruments capable of imaging and manipulating nanoscale structures were first developed. The invention of the scanning tunneling microscope (STM) in 1981 by Gerd Binnig and Heinrich Rohrer at IBM Zurich Research Laboratory marked a pivotal moment, allowing scientists to visualize individual atoms for the first time. This breakthrough earned Binnig and Rohrer the Nobel Prize in Physics in 1986 and catalyzed rapid advancements in nanoscale observation and manipulation.

CHAPTER 1   INTRODUCTION TO NANOBIOTECHNOLOGY

The term "nanotechnology" itself was coined by Norio Taniguchi of Tokyo Science University in 1974, referring to precision engineering at scales below one micron. The concept was later popularized and expanded by K. Eric Drexler in his 1986 book "Engines of Creation," which envisioned molecular manufacturing and self-replicating machines operating at the nanoscale. Throughout the 1990s, government initiatives worldwide recognized the transformative potential of nanotechnology, leading to substantial funding increases. The United States launched the National Nanotechnology Initiative (NNI) in 2000, committing billions of dollars to accelerate nanoscience research and development.

As instrumentation and fabrication techniques advanced, researchers began developing practical applications across diverse fields. The creation of carbon nanotubes, quantum dots, and various nanoparticle systems opened new possibilities for materials with unprecedented properties. Early commercial applications included stronger, lighter materials for sporting equipment, stain-resistant fabrics, and more effective sunscreens utilizing nano-sized particles (Table 1-1).

Table 1-1. Key Milestones in Early Nanotechnology Development

Year	Milestone	Significance
1959	Richard Feynman's lecture "There's Plenty of Room at the Bottom"	First conceptual proposal for atomic-scale manipulation
1974	Norio Taniguchi coins the term "nanotechnology"	Formal naming of the emerging field
1981	Invention of the scanning tunneling microscope (STM)	First tool to visualize individual atoms
1985	Discovery of fullerenes	New class of carbon nanomaterials
1986	Development of atomic force microscope (AFM)	Expanded capabilities for nanoscale imaging
1991	Discovery of carbon nanotubes	Revolutionary nanomaterial with exceptional properties
2000	Launch of US National Nanotechnology Initiative	Major government commitment to nanoscience R&D

The historical development of nanotechnology reveals a pattern of convergence between theoretical concepts and enabling technologies. Each advance in instrumentation expanded the boundaries of what scientists could observe and manipulate, while theoretical frameworks provided direction for experimental exploration. This interplay between theory and practice continues to characterize the field today, with new applications emerging as researchers gain greater control over matter at the nanoscale.

1.2 Evolution of Nanobiotechnology

Nano-biotechnology represents the synergistic integration of nanotechnology with biological systems, emerging as a distinct discipline in the late 1990s and early 2000s. This convergence occurred naturally as researchers recognized the potential of applying nanoscale engineering principles to biological challenges. The field developed at the intersection of multiple disciplines, including biology, chemistry, physics, engineering, and medicine, creating a uniquely collaborative research environment.

The evolution of nano-biotechnology can be conceptualized in three distinct phases. The first phase, spanning roughly 1990–2000, focused primarily on developing basic tools for biological observation and manipulation at the nanoscale. During this period, researchers adapted atomic force microscopy and other scanning probe techniques to study biological structures such as DNA, proteins, and cell membranes under physiological conditions. These capabilities enabled unprecedented insights into biomolecular structures and interactions.

The second phase, from approximately 2000 to 2010, saw a shift toward creating functional nano-biointerfaces and systems. Scientists developed biocompatible nanoparticles, quantum dots for biological imaging, and the first generation of nanoscale drug delivery systems. This period was characterized by proof-of-concept demonstrations showing how engineered nanomaterials could interact with biological systems in controlled ways. The development of DNA origami techniques by Paul Rothemund in 2006 exemplified this era's advances, enabling the precise folding of DNA molecules into predetermined nanoscale shapes with potential applications in drug delivery and molecular computing.

The current third phase, from 2010 onward, has focused on practical applications and systems integration. Advanced nano-biotechnological platforms have moved from laboratories into clinical trials and commercial products. Nano-enabled diagnostic systems, targeted therapeutics, and tissue engineering approaches have demonstrated

CHAPTER 1 INTRODUCTION TO NANOBIOTECHNOLOGY

tangible benefits in healthcare settings. Similarly, agricultural applications have progressed from laboratory demonstrations to field trials. This phase has been characterized by increased attention to safety, regulatory considerations, and scale-up challenges necessary for widespread implementation.

Throughout this evolution, the relationship between nanotechnology and biotechnology has been remarkably productive. Biological systems have inspired the design of novel nanomaterials and self-assembly strategies, while nanotechnology has provided tools to probe and manipulate biological systems with unprecedented precision. This bidirectional exchange of ideas and methodologies has accelerated innovation in both fields.

The integration of nano-biotechnology with other emerging technologies has further expanded its capabilities. Advances in computational biology, artificial intelligence, and high-throughput screening have complemented experimental approaches, enabling more systematic exploration of nano-bio interactions. Meanwhile, developments in advanced manufacturing, including 3D bioprinting and microfluidics, have facilitated the creation of more complex nano-biotechnological systems with potential applications in tissue engineering and organ-on-chip platforms (Figure 1-1).

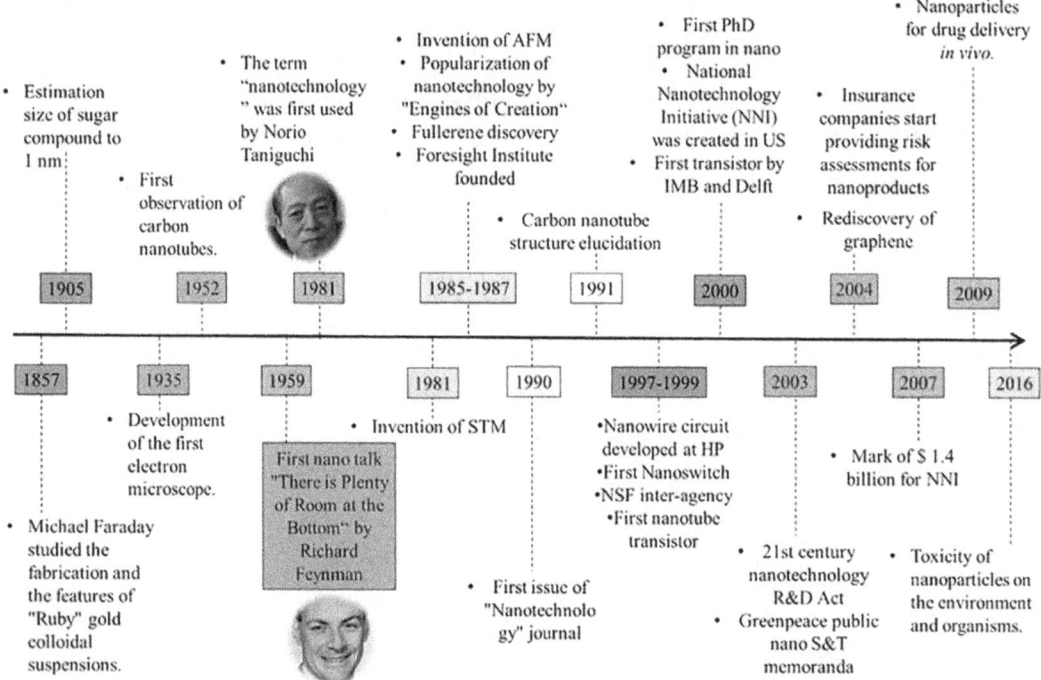

Figure 1-1. *Evolution of Nano-biotechnology Research Focus Areas*

Looking forward, nano-biotechnology continues to evolve toward greater sophistication and integration. The boundaries between traditional disciplines are increasingly blurred as researchers focus on solving complex biological challenges using convergent approaches that incorporate nanoscale materials, structures, and devices. This interdisciplinary character remains one of nano-biotechnology's greatest strengths, fostering innovation through the cross-pollination of ideas and methodologies.

1.3 Core Concepts and Terminology

Understanding nano-biotechnology requires familiarity with fundamental concepts and specialized terminology that bridge the nanoscience and biological domains. At its core, this field operates within the nanoscale regime, typically defined as structures and systems within the 1–100 nanometer size range. To provide perspective, a typical human hair is approximately 80,000–100,000 nanometers in diameter, while a DNA double helix measures roughly 2 nanometers in width. Operating at these dimensions allows direct interaction with cellular and biomolecular structures, many of which naturally function at the nanoscale.

A defining characteristic of nanoscale materials is their unique physicochemical properties, which often differ significantly from those of the same substances in bulk form. These distinctions arise from two primary factors: the dramatically increased surface-to-volume ratio of nanomaterials and quantum effects that emerge at the nanoscale. For instance, gold nanoparticles exhibit different optical properties than bulk gold, appearing red or purple rather than gold-colored, and demonstrating size-dependent absorption and scattering behaviors that enable applications in biological imaging and sensing.

The field employs several specialized categories of nanomaterials for biological applications:

> **Nanoparticles** are particulate structures with all three dimensions in the nanoscale range. They can be composed of various materials, including metals (gold, silver), metal oxides (iron oxide, titanium dioxide), polymers, lipids, or carbon-based materials. Their surfaces are frequently functionalized with biomolecules such as antibodies, nucleic acids, or targeting peptides to enable specific biological interactions.

Nanowires and nanotubes possess two dimensions in the nanoscale range, with one dimension extended. Carbon nanotubes, for example, exhibit exceptional mechanical strength and electrical conductivity, making them valuable for biosensing applications and as scaffolds for tissue engineering.

Nanosheets and nanolayers feature one dimension in the nanoscale range. Examples include graphene (a single layer of carbon atoms arranged in a two-dimensional honeycomb lattice) and various two-dimensional nanomaterials that can serve as platforms for biomolecule detection or drug delivery.

Nanocomposites combine multiple materials at the nanoscale to create structures with enhanced properties. Polymer-nanoparticle composites, for instance, may incorporate magnetic nanoparticles within a biocompatible polymer matrix to create systems responsive to external magnetic fields for targeted drug delivery.

Beyond these material classifications, several key conceptual frameworks guide nano-biotechnological development:

Biocompatibility refers to a nanomaterial's ability to perform its intended function without eliciting undesirable local or systemic effects in the biological host. This consideration is paramount for applications involving direct contact with living systems, especially those intended for in vivo use.

Bio-nano interface describes the critical boundary where engineered nanomaterials interact with biological systems. Understanding and controlling these interfaces—including protein corona formation, cellular uptake mechanisms, and immune system interactions—is essential for successful applications.

Self-assembly refers to the spontaneous organization of molecules or components into ordered structures without external direction. This phenomenon, commonly observed in biological systems (such as protein folding or DNA hybridization), is frequently leveraged in nano-biotechnology to create complex functional structures through bottom-up approaches.

Biomimetics involves drawing inspiration from biological systems to design nanomaterials and devices. Examples include nanoparticles that mimic the structure of viruses for efficient cellular entry or synthetic membranes that incorporate biological channel proteins for selective transport.

The field also employs specialized terminology for various nano-biotechnological approaches:

Table 1-2. Key Terminology in Nano-biotechnology

Term	Definition	Example Application
Biofunctionalization	Process of attaching biological molecules to nanomaterial surfaces	Antibody-conjugated nanoparticles for targeted cancer therapy
Theranostics	Nanomaterials designed to provide both therapeutic and diagnostic functions	Gold nanoshells for simultaneous imaging and photothermal therapy
Nano-biosensors	Detection systems combining nanomaterials with biological recognition elements	Graphene-based electrochemical sensors for glucose monitoring
Nanomedicine	Application of nanotechnology to medical diagnosis and treatment	Liposomal drug delivery systems for reduced side effects
Bio-nanofabrication	Creation of nanoscale structures using biological components or principles	DNA origami structures for drug encapsulation
Nano-biophotonics	Study of light-matter interactions at nanoscale in biological contexts	Quantum dot fluorescent probes for cellular imaging

This terminology provides the conceptual foundation for understanding nano-biotechnological approaches and applications, creating a shared language for this inherently interdisciplinary field (Table 1-2). As research continues to advance, this vocabulary continues to evolve, with new terms emerging to describe novel approaches and applications at the interface of nanotechnology and biology.

1.4 Key Application Areas

Nano-biotechnology has catalyzed transformative advances across diverse sectors, with applications ranging from healthcare to agriculture and environmental remediation. This section explores the primary domains where nano-biotechnological approaches are making significant impacts, examining both current implementations and promising developmental trajectories (Figure 1-2).

Medical Applications

The medical domain represents the most extensively developed area for nano-biotechnology, encompassing diagnostics, therapeutics, and regenerative medicine approaches. Nanoscale diagnostic platforms have revolutionized disease detection through increased sensitivity and multiplexing capabilities. Quantum dots—semiconductor nanocrystals with size-dependent fluorescence properties—enable simultaneous detection of multiple biomarkers with exceptional brightness and photostability. Similarly, gold nanoparticle-based lateral flow assays have enhanced the sensitivity of point-of-care diagnostics for conditions ranging from infectious diseases to cancer biomarkers.

In therapeutics, nano-enabled drug delivery systems address fundamental challenges in pharmacology. Liposomal formulations such as Doxil® (liposomal doxorubicin) and Abraxane® (albumin-bound paclitaxel nanoparticles) represent commercially successful examples that enhance drug efficacy while reducing systemic toxicity. These platforms achieve targeted delivery through both passive mechanisms (exploiting the enhanced permeability and retention effect in tumors) and active targeting (utilizing surface-conjugated ligands that bind specifically to disease-associated receptors).

Gene therapy has been significantly advanced through nanomaterial-based delivery vectors. Lipid nanoparticles (LNPs) provide effective encapsulation and cellular delivery of nucleic acid therapeutics, as demonstrated by their successful implementation in mRNA vaccines. Polymeric nanoparticles offer tunable degradation profiles for controlled release of genetic material, while inorganic nanostructures provide additional functionalities such as magnetic guidance or photothermal activation.

Regenerative medicine applications leverage nanomaterials as scaffolds for tissue engineering, providing structural support while mimicking extracellular matrix properties. Electrospun nanofibers create biomimetic environments for cell growth, while nanopatterned surfaces guide cellular adhesion, migration, and differentiation. Self-assembling peptide nanostructures form hydrogels with tunable mechanical properties for three-dimensional cell culture and tissue repair.

Agricultural Applications

In agriculture, nano-biotechnology offers solutions to enhance crop productivity, resilience, and resource utilization efficiency. Nanoscale formulations of fertilizers enable precise nutrient delivery with controlled release profiles, reducing runoff and environmental contamination while improving nutrient uptake efficiency. Similarly, nanopesticide systems provide targeted pest control with reduced active ingredient requirements, minimizing environmental impact and nontarget effects.

Nanosensors for soil and crop monitoring enable precision agriculture through real-time detection of nutrient deficiencies, pathogen presence, and plant stress hormones. These systems support data-driven decision-making for optimized resource allocation and early intervention against threats. Seed treatment technologies utilizing nanomaterials enhance germination rates, seedling vigor, and resistance to environmental stresses.

Genetic modification approaches benefit from nanomaterial-based delivery systems that facilitate DNA or RNA transfer into plant cells without viral vectors. Carbon nanotubes and mesoporous silica nanoparticles have demonstrated efficient biomolecule transport across plant cell walls and membranes, opening new possibilities for crop improvement with reduced regulatory complications compared to traditional transgenic approaches.

Environmental Applications

Environmental applications leverage nano-biotechnology for monitoring, remediation, and pollution prevention. Advanced nanosensors provide ultrasensitive detection of environmental contaminants, including heavy metals, organic pollutants, and pathogens, at concentrations previously below detection limits. These systems enable real-time environmental monitoring for early warning of contamination events and compliance verification.

CHAPTER 1   INTRODUCTION TO NANOBIOTECHNOLOGY

Nanomaterial-based remediation approaches address water and soil contamination through enhanced adsorption, catalytic degradation, or biological transformation of pollutants. Engineered nanomaterials such as zero-valent iron nanoparticles facilitate reductive transformation of chlorinated compounds and heavy metals in groundwater, while photocatalytic nanomaterials like titanium dioxide degrade organic contaminants under solar irradiation.

Membrane filtration technologies incorporating nanomaterials achieve superior selectivity for water purification and desalination. Nanocomposite membranes with embedded silver nanoparticles combine antimicrobial properties with enhanced flux rates, while carbon nanotube and graphene-based membranes provide precise molecular sieving capabilities with reduced energy requirements compared to conventional membrane processes.

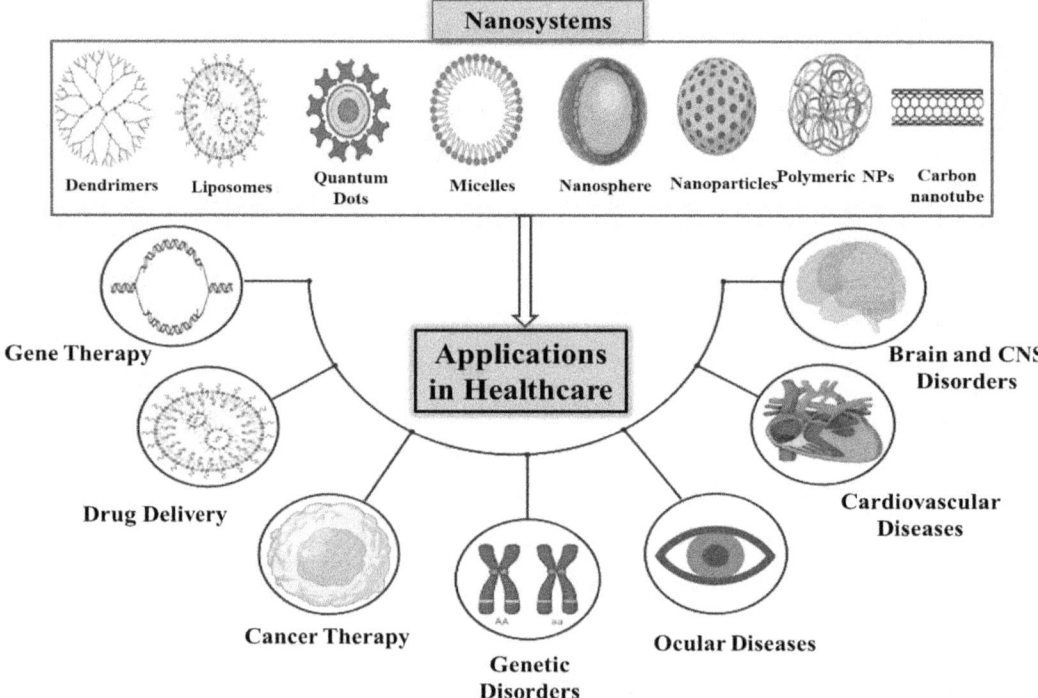

Figure 1-2. *Major Application Areas of Nano-biotechnology with Key Examples*

Industrial Bioprocessing

In industrial bioprocessing, nano-biotechnology enhances efficiency and selectivity across biocatalysis, fermentation, and downstream processing. Enzyme immobilization on nanomaterials improves stability and reusability while often enhancing catalytic activity through favorable microenvironments and increased surface area. Magnetic nanoparticle supports enable simple separation and recovery of biocatalysts from reaction mixtures.

Nanoscale monitoring systems provide real-time data on bioprocess parameters, supporting process optimization and quality control. Nanostructured materials for bioreactor design offer improved mass transfer characteristics and cell attachment surfaces for immobilized cell systems. Moreover, enhanced functionality is derived through the integration of Artificial Intelligence (AI) and the Internet of Things (IoT), enabling precision data collection and intelligent data processing for more accurate and adaptive bioprocess control. In downstream processing, nano-enabled separation technologies such as affinity magnetic nanoparticles facilitate selective product recovery through affinity binding, reducing processing steps and solvent requirements.

The code above demonstrates how researchers might analyze nanoparticle size distribution data, a critical quality parameter for many nano-biotechnological applications. The normal distribution observed in many synthetic nanoparticle preparations can significantly impact biological interactions and therapeutic efficacy.

This diverse application landscape illustrates the versatility of nano-biotechnological approaches in addressing challenges across sectors. The field's impact continues to expand as fundamental nanoscience advances translate into practical applications with commercial and societal benefits. Cross-pollination between application domains further accelerates innovation, with advances in one area often finding unexpected utility in others.

1.5 Emerging Trends and Prospects

Nano-biotechnology stands at an inflection point, with several emerging trends poised to redefine its capabilities and applications in the coming decade. These developments reflect both technological advancements and evolving research priorities focused on addressing global challenges in healthcare, food security, and environmental sustainability.

CHAPTER 1   INTRODUCTION TO NANOBIOTECHNOLOGY

A prominent trend is the move toward increasingly complex and hierarchical nano-biosystems that mimic the sophisticated organization of natural biological structures. Rather than relying on single-component nanomaterials, researchers are developing integrated multicomponent systems that combine diverse functional elements to achieve more sophisticated behaviors. DNA nanotechnology exemplifies this trend, with researchers creating programmable structures capable of dynamic reconfiguration in response to environmental stimuli. Similarly, biomimetic nanoparticle assemblies that replicate the structure and function of natural entities like viruses or exosomes demonstrate enhanced capabilities for targeted delivery and cellular interaction.

Stimulus-responsive nanomaterials represent another frontier with significant potential for intelligent nano-biotechnological systems. These materials undergo predictable physical or chemical changes in response to specific triggers such as pH, temperature, light, or biomolecular recognition events. Applications include drug delivery systems that release therapeutic cargo only under disease-specific conditions, biosensors that amplify signals upon target detection, and tissue engineering scaffolds that adapt their properties to support different stages of tissue development. The programmability of these responsive behaviors enables unprecedented control over nano-bio interactions in complex biological environments.

The integration of living and synthetic components into hybrid systems is generating entirely new capabilities that transcend the limitations of purely synthetic approaches. Cell-nanoparticle hybrids, such as nanoparticle-loaded immune cells for enhanced cancer immunotherapy, leverage cellular targeting and migration abilities while adding synthetic functionalities. Bacteria-nanoparticle conjugates combine bacterial motility with nanoscale sensing or delivery capabilities. These hybrid approaches represent a paradigm shift from using nanomaterials to simply deliver therapeutic agents toward creating symbiotic systems where biological and synthetic components complement each other's capabilities.

Sustainable nano-biotechnology is emerging as an essential research direction, with increased emphasis on environmentally benign fabrication methods and biodegradable nanomaterials. Green synthesis approaches utilize natural reducing agents and stabilizers derived from plant extracts, microorganisms, or biomass to produce metallic nanoparticles with reduced environmental impact. Biodegradable nanomaterials based on natural polymers such as chitosan, alginate, and cellulose nanocrystals offer alternatives to persistent synthetic materials. These developments align nano-biotechnology with circular economy principles while addressing safety concerns associated with nanomaterial accumulation in environmental and biological systems.

The field is also experiencing a shift from generalized approaches toward precision nano-biotechnology tailored to specific biological contexts or individual patients. This trend is particularly evident in nanomedicine, where researchers are developing personalized nanoformulations based on individual patient characteristics such as disease molecular profiles, genetic factors, and immune system status. Similar personalization approaches are emerging in agricultural applications, with nanomaterial-based delivery systems designed for specific crop varieties and growing conditions.

Translational research has gained increased prominence, with greater emphasis on bridging the "valley of death" between laboratory discoveries and commercial applications. Standardized characterization methods, reproducible manufacturing protocols, and systematic safety evaluations are becoming standard elements of nano-biotechnology research programs. Regulatory frameworks specific to nanomaterials are maturing, providing clearer pathways for clinical translation and commercial deployment. These developments are accelerating the real-world impact of nano-biotechnology innovations while ensuring safety for humans and the environment.

Table 1-3. Emerging Trends in Nano-biotechnology Research (2020–2025)

Trend	Description	Potential Impact
Hierarchical nano-biosystems	Integration of multiple nanomaterials into functional assemblies with increased complexity	Enables more sophisticated functionalities mimicking natural biological structures
Stimulus-responsive materials	Nanomaterials that change properties in response to specific triggers	Creates intelligent systems capable of autonomous adaptation to environmental conditions
Biohybrid approaches	Combination of living components with synthetic nanomaterials	Leverages advantages of both biological and synthetic systems for enhanced performance
Sustainable nanomaterials	Development of environmentally friendly synthesis methods and biodegradable materials	Reduces environmental impact and addresses safety concerns
Precision nano-biotechnology	Customization of nanomaterials for specific biological contexts or individuals	Enhances efficacy through tailored approaches for specific applications
Accelerated translation	Focus on standardization, reproducibility, and regulatory considerations	Bridges the gap between laboratory discoveries and practical applications
Convergence with digital technologies	Integration with AI, IoT, and advanced computing	Enables data-driven design and real-time monitoring of nano-bio interactions

Looking forward, several emerging application areas show particular promise. Extracellular vesicle engineering, combining natural cell-derived nanoparticles with synthetic modifications, offers new approaches for targeted drug delivery with reduced immunogenicity. Nano-enabled neural interfaces provide unprecedented capabilities for brain monitoring and modulation with potential applications in neurological disease treatment. Agricultural microbiome engineering using nanomaterials to deliver beneficial microorganisms or modulate microbial communities shows promise for sustainable crop production. These emerging applications illustrate the continuing expansion of nano-biotechnology into new domains with significant societal impact (Table 1-3).

As the field matures, addressing ethical, legal, and social implications has become increasingly important. Questions regarding nanomaterial safety, equitable access to nano-biotechnology benefits, and potential unintended consequences require thoughtful consideration alongside technical development. Proactive engagement with these dimensions will be essential for the responsible advancement of nano-biotechnology and its acceptance by society.

1.6 Role of AI and IoT in Nanobiotechnology

The convergence of nano-biotechnology with artificial intelligence (AI) and Internet of Things (IoT) technologies is creating powerful synergies that amplify capabilities across research, development, and application domains. This integration represents more than a simple technology combination—it enables fundamentally new approaches to understanding and manipulating biological systems at the nanoscale.

Artificial intelligence, particularly machine learning and deep learning methods, is transforming multiple aspects of nano-biotechnology. In materials discovery and design, AI algorithms accelerate the identification of novel nanomaterials with desired properties by exploring vast compositional and structural parameter spaces more efficiently than traditional experimental approaches. These methods leverage existing experimental data to build predictive models that guide synthesis efforts toward promising candidates, reducing the need for extensive trial-and-error experimentation.

For example, researchers have utilized machine learning to predict the protein corona formation on nanoparticles—a critical determinant of biological interactions and therapeutic efficacy. By analyzing relationships between nanoparticle physicochemical properties and protein adsorption patterns, these models enable rational design of nanomaterials with specific biological behaviors. Similarly, deep learning approaches have been applied to optimize the composition and structure of lipid nanoparticles for nucleic acid delivery, identifying formulations with enhanced transfection efficiency.

Image analysis represents another domain where AI significantly enhances nano-biotechnology research. Convolutional neural networks and other deep learning architectures facilitate automated interpretation of microscopy data from techniques such as atomic force microscopy, transmission electron microscopy, and super-resolution optical microscopy. These approaches enable higher throughput characterization of nanomaterials and their biological interactions while extracting quantitative information that might elude human observers.

In clinical and agricultural applications, AI enables personalized approaches by identifying patterns in biological data that can guide the design of 2D and 3D nanomaterials for specific contexts. Machine learning algorithms analyzing patient genomic, proteomic, and metabolomic profiles can inform the development of personalized nanomedicine formulations. Similarly, AI systems processing crop phenotypic data and environmental parameters can optimize 2D and 3D nanoformulations tailored for specific agricultural applications.

The Internet of Things complements these AI capabilities by connecting physical systems to digital networks, enabling real-time data collection, remote monitoring, and automated interventions. In nano-biotechnology, IoT integration creates several transformative capabilities:

Networked nanosensor systems represent a powerful convergence of nanotechnology, biotechnology, and IoT. These systems combine nanoscale sensing elements with wireless communication capabilities to enable continuous monitoring of biological parameters. Applications include wearable or implantable medical sensors that track biomarkers in real-time, agricultural monitoring systems that detect plant pathogens or nutrient deficiencies, and environmental sensing networks that provide early warning of contamination events. Data from these distributed nanosensors feed into AI analysis platforms, creating intelligent monitoring systems capable of detecting subtle patterns that precede disease outbreaks or crop failures (Figure 1-3).

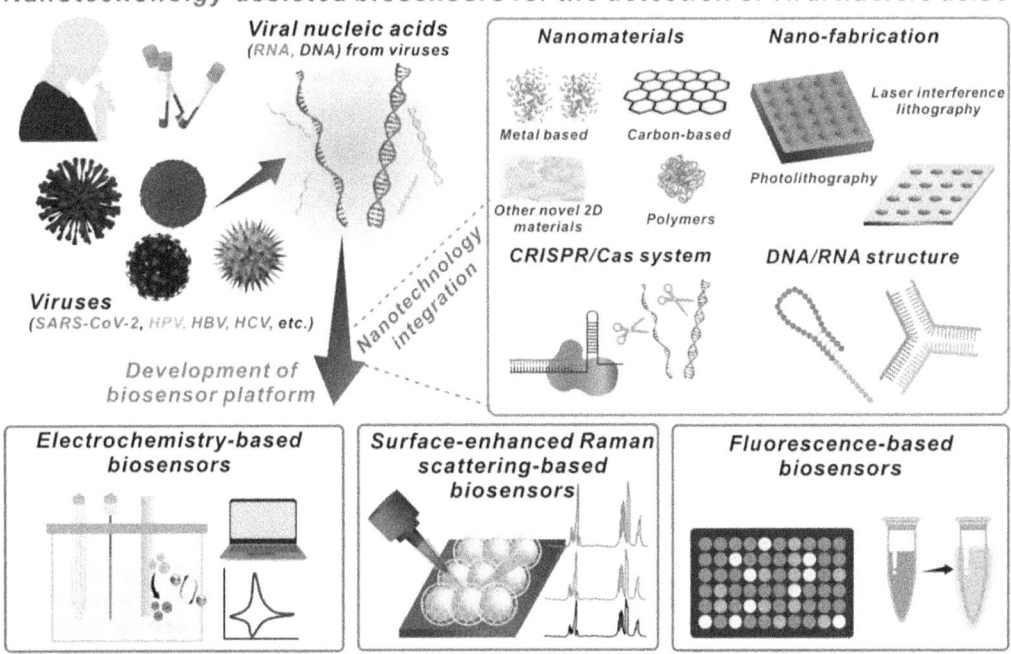

Figure 1-3. *Integration of Nano-biotechnology with AI and IoT Technologies for Advanced Biosensing*

Smart drug delivery systems combine nanomaterial carriers with sensing capabilities and wireless connectivity to enable dynamic, responsive therapeutic interventions. These platforms can adjust dosing based on real-time physiological measurements, be remotely triggered by healthcare providers, or operate autonomously based on programmed parameters. The integration of closed-loop control systems guided by AI algorithms allows these platforms to learn from treatment responses and optimize therapy over time.

In research and development, IoT-enabled laboratory automation accelerates nanomaterial discovery and optimization. Connected synthesis platforms can execute experimental protocols with minimal human intervention while collecting comprehensive data on process parameters and outcomes. This approach enables high-throughput exploration of synthesis conditions while generating rich datasets for AI-guided optimization. Similarly, automated testing systems for nanomaterial biological interactions provide standardized, reproducible evaluation across multiple parameters simultaneously. These systems are designed with scalability to accommodate varied data sizes, ensuring compatibility with diverse platforms and data streams for broader applicability and integration.

Digital twin technology—the creation of virtual replicas of physical systems—represents an emerging approach at the intersection of nano-biotechnology, AI, IoT, and robotics. By combining real-time data from physical nano-biosystems with computational models, digital twins enable simulation-based prediction, optimization, and control. Robotics-driven nanofabrications, integrated through IoT frameworks, further enhance the physical-digital interface by enabling precise, automated manipulation at the nanoscale. Applications include digital twins of nanomedicine formulations for personalized dosing optimization, virtual models of nano-enabled agricultural systems for intervention planning, and simulated testing of nanomaterials for safety assessment.

The integration of these technologies creates a virtuous cycle of advancement: IoT systems generate comprehensive data on nano-bio interactions, AI algorithms extract insights from these complex datasets, and these insights guide the design of improved nanomaterials and systems. This iterative process accelerates development while enabling more sophisticated control over biological processes at the nanoscale.

However, this convergence also presents significant challenges. Data security and privacy concerns are paramount, particularly for medical applications involving sensitive patient information. Technical challenges in miniaturizing IoT capabilities for integration with nanoscale systems require innovative approaches to power management, wireless communication, and sensor design. Ethical considerations around agentic nano-biosystems that make decisions without human intervention necessitate careful governance frameworks.

Despite these challenges, the integration of AI and IoT with nano-biotechnology continues to accelerate, driven by the transformative potential of these combined technologies. As computational capabilities advance and IoT infrastructure expands, we can anticipate increasingly sophisticated nano-biosystems capable of addressing complex challenges in healthcare, agriculture, and environmental management with unprecedented precision, effectiveness, and scalability.

1.7 Summary

The field of nano-biotechnology represents a powerful convergence of disciplines that is revolutionizing our approach to biological challenges across multiple sectors. By manipulating materials and systems at the nanoscale—a dimension where the fundamental building blocks of biology naturally operate—researchers have created unprecedented capabilities for interacting with living systems with molecular precision. The applications span from targeted medical therapies that minimize side effects to agricultural nanotechnologies that enhance food production with reduced environmental impact.

As explored throughout this chapter, nano-biotechnology has evolved from theoretical concepts and basic tools to sophisticated functional systems with demonstrated real-world benefits. The field's inherently interdisciplinary nature has fostered innovation through cross-pollination of ideas and methodologies from diverse scientific traditions. This collaborative approach continues to accelerate development as researchers from biology, chemistry, physics, engineering, and computational sciences bring complementary perspectives to common challenges.

The integration of artificial intelligence and Internet of Things technologies represents a particularly significant development, creating systems capable of autonomous adaptation, real-time monitoring, and data-driven optimization. These capabilities are transforming nano-biotechnology from a collection of static technologies into dynamic, responsive systems that can learn and improve over time. This evolution mirrors natural biological systems, which have evolved sophisticated mechanisms for sensing and responding to their environments.

Looking forward, nano-biotechnology faces both exciting opportunities and substantial challenges. Realizing the field's full potential will require addressing technical hurdles in areas such as scalable manufacturing, standardization, and long-term safety assessment. Equally important will be thoughtful consideration of ethical, legal, and social implications to ensure that nano-biotechnological advances benefit humanity broadly while minimizing potential risks.

As this chapter has illustrated, nano-biotechnology represents not merely an incremental improvement over existing approaches but rather a fundamental reconceptualization of how we interact with biological systems. By working at the same scale as nature's own machinery, researchers can achieve unprecedented control and precision while leveraging billions of years of evolutionary optimization. This symbiotic relationship between natural biological principles and engineered nanosystems promises continued breakthroughs in addressing some of society's most pressing challenges in healthcare, food security, and environmental sustainability.

CHAPTER 2

Nanomaterials and Their Properties

This chapter provides a comprehensive exploration of nanomaterials, examining their diverse types, unique physical and chemical properties, and classification based on applications. It delves into the revolutionary medical applications of nanomaterials, from targeted drug delivery to diagnostic imaging. The chapter addresses the significant challenges in nanomaterial development, including scalability, standardization, and safety concerns. Finally, it explores the integration of artificial intelligence and Internet of Things technologies in nanomaterial analysis, highlighting how these advanced computational methods are accelerating discovery and optimization. Through detailed examination of structure-property relationships, this chapter establishes the fundamental knowledge necessary for understanding nanomaterial applications across multiple disciplines.

2.1 Types of Nanomaterials

The realm of nanotechnology revolves around materials with dimensions measured in nanometers (10^{-9} meters), where unique properties emerge that differ significantly from their bulk counterparts. Understanding the various types of nanomaterials provides a foundation for appreciating their diverse applications and behaviors. Nanomaterials are typically categorized based on their dimensionality, composition, morphology, and production method, each classification offering insights into their potential applications (Table 2-1).

CHAPTER 2 NANOMATERIALS AND THEIR PROPERTIES

Dimensionality-Based Classification

Nanomaterials can be classified based on the number of dimensions that are confined to the nanoscale (1–100 nm):

Zero-dimensional (0D) nanomaterials have all three dimensions within the nanoscale. The most prominent examples are quantum dots and nanoparticles, which exhibit properties heavily influenced by quantum confinement effects. Quantum dots, typically composed of semiconductor materials like cadmium selenide or zinc sulfide, demonstrate size-dependent optical and electronic properties that make them valuable for applications ranging from display technologies to biological imaging.

One-dimensional (1D) nanomaterials have two dimensions in the nanoscale while one dimension extends beyond this range. This category includes nanotubes, nanowires, and nanofibers. Carbon nanotubes (CNTs), discovered in 1991, represent one of the most studied 1D nanomaterials. With their exceptional mechanical strength (approximately 100 times stronger than steel by weight), high thermal conductivity, and unique electrical properties, CNTs have found applications in electronics, composite materials, and sensing technologies.

Two-dimensional (2D) nanomaterials have only one dimension in the nanoscale. These sheet-like structures include graphene, molybdenum disulfide, and hexagonal boron nitride. Graphene, a single layer of carbon atoms arranged in a honeycomb lattice, has garnered immense attention since its isolation in 2004. With its extraordinary electron mobility (up to 200,000 $cm^2/V \cdot s$), thermal conductivity (~5000 $W/m \cdot K$), and mechanical strength (breaking strength of ~42 N/m), graphene has been hailed as a revolutionary material for next-generation electronics and composite materials.

Three-dimensional (3D) nanomaterials feature nanoscale structural elements in a three-dimensional configuration. These include nanocomposites, nanoporous materials, and interconnected nanostructures. Materials like aerogels, which consist of a network of nanoparticles with air-filled pores, exemplify this category, offering properties like ultralow density and exceptional thermal insulation.

Composition-Based Classification

Based on their chemical composition, nanomaterials can be divided into several categories:

Carbon-based nanomaterials include fullerenes, carbon nanotubes, graphene, and carbon nanofibers. These materials derive their unique properties from the diverse bonding capabilities of carbon atoms. Fullerenes, soccer ball-shaped carbon molecules like C60, possess remarkable stability and have applications in drug delivery and electronic devices.

Metal and metal oxide nanomaterials encompass noble metal nanoparticles (gold, silver), magnetic nanoparticles (iron oxide), and semiconductor quantum dots (cadmium selenide, zinc oxide). Gold nanoparticles, for instance, exhibit surface plasmon resonance effects that change their optical properties based on size and shape, making them valuable for sensing applications and medical diagnostics.

Organic nanomaterials include dendrimers, liposomes, and polymeric nanoparticles. Dendrimers, tree-like branched molecules with precise size and structure, offer controlled functionality for drug delivery and catalysis. Liposomes, composed of phospholipid bilayers, mimic cell membranes and can encapsulate both hydrophilic and hydrophobic compounds, making them ideal for pharmaceutical applications.

Composite nanomaterials combine different materials to achieve enhanced properties or multifunctionality. Examples include polymer-metal nanocomposites and core-shell nanostructures. These materials often demonstrate synergistic effects where the combined properties exceed those of the individual components.

CHAPTER 2 NANOMATERIALS AND THEIR PROPERTIES

Morphology-Based Classification

The shape and structure of nanomaterials significantly influence their behavior:

> **Spherical nanoparticles** represent the most common and easily synthesized morphology. Their uniform surface area-to-volume ratio facilitates consistent properties and interactions.
>
> **Rod-shaped nanomaterials** include nanorods and nanowires, which often display anisotropic properties that vary based on the direction of measurement.
>
> **Plate-like structures** such as nanosheets and nanoplatelets offer high surface areas with minimal thickness, valuable for catalysis and sensing applications.
>
> **Complex morphologies** include star-shaped, hollow, and mesoporous nanostructures, which provide specialized functionalities for applications like controlled release and enhanced catalytic activity.

Table 2-1. Summarizes the Major Types of Nanomaterials and Their Key Characteristics

Classification	Examples	Key Characteristics	Major Applications
0D nanomaterials	Quantum dots, nanoparticles	Quantum confinement effects, high surface-to-volume ratio	Bioimaging, displays, sensors
1D nanomaterials	Carbon nanotubes, nanowires	Directional electrical and thermal conductivity, high aspect ratio	Electronics, reinforcement in composites, field emission devices
2D nanomaterials	Graphene, MoS_2, h-BN	Exceptional in-plane properties, flexibility, high surface area	Flexible electronics, barrier materials, energy storage
3D nanomaterials	Aerogels, nanoporous materials	Complex architecture, controlled porosity	Catalysis, energy storage, thermal insulation

The production methods for these materials vary widely, from top-down approaches like lithography and milling to bottom-up methods such as chemical vapor deposition and sol-gel processing. Each fabrication technique imparts specific characteristics to the resulting nanomaterials, further diversifying their properties and potential applications.

Understanding the fundamental types of nanomaterials provides a crucial foundation for exploring their unique properties and diverse applications across fields ranging from medicine to electronics. The following sections will delve deeper into these properties and applications, illustrating how the nanoscale dimensions fundamentally transform material behavior.

2.2 Physical and Chemical Properties

At the nanoscale, materials exhibit remarkable properties that differ significantly from their bulk counterparts. These unique characteristics stem from two primary factors: the increased surface-to-volume ratio and quantum confinement effects. Understanding these properties is crucial for harnessing the full potential of nanomaterials across various applications.

Surface Effects and Surface-to-Volume Ratio

As materials decrease in size to the nanoscale, the proportion of atoms at the surface increases dramatically relative to those in the bulk. For a spherical nanoparticle, the surface-to-volume ratio is inversely proportional to its radius, meaning that smaller particles have exponentially larger relative surface areas. This phenomenon fundamentally alters material behavior in several ways:

> **Enhanced Reactivity**: The abundance of surface atoms with unsatisfied bonds leads to increased chemical reactivity. Gold, which is chemically inert in bulk form, becomes highly reactive as nanoparticles, serving as excellent catalysts for various chemical reactions. Silver nanoparticles demonstrate exceptional antimicrobial properties not observed in larger silver particles due to their increased reactivity with bacterial cell membranes.

> **Adsorption Properties**: Nanomaterials can adsorb gases, liquids, and biomolecules with remarkable efficiency due to their high surface area. Mesoporous silica nanoparticles can adsorb over 1000 m^2/g of material, making them excellent candidates for drug delivery systems and environmental remediation applications.
>
> **Surface Energy**: The substantial surface energy of nanomaterials affects their thermodynamic stability, melting point, and interaction with other materials. Gold nanoparticles melt at temperatures significantly lower than bulk gold (1064°C), with 2 nm particles melting at approximately 500°C due to the increased proportion of surface atoms with higher mobility.

Quantum Confinement Effects

When the dimensions of materials approach the wavelength of electrons (typically a few nanometers), quantum mechanics begins to dominate their behavior, leading to size-dependent properties (Figure 2-1).

> **Electronic Properties**: Quantum confinement alters electronic band structures, creating discrete energy levels rather than continuous bands found in bulk materials. This effect is most pronounced in semiconductor quantum dots, where the band gap energy increases as particle size decreases, resulting in size-tunable emission colors. CdSe quantum dots, for example, can emit light across the entire visible spectrum simply by varying their diameter from 2 to 7 nm.
>
> **Optical Properties**: Nanomaterials interact with light in unique ways, often displaying phenomena not observed in bulk materials. Noble metal nanoparticles exhibit localized surface plasmon resonance (LSPR), a collective oscillation of conduction electrons in response to light. This property gives gold nanoparticles their characteristic ruby-red color in solution and enables applications in biosensing and photothermal therapy.

Magnetic Properties: Nanoscale magnetic materials often transition from multi-domain to single-domain magnetic structures, leading to superparamagnetism. Superparamagnetic iron oxide nanoparticles (SPIONs) behave as paramagnets with extraordinarily high magnetic susceptibility, allowing them to be magnetized in the presence of an external magnetic field but revert to a nonmagnetic state when the field is removed—a critical property for biomedical applications.

Mechanical Properties

The mechanical behavior of nanomaterials often defies conventional wisdom:

Strength and Hardness: Nanomaterials frequently demonstrate extraordinary mechanical properties. Graphene exhibits a breaking strength of approximately 42 N/m, making it the strongest material ever measured in terms of its weight. Carbon nanotubes possess tensile strengths of approximately 100 GPa, compared to about 1–2 GPa for high-strength steel.

Ductility and Plasticity: Nanocrystalline metals can demonstrate both increased strength and unique deformation behaviors. While conventional metals follow the Hall-Petch relationship (strength increases as grain size decreases) down to grain sizes of about 100 nm, further reduction in grain size can sometimes lead to an inverse Hall-Petch effect, where different deformation mechanisms begin to dominate.

Viscoelastic Properties: Nanomaterials often display modified viscoelastic behavior compared to bulk materials. Polymer nanocomposites incorporating small amounts of nanomaterials like clay platelets or carbon nanotubes can exhibit dramatically enhanced mechanical properties, including increased stiffness, strength, and impact resistance.

CHAPTER 2   NANOMATERIALS AND THEIR PROPERTIES

Thermal Properties

Thermal behavior at the nanoscale often deviates significantly from bulk materials:

>**Thermal Conductivity**: Nanomaterials can exhibit either enhanced or reduced thermal conductivity depending on their structure. Single-layer graphene demonstrates exceptional in-plane thermal conductivity (~5000 W/m·K), while nanostructured materials with numerous interfaces can effectively scatter phonons, reducing thermal conductivity—a property exploited in thermoelectric materials.
>
>**Melting Point Depression**: Nanomaterials typically display lower melting points than their bulk counterparts due to the increased proportion of surface atoms with higher energy and mobility. Gold nanoparticles begin to show significant melting point depression below 10 nm, with the relationship between particle radius (r) and melting temperature following the Gibbs-Thomson equation.

Chemical Properties

The chemical behavior of nanomaterials is often dramatically different from bulk materials:

>**Catalytic Activity**: Many nanomaterials demonstrate remarkable catalytic properties due to their high surface area and abundance of active sites. Platinum nanoparticles as small as 2–3 nm maximize the surface-to-volume ratio while maintaining sufficient coordination for optimal catalytic activity in fuel cells and other applications.
>
>**Redox Properties**: The oxidation and reduction potentials of materials can shift at the nanoscale. This property is utilized in nanostructured electrodes for batteries and supercapacitors, where the altered redox behavior enables faster charge/discharge rates and improved cycle life.

CHAPTER 2   NANOMATERIALS AND THEIR PROPERTIES

Self-Assembly Capabilities: Many nanomaterials can spontaneously organize into ordered structures through noncovalent interactions. This property enables the bottom-up fabrication of complex nanostructures and facilitates their integration into functional devices.

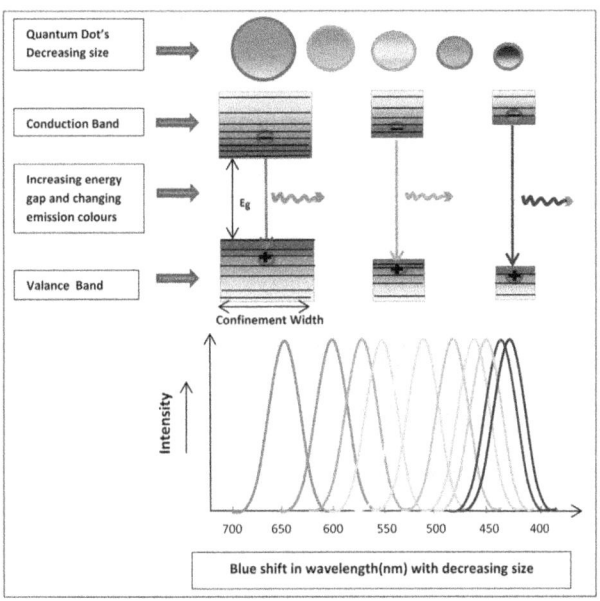

Figure 2-1. Quantum Confinement Effects in Semiconductor Quantum Dots

CHAPTER 2   NANOMATERIALS AND THEIR PROPERTIES

Table 2-2. *Summarizes the Key Property Changes Observed as Materials Transition from Bulk to Nanoscale*

Property Category	Bulk Material Behavior	Nanomaterial Behavior	Underlying Mechanism
Optical	Fixed absorption/emission	Size-tunable color	Quantum confinement
Melting point	Size-independent	Decreases with size reduction	Surface energy effects
Reactivity	Lower surface activity	Highly reactive	Increased surface-to-volume ratio
Mechanical strength	Lower yield strength	Significantly enhanced strength	Restricted dislocation movement
Electrical conductivity	Continuous bands	Discrete energy levels	Quantum confinement
Magnetic behavior	Multi-domain	Single-domain, superparamagnetic	Domain wall energetics

The unique properties of nanomaterials stem from fundamental physical principles but manifest in ways that enable revolutionary applications across numerous fields (Table 2-2). Understanding the relationship between nanomaterial structure and resulting properties is essential for designing materials with tailored characteristics for specific applications. The next section explores how these properties translate into practical applications across various fields.

2.3 Application-Based Classification

Nanomaterials have demonstrated exceptional versatility across numerous fields, driving innovation and enabling novel solutions to complex challenges. Classifying nanomaterials based on their applications provides a practical framework for understanding their implementation across diverse sectors. This classification approach helps bridge the gap between fundamental properties and real-world utility, guiding both research directions and commercial development (Table 2-3).

Energy Applications

Nanomaterials have revolutionized energy generation, storage, and conversion technologies through their unique properties:

> **Solar energy conversion** has been dramatically enhanced by nanomaterials. Perovskite solar cells utilize nanostructured materials to achieve power conversion efficiencies exceeding 25%, approaching those of conventional silicon cells but with potentially lower manufacturing costs. Quantum dot solar cells leverage size-tunable band gaps to capture broader portions of the solar spectrum. In dye-sensitized solar cells, TiO_2 nanoparticles provide high surface area scaffolds that maximize light absorption by attached dye molecules.

Characterization and Standardization Challenges

Accurate characterization and standardization of nanomaterials pose significant challenges that impact research reproducibility, regulatory approval, and commercial development:

> **Measurement limitations and techniques** present fundamental challenges for nanomaterial characterization. No single analytical technique provides comprehensive information about nanomaterial properties, necessitating complementary approaches. Transmission electron microscopy (TEM) offers excellent spatial resolution for morphological analysis but requires sample preparation that may alter nanomaterial states and provides limited statistical sampling. Dynamic light scattering (DLS) measures particle size distributions in solution but struggles with polydisperse or nonspherical particles. Surface characterization techniques like X-ray photoelectron spectroscopy (XPS) provide valuable information about surface chemistry but require high vacuum conditions that may not reflect real-world environments.

Characterization in complex environments remains particularly challenging. Nanomaterials often behave differently in biological fluids, environmental matrices, or product formulations compared to idealized laboratory conditions. Protein coronas that form around nanoparticles in biological media dramatically alter their surface properties and biological interactions. Developing methods to characterize nanomaterials in situ without disrupting these complex interactions represents an ongoing challenge for the field.

Standardization of terminology, methods, and reference materials is critical for ensuring reproducibility across laboratories and enabling meaningful comparisons between studies. Despite significant efforts by organizations like the International Organization for Standardization (ISO) and the National Institute of Standards and Technology (NIST), the rapid pace of nanomaterial development often outstrips standardization efforts. Reference materials certified for specific nanomaterial properties remain limited, particularly for complex or novel nanomaterial types.

Metrology at the nanoscale presents unique challenges due to quantum effects, surface phenomena, and statistical variations that become prominent at these dimensions. Quantifying properties like surface area, porosity, or defect density requires specialized approaches that may not translate well between different nanomaterial types. Developing universally applicable metrological frameworks remains an active area of research and development.

Safety and Environmental Challenges

Understanding and mitigating the potential risks associated with nanomaterials constitute critical challenges for sustainable development:

Nanotoxicology is an evolving field addressing the unique biological interactions of nanomaterials. Unlike conventional materials, nanomaterials can cross biological barriers, interact with cellular machinery, and exhibit toxicity mechanisms distinct from their bulk counterparts. The diversity of nanomaterial types, surface chemistries, and physical properties creates a vast parameter space for toxicological assessment. High-throughput screening methods and predictive toxicology approaches are being developed but still require extensive validation.

Environmental fate and behavior of nanomaterials remain incompletely understood. Aggregation, dissolution, and transformation processes in environmental media can dramatically alter nanomaterial properties and bioavailability. Silver nanoparticles, for example, may gradually release silver ions in aquatic environments, with toxicity mechanisms shifting from particle-specific effects to ionic silver toxicity. Developing standardized protocols for assessing nanomaterial persistence, bioaccumulation, and toxicity in environmental contexts remains challenging.

Occupational exposure during nanomaterial manufacturing, processing, and handling presents health and safety concerns. Conventional personal protective equipment may not effectively shield workers from nanomaterial exposure through inhalation or dermal contact. Implementing engineering controls and developing specialized monitoring techniques for airborne nanomaterials represent important areas for continued development.

Lifecycle assessment of nanomaterial-containing products presents methodological challenges due to limited data availability and the complexity of nanomaterial interactions throughout the product lifecycle. Energy requirements for nanomaterial production, potential releases during product use, and end-of-life considerations all factor into comprehensive environmental impact assessments. Standardized frameworks for nano-specific lifecycle assessment are still under development.

CHAPTER 2   NANOMATERIALS AND THEIR PROPERTIES

Regulatory and Commercialization Challenges

Navigating regulatory frameworks and commercialization pathways presents significant hurdles for nanomaterial development:

> **Regulatory considerations** for nanomaterials continue to evolve as scientific understanding advances. Different jurisdictions apply varying approaches to nanomaterial regulation, creating a complex landscape for developers and manufacturers. The European Union's Registration, Evaluation, Authorization and Restriction of Chemicals (REACH) regulation requires specific information for nanomaterials, while the US Food and Drug Administration (FDA) generally regulates nanomaterials within existing frameworks based on their intended use rather than their nanoscale dimensions.
>
> **Risk assessment methodologies** for nanomaterials require adaptation from conventional approaches. Dose metrics based solely on mass concentration may inadequately capture nanomaterial hazards, with surface area, particle number, or specific surface functionalization potentially serving as more relevant parameters. Developing scientifically sound yet practical risk assessment frameworks continues to challenge regulatory scientists and agencies.
>
> **Intellectual property landscape** for nanomaterials features overlapping patent claims, platform technologies with broad applications, and rapidly evolving scientific understanding. Navigating this complex IP environment can delay commercialization and increase development costs, particularly for startups and small enterprises with limited legal resources.
>
> **Market acceptance and public perception** significantly impact nanomaterial commercialization. Consumer concerns about "nanotechnology" broadly, even when scientifically unfounded, can influence market adoption. Effective science communication and stakeholder engagement represent important components of successful nanomaterial commercialization strategies.

Table 2-3. *Summarizes Key Challenges in Nanomaterial Development and Potential Mitigation Strategies*

Challenge Category	Specific Challenges	Potential Mitigation Approaches	Current Status
Synthesis and manufacturing	Scalability, reproducibility, cost-effectiveness	Continuous flow processes, automated synthesis platforms, green chemistry approaches	Varies by nanomaterial type; metals and oxides generally more mature than complex nanostructures
Characterization	Measurement limitations, behavior in complex media, reference materials	Multi-technique approaches, in situ characterization methods, international standardization efforts	Significant progress for common nanomaterials; challenges remain for novel types and complex systems
Safety and environmental	Nanotoxicology, environmental fate, exposure assessment	High-throughput screening, predictive modeling, safer-by-design approaches	Expanding knowledge base, but significant gaps remain, particularly for chronic exposures
Regulatory and commercial	Evolving regulations, risk assessment methodologies, market acceptance	Harmonized international approaches, stakeholder engagement, transparent reporting	Progressive implementation with continuing refinement as scientific understanding advances

Integration Challenges

Beyond the challenges specific to individual nanomaterials, significant hurdles exist in integrating nanomaterials into functional devices and systems:

> **Interface engineering** between nanomaterials and other components represents a critical challenge. Creating stable interfaces while preserving nanomaterial properties requires careful consideration of surface chemistry, mechanical

compatibility, and electronic structure. Carbon nanotube-polymer composites, for example, require effective interfacial bonding to translate the exceptional mechanical properties of individual nanotubes to macroscale performance enhancements.

Scale bridging from nanoscale to macroscale represents both a scientific and engineering challenge. Maintaining nanoscale properties while achieving macroscale functionality often requires hierarchical structures with precisely controlled organization across multiple length scales. Developing fabrication techniques that preserve nanoscale features while enabling macroscale production remains an active area of research.

Stability and aging of nanomaterials under operational conditions impact long-term performance and reliability. Quantum dots may experience photobleaching or surface oxidation that alters their optical properties over time. Metal nanoparticles can undergo sintering at elevated temperatures, losing their nanoscale dimensions and associated catalytic properties. Understanding and mitigating these aging mechanisms represents an important aspect of nanomaterial development for practical applications.

System integration challenges emerge when incorporating nanomaterials into complex devices or systems. Compatibility with existing manufacturing processes, consistency across production batches, and quality control methodologies all require adaptation for nanomaterial-based components. The electronics industry, for instance, has invested significant resources in developing integration protocols for carbon nanotubes and graphene that maintain their exceptional properties while remaining compatible with established semiconductor manufacturing processes.

Addressing these diverse challenges requires interdisciplinary collaboration among scientists, engineers, toxicologists, regulatory experts, and industry stakeholders. As the field continues to mature, overcoming these barriers will facilitate the transition from promising laboratory demonstrations to commercially viable and socially beneficial nanomaterial applications. The next section explores how advanced computational methods, particularly artificial intelligence and Internet of Things technologies, are accelerating progress in nanomaterial development and helping to address many of these challenges.

2.4 AI and IoT in Nanomaterials Analysis

The convergence of artificial intelligence (AI), Internet of Things (IoT) technologies, and nanotechnology is creating unprecedented opportunities for accelerating nanomaterial discovery, optimization, and implementation (Figure 2-2). These advanced computational and connectivity approaches address many of the challenges discussed in the previous section by enhancing data acquisition, analysis, and knowledge generation. This rapidly evolving interdisciplinary field is transforming nanomaterials research from a largely empirical endeavor to a more systematic, data-driven enterprise (Table 2-4).

AI-Driven Nanomaterial Discovery and Design

Artificial intelligence has emerged as a powerful tool for exploring the vast chemical and structural space of potential nanomaterials:

> **Machine learning for property prediction** enables rapid screening of candidate nanomaterials without extensive experimental testing. Supervised learning algorithms trained on experimental datasets can establish quantitative structure-property relationships (QSPRs) that predict nanomaterial behaviors based on structural features, composition, and processing conditions. Convolutional neural networks (CNNs) have demonstrated remarkable success in predicting quantum dot properties from structural inputs, achieving over 95% accuracy in band gap prediction for various semiconductor compositions. Graph neural networks (GNNs) effectively model nanomaterial properties by representing atomic structures as graphs, capturing the local chemical environments critical for property determination.

Materials informatics approaches combine diverse datasets, computational models, and machine learning algorithms to accelerate materials discovery. Feature engineering techniques identify the most relevant descriptors for nanomaterial performance, while dimensionality reduction methods like principal component analysis (PCA) and t-distributed stochastic neighbor embedding (t-SNE) help visualize complex property spaces. These approaches have enabled the identification of promising nanoparticle catalysts for hydrogen evolution reactions, reducing development time from years to months.

Inverse design strategies reverse the traditional design process by starting with desired properties and working backward to identify nanomaterial structures that would exhibit those characteristics. Generative adversarial networks (GANs) and variational autoencoders (VAEs) can generate novel nanomaterial designs that satisfy multiple property constraints simultaneously. Researchers have employed these approaches to design plasmonic nanostructures with specific optical responses for applications in biosensing and photonic devices.

Active learning frameworks iteratively improve predictive models by strategically selecting experiments that maximize information gain. These approaches efficiently explore the vast parameter space of nanomaterial synthesis by focusing experimental efforts on regions with high uncertainty or predicted promising properties. Such Bayesian optimization techniques have demonstrated 3- to 5-fold reductions in the number of experiments required to identify optimal synthesis conditions for quantum dots with specific emission characteristics.

IoT Integration in Nanomaterial Synthesis and Characterization

Internet of Things technologies enable unprecedented monitoring, control, and automation of nanomaterial research and manufacturing:

Smart synthesis platforms equipped with multiple sensors continuously monitor reaction parameters like temperature, pressure, pH, and spectroscopic signatures during nanomaterial synthesis. These systems can detect deviations from optimal conditions and make real-time adjustments to maintain product quality. For instance, microfluidic reactors for quantum dot synthesis incorporate in-line optical sensors that monitor nucleation and growth processes, enabling precise control over particle size distributions through automated feedback loops.

Connected characterization instruments form networks that facilitate comprehensive nanomaterial analysis. Distributed systems linking electron microscopes, spectroscopic tools, and mechanical testing instruments generate multi-modal datasets that provide complementary information about nanomaterial properties. Standardized data formats and communication protocols enable seamless information sharing across instruments and research groups, accelerating collaborative research efforts.

Digital twins of nanomaterial synthesis processes create virtual replicas that simulate physical systems in real-time. These computational models incorporate physics-based simulations and empirical data to predict process outcomes under various conditions. By continuously updating these models with sensor data from actual synthesis runs, researchers can identify optimal process parameters, troubleshoot issues, and scale up production while maintaining nanomaterial quality. Digital twins may also help resolve issues within the simulation setup, saving significant time, investment, and debugging efforts when addressing real-world challenges.

Blockchain integration ensures data integrity and provenance throughout the nanomaterial development lifecycle. This technology creates immutable records of synthesis conditions, characterization results, and property measurements, facilitating regulatory compliance and enhancing reproducibility. Smart contracts can automate material transfers between research groups while maintaining appropriate controls over proprietary information using secure blockchain credentials.

CHAPTER 2   NANOMATERIALS AND THEIR PROPERTIES

High-Throughput Experimentation and Automation

The combination of AI and IoT enables unprecedented experimental throughput in nanomaterial research:

Robotic experimentation systems automate synthesis, processing, and characterization workflows. These platforms can execute complex experimental protocols with minimal human intervention, significantly increasing throughput while reducing variability. Automated nanoparticle synthesis robots capable of performing hundreds of reactions daily have accelerated the optimization of quantum dot synthesis, identifying optimal conditions for specific emission wavelengths in days rather than months.

Self-optimizing systems combine automated experimentation with machine learning algorithms that interpret results and design subsequent experiments. These closed-loop platforms iteratively refine synthesis conditions to achieve target nanomaterial properties. Bayesian optimization algorithms have proven particularly effective for navigating complex parameter spaces, converging on optimal conditions more efficiently than traditional design of experiments approaches.

Standardized data collection ensures that information generated across different laboratories and instruments remains comparable and interoperable. Nanoinformatics initiatives have developed ontologies and data schemas specifically for nanomaterials, enabling seamless integration of diverse datasets. These standardized approaches facilitate data sharing, meta-analyses, and the development of more robust predictive models.

Cloud-based collaborative platforms connect researchers, instruments, and computational resources across geographic boundaries. These systems enable real-time sharing of experimental results, collaborative analysis, and distributed computing for resource-intensive simulations. The resulting research networks accelerate discovery by leveraging complementary expertise and resources across institutions.

Advanced Analytics for Nanomaterial Characterization

AI techniques are transforming how nanomaterial characterization data is analyzed and interpreted:

Image analysis automation employs computer vision algorithms to extract quantitative information from electron microscopy and other imaging techniques. Convolutional neural networks can automatically identify, count, and measure nanoparticles in TEM images with accuracy comparable to human experts but at much higher throughput. Semantic segmentation techniques differentiate nanomaterial features from backgrounds and artifacts, enabling more reliable morphological analysis. In parallel, transformer-based models are rapidly transforming image analysis in nanotechnology by offering powerful capabilities for extracting patterns, structures, and insights from complex nanoscale imaging data. Unlike traditional CNNs, transformer architectures such as Vision Transformers (ViT), Swin Transformers, and MaskFormer use self-attention mechanisms to capture global contextual relationships within an image, making them highly suitable for tasks involving irregular nanoparticle shapes, subtle defects, or high-resolution electron microscopy. These models enable a range of applications—from automated nanoparticle classification and segmentation to defect detection in 2D materials, image restoration, and even 3D reconstruction from tomography data. By combining pretrained transformer backbones with domain-specific pipelines, researchers can accelerate image annotation, improve reproducibility, and drive discovery in nano-enabled fields such as drug delivery, catalysis, and quantum materials. As the field advances, integrating self-supervised learning, edge inference, and hybrid transformer-CNN architectures will further unlock transformer potential for real-time, high-throughput nanoscale analysis.

Spectral data interpretation benefits from machine learning approaches that identify patterns in complex spectroscopic datasets. Principal component analysis (PCA) and other dimensionality reduction techniques help visualize relationships between samples and identify key spectral features associated with specific nanomaterial properties. Neural networks trained on reference spectra can identify nanomaterial components in mixtures and quantify their relative abundances with high accuracy.

Anomaly detection algorithms identify unusual patterns in synthesis or characterization data that may indicate process deviations or novel phenomena. These approaches help researchers identify unexpected behavior that might otherwise be overlooked in large datasets. Unsupervised learning techniques like autoencoders excel at detecting anomalies by identifying data points that deviate significantly from learned normal patterns.

Multi-modal data fusion combines information from complementary characterization techniques to provide more comprehensive nanomaterial analysis. Bayesian inference frameworks can integrate data with different resolutions, sensitivities, and information content while appropriately weighting each source based on its reliability. These approaches have enabled more accurate determination of nanoparticle size distributions by combining dynamic light scattering, electron microscopy, and small-angle X-ray scattering data.

CHAPTER 2 NANOMATERIALS AND THEIR PROPERTIES

Table 2-4. *Summarizes Key AI and IoT Applications in Nanomaterial Research*

Technology Area	Specific Applications	Benefits	Implementation Examples
Machine learning	Property prediction, structure-property relationships, inverse design	Accelerated screening, design space exploration, reduced experimental load	Neural networks for quantum dot band gap prediction, GANs for nanostructure design
IoT integration	Sensor networks, digital twins, connected instruments	Real-time monitoring, process control, enhanced reproducibility	Microfluidic reactors with in-line monitoring, networked characterization facilities
Automated experimentation	Robotic synthesis, self-optimizing systems	Increased throughput, reduced human error, systematic optimization	High-throughput nanoparticle synthesis platforms, closed-loop optimization systems
Advanced analytics	Automated image analysis, multi-modal data fusion	Enhanced data extraction, more comprehensive characterization	CNN-based particle analysis, Bayesian integration of spectroscopic data

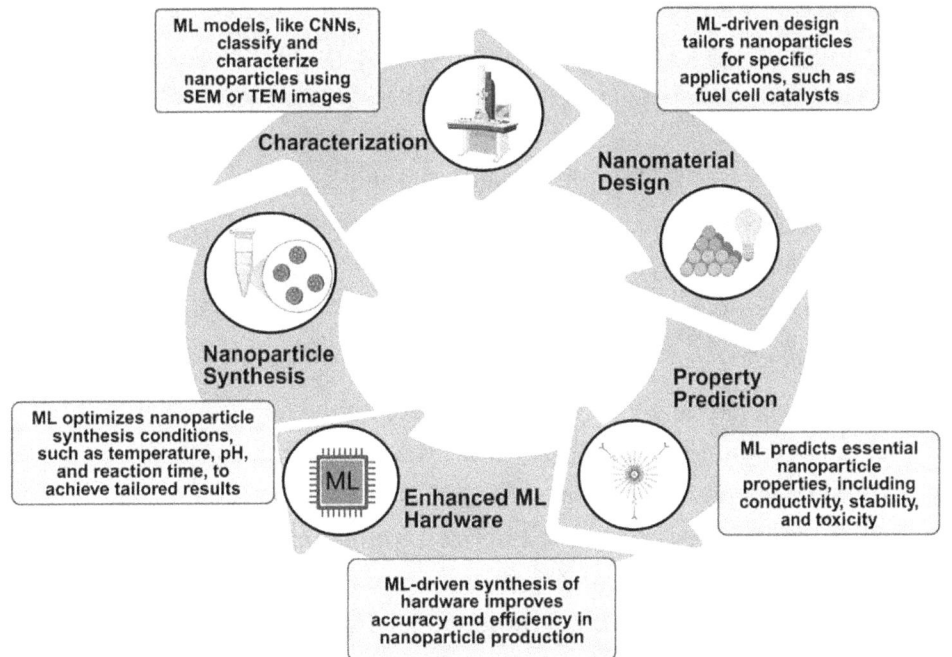

Figure 2-2. *AI and IoT Integration in Nanomaterial Research*

CHAPTER 2   NANOMATERIALS AND THEIR PROPERTIES

Future Directions and Challenges

The integration of AI and IoT in nanomaterials research continues to evolve rapidly, with several emerging trends and challenges:

> **Explainable AI** approaches are becoming increasingly important as researchers seek to understand the scientific principles underlying machine learning predictions. While black-box models can make accurate predictions, understanding the physical mechanisms and structure-property relationships remains crucial for scientific advancement. Techniques like attention mechanisms, feature importance analysis, and model distillation are being developed to provide interpretable insights from complex models.
>
> In particular, transformer-based architectures such as Vision Transformers (ViT) and Swin Transformers offer built-in explainability through their self-attention mechanisms, which can highlight the specific regions or features of an image that influence the model's decisions. These attention maps enable researchers to trace how the model prioritizes features related to nanoparticle morphology, defects, or spatial distributions. Additionally, techniques such as saliency maps, SHAP (SHapley Additive exPlanations), and integrated gradients are being adapted to transformer models for both image and sequence data, offering granular insight into model behavior. Such interpretability not only builds trust in AI-driven discoveries but also uncovers novel structure-function relationships critical to advancing nano-biotechnology, materials science, and related disciplines.
>
> **Federated learning** enables collaborative model development while maintaining data privacy and security. This approach allows multiple institutions to train shared models using local data that never leaves secure servers, addressing confidentiality concerns in competitive research environments. Such distributed approaches facilitate the development of more robust predictive models by incorporating diverse datasets without compromising intellectual property.

Edge computing brings computational capabilities closer to experimental instruments, enabling real-time data analysis and decision-making without reliance on cloud connectivity. This approach is particularly valuable for time-sensitive experiments where immediate feedback is necessary to adjust synthesis parameters or characterization settings. Edge devices with specialized hardware accelerators can execute complex neural network inference with minimal latency, facilitating closed-loop experimental control.

Data quality and bias concerns remain significant challenges, as AI systems are only as good as their training data. Ensuring representative, well-characterized datasets free from systematic biases is essential for developing reliable predictive models. Interdisciplinary collaboration between nanomaterial scientists, data scientists, and domain experts is crucial for identifying and addressing data quality issues.

Computational infrastructure requirements for advanced AI applications in nanomaterial research are substantial, potentially limiting access for smaller research groups or institutions. Developing more efficient algorithms, accessible cloud resources, and collaborative platforms can help democratize these technologies and ensure broader participation in AI-driven nanomaterial discovery.

The convergence of AI, IoT, and nanotechnology represents a paradigm shift in how nanomaterials are discovered, optimized, and implemented. These advanced computational and connectivity approaches address many traditional challenges in nanomaterial development by enhancing experimental efficiency, enabling more sophisticated data analysis, and facilitating knowledge sharing across disciplines. As these technologies continue to mature and become more accessible, they promise to accelerate innovation across the diverse application domains discussed throughout this chapter.

2.5 Summary

Nanomaterials represent a transformative class of materials whose properties and applications span virtually every technological domain. This chapter has explored the fundamental types, properties, and applications of nanomaterials, highlighting both their remarkable potential and the significant challenges associated with their development and implementation.

The diverse types of nanomaterials—from zero-dimensional quantum dots to three-dimensional nanostructured networks—derive their unique properties from quantum confinement effects and dramatically increased surface-to-volume ratios. These properties enable revolutionary applications across energy, environmental, electronic, and medical fields. As explored in this chapter, nanomaterials have already transformed medical diagnostics and therapeutics, catalysis, energy conversion and storage, and numerous other technological domains.

Despite substantial progress, significant challenges remain in nanomaterial synthesis, characterization, standardization, and safety assessment. The increasing integration of artificial intelligence and Internet of Things technologies is accelerating progress by enabling more systematic exploration of nanomaterial design spaces, automating experimental workflows, and extracting deeper insights from characterization data. These computational approaches, combined with continued advances in synthesis techniques and characterization methods, promise to address many current limitations.

The future of nanomaterial development lies at the intersection of multiple disciplines, requiring collaboration among materials scientists, chemists, biologists, computational experts, and engineers. Such interdisciplinary efforts will be essential for translating the remarkable properties of nanomaterials into transformative technologies that address global challenges in healthcare, energy, environmental protection, and beyond.

As nanotechnology continues to mature, balancing innovation with responsible development will remain crucial. Addressing safety concerns, establishing appropriate regulatory frameworks, and ensuring sustainable manufacturing practices will be essential for realizing the full potential of nanomaterials while minimizing potential risks. With these considerations in mind, nanomaterials will undoubtedly continue to drive technological advancement across numerous fields in the coming decades.

CHAPTER 3

Cellular Nanostructures and Biomolecular Motors

This chapter explores the intricate world of cellular nanostructures and biomolecular motors that exist naturally within biological systems. Beginning with an overview of fundamental cellular nanostructures, the chapter examines how these molecular machines perform critical functions in living organisms. It delves into the mechanisms and applications of biomolecular motors, which convert chemical energy into mechanical work at the nanoscale. The chapter further investigates nanopores—natural and synthetic channels that facilitate selective transport across membranes—and their technological applications. Bio-inspired structures that mimic natural nanomachinery are discussed, illustrating how principles from nature inform nanotechnological innovation. The chapter concludes by examining the technological significance of these cellular nanostructures in fields including medicine, biosensing, energy conversion, and nanorobotics, highlighting how understanding these natural nanomachines drives advances in nanotechnology with transformative potential across multiple disciplines.

3.1 Overview of Cellular Nanostructures

The cellular environment represents nature's most sophisticated nanofactory, filled with molecular machines that operate with remarkable precision and efficiency. At the nanoscale, cells contain a diverse array of structural and functional components that carry out the complex business of life. These cellular nanostructures are not merely passive architectural elements but dynamic systems that continuously respond to internal and external stimuli, maintaining the delicate balance required for life.

CHAPTER 3   CELLULAR NANOSTRUCTURES AND BIOMOLECULAR MOTORS

Biomolecules such as proteins, nucleic acids, lipids, and carbohydrates serve as the building blocks for these cellular nanostructures. Through a process of molecular self-assembly—driven by noncovalent interactions including hydrogen bonding, van der Waals forces, electrostatic interactions, and hydrophobic effects—these molecules organize themselves into complex functional units. This self-assembly creates structures with precise spatial arrangements that are essential for their biological functions.

The cytoskeleton represents one of the most remarkable examples of cellular nanostructures. Composed primarily of three types of protein filaments—microfilaments (actin filaments), intermediate filaments, and microtubules—the cytoskeleton provides structural support to the cell while also serving as tracks for the movement of cellular cargo. Microtubules, with their hollow cylindrical structure approximately 25 nm in diameter, exemplify nature's engineering precision at the nanoscale (Figure 3-1).

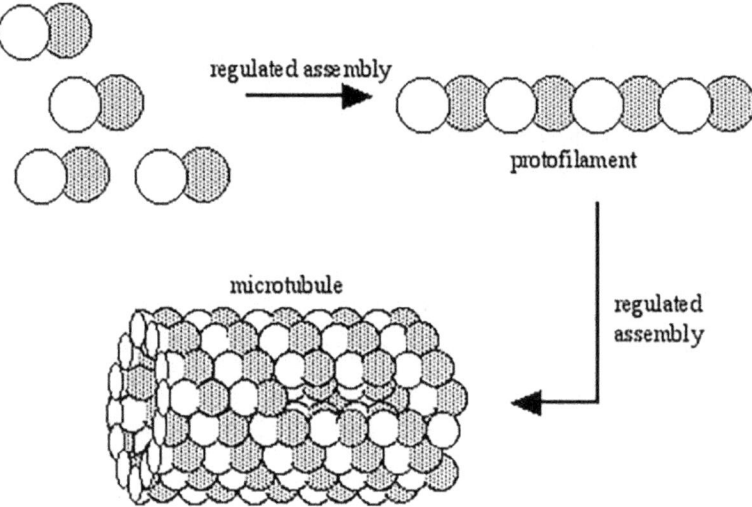

Figure 3-1. Structure of Microtubules and Their Organization in Cells

The cell membrane itself is a sophisticated nanostructure, consisting of a phospholipid bilayer embedded with various proteins that serve as channels, receptors, and transporters. This membrane, approximately 5-10 nm thick, selectively controls the passage of materials into and out of the cell, maintaining cellular homeostasis. Membrane proteins exhibit remarkable specificity, allowing the transport of particular molecules while excluding others—a principle that has inspired the development of synthetic nanopores and selective filters.

CHAPTER 3 CELLULAR NANOSTRUCTURES AND BIOMOLECULAR MOTORS

Ribosomes, the cellular protein factories, represent another fascinating example of natural nanostructures. These complex molecular assemblies, approximately 20–30 nm in diameter, translate genetic information into proteins with extraordinary precision. Comprised of RNA and protein components that fit together like pieces of a three-dimensional puzzle, ribosomes demonstrate how nanoscale structures can perform complex functions through precise molecular arrangements.

Within the nucleus, chromatin—the complex of DNA and proteins—exemplifies hierarchical organization at the nanoscale. DNA, with its diameter of approximately 2 nm, wraps around histone proteins to form nucleosomes (11 nm in diameter), which further compact into chromatin fibers and, ultimately, chromosomes. This hierarchical organization allows the cell to pack nearly two meters of DNA within a nucleus just a few micrometers in diameter while maintaining accessibility for replication and transcription processes.

Cellular organelles such as mitochondria and chloroplasts contain their own intricate nanostructures. The inner mitochondrial membrane, for instance, is folded into cristae that house the molecular machinery for cellular respiration. These membrane-bound compartments create specialized nanoenvironments optimized for specific biochemical reactions, highlighting how spatial organization at the nanoscale enhances functional efficiency.

Molecular chaperones represent another class of cellular nanostructures that assist in protein folding and prevent aggregation. These molecular machines, such as the barrel-shaped GroEL-GroES complex, provide a protected environment where newly synthesized proteins can fold correctly, illustrating how cells have evolved specialized nanostructures to ensure quality control at the molecular level.

The study of these cellular nanostructures has profound implications for nanotechnology. By understanding the principles that govern their formation, function, and regulation, scientists can develop biomimetic nanomaterials and devices with properties inspired by nature's designs. The following sections will explore specific examples of cellular nanomachines—biomolecular motors, nanopores, and other bio-inspired structures—and their technological applications.

3.2 Functions of Biomolecular Motors

Biomolecular motors represent nature's solution to the challenge of directed movement at the nanoscale. These remarkable protein machines convert chemical energy, typically from ATP hydrolysis, into mechanical work with efficiency that surpasses human-engineered motors. Their ability to function in the thermally noisy cellular environment, where Brownian motion dominates, represents a triumph of natural evolution and continues to inspire nanotechnological innovation.

Kinesin and dynein are two families of motor proteins that transport cellular cargo along microtubule tracks. Kinesin, approximately 80 nm in length, moves toward the plus end of microtubules, while dynein travels toward the minus end. These motors literally "walk" along microtubules, with their two motor domains (heads) taking alternating steps in a hand-over-hand fashion. Each step covers approximately 8 nm—the distance between adjacent tubulin dimers in a microtubule—and generates forces of around 5–7 piconewtons. This force, though seemingly minute, is sufficient to transport vesicles, organelles, and other cellular cargo through the crowded cytoplasm.

The mechanochemical cycle of kinesin illustrates how these motors function at the molecular level (Table 3-1). ATP binding causes conformational changes in the motor domain attached to the microtubule, leading to movement of the tethered motor domain forward to the next binding site. ATP hydrolysis and release of the products (ADP and phosphate) then trigger detachment of the rear motor domain, completing one cycle of the stepping mechanism. Through this coordinated sequence of molecular events, kinesin can take hundreds of steps before detaching from the microtubule, achieving remarkable processivity.

Table 3-1. Mechanochemical Cycle of Kinesin

Step	Molecular Event	Structural Change	Functional Consequence
1	ATP binding to the leading head	Conformational change in neck linker	Power stroke, positioning trailing head forward
2	Attachment of trailing head to next binding site	Strain between heads	Both heads bound to microtubule
3	ATP hydrolysis in the leading head	Generation of ADP and phosphate	Preparation for detachment
4	Phosphate release from leading head	Weakening of microtubule attachment	Detachment of original leading head
5	Cycle repeats with roles reversed	Step completed	8 nm movement along microtubule

Myosin represents another family of biomolecular motors that interact with actin filaments rather than microtubules. Myosin II, found in muscle cells, forms thick filaments that interact with thin actin filaments to generate contractile force. The power stroke of myosin involves conformational changes triggered by ATP hydrolysis, causing the myosin head to pull actin filaments toward the center of the sarcomere, the fundamental unit of muscle contraction. Through the coordinated action of billions of myosin motors, muscles can generate macroscopic forces and movement.

Myosin V, a nonmuscle myosin, functions as a cargo transporter similar to kinesin. With its two motor domains connected by a long lever arm, myosin V takes 36 nm steps along actin filaments, much larger than kinesin's 8 nm steps. This difference in step size corresponds to the structural repeat of their respective tracks: actin's helical repeat versus the tubulin dimer spacing in microtubules.

The F1-ATP synthase represents a rotary biomolecular motor of extraordinary efficiency. Located in the inner mitochondrial membrane, this enzyme synthesizes ATP from ADP and phosphate using the energy of a proton gradient. The F0 portion of the enzyme acts as a proton channel, converting the potential energy of the proton gradient into rotational motion. This rotation drives conformational changes in the F1 portion, facilitating ATP synthesis. Remarkably, when operating in reverse, the F1-ATP synthase can hydrolyze ATP to pump protons against their concentration gradient, demonstrating the reversibility of these nanomachines (Figure 3-2).

CHAPTER 3 CELLULAR NANOSTRUCTURES AND BIOMOLECULAR MOTORS

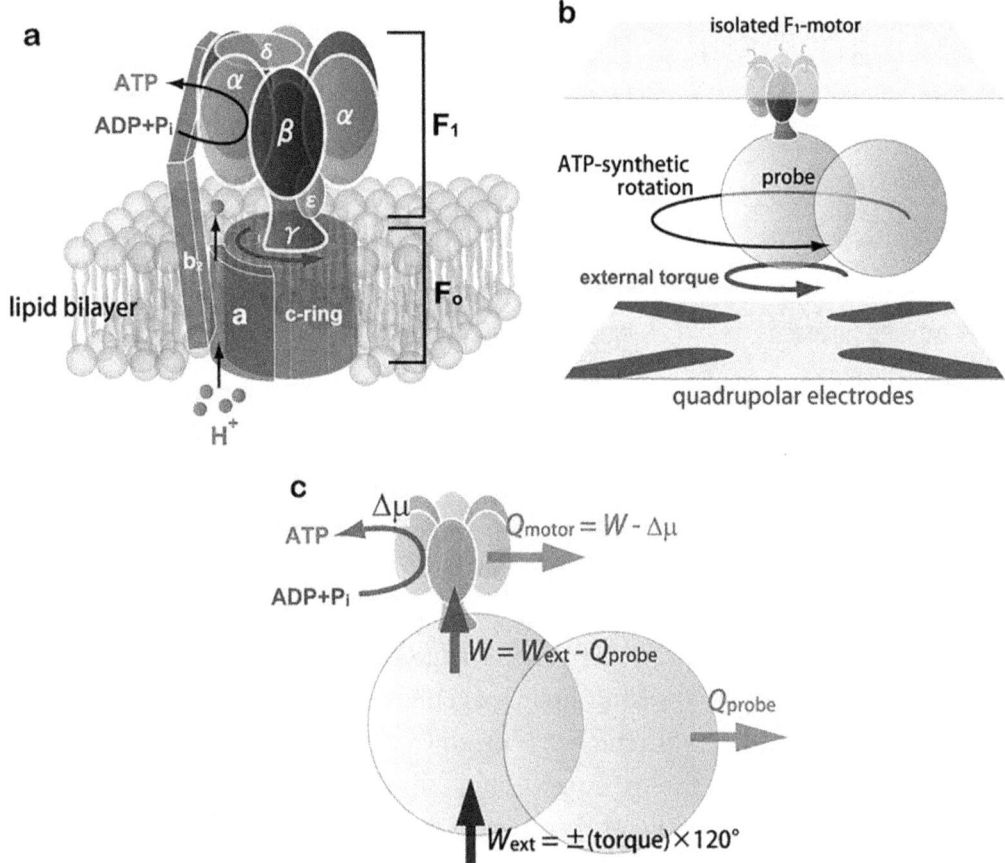

Figure 3-2. Structure and Rotational Mechanism of F1-ATP Synthase

Flagellar motors drive bacterial motility through the rotation of a helical flagellum. This complex molecular machine, embedded in the bacterial cell envelope, converts the energy of an ion gradient (typically protons or sodium ions) into rotational motion. With over 40 different proteins organized into the rotor, stator, and switching apparatus, the bacterial flagellar motor represents one of the most complex biomolecular machines known. Capable of rotating at speeds exceeding 100 Hz and generating torques of up to 4,000 pN·nm, this nanomotor demonstrates how natural selection has optimized molecular machines for specific functions.

Viral DNA packaging motors, such as those found in bacteriophages, represent another class of powerful biomolecular motors. These motors generate forces exceeding 50 piconewtons to package DNA into preformed viral capsids against enormous internal pressure. Through a mechanism involving conformational changes coupled to ATP hydrolysis, these motors can compact DNA to near-crystalline density within the confined space of the viral capsid.

RNA polymerase and ribosomes, though not traditionally classified as motor proteins, also exhibit motor-like behavior. RNA polymerase translocates along DNA during transcription, unwinding the double helix and synthesizing RNA while generating forces sufficient to displace nucleosomes. Similarly, ribosomes move along mRNA during translation, coordinating the complex process of protein synthesis with precise movements at the nanoscale.

The study of biomolecular motors has profound implications for nanotechnology. These natural nanomachines demonstrate principles of energy transduction, mechanochemical coupling, and coordinated motion that inspire the design of synthetic molecular motors. By understanding how these motors function at the molecular level, scientists are developing artificial nanomotors for applications ranging from targeted drug delivery to nanorobotics. The efficiency, specificity, and adaptability of biomolecular motors represent benchmarks for synthetic systems, driving innovation in molecular engineering and nanoscale design.

3.3 Nanopores and Uses

Nanopores represent a fascinating class of biological and synthetic nanostructures that form channels or pores with diameters in the nanometer range. These nanoscale channels facilitate the selective transport of ions, molecules, and even macromolecules across otherwise impermeable barriers. In biological systems, nanopores play crucial roles in cellular processes such as ion conduction, molecular transport, and cell signaling. Inspired by these natural systems, synthetic nanopores have emerged as powerful tools with applications spanning biosensing, molecular separation, energy conversion, and DNA sequencing.

Biological nanopores exist in cellular membranes as integral membrane proteins that create passage channels across the lipid bilayer. One of the most well-studied examples is α-hemolysin, a toxin produced by Staphylococcus aureus that self-assembles into a mushroom-shaped heptameric pore with an internal diameter of approximately 1.4 nm at its narrowest point. This pore allows ions and small molecules to pass through the membrane, disrupting cellular homeostasis in the host organism. Other biological nanopores include gramicidin A, which forms a narrow channel specific for monovalent cations, and porins, which create larger pores in the outer membrane of gram-negative bacteria.

The ion channels that regulate cellular electrical activity represent another important class of biological nanopores. These specialized membrane proteins undergo conformational changes in response to specific stimuli—voltage differences, ligand binding, or mechanical stress—transitioning between open and closed states. Potassium channels, for instance, achieve remarkable selectivity, allowing potassium ions to pass while excluding sodium ions, despite their smaller size. This selectivity arises from precise arrangements of amino acids in the channel that mimic the hydration shell of potassium ions, illustrating how atomic-scale geometry determines nanopore function.

Synthetic nanopores can be fabricated using various approaches, each offering unique advantages and challenges. Solid-state nanopores are typically created by drilling holes in thin membranes of materials such as silicon nitride, graphene, or molybdenum disulfide using techniques such as focused ion beam milling or controlled dielectric breakdown. These nanopores offer excellent mechanical stability and the possibility of integration with electronic detection systems, though they generally lack the precise structural control achieved in biological systems.

Hybrid approaches combine biological components with synthetic materials to create nanopores with tailored properties. For example, biological pores such as α-hemolysin can be embedded in synthetic lipid bilayers or polymer membranes, creating platforms that harness the specificity of biological systems while improving stability and control. DNA origami, which uses DNA as a structural material to create predetermined nanoscale shapes, has also been employed to design artificial nanopores with programmable dimensions and surface chemistry.

The unique properties of nanopores—their confined dimensions, controlled surface chemistry, and selective transport characteristics—have led to numerous technological applications. Perhaps the most transformative has been nanopore-based DNA sequencing, which enables the direct reading of DNA sequences without the need for amplification or labeling. As DNA molecules pass through the nanopore, they disrupt the ionic current in a sequence-dependent manner, producing electrical signals that can be decoded to determine the nucleotide sequence (Figure 3-3).

CHAPTER 3   CELLULAR NANOSTRUCTURES AND BIOMOLECULAR MOTORS

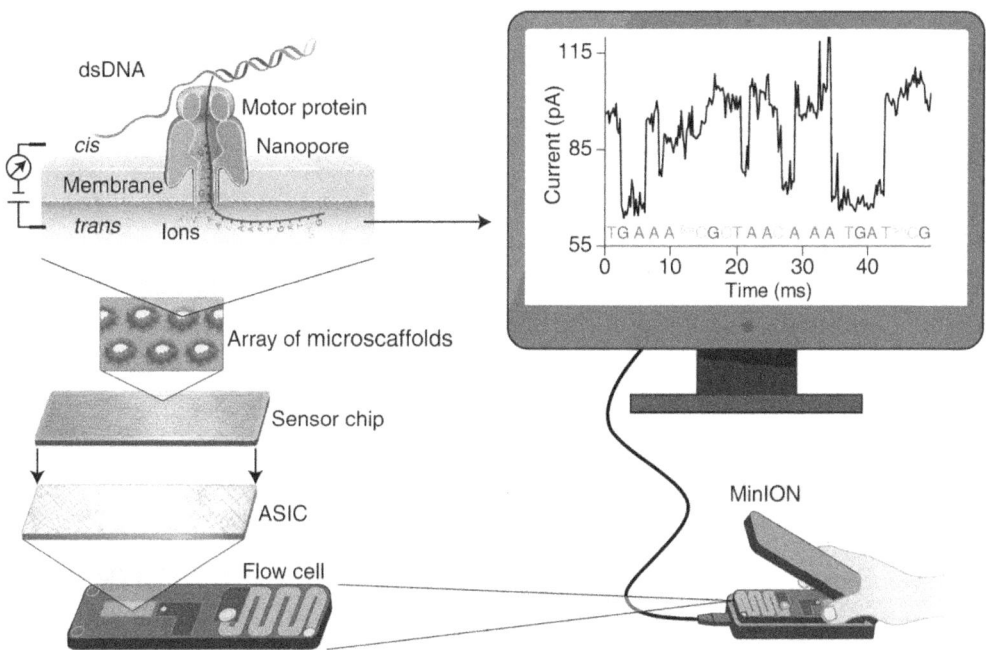

Figure 3-3. Nanopore-Based DNA Sequencing

Nanopore sensing has expanded beyond DNA sequencing to detect and characterize a wide range of analytes, from small molecules to proteins and even viruses. The principle remains similar: the passage or binding of an analyte within the nanopore creates a characteristic signal—typically a change in ionic current—that provides information about the analyte's identity, concentration, and properties. By functionalizing nanopores with specific recognition elements such as aptamers or antibodies, researchers have developed highly selective sensors for targets ranging from biomarkers of disease to environmental contaminants.

The selective transport properties of nanopores have also been exploited for molecular separation and filtration. Nanoporous membranes with precisely controlled pore sizes can separate molecules based on size and shape, offering potential applications in water purification, gas separation, and biomolecule isolation. When combined with surface functionalization to introduce chemical selectivity, these membranes can achieve separations beyond what is possible with size exclusion alone.

CHAPTER 3   CELLULAR NANOSTRUCTURES AND BIOMOLECULAR MOTORS

Energy conversion represents another promising application of nanopore technology. Inspired by biological systems such as the F0F1-ATP synthase, researchers are developing nanopore-based devices that convert osmotic, electrochemical, or thermal gradients into electrical energy. These systems harness the controlled movement of ions through nanopores to generate electrical power, potentially enabling energy harvesting from sources such as salinity gradients in estuaries or waste heat.

Controlled drug delivery systems utilizing nanopores have been developed to achieve precise spatial and temporal control over the release of therapeutic agents. By incorporating stimuli-responsive elements that alter nanopore permeability in response to specific triggers—pH changes, temperature, light, or biomarkers—these systems can deliver drugs only when and where needed, potentially reducing side effects and improving treatment efficacy.

The field of nanopore technology continues to advance rapidly, driven by improvements in fabrication techniques, detection methods, and theoretical understanding. As researchers gain greater control over nanopore geometry, surface chemistry, and integration with other systems, the applications of these remarkable nanostructures will likely expand, potentially revolutionizing fields from healthcare to environmental monitoring and energy production.

3.4 Bio-inspired Structures

The extraordinary efficiency, specificity, and adaptability of biological nanostructures have long served as inspiration for human-engineered nanotechnological systems. Bio-inspired nanomaterials and devices draw on principles refined through billions of years of evolution, translating nature's solutions into innovative technologies with applications across multiple disciplines. This biomimetic approach leverages the sophisticated molecular machinery of living systems to design synthetic structures with enhanced functionality and performance.

DNA nanotechnology represents one of the most successful implementations of bio-inspired design at the nanoscale. Pioneered by Nadrian Seeman in the 1980s, this field exploits the specific base-pairing interactions of DNA not for its genetic information but as a structural material. Through careful sequence design, DNA can be programmed to self-assemble into complex two- and three-dimensional structures with nanometer precision. DNA origami, a technique developed by Paul Rothemund, enables the folding of a long single-stranded DNA scaffold into virtually any desired shape using hundreds

CHAPTER 3   CELLULAR NANOSTRUCTURES AND BIOMOLECULAR MOTORS

of short "staple" strands. This approach has produced DNA nanostructures ranging from simple geometric shapes to complex objects like boxes with controllable lids, molecular robots, and logic gates.

The applications of DNA nanotechnology extend beyond structural designs to functional devices. DNA nanomachines can perform tasks such as molecular sensing, cargo transport, and even rudimentary computation. For example, DNA walkers inspired by natural motor proteins can move along predefined tracks, carrying molecular cargo from one location to another. These synthetic molecular motors, though currently less efficient than their biological counterparts, demonstrate how principles from natural systems can be adapted to create novel functional nanomachines.

Peptide-based nanostructures offer another avenue for bio-inspired design. Peptides, with their diverse chemical functionalities and ability to form secondary structures (α-helices, β-sheets), provide versatile building blocks for self-assembling nanomaterials. Peptide amphiphiles, which combine a hydrophobic tail with a hydrophilic peptide head group, can self-assemble into various nanostructures, including fibers, ribbons, tubes, and vesicles. These materials have shown promise for applications in tissue engineering, drug delivery, and biomineralization.

Protein engineering has enabled the design of custom protein nanostructures with tailored properties and functions. Using computational design tools and directed evolution approaches, researchers have created artificial protein assemblies ranging from nanoscale cages to extended crystalline frameworks. These protein-based materials can incorporate specific binding sites, catalytic activities, or stimuli-responsive elements, mimicking the functional versatility of natural proteins while expanding beyond the constraints of evolved systems.

Lipid-based nanostructures, inspired by cellular membranes, have found widespread applications, particularly in drug delivery. Liposomes—spherical vesicles composed of phospholipid bilayers—encapsulate and protect therapeutic agents, improving their pharmacokinetics and reducing side effects. More complex lipid nanostructures, such as cubosomes and hexosomes, offer alternative delivery platforms with unique properties, including high internal surface area and multiple compartments for combination therapies.

Biohybrid systems represent a growing area of bio-inspired nanotechnology, combining biological components with synthetic materials to create devices with enhanced functionality. For instance, nanomotors powered by enzymes or whole cells attached to synthetic nanomaterials harness biological energy conversion systems to drive mechanical motion. These biohybrid motors demonstrate higher efficiency than fully synthetic systems, particularly in biological environments where they can use naturally available fuels.

Surface functionalization with biomolecules has produced materials with specialized properties such as antifouling, self-cleaning, or tissue integration. For example, surfaces patterned with antimicrobial peptides can prevent bacterial colonization, while those modified with cell-adhesion peptides promote specific cellular interactions—principles derived from natural defense mechanisms and extracellular matrices, respectively.

Biomineralization, the process by which living organisms produce minerals, has inspired approaches for synthesizing inorganic nanomaterials under mild conditions. By mimicking the proteins and processes involved in natural biomineralization, researchers have developed methods to control the nucleation, growth, and morphology of nanocrystals. These bio-inspired synthesis routes typically operate at ambient temperature and pressure, using environmentally benign reagents—a stark contrast to many traditional nanomaterial synthesis methods that require harsh conditions.

Nature's hierarchical organization, where nanoscale building blocks assemble into increasingly complex structures across multiple length scales, provides a blueprint for designing advanced materials with emergent properties. Bio-inspired hierarchical materials combine precisely defined nanoscale components with controlled organization at micro-, meso-, and macroscales, resulting in properties that cannot be achieved through uniform structuring alone. Examples include nacre-inspired composites with exceptional mechanical properties and bone-inspired materials that combine strength with porosity (Table 3-2).

Table 3-2. Examples of Bio-inspired Hierarchical Materials

Natural System	Key Features	Bio-inspired Material	Enhanced Properties
Nacre (mother of pearl)	Layered arrangement of aragonite platelets with organic matrix	Layered polymer-ceramic composites	High strength and toughness, crack deflection
Bone	Mineralized collagen fibrils organized into osteons	Mineralized polymer scaffolds with controlled porosity	Combination of strength, lightness, and bioactivity
Lotus leaf	Hierarchical surface roughness with waxy coating	Superhydrophobic surfaces with micro-/nanotexturing	Self-cleaning, water repellency
Spider silk	Proteins with ordered and disordered regions	Recombinant or synthetic silk-inspired fibers	High tensile strength with elasticity
Gecko foot	Hierarchical branching setae with nanoscale spatulae	Microstructured adhesives with nanoscale tips	Reversible adhesion, clean detachment

The development of bio-inspired smart materials that respond dynamically to environmental changes represents an ongoing frontier in nanotechnology. Drawing inspiration from biological systems that sense and adapt to their surroundings, these materials incorporate mechanisms for stimuli-responsiveness, self-regulation, and even self-healing. Shape-memory materials that change form in response to temperature, pH-responsive polymers that swell or contract, and self-healing composites that repair damage all demonstrate how principles from living systems can create materials with lifelike behaviors.

As our understanding of biological nanostructures deepens, so too does our ability to extract and implement their design principles in synthetic systems. The convergence of nanotechnology with fields such as synthetic biology, materials science, and computational modeling continues to expand the possibilities for bio-inspired innovation. By learning from and building upon nature's designs, researchers are developing nanomaterials and devices with unprecedented capabilities, potentially revolutionizing fields from medicine to energy conversion and environmental remediation.

3.5 Technological Significance

The study of cellular nanostructures and biomolecular motors has profound technological implications that extend across numerous disciplines, from medicine to materials science and computational systems. By understanding and harnessing the principles that govern these natural nanomachines, researchers are developing technologies that not only address current challenges but also open entirely new possibilities for human innovation.

In medicine, nanotechnologies inspired by cellular structures have revolutionized drug delivery systems. Liposomes and polymeric nanoparticles, mimicking the structure and function of cellular vesicles, can encapsulate therapeutic agents and deliver them specifically to diseased tissues, minimizing side effects and improving efficacy. More sophisticated drug delivery platforms incorporate targeting ligands, stimuli-responsive elements, and controlled release mechanisms inspired by cellular transport systems. For instance, nanoparticles designed to respond to the unique microenvironment of tumors—such as lower pH or higher temperature—can release their cargo selectively at the disease site, increasing therapeutic efficacy while reducing systemic toxicity.

Nanomedicine extends beyond drug delivery to diagnostic applications, where principles from cellular sensing mechanisms inform the development of advanced biosensors. Nanopore-based sensing platforms, drawing inspiration from ion channels, can detect individual molecules with extraordinary sensitivity. These systems have enabled breakthrough technologies such as nanopore sequencing, which allows for direct, label-free reading of DNA sequences with implications for personalized medicine, pathogen detection, and basic research. The commercialization of nanopore sequencing devices has already transformed genomic analysis, making it more accessible, portable, and real time.

The field of regenerative medicine has benefited tremendously from bio-inspired scaffolds that mimic the extracellular matrix's nanoscale architecture. These scaffolds provide structural support while incorporating biochemical and mechanical cues that guide cell behavior, promoting tissue regeneration. By replicating the hierarchical organization of natural tissues—from nanoscale protein structures to microscale cellular arrangements—these materials create environments conducive to proper cell function and tissue development.

In medical imaging, nanoparticles with properties derived from or enhanced by biomolecular principles have improved contrast, specificity, and functionality. Multimodal imaging agents that combine different contrast mechanisms—such as magnetic resonance and optical imaging—within a single nanoparticle platform allow comprehensive visualization of biological processes. Active targeting strategies, inspired by cellular recognition mechanisms, direct these agents to specific tissues or cell types, enhancing diagnostic specificity.

Beyond medicine, cellular nanostructures have influenced the development of advanced materials with exceptional properties. Structural proteins like collagen, elastin, and silk have inspired synthetic materials that combine strength, toughness, and elasticity in ways difficult to achieve with traditional engineering approaches. These bio-inspired materials find applications ranging from high-performance textiles to medical implants and tissue engineering scaffolds.

Energy conversion and storage technologies have drawn significant inspiration from biological energy transduction systems. Artificial photosynthetic systems, mimicking the nanoscale organization of natural light-harvesting complexes, aim to convert sunlight into chemical fuels with efficiencies approaching those of plants. Bio-inspired catalysts, designed based on principles from enzymatic active sites, can accelerate chemical reactions under mild conditions, potentially reducing the environmental impact of industrial processes. Batteries with nanostructured electrodes inspired by biological ion transport systems offer improved energy density, faster charging rates, and longer lifespans compared to conventional designs.

The field of nanorobotics represents perhaps the most ambitious application of principles from cellular nanomachines. Drawing inspiration from molecular motors like kinesin and dynein, researchers are developing synthetic nanomotors capable of directed motion at the nanoscale. These motors, powered by chemical reactions, light, or external fields, could eventually perform tasks such as targeted drug delivery, environmental remediation, or microscale manufacturing. While current synthetic nanomotors remain far less sophisticated than their biological counterparts, steady progress in understanding and implementing biomolecular principles brings the vision of functional nanorobots closer to reality.

Computational systems have also benefited from insights into cellular information processing. DNA computing and molecular logic gates, inspired by cellular signaling pathways, offer alternative approaches to information processing that could eventually complement traditional electronic systems. These biochemical computing platforms operate in parallel, potentially solving certain classes of problems more efficiently than conventional computers. Moreover, the extreme information density of DNA—approximately 1 bit per cubic nanometer—suggests possibilities for ultra-high-density data storage systems, with demonstrations already achieving storage densities millions of times greater than conventional flash memory.

Environmental applications of bio-inspired nanotechnology include advanced filtration membranes that mimic the selective permeability of cellular membranes. These materials can address challenges in water purification, separating contaminants based on size, charge, or specific molecular interactions. Bioremediation approaches using engineered nanoparticles or biohybrid systems leverage principles from cellular detoxification mechanisms to neutralize or sequester environmental pollutants.

The convergence of nanotechnology with synthetic biology creates particularly promising opportunities for technological innovation. Engineered cellular systems that incorporate synthetic nanomaterials can perform functions beyond what either could achieve alone. For instance, bacteria modified to express proteins that interact with magnetic nanoparticles can be guided by external magnetic fields, potentially enabling targeted delivery of therapeutic payloads or environmental sensing in otherwise inaccessible locations.

As our understanding of cellular nanostructures deepens and fabrication techniques advance, the technological applications will likely expand in both predicted and unexpected directions. The principles that govern biomolecular motors—energy transduction, mechanical coupling, and information processing at the nanoscale—will continue to inform developments across disciplines, potentially leading to transformative technologies that address global challenges in healthcare, energy, environment, and information processing.

3.6 Summary

The exploration of cellular nanostructures and biomolecular motors reveals nature's extraordinary engineering at the molecular level. From the precise architecture of microtubules to the coordinated stepping of kinesin motors and the selective transport through nanopores, biological systems demonstrate principles of nanoscale design and function that continue to inspire technological innovation. The remarkable efficiency, specificity, and adaptability of these natural nanomachines—operating in the thermally noisy cellular environment where conventional engineering principles often break down—represent benchmarks for synthetic systems.

Bio-inspired nanotechnology has already produced significant advances across multiple disciplines, from nanopore sequencing devices that read DNA with single-nucleotide precision to drug delivery systems that target specific tissues and responsive materials that adapt to environmental changes. As techniques for nanofabrication, biomolecular engineering, and characterization continue to improve, the gap between natural and synthetic nanomachines gradually narrows, opening possibilities for technologies that combine the best aspects of both.

The ongoing dialogue between biological discovery and technological implementation drives progress in nanoscience. Each new insight into the structure and function of cellular nanomachines suggests novel approaches for synthetic systems, while challenges in technology development highlight gaps in our understanding of biological mechanisms. This reciprocal relationship promises to yield increasingly sophisticated nanotechnologies that harness the principles refined through billions of years of evolution.

The future of this field likely lies in hybrid approaches that integrate biological components with synthetic materials, creating systems that leverage the precision and efficiency of biomolecular machines while enhancing stability, control, and functionality through engineered elements. Such biohybrid nanosystems could eventually perform complex tasks in areas ranging from medicine to environmental remediation and information processing, potentially addressing global challenges while opening new frontiers in human technological capability.

Understanding cellular nanostructures and biomolecular motors thus represents not merely an academic pursuit but a practical foundation for technological innovation with transformative potential. By learning from and building upon nature's designs, we continue to expand the boundaries of what is possible at the nanoscale, with implications that extend from individual health to planetary sustainability.

CHAPTER 4

Nanomaterial Synthesis

This chapter examines diverse methodologies for nanomaterial synthesis, covering physical, chemical, and biological approaches. It explores fundamental principles of top-down and bottom-up fabrication techniques, including mechanical milling, laser ablation, sol-gel processing, and green synthesis methods. The chapter investigates hybrid nanocomposite formation and advanced synthesis technologies such as microreactors and 3D printing at the nanoscale. Throughout, emphasis is placed on the relationship between synthesis parameters and resulting nanomaterial properties, providing readers with a comprehensive understanding of how synthesis techniques influence nanomaterial characteristics for various applications.

4.1 Introduction

Nanomaterial synthesis represents a cornerstone of nanotechnology, determining the properties, performance, and applicability of nanoscale structures across various fields. At dimensions between 1 and 100 nanometers, materials exhibit unique physical, chemical, and biological properties vastly different from their bulk counterparts due to quantum confinement effects and increased surface-to-volume ratios.

Precise control over size, shape, composition, and surface chemistry has revolutionized numerous industries from electronics to medicine. This chapter explores nanomaterial synthesis strategies categorized broadly into physical, chemical, and biological approaches, examining how each method influences nanomaterial characteristics and their suitability for different applications.

CHAPTER 4 NANOMATERIAL SYNTHESIS

4.2 Physical Synthesis Techniques

Physical synthesis methods typically employ mechanical forces, thermal processes, or high-energy inputs to transform bulk materials into nanoscale structures, generally following a top-down approach.

Mechanical Milling and Ball Milling

Mechanical milling represents an established technique for nanomaterial synthesis, offering simplicity and scalability. In this process, mechanical forces break down bulk materials into nanoparticles through repeated deformation, fracturing, and cold welding. Ball milling utilizes high-energy collisions between grinding media and precursor material within a rotating chamber (Figure 4-1).

Key parameters affecting this process include milling time, rotation speed, ball-to-powder ratio, and milling atmosphere. The technique is versatile, capable of processing metals, alloys, ceramics, and composites, and enables the production of metastable phases difficult to achieve through equilibrium processes.

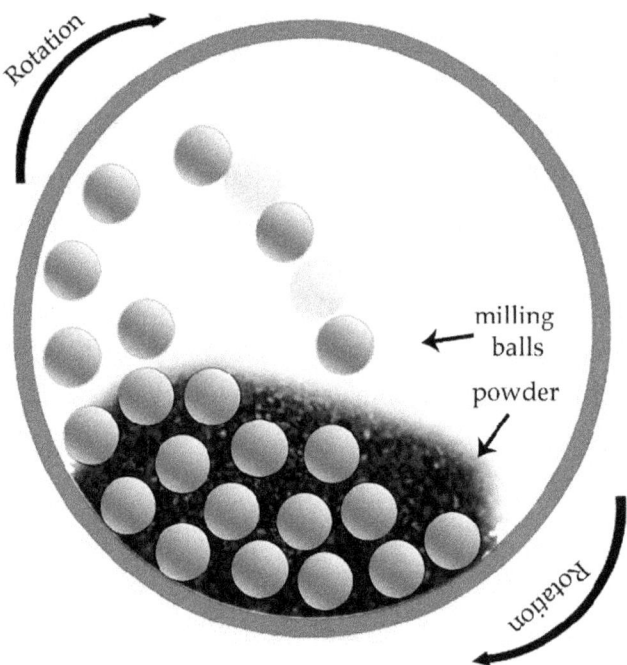

Figure 4-1. *Schematic Diagram of High-Energy Ball Milling Process Showing the Transformation from Bulk to Nanoscale Particles*

Limitations include contamination from milling media, broad particle size distribution, and potential agglomeration. Recent advances include surfactant-assisted milling and cryogenic milling to minimize these issues.

Laser Ablation

Laser ablation utilizes intense laser irradiation to remove material from a target and generate nanoparticles. A high-power pulsed laser beam focused onto a solid target causes rapid heating, melting, and vaporization, forming a plasma plume that expands and cools to form nanoparticles.

This technique can be performed in various media, including vacuum, gases, or liquids. Laser ablation in liquid (LAL) produces pure colloidal nanoparticles without chemical additives, while pulsed laser deposition (PLD) is primarily used for thin film deposition (Table 4-1).

Table 4-1. Key Parameters in Laser Ablation Synthesis of Nanomaterials

Parameter	Range	Effect on Nanoparticle Properties
Laser wavelength	193–1064 nm	Influences absorption efficiency
Pulse duration	Femtosecond to nanosecond	Affects heat dissipation
Fluence	0.1–10 J/cm^2	Determines ablation threshold
Target material	Metals, semiconductors, ceramics	Defines chemical composition
Medium	Vacuum, gas, liquid	Impacts cooling rate

Advantages include high-purity products without chemical reagents, but production rates are typically lower than chemical methods.

Physical Vapor Deposition (PVD)

PVD encompasses vacuum-based techniques that convert solid materials into the vapor phase through physical processes, followed by condensation onto a substrate. The main variants include

- **Thermal Evaporation**: A simple method where source material is heated to its evaporation point
- **Sputtering**: Uses energetic ions to bombard a target material, ejecting atoms
- **Electron Beam Evaporation**: Utilizes focused electron beams to heat and evaporate source materials

PVD techniques offer precise control over film thickness down to the nanometer scale. By manipulating substrate temperature, deposition angle, and rotation, various nanostructures can be created, including nanorods and nanocolumns (Figure 4-2).

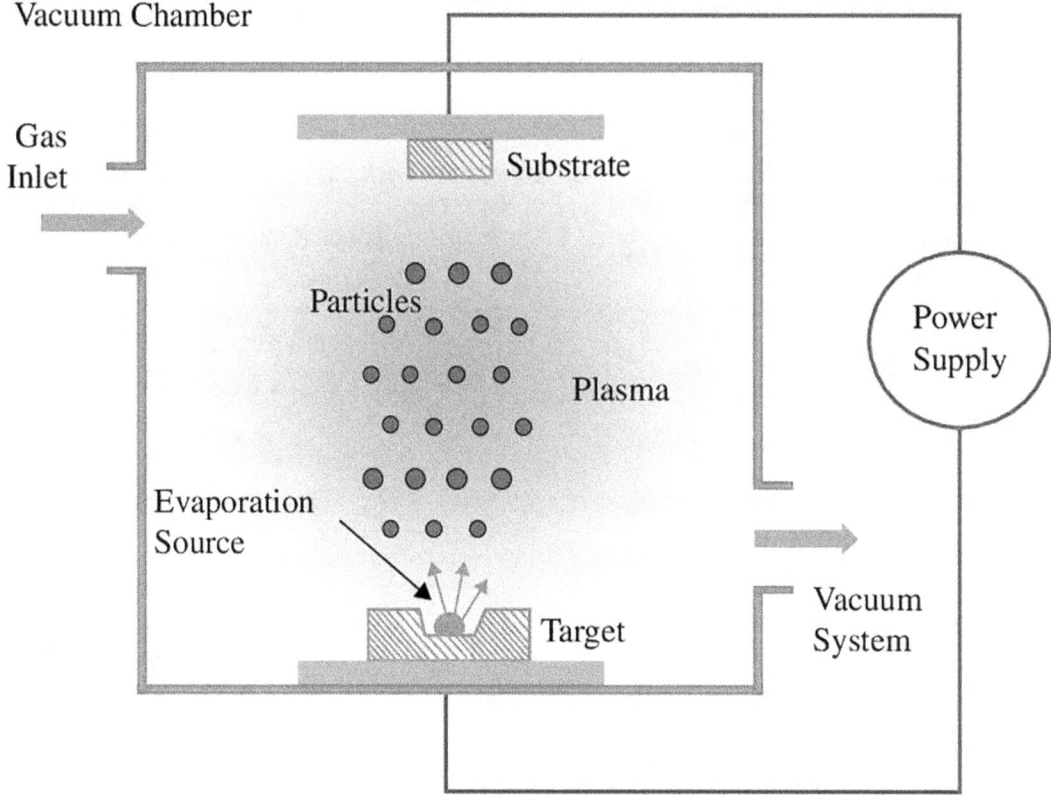

Figure 4-2. Angle-Dependent Physical Vapor Deposition

Inert Gas Condensation

Inert gas condensation (IGC) specializes in synthesizing ultra-pure metal and alloy nanoparticles with a narrow size distribution. The source material is evaporated in a chamber partially filled with inert gas at low pressure. Evaporated atoms collide with inert gas molecules, cool, and nucleate to form nanoclusters.

The technique offers precise control over particle size through adjustment of process parameters like gas pressure and evaporation temperature. IGC produces metallic nanoparticles with exceptional purity due to the ultra-high vacuum environment.

4.3 Chemical Synthesis Methods

Chemical synthesis approaches typically employ bottom-up strategies, building nanomaterials from atomic or molecular precursors through chemical reactions and assembly processes.

Sol-Gel Processing

Sol-gel processing transforms a solution (sol) into a three-dimensional network (gel) through hydrolysis and condensation reactions of molecular precursors, typically metal alkoxides. As these reactions progress, the solution transitions from a colloidal suspension to a network that entraps the remaining solvent.

The method offers remarkable control over nanomaterial properties through adjustment of parameters including precursor type, solvent choice, pH, and reaction temperature (Table 4-2).

Table 4-2. Influence of Sol-Gel Processing Parameters on Nanomaterial Properties

Parameter	Effect on Nanomaterial Properties
pH	Acidic: linear polymersBasic: branched networks
Water ratio	Higher ratios: smaller particlesLower ratios: larger structures
Solvent type	Affects reaction rates and drying behavior
Aging temperature	Higher temperatures increase crystallinity
Drying method	Conventional: causes shrinkageSupercritical: preserves porosity

Sol-gel-derived nanomaterials find applications across diverse fields, including catalysis, sensors, and optical coatings.

Chemical Precipitation and Co-precipitation

Chemical precipitation creates nanomaterials through the formation of insoluble products from soluble precursors. When reactants containing metal ions are mixed under controlled conditions, supersaturation leads to nucleation and growth of nanoparticles.

Co-precipitation extends this approach to multi-component systems, where multiple metal ions precipitate simultaneously to form mixed-metal compounds. Key parameters affecting the process include supersaturation level, temperature, pH, and surfactants.

These methods offer simplicity, scalability, and cost-effectiveness, though challenges include potential inhomogeneity in particle size and impurity incorporation.

Hydrothermal and Solvothermal Synthesis

These methods leverage elevated temperatures and pressures to dissolve and recrystallize materials that would otherwise be insoluble under ambient conditions. Reactions occur in sealed vessels called autoclaves, with water (hydrothermal) or nonaqueous solvents (solvothermal) as the medium.

Both techniques excel in producing highly crystalline nanomaterials with controlled morphology. Critical parameters include temperature, pressure, reaction duration, and structure-directing agents.

These methods are particularly valuable for creating one-dimensional (nanorods, nanowires) and two-dimensional (nanosheets) structures.

Chemical Vapor Deposition (CVD)

CVD utilizes gas-phase chemical reactions to deposit solid materials onto substrates. Unlike physical methods, CVD involves chemical reactions of volatile precursors at or near a heated substrate surface.

Variants include plasma-enhanced CVD (PECVD), metal-organic CVD (MOCVD), and atomic layer deposition (ALD). The technique excels in creating conformal coatings and one-dimensional nanostructures such as carbon nanotubes and semiconductor nanowires (Table 4-3).

Table 4-3. Key Parameters in Chemical Vapor Deposition of Nanomaterials

Parameter	Effect on Nanomaterial Properties
Substrate temperature	Determines reaction kinetics and crystallinity
Precursor chemistry	Defines growth rate and potential contamination
Pressure	Influences precursor residence time
Gas flow rate	Affects mass transport and uniformity
Catalyst type/size	Determines nanostructure diameter

CVD enables selective deposition, where growth occurs preferentially on specific substrate regions, valuable for device integration.

4.4 Biological Synthesis Approaches

Biological synthesis harnesses living organisms or their derivatives to produce nanomaterials under mild, environmentally friendly conditions.

Microorganism-Mediated Synthesis

Microorganisms, including bacteria, fungi, and yeasts, can transform metal ions into nanoparticles through various cellular mechanisms. The synthesis can occur

1. **Extracellularly**: Through enzymes secreted into the surrounding medium
2. **Intracellularly**: Within the cytoplasm after metal ions penetrate the cell
3. **At the Cell Surface**: Through membrane-bound enzymes

Different microorganisms demonstrate varied capabilities based on their enzymatic machinery. A significant advantage is the natural capping of nanoparticles with biomolecules, enhancing stability and biocompatibility.

CHAPTER 4 NANOMATERIAL SYNTHESIS

Plant-Mediated Synthesis

This method utilizes plant extracts containing biomolecules that function as reducing and stabilizing agents. The process involves mixing aqueous plant extract with metal salt solution, resulting in nanoparticle formation through the action of phytochemicals, including polyphenols, terpenoids, alkaloids, and proteins (Figure 4-3).

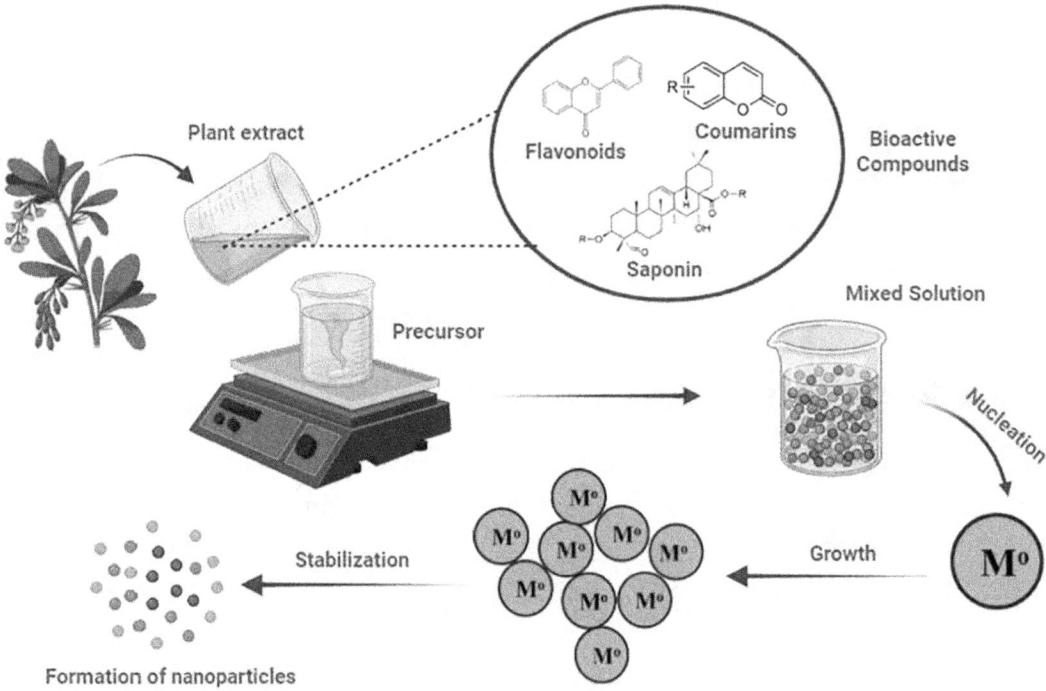

Figure 4-3. Schematic of plant-mediated nanoparticle synthesis showing different phytochemicals' roles

Advantages include elimination of hazardous chemicals, ambient reaction conditions, and biocompatible surface coating. Parameters such as extract concentration, pH, and temperature influence the final nanomaterial properties.

Biomolecule-Assisted Synthesis

This refined approach employs purified biomolecules rather than whole organisms or crude extracts. Effective biomolecules include

1. Proteins and enzymes (BSA, lysozyme, nitrate reductase)
2. Polysaccharides (chitosan, starch, alginate)
3. DNA and nucleic acids
4. Peptides and amino acids
5. Vitamins (especially ascorbic acid)

This approach offers better reproducibility and mechanistic understanding compared to using whole organisms or crude extracts.

4.5 Hybrid Nanocomposites

Hybrid nanocomposites integrate different nanomaterials to achieve enhanced properties beyond those of individual components. These materials combine organic and inorganic constituents at the nanoscale, creating synergistic effects.

Common hybrid combinations include polymer-metal nanoparticle composites, carbon nanotube-ceramic hybrids, and metal oxide-quantum dot systems. Integration strategies include physical blending, in situ synthesis, layer-by-layer assembly, and template-directed approaches.

Applications span structural materials, energy storage, catalysis, and biomedical systems. Recent advances focus on stimuli-responsive nanocomposites that change properties in response to external triggers like light, pH, or temperature.

4.6 Advanced Synthesis Technologies

Recent innovations are pushing the boundaries of nanomaterial fabrication through novel methodologies and equipment.

Microfluidic and Continuous Flow Synthesis

Microfluidic devices offer precise control over reaction conditions in miniaturized channels. Benefits include rapid mixing, enhanced heat transfer, uniform residence times, and reduced reagent consumption. These systems enable continuous production of nanomaterials with consistent properties.

Electrospinning and Electrospraying

These techniques apply high voltage to liquid solutions or melts, creating charged jets that solidify into nanofibers (electrospinning) or nanoparticles (electrospraying). Parameters including voltage, flow rate, and working distance determine the resulting nanomaterial morphology.

Atomic and Molecular Layer Deposition

These methods deposit materials with atomic precision through sequential, self-limiting surface reactions. Each reaction cycle adds a single layer of atoms or molecules, enabling unprecedented control over thickness and composition for ultrathin films and conformal coatings.

3D Printing at the Nanoscale

Two-photon polymerization and directed energy deposition techniques enable three-dimensional fabrication with nanoscale precision. These approaches create complex architectures for applications in photonics, tissue engineering, and microfluidic devices.

4.7 Summary

The synthesis of nanomaterials represents a dynamic field that bridges fundamental science with practical applications. This chapter has examined diverse synthesis methodologies across physical, chemical, and biological domains, highlighting how each approach offers distinct advantages for controlling nanomaterial properties.

The choice of synthesis method significantly influences the characteristics of resulting nanomaterials, including size, shape, composition, crystallinity, and surface chemistry. Understanding these relationships enables researchers to tailor nanomaterials for specific applications, from electronics and energy to medicine and environmental remediation.

As nanotechnology continues to advance, synthesis methodologies evolve toward greater precision, sustainability, and scalability. Hybrid approaches that combine multiple techniques often yield the most promising results, leveraging the strengths of different methods to achieve nanomaterials with unprecedented properties and performance.

Future directions in nanomaterial synthesis will likely focus on in situ monitoring and feedback control systems, computational modeling for predictive synthesis, and environmentally benign processes that minimize energy consumption and hazardous waste. Through these innovations, nanomaterial synthesis will continue to enable technological breakthroughs across diverse fields, addressing critical challenges in health, energy, and sustainability.

CHAPTER 5

Characterization of Nanomaterials

This chapter provides a comprehensive analysis of the principal techniques employed in the characterization of nanomaterials, which is essential for understanding their properties and potential applications. The chapter begins with optical techniques such as UV-Vis spectroscopy and photoluminescence, which reveal critical information about electronic structure and physical properties. X-ray diffraction techniques for crystallographic analysis are then explored, followed by electron microscopy methods that allow direct visualization of nanomaterials. The discussion extends to size and surface analysis techniques, including dynamic light scattering and BET surface area analysis, which provide crucial data on particle dimensions and surface properties. The chapter concludes with a methodological comparison that guides researchers in selecting appropriate techniques based on specific research requirements, highlighting the complementary nature of these characterization methods and their synergistic use in nanotechnology research and development.

5.1 Introduction

The characterization of nanomaterials represents a critical junction in nanotechnology where theory meets experimental validation. As materials transition into the nanoscale realm (1–100 nm), their properties often diverge significantly from their bulk counterparts due to quantum confinement effects, increased surface-to-volume ratios, and unique structural arrangements. Accurate characterization is therefore not merely descriptive but fundamentally predictive of how nanomaterials will perform in various applications ranging from medicine to electronics.

CHAPTER 5   CHARACTERIZATION OF NANOMATERIALS

The multifaceted nature of nanomaterials necessitates a diverse arsenal of characterization techniques, each providing distinct but complementary information about material properties. No single technique offers a complete picture; rather, researchers must strategically employ multiple methods to construct a comprehensive understanding of nanomaterial structure, composition, and behavior.

This chapter navigates through the principal characterization methodologies employed in modern nanotechnology laboratories. We begin with optical techniques that probe electronic structure, then progress to X-ray methods that reveal crystallographic information, followed by electron microscopy techniques that provide direct visual confirmation of nanoscale features. Size and surface analysis methods are then examined, concluding with a comparative analysis of these diverse approaches to guide researchers in selecting appropriate techniques for specific research questions.

Throughout this exploration, we emphasize not only the theoretical foundations of each technique but also their practical implementation, limitations, and complementary relationships. The field of nanomaterial characterization continues to evolve rapidly, with innovations in instrumentation and methodology continuously enhancing our ability to understand these remarkable materials at increasingly fundamental levels.

5.2 Optical Techniques

Introduction to Optical Characterization

Optical characterization techniques rely on the interaction between light and matter to extract valuable information about nanomaterials. These methods are particularly powerful because they are often nondestructive, provide rapid analysis, and can reveal critical information about electronic structure, physical dimensions, and chemical composition. The nanoscale dimensions of materials create unique optical phenomena that can be leveraged for characterization, including quantum confinement effects, surface plasmon resonance, and enhanced light scattering.

UV-Visible Spectroscopy

UV-Visible spectroscopy represents one of the most accessible yet powerful techniques for nanomaterial characterization. This method measures the absorption or transmission of ultraviolet and visible light through a sample, providing insights into electronic transitions and band structure. For nanomaterials, UV-Vis spectroscopy is particularly valuable due to size-dependent optical properties.

In semiconductor quantum dots, for instance, the absorption edge shifts to higher energies (blue shift) as particle size decreases due to quantum confinement effects. This relationship between particle size and absorption characteristics allows researchers to estimate nanoparticle dimensions through spectroscopic analysis. Gold and silver nanoparticles exhibit strong absorption bands in the visible region due to surface plasmon resonance (SPR), with peak positions highly sensitive to particle size, shape, and surrounding medium (Table 5-1).

The Beer-Lambert law forms the fundamental basis for quantitative analysis using UV-Vis spectroscopy:

$$A = \varepsilon c l$$

Where A represents absorbance, ε is the molar extinction coefficient, c denotes concentration, and l is the path length of the sample cell. For nanomaterials, the extinction coefficient is often size-dependent, requiring careful calibration for accurate concentration determination.

Table 5-1. *Typical UV-Vis Absorption Characteristics of Common Nanomaterials*

Nanomaterial Type	Typical Absorption Range (nm)	Size-Dependent Features
Gold nanoparticles	520–580	Red shift with increasing size
Silver nanoparticles	380–450	Red shift with increasing size
CdSe quantum dots	400–650	Blue shift with decreasing size
Carbon nanotubes	400–1400	Multiple peaks based on chirality
Graphene oxide	230–300	Reduction state dependent

CHAPTER 5   CHARACTERIZATION OF NANOMATERIALS

Photoluminescence Spectroscopy

Photoluminescence (PL) spectroscopy examines the light emitted by a nanomaterial following photoexcitation. This technique provides crucial information about electronic band structure, defect states, and energy transfer processes. For semiconductor nanomaterials, PL spectroscopy reveals quantum confinement effects through emission wavelength dependence on particle size.

The PL process involves several steps: photoexcitation of electrons from the valence to the conduction band, relaxation to the band edge, and radiative recombination resulting in photon emission. The emission wavelength correlates directly with the band gap energy, which varies with nanoparticle size due to quantum confinement. Additionally, the PL intensity and spectral width provide insights into surface defects and size distribution, respectively.

Time-resolved photoluminescence (TRPL) extends conventional PL by measuring the time dependence of emission, yielding information about carrier lifetimes and recombination dynamics. Fluorescence lifetime measurements are particularly valuable for biological applications of nanomaterials, including sensors and imaging agents.

Surface-Enhanced Raman Spectroscopy (SERS)

Raman spectroscopy detects vibrational modes in materials through inelastic scattering of monochromatic light. While conventional Raman signals are often weak, nanomaterials—particularly noble metal nanostructures—can enhance these signals by factors of 10^6 to 10^{10} through a phenomenon known as surface-enhanced Raman spectroscopy (SERS).

SERS enhancement occurs primarily through two mechanisms: electromagnetic enhancement due to localized surface plasmon resonance and chemical enhancement via charge transfer between the adsorbed molecule and the metal surface. The electromagnetic mechanism typically contributes the majority of the enhancement and is highly dependent on nanostructure morphology.

This technique has revolutionized trace detection capabilities, enabling single-molecule sensitivity in optimal conditions. For nanomaterial characterization, SERS provides information about surface chemistry, adsorbed species, and molecular interactions at interfaces. Furthermore, SERS substrate design itself represents an important area of nanomaterial research, with structures including nanoparticle aggregates, nanorods, and nanostars offering varying degrees of enhancement and reproducibility.

Optical Microscopy Techniques

While conventional optical microscopy is diffraction-limited (resolving features no smaller than approximately half the wavelength of light), several advanced techniques circumvent this limitation for nanomaterial visualization:

Near-field scanning optical microscopy (NSOM) achieves subwavelength resolution by positioning a probe with an aperture smaller than the wavelength of light very close to the sample surface. The probe collects evanescent waves that contain high-frequency spatial information, enabling resolution down to tens of nanometers.

Dark-field microscopy selectively collects scattered light while excluding direct illumination, making it particularly effective for visualizing noble metal nanoparticles that exhibit strong scattering due to plasmonic effects. Individual gold and silver nanoparticles can be observed as bright spots against a dark background, with colors corresponding to their dimensions and morphologies.

These optical techniques offer complementary information to electron microscopy methods, with advantages including simpler sample preparation, compatibility with aqueous environments, and the potential for real-time monitoring of dynamic processes (Figure 5-1).

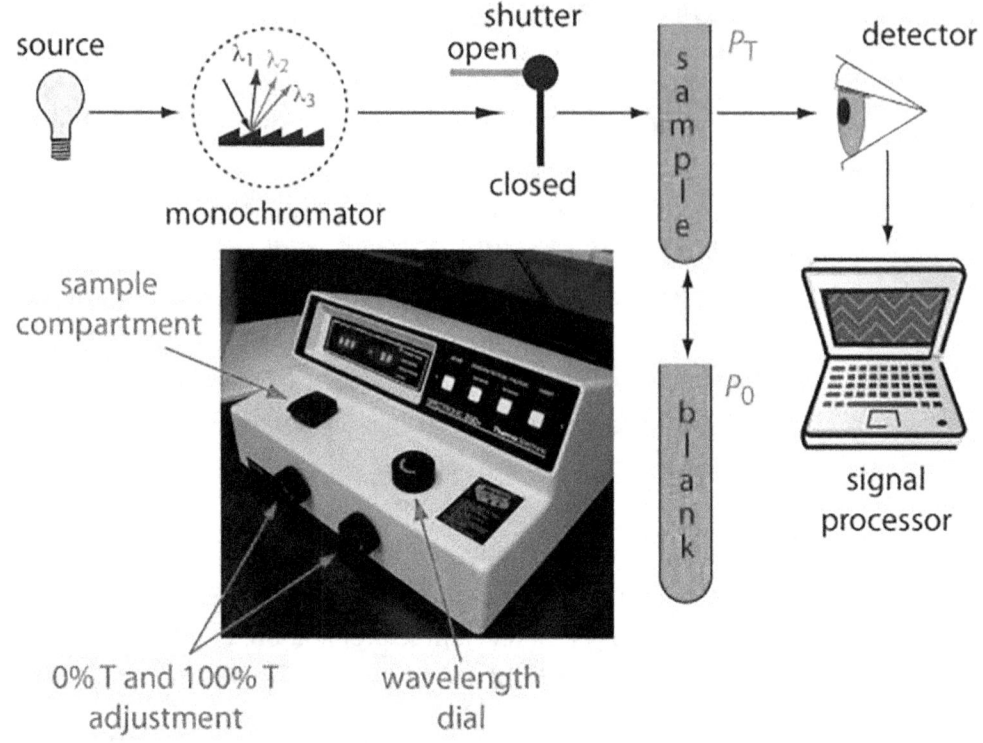

Figure 5-1. Schematic Representation of UV-Vis Spectroscopy Setup for Nanomaterial Characterization Showing Light Source, Monochromator, Sample Holder, Detector, and Data Acquisition System

5.3 X-ray Diffraction

Principles of X-ray Diffraction

X-ray diffraction (XRD) stands as a cornerstone technique in nanomaterial characterization, providing definitive information about crystallographic structure, phase composition, and crystallite size. The technique relies on the diffraction of X-rays by the periodic arrangement of atoms in crystalline materials, following Bragg's law:

$$n\lambda = 2d \sin \theta$$

Where n is an integer representing the diffraction order, λ is the X-ray wavelength, d is the interplanar spacing in the crystal lattice, and θ is the diffraction angle. When this condition is satisfied, constructive interference occurs, resulting in diffraction peaks at specific angles.

For nanomaterials, XRD patterns exhibit distinctive broadening of diffraction peaks compared to their bulk counterparts. This broadening primarily results from the finite size of crystallites and can be quantitatively related to crystallite dimensions through the Scherrer equation:

$$D = K\lambda/\beta \cos\theta$$

where D represents the mean crystallite size, K is a shape factor (typically 0.9), λ is the X-ray wavelength, β is the line broadening at half the maximum intensity (FWHM) in radians, and θ is the Bragg angle. This relationship makes XRD an invaluable tool for estimating nanocrystal dimensions, typically applicable to crystallites between 5 and 200 nm.

Powder X-ray Diffraction

Powder XRD represents the most common configuration for nanomaterial analysis, where the sample consists of randomly oriented crystallites, ideally sampling all possible crystallographic orientations. The resulting diffraction pattern contains concentric rings (captured as peaks in a 2θ scan) corresponding to different crystal planes (Figure 5-2).

For nanomaterial characterization, powder XRD provides several critical pieces of information:

Phase identification is achieved by comparing experimental diffraction patterns with reference databases such as the International Centre for Diffraction Data (ICDD) Powder Diffraction File (PDF). This enables confirmation of synthesis success and detection of impurity phases.

Quantitative phase analysis determines the relative proportions of different crystalline phases in mixed nanomaterials through methods such as Rietveld refinement. This is particularly valuable for catalytic nanomaterials, where performance depends on phase composition.

Lattice parameter determination reveals subtle structural changes resulting from doping, strain, or size effects. For nanomaterials, lattice expansion or contraction compared to bulk values often occurs due to surface tension and increased significance of surface atoms.

Texture analysis identifies preferred orientations of crystallites, which can significantly impact material properties, especially in nanostructured thin films and coatings.

Small-Angle X-ray Scattering (SAXS)

While conventional XRD examines atomic-scale periodicities, small-angle X-ray scattering (SAXS) probes larger-scale structures ranging from approximately 1 to 100 nm. SAXS measures the scattering of X-rays at very small angles (typically 0.1–10°), providing information about particle size, shape, distribution, and internal structure.

For nanomaterial characterization, SAXS offers several unique advantages:

The technique works with samples in various forms, including powders, solutions, and colloidal suspensions, making it particularly valuable for in situ studies of nanomaterial formation and transformation.

Unlike microscopy techniques, SAXS provides statistically significant information averaged over a large sample volume, yielding more representative data on size distribution and morphology.

SAXS can analyze internal structure and porosity, revealing information about core-shell architectures, hollow nanoparticles, and mesoporous materials.

The analysis of SAXS data typically involves fitting scattering profiles to theoretical models based on particle geometry. For monodisperse spherical particles, for instance, the scattering intensity I(q) as a function of the scattering vector q follows the relationship:

$$I(q) \propto [3(\sin(qR) - qR\cos(qR))/(qR)^3]^2$$

where R represents the particle radius. More complex morphologies require correspondingly sophisticated models, often implemented in specialized software packages.

Grazing Incidence X-ray Diffraction (GIXRD)

Grazing incidence X-ray diffraction represents a specialized configuration particularly suited for thin films and surface-supported nanomaterials. By directing X-rays at a very shallow angle (typically 0.1–5°) relative to the sample surface, GIXRD enhances surface sensitivity and minimizes substrate contributions.

For nanomaterial thin films, GIXRD provides several key insights:

Film crystallinity and phase composition can be determined with minimal interference from substrate signals.

CHAPTER 5   CHARACTERIZATION OF NANOMATERIALS

Depth profiling becomes possible by varying the incidence angle, exploiting the dependency of X-ray penetration depth on this parameter.

In-plane ordering information emerges from the analysis of diffraction patterns collected parallel to the sample surface, revealing epitaxial relationships and in-plane strain.

The technique proves especially valuable for studying catalytic nanoparticles on supports, semiconductor quantum dot arrays, and self-assembled nanostructures on surfaces.

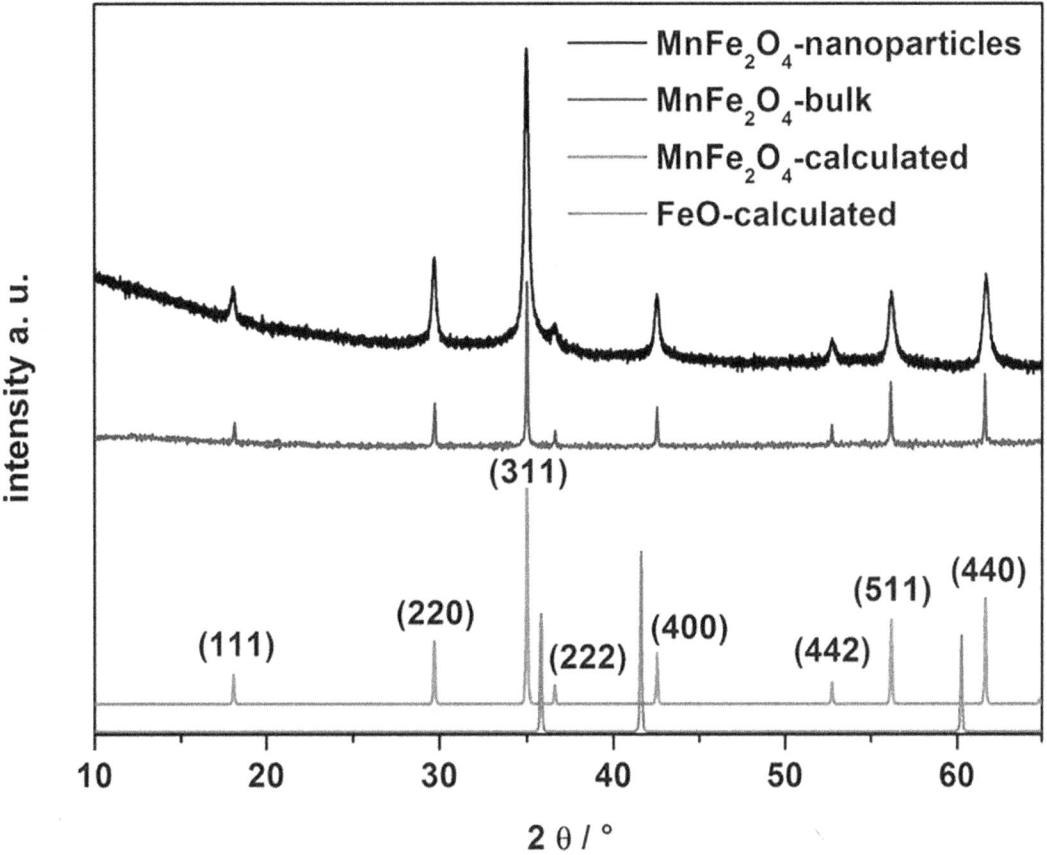

Figure 5-2. Comparison of XRD Patterns for Bulk and Nanoscale Crystalline Materials Showing Peak Broadening Effect with Decreasing Crystallite Size

5.4 Electron Microscopy

Transmission Electron Microscopy (TEM)

Transmission electron microscopy (TEM) stands as perhaps the most direct and powerful technique for visualizing nanomaterials, capable of revealing structural details down to the atomic level. The technique operates by transmitting a high-energy electron beam (typically 80–300 keV) through an ultra-thin specimen, with image formation resulting from the interaction of electrons with the sample.

For nanomaterial characterization, TEM provides unparalleled insights into morphology, crystal structure, and defects. The technique can operate in several complementary modes:

Bright-field imaging, the most common configuration, forms images based on amplitude contrast resulting from mass-thickness and diffraction effects. Regions of the specimen that scatter electrons strongly (thicker areas or heavier elements) appear darker, while regions that allow more electrons to pass through appear brighter. This mode excels at revealing the overall morphology and size distribution of nanomaterials.

High-resolution TEM (HRTEM) utilizes phase contrast to reveal atomic-scale details, including crystal lattice planes and atomic arrangements. This enables direct visualization of crystal structure, grain boundaries, and lattice defects in nanomaterials. The technique proves invaluable for characterizing quantum dots, nanowires, and complex nanoarchitectures where atomic precision is critical.

Selected area electron diffraction (SAED) complements imaging by providing crystallographic information from specific regions as small as a few hundred nanometers in diameter. The resulting diffraction patterns reveal crystal structure, orientation relationships, and phase identification. For polycrystalline nanomaterials, SAED patterns consist of concentric rings, while single-crystal regions produce discrete spot patterns.

Despite its remarkable capabilities, TEM presents several challenges for nanomaterial characterization. Sample preparation requires considerable expertise to produce electron-transparent specimens without altering the material's native structure. Additionally, beam damage can significantly affect sensitive nanomaterials, particularly those containing organic components or light elements.

Scanning Electron Microscopy (SEM)

Scanning electron microscopy complements TEM by providing excellent surface topography information with relatively simpler sample preparation and handling. SEM operates by scanning a focused electron beam across the sample surface while detecting various signals generated by electron-specimen interactions (Figure 5-3).

For nanomaterial characterization, several detection modes offer complementary information:

Secondary electron (SE) imaging provides the highest spatial resolution and greatest topographic contrast. Secondary electrons, generated within a few nanometers of the sample surface, create images that reveal surface texture and morphology with a remarkable three-dimensional appearance. This mode excels at visualizing nanomaterial surface features, particle arrangements, and hierarchical structures.

Backscattered electron (BSE) imaging offers strong atomic number (Z) contrast, with heavier elements appearing brighter. This proves particularly valuable for heterogeneous nanomaterials containing elements with significant Z differences, enabling compositional mapping at the nanoscale.

Energy-dispersive X-ray spectroscopy (EDS), while technically a spectroscopic rather than imaging technique, is commonly integrated with SEM to provide elemental analysis. The technique detects characteristic X-rays generated when the electron beam excites inner-shell electrons in sample atoms. For nanomaterials, EDS enables composition verification, detection of dopants, and elemental mapping with spatial resolution approaching 10 nm in modern instruments.

Modern SEM instruments achieve resolution better than 1 nm under optimal conditions, making them suitable for all but the smallest nanomaterials. The technique offers several advantages over TEM, including simpler sample preparation, larger field of view, and compatibility with bulkier specimens. However, SEM provides limited internal structural information compared to TEM.

CHAPTER 5   CHARACTERIZATION OF NANOMATERIALS

Scanning Transmission Electron Microscopy (STEM)

Scanning transmission electron microscopy combines principles from both TEM and SEM, scanning a highly focused electron probe across a thin specimen while collecting transmitted electrons. This hybrid approach offers several unique advantages for nanomaterial characterization:

High-angle annular dark-field (HAADF) imaging, often called Z-contrast imaging, produces image intensity approximately proportional to Z^2 (atomic number squared). This makes HAADF-STEM exceptionally powerful for visualizing heterogeneous nanomaterials, core-shell structures, and supported catalytic nanoparticles, particularly when elements with significant Z differences are involved.

Electron energy loss spectroscopy (EELS), frequently coupled with STEM, analyzes the energy distribution of transmitted electrons that have interacted inelastically with the specimen. The resulting spectra provide information about elemental composition, chemical bonding states, and electronic structure. For nanomaterials, STEM-EELS enables chemical state mapping with atomic resolution, revealing oxidation states, bonding environments, and interface chemistry.

Tomographic reconstruction, achieved by collecting STEM images at multiple tilt angles, allows three-dimensional visualization of nanomaterials. This approach has revolutionized our understanding of complex nanostructures by revealing internal architectures, connectivity, and spatial distributions that cannot be discerned from two-dimensional projections alone.

Recent advances in aberration-corrected STEM have pushed spatial resolution below 50 pm, enabling the routine imaging of individual atoms and bond details in many nanomaterials. This capability has proven transformative for fields like catalysis, where active site identification at the atomic scale directly informs rational design principles.

Environmental and In Situ Electron Microscopy

Conventional electron microscopy requires high vacuum conditions, limiting observations to static, vacuum-compatible specimens. However, recent advances have introduced environmental and in situ capabilities that expand the technique's applicability to dynamic nanomaterial processes:

Environmental TEM/SEM permits imaging in the presence of gases or vapors at pressures up to several thousand Pa, enabling direct observation of gas-solid interactions relevant to catalysis, gas sensing, and environmental remediation applications of nanomaterials.

Liquid-cell TEM allows visualization of nanomaterials in liquid environments, opening unprecedented windows into nucleation, growth, and self-assembly processes. This capability has transformed our understanding of nanoparticle synthesis mechanisms and behavior in solution-phase environments.

In situ heating, cooling, mechanical testing, and electrical biasing holders enable real-time observation of phase transformations, sintering behavior, mechanical properties, and electron transport phenomena in nanomaterials. These studies provide direct links between structure and functional properties across multiple length scales.

These advanced electron microscopy techniques continue to evolve rapidly, with ongoing developments in detector technology, data processing algorithms, and in situ capabilities continuously expanding the frontier of nanomaterial characterization (Table 5-2).

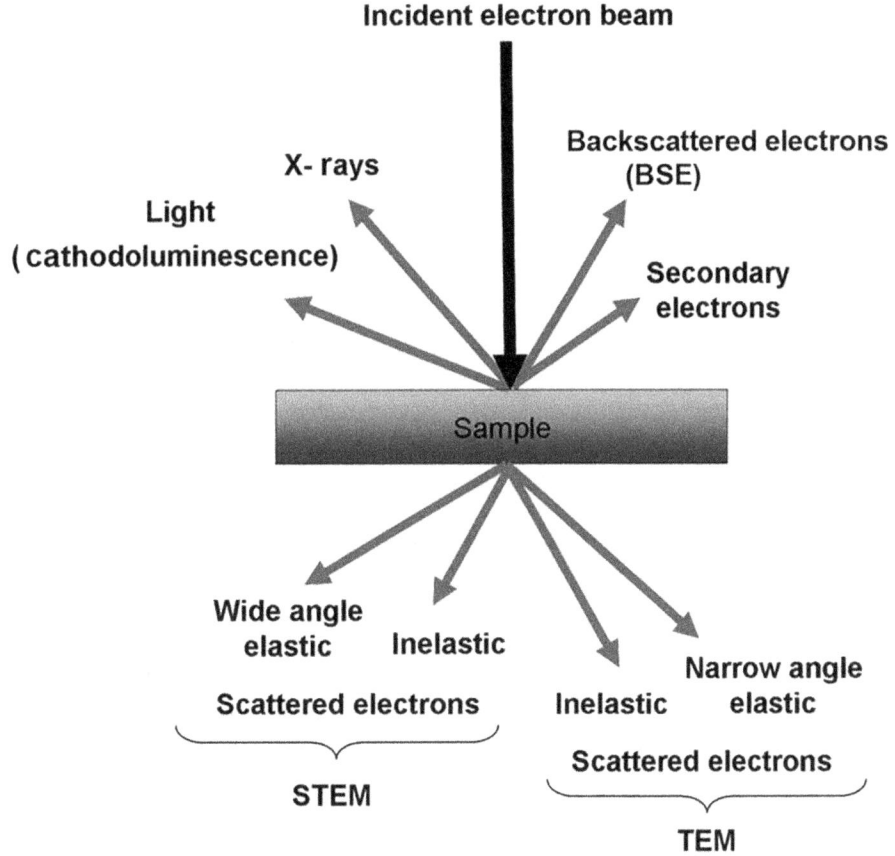

Figure 5-3. *Comparative Diagram of Electron Beam—Sample Interactions in TEM, SEM, and STEM Showing Various Signals Generated and Detected*

Table 5-2. Comparison of Electron Microscopy Techniques for Nanomaterial Characterization

Feature	TEM	SEM	STEM
Resolution	0.05–0.2 nm	0.5–4 nm	0.05–0.2 nm
Sample requirements	Electron transparent (<100 nm)	Conductive surface	Electron transparent (<100 nm)
Depth information	2D projection of 3D structure	Surface topography	2D projection with depth sensitivity
Elemental analysis	EDS, EELS (limited spatial resolution)	EDS (μm resolution)	EDS, EELS (atomic resolution possible)
Primary advantages	Atomic structure visualization	Surface morphology, ease of use	Z-contrast imaging, spectroscopic mapping
Limitations	Complex sample preparation, beam damage	Limited resolution, surface only	Similar to TEM, with higher beam damage

5.5 Size and Surface Analysis
Dynamic Light Scattering (DLS)

Dynamic light scattering represents one of the most widely employed techniques for determining the hydrodynamic size distribution of nanomaterials in suspension. The technique measures fluctuations in scattered light intensity caused by Brownian motion of particles, with smaller particles diffusing more rapidly than larger ones.

The fundamental relationship governing DLS analysis is the Stokes-Einstein equation:

$$D = kT/6\pi\eta R$$

where D represents the diffusion coefficient derived from light scattering measurements, k is the Boltzmann constant, T is absolute temperature, η is solvent viscosity, and R is the hydrodynamic radius of the particle. The hydrodynamic radius encompasses both the solid particle and any associated solvation layer or surface coating, making it generally larger than the physical radius determined by electron microscopy.

For nanomaterial characterization, DLS offers several significant advantages:

The technique provides ensemble measurements averaged over thousands to millions of particles, yielding statistically robust size distributions. This complements microscopy techniques that typically analyze much smaller sample populations.

Measurements can be performed in native suspension media, avoiding potential artifacts introduced by sample drying or vacuum exposure required for electron microscopy.

Real-time data acquisition enables monitoring of dynamic processes, including aggregation, dissolution, and protein corona formation around nanoparticles in biological environments.

Modern DLS instruments typically report size distributions in three formats: intensity-weighted (most sensitive to larger particles), volume-weighted, and number-weighted (most closely resembling microscopy-based distributions). Interpretation requires careful consideration of these different distribution bases, particularly for polydisperse or multimodal samples.

While DLS excels at measuring monodisperse spherical particles, several limitations arise for complex nanomaterials:

The technique assumes spherical morphology, leading to inaccuracies for anisotropic shapes like nanorods or nanoplates. For such materials, the reported hydrodynamic diameter represents an equivalent sphere with the same diffusion coefficient.

Resolution becomes limited for polydisperse samples, with larger particles dominating scattering intensity and potentially masking smaller populations.

Multiple scattering effects in concentrated samples can distort results, necessitating appropriate dilution for accurate measurements.

Zeta Potential Analysis

Zeta potential measurements provide crucial information about the surface charge and colloidal stability of nanomaterials in suspension. The zeta potential represents the electrical potential at the slipping plane of the electrical double layer surrounding a charged particle in solution, rather than the actual surface potential (Figure 5-4).

For nanomaterial characterization, zeta potential offers several important insights:

Colloidal stability prediction relies heavily on zeta potential magnitude, with values beyond ±30 mV typically indicating good electrostatic stabilization against aggregation. This parameter proves critical for applications requiring stable dispersions, including drug delivery systems and printing inks.

Surface modification confirmation can be achieved through zeta potential shifts. For instance, coating negatively charged nanoparticles with cationic polymers typically produces a sign reversal and magnitude change in zeta potential, verifying successful functionalization.

pH-dependent behavior reveals information about surface functional groups through zeta potential titration curves. The isoelectric point (pH at which zeta potential equals zero) serves as a characteristic parameter for different nanomaterials and their surface modifications.

Biological interaction prediction correlates strongly with zeta potential, as this parameter influences protein adsorption, cellular uptake, and biodistribution of nanomaterials. Positively charged nanoparticles, for example, typically demonstrate enhanced cellular internalization compared to negative or neutral counterparts due to electrostatic attraction with negatively charged cell membranes.

Zeta potential measurements typically employ electrophoretic light scattering techniques, where an applied electric field induces charged particle movement detected through Doppler shift of scattered light. The electrophoretic mobility μ relates to zeta potential ζ through the Henry equation:

$$\mu = 2\varepsilon\zeta f(\kappa a)/3\eta$$

where ε represents the dielectric constant of the medium, η is viscosity, $f(\kappa a)$ is Henry's function, and κa relates to the ratio of particle radius to electrical double layer thickness.

Brunauer-Emmett-Teller (BET) Surface Area Analysis

Surface area represents a defining characteristic of nanomaterials, often directly correlating with performance in applications including catalysis, gas sensing, and energy storage. The Brunauer-Emmett-Teller (BET) method stands as the gold standard for determining specific surface area through gas adsorption measurements.

The technique quantifies the amount of adsorbed gas (typically nitrogen) required to form a complete monolayer on the material surface. This value, combined with knowledge of the adsorbate molecular cross-sectional area, enables calculation of total surface area. The specific surface area, expressed in square meters per gram (m^2/g), represents one of the most important parameters for comparing nanomaterial variants.

For nanomaterial characterization, BET analysis provides several critical insights:

Verification of nanoscale dimensions often relies on surface area measurements. For spherical particles, specific surface area S relates inversely to particle diameter d through the relationship $S = 6/(\rho d)$, where ρ represents material density. Deviations from this relationship can indicate nonspherical morphologies or internal porosity.

Porosity characterization extends beyond surface area to pore size distribution, pore volume, and pore geometry through analysis of the complete adsorption-desorption isotherm. The IUPAC classification identifies six isotherm types corresponding to different material classes, with Type IV isotherms characteristic of many mesoporous nanomaterials.

Quality control in nanomaterial production frequently employs BET analysis as a sensitive indicator of synthesis reproducibility. Changes in specific surface area can reveal variations in particle size, aggregation state, or porosity that might not be immediately apparent through other techniques.

Despite its prevalence, BET analysis presents several considerations for nanomaterial characterization:

Sample pretreatment, including degassing to remove adsorbed contaminants, can potentially alter sensitive nanomaterials through thermal or vacuum-induced changes.

The technique measures all accessible surfaces, including both external particle surfaces and internal pore surfaces, potentially complicating interpretation for porous nanomaterials.

Aggregation state significantly impacts measured surface area, with dense agglomerates preventing complete nitrogen access to all particle surfaces. This necessitates careful sample preparation to maintain representative dispersion states.

Atomic Force Microscopy (AFM)

Atomic Force Microscopy offers exceptional vertical resolution for nanomaterial characterization, capable of subnanometer precision in height measurements while providing three-dimensional topographic information. Unlike electron microscopy techniques, AFM operates in ambient conditions without requiring vacuum or conductive samples.

The technique employs a sharp probe mounted on a flexible cantilever that interacts with the sample surface. Probe-surface interactions cause cantilever deflections measured by reflecting a laser beam off the cantilever onto a position-sensitive photodetector. For nanomaterial characterization, several operational modes offer complementary information:

Contact mode maintains constant contact between the probe and sample, providing high-resolution topographic images but potentially disturbing weakly bound nanomaterials or soft structures.

Tapping mode (intermittent contact) oscillates the cantilever near its resonant frequency, with the probe briefly contacting the surface during each oscillation cycle. This reduces lateral forces and sample damage, making it suitable for most nanomaterial imaging applications.

Noncontact mode maintains probe-sample separation while detecting long-range forces, minimizing sample disturbance but typically yielding lower resolution than other modes.

Beyond basic topography, AFM enables numerous specialized measurements for nanomaterial characterization:

Force spectroscopy quantifies mechanical properties including elasticity, adhesion, and hardness at the nanoscale by analyzing force-distance curves at specific surface locations. This proves particularly valuable for heterogeneous nanomaterials with spatially varying mechanical characteristics.

Kelvin probe force microscopy (KPFM) maps surface potential variations across nanomaterials, providing insights into electronic properties, work function, and charge distribution with nanometer spatial resolution.

Magnetic force microscopy (MFM) visualizes magnetic domain structures in ferromagnetic and ferrimagnetic nanomaterials by detecting magnetic field gradients near the sample surface.

For nanomaterial size determination, AFM offers several advantages over other techniques:

The exceptional vertical resolution (typically <0.1 nm) enables precise height measurements of even monolayer materials like graphene.

Minimal sample preparation requirements allow characterization under ambient conditions in their native state.

CHAPTER 5   CHARACTERIZATION OF NANOMATERIALS

Three-dimensional data acquisition permits differentiation between true three-dimensional particles and two-dimensional flakes or sheets that might appear similar in projection techniques like TEM.

However, several considerations apply to AFM analysis of nanomaterials:

Lateral resolution remains limited by probe dimensions (typically 5–10 nm) rather than the inherent resolution capabilities of the technique.

Tip convolution effects can artificially broaden the lateral dimensions of small nanostructures, necessitating deconvolution algorithms for accurate width measurements.

Sample substrate interactions may affect nanoparticle dispersion and morphology compared to their solution-phase behavior.

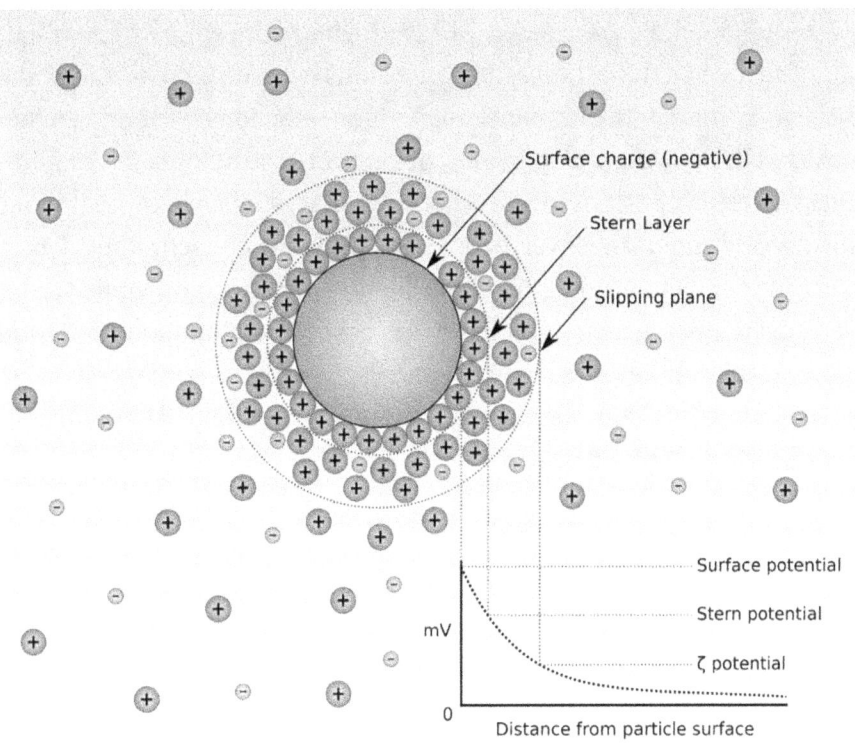

Figure 5-4. Schematic Diagram of the Electric Double Layer Surrounding a Charged Nanoparticle in Solution, Showing the Relationship Between Surface Potential, Stern Potential, and Zeta Potential

5.6 Method Comparison

Complementary Nature of Characterization Techniques

The comprehensive characterization of nanomaterials invariably requires multiple analytical techniques, as each method provides distinct information with inherent strengths and limitations. Rather than viewing these techniques as alternatives, researchers should recognize their complementary nature and strategic integration for complete material understanding.

Several key principles guide effective technique selection and integration:

Information hierarchy considerations recognize that techniques vary in their information depth, from basic confirmation of nanoscale dimensions to detailed atomic structure determination. Researchers typically progress from simpler screening methods to more sophisticated analyses as research questions become increasingly specific.

Sample state compatibility influences technique selection based on whether materials exist as dry powders, dispersions, or supported structures. Techniques like DLS apply exclusively to suspensions, while others like SEM typically require dry samples.

Statistical representativeness varies dramatically between techniques. Microscopy methods provide detailed information about small sample regions, while scattering and spectroscopy techniques average over much larger volumes, potentially offering more representative results for heterogeneous materials. Table 5-3 summarizes the primary strengths, limitations, and complementary relationships between key characterization techniques discussed in this chapter.

Table 5-3. Comparative Analysis of Nanomaterial Characterization Techniques

Technique	Primary Information	Strengths	Limitations	Complementary Techniques
UV-Vis spectroscopy	Electronic structure, size-dependent optical properties	Rapid, nondestructive, solution-compatible	Limited structural information	TEM for structural verification
XRD	Crystal structure, phase composition, crystallite size	Quantitative, well-established databases	Limited for amorphous materials	TEM for local structure, SAXS for amorphous systems
TEM	Direct visualization, atomic structure	Atomic resolution, internal structure	Small sampling area, vacuum required	DLS for ensemble measurements, XRD for bulk crystallinity
SEM	Surface morphology, particle distribution	Large field of view, minimal preparation	Limited resolution, surface only	TEM for internal structure
DLS	Hydrodynamic size distribution	Rapid, solution-phase, statistical averaging	Assumes spherical particles	Microscopy for shape information
Zeta potential	Surface charge, colloidal stability	Predictive of stability and interactions	Limited to charged particles in solution	Surface spectroscopy for chemical composition
BET	Surface area, porosity	Quantitative, well-established	Requires dry samples, time-consuming	Microscopy for morphology verification
AFM	3D topography, height measurements	Exceptional height resolution, ambient conditions	Limited lateral resolution	SEM for larger scan areas, faster imaging

CHAPTER 5   CHARACTERIZATION OF NANOMATERIALS

Selection Criteria for Characterization Methods

When designing characterization strategies for nanomaterials, researchers should consider several key selection criteria:

Research question specificity determines technique selection, with different methods appropriate for fundamental characterization versus application-specific performance evaluation. Initial screening might employ rapid techniques like UV-Vis or DLS, while mechanistic investigations might require high-resolution TEM or surface spectroscopy.

Material properties influence technique suitability, with considerations including

- Composition (organic vs. inorganic)
- Stability (beam-sensitive vs. robust)
- Conductivity (charging issues in electron microscopy)
- Dispersibility (solution vs. solid-state techniques)

Sample availability impacts technique selection, with some methods requiring milligram quantities while others can function with microgram amounts. Additionally, destructive techniques might be unsuitable for limited samples.

Time and cost constraints often determine practical characterization strategies. Technique accessibility, equipment costs, and analysis timeframes vary dramatically, necessitating prioritization based on critical information needs.

Multi-technique Characterization Strategies

Effective nanomaterial characterization typically follows strategic workflows that maximize information while minimizing redundancy:

Screening-to-detailed progression often begins with rapid techniques that confirm basic parameters before advancing to more sophisticated analyses. For instance, DLS might verify nanoparticle formation before proceeding to TEM for detailed morphological analysis.

Correlative microscopy approaches combine information from multiple imaging modalities applied to the same sample region. For example, correlative light-electron microscopy (CLEM) provides both functional information (fluorescence) and structural details (electron microscopy) for the same nanostructures.

Multi-parameter analysis recognizes that single techniques rarely provide complete characterization. A comprehensive nanomaterial analysis might include

- Size and morphology (TEM/SEM)
- Crystal structure (XRD)
- Surface chemistry (FTIR/XPS)
- Colloidal properties (DLS/zeta potential)
- Surface area (BET)

In situ and operando approaches represent the frontier of nanomaterial characterization, examining materials under realistic operating conditions rather than idealized laboratory states. These techniques provide crucial insights into dynamic processes, including catalysis, sensing, and energy storage, that cannot be captured by conventional ex situ methods.

Limitations and Challenges in Nanomaterial Characterization

Despite significant advances in characterization methodology, several universal challenges persist in nanomaterial analysis:

Sample preparation artifacts remain a persistent concern across multiple techniques. The preparation processes required for certain methods can potentially alter material properties, introducing uncertainties into interpretation. For example, the high vacuum environment of electron microscopy may induce structural changes in sensitive nanomaterials, while drying processes can cause irreversible aggregation that misrepresents solution behavior.

Statistical representation issues arise from the inherent variability in nanomaterial samples. The inevitable heterogeneity in size, shape, and structure necessitates analysis of sufficiently large sample populations to ensure representative results. This proves particularly challenging for techniques like TEM that examine relatively small sample regions, potentially missing important subpopulations or rare features.

Instrumental limitations constrain information accessibility across techniques. Resolution limits, both spatial and temporal, may obscure critical details of nanomaterial structure and dynamics. Additionally, beam damage in electron microscopy techniques can degrade sensitive samples during observation, altering the very structures being studied.

Interpretation complexities emerge from the multifaceted nature of nanomaterial properties. Data analysis often requires sophisticated modeling and assumptions that may introduce biases or oversimplifications. Furthermore, correlating results across different techniques with varying sample states, preparation methods, and physical principles requires careful consideration of potential inconsistencies.

Future Directions in Nanomaterial Characterization

The field of nanomaterial characterization continues to evolve rapidly, with several emerging trends promising to address current limitations:

Artificial intelligence and machine learning approaches increasingly assist in data interpretation, feature extraction, and correlation across multiple techniques. These computational methods enable more efficient processing of large datasets while potentially revealing patterns and relationships not immediately apparent through conventional analysis.

Multimodal and correlative approaches gain prominence as researchers develop integrated instruments and workflows that combine complementary techniques. These approaches enable examination of the same nanomaterial features across multiple dimensions, providing more comprehensive characterization while minimizing sample preparation variations.

In situ and operando characterization continues to advance, with new instruments enabling observation of nanomaterials under increasingly realistic conditions. These developments bridge the gap between laboratory characterization and real-world performance, providing insights into dynamic processes including catalysis, energy storage, and biological interactions.

Probe-based tomographic techniques enable three-dimensional visualization with nanoscale resolution, overcoming the projection limitations of conventional microscopy. Methods including electron tomography, atom probe tomography, and scanning probe tomography provide unprecedented insights into complex nanostructured materials with heterogeneous compositions and morphologies.

As nanomaterials increasingly transition from laboratory curiosities to commercial products, characterization methods continue to adapt, addressing the demands for higher throughput, greater accessibility, and enhanced relevance to practical applications. This evolution ensures that our understanding of nanomaterial structure-property relationships remains foundational to technological advancement across diverse fields.

5.7 Summary

The characterization of nanomaterials represents a multifaceted challenge requiring strategic implementation of complementary analytical techniques. This chapter has navigated through the principal methodologies employed in modern nanotechnology research, from optical techniques that probe electronic structure to advanced microscopy methods that visualize atomic arrangements directly. Each approach offers unique insights while presenting specific limitations, emphasizing the necessity of multi-technique characterization strategies.

Optical techniques, including UV-Vis spectroscopy and photoluminescence, provide rapid, nondestructive assessment of electronic properties and quantum confinement effects. X-ray diffraction methods reveal crystallographic details essential for structure-property correlations, while electron microscopy techniques offer direct visualization across multiple length scales from atomic structure to ensemble arrangements. Size and surface analysis methods, including dynamic light scattering and BET surface area analysis, provide critical information about dimensions and interfacial properties that often determine functional performance.

The complementary nature of these techniques cannot be overstated. No single method provides complete characterization; rather, researchers must strategically combine approaches based on specific research questions, material properties, and practical constraints. This combinatorial approach yields a comprehensive understanding of nanomaterial structure, composition, and behavior across relevant length scales and environmental conditions.

As nanotechnology continues its rapid evolution from fundamental science to practical application, characterization methodologies likewise advance. Emerging capabilities in in situ observation, three-dimensional reconstruction, and artificial intelligence-assisted analysis promise even deeper insights into nanomaterial properties. These developments will prove essential in addressing grand challenges across diverse fields, including energy, medicine, electronics, and environmental remediation, where nanomaterials increasingly play pivotal roles.

The characterization techniques discussed throughout this chapter serve not merely as analytical tools but as the essential bridge between nanomaterial synthesis and application. Through rigorous, multi-technique characterization, researchers establish the critical structure-property relationships that enable rational design of next-generation nanomaterials with tailored functionalities and enhanced performance.

CHAPTER 6

Thin Films and Colloidal Nanostructures

This chapter explores the fundamental concepts and applications of thin films and colloidal nanostructures, two critical areas in nanotechnology. Beginning with an introduction to thin film technology, the chapter examines various synthesis and characterization techniques essential for creating and analyzing these nanoscale structures. It then delves into the complex dynamics of colloidal systems, highlighting their unique physical and chemical properties. The practical applications of these technologies in medicine and electronics are thoroughly explored, demonstrating their transformative potential across industries. The chapter also investigates emerging trends in thin film and colloidal nanotechnology and examines how artificial intelligence and Internet of Things technologies are revolutionizing these applications. Through comprehensive analysis and detailed examples, this chapter provides readers with a thorough understanding of how thin films and colloidal nanostructures are advancing modern technological capabilities.

6.1 Introduction to Thin Films

Thin films represent one of the most fundamental and widely utilized structures in nanotechnology. At their core, thin films are layers of material with thicknesses ranging from a few nanometers to several micrometers—dimensions that place them firmly within the realm of nanoscale engineering. The significance of thin films in modern technology cannot be overstated, as they serve as the building blocks for countless applications across industries ranging from electronics and optics to medicine and energy production.

CHAPTER 6   THIN FILMS AND COLLOIDAL NANOSTRUCTURES

The history of thin film technology dates back to the early 20th century, but it was not until the development of advanced deposition techniques in the 1960s and 1970s that the field truly began to flourish. Today, thin films have become ubiquitous in our technological landscape, enabling the miniaturization and enhanced performance of electronic devices, improved optical coatings, more efficient solar cells, and numerous other applications that underpin our modern society.

What makes thin films particularly fascinating from a scientific and engineering perspective is their unique properties, which often differ significantly from those of the same materials in bulk form. When materials are confined to nanoscale dimensions in one direction (as in thin films), quantum effects begin to dominate, leading to novel electronic, optical, magnetic, and mechanical behaviors. For instance, thin films can exhibit enhanced conductivity, altered band gaps, unique optical interference patterns, and modified mechanical strength compared to their bulk counterparts.

The physics governing thin film behavior encompasses several complex phenomena. Surface and interface effects become predominant at the nanoscale, with a significantly higher proportion of atoms residing at surfaces or interfaces rather than within the bulk. This leads to modified atomic bonding arrangements and energy states, which in turn affect the material's overall properties. Additionally, the growth processes of thin films often induce specific crystallographic orientations or amorphous structures that further influence their characteristics.

From a practical standpoint, thin films can be broadly categorized based on their composition, structure, and functional properties:

1. **Metallic Films**: Used primarily for their electrical conductivity, reflectivity, and, in some cases, magnetic properties

2. **Semiconductor Films**: The foundation of modern microelectronics and optoelectronic devices

3. **Dielectric Films**: Essential for insulation, optical coatings, and capacitive elements

4. **Organic Films**: Including polymers and biological materials, applied in flexible electronics and biomedical devices

The thickness uniformity and interface quality of thin films are critical parameters that determine their performance in practical applications. Even atomic-scale variations can significantly impact functionality, particularly in high-precision applications such as integrated circuits or optical filters. This necessitates precise control over deposition processes and sophisticated characterization techniques, topics that will be explored in the subsequent section.

Recent advances in thin film technology have opened new frontiers in materials science, enabling the creation of metamaterials with properties not found in nature, ultra-barrier films with exceptional impermeability to gases and liquids, and atomically precise heterostructures with tailored electronic properties. These developments continue to push the boundaries of what is possible in fields ranging from quantum computing to flexible displays and beyond.

6.2 Synthesis and Characterization

The synthesis and characterization of thin films and colloidal nanostructures represent critical processes in nanomaterial engineering, requiring precise control and sophisticated analytical techniques to achieve desired properties and functionality. This section explores the diverse methodologies employed in creating these nanomaterials and the advanced tools used to evaluate their characteristics.

Synthesis Methods for Thin Films

The creation of thin films relies on several well-established deposition techniques, each offering distinct advantages for specific applications and material systems. These methods can be broadly categorized into physical vapor deposition (PVD), chemical vapor deposition (CVD), and solution-based approaches.

Physical vapor deposition encompasses techniques such as thermal evaporation, sputtering, and pulsed laser deposition. In thermal evaporation, the source material is heated to its vapor pressure in a vacuum environment, allowing vaporized atoms to travel directly to the substrate, where they condense to form a film. This method is particularly valuable for materials with relatively low melting points and is widely used in manufacturing metallic contacts and optical coatings.

Sputtering, another prominent PVD technique, involves bombarding a target material with energetic ions (typically argon) to eject atoms, which then deposit onto a nearby substrate. As Dr. Richard Thompson notes in his seminal work on thin film deposition, "Sputtering offers exceptional control over film composition and structure, enabling the creation of complex alloys and compounds with precise stoichiometry"

(Thompson, 2023). The versatility of sputtering has made it the method of choice for numerous applications, including thin film transistors, magnetic storage media, and architectural glass coatings.

Chemical vapor deposition methods utilize chemical reactions to form solid materials from gaseous precursors. In conventional CVD, precursor gases react at or near a heated substrate surface to form a solid film. Atomic layer deposition (ALD), a specialized form of CVD, uses sequential, self-limiting surface reactions to achieve exceptional thickness control at the atomic level. This precision has proven invaluable for fabricating high-k dielectric layers in advanced microelectronics and conformal coatings on complex three-dimensional structures.

Solution-based deposition techniques include spin coating, dip coating, and various printing methods. These approaches offer advantages in terms of scalability, cost-effectiveness, and compatibility with temperature-sensitive substrates. They have gained significant traction in emerging fields such as flexible electronics, where organic semiconductors and metal oxide films can be deposited from solution precursors under mild conditions.

Synthesis of Colloidal Nanostructures

The creation of colloidal nanostructures typically involves chemical synthesis routes that enable precise control over particle size, shape, and surface chemistry. Bottom-up approaches predominate in this domain, with particles forming through nucleation and growth processes in solution.

One of the most widely employed methods is the reduction of metal salts in the presence of stabilizing agents. For instance, gold nanoparticles can be synthesized through the reduction of chloroauric acid ($HAuCl_2$) using citrate, which simultaneously acts as both a reducing agent and a stabilizer. By carefully controlling reaction parameters such as temperature, concentration, and pH, researchers can tune the size distribution and morphology of the resulting particles.

Hot injection techniques have revolutionized the synthesis of semiconductor quantum dots, allowing for the production of highly monodisperse nanocrystals with precisely controlled optical properties. In this approach, precursor compounds are rapidly injected into a hot coordinating solvent, triggering burst nucleation followed by controlled growth. This temporal separation of nucleation and growth phases is key to achieving narrow size distributions.

Sol-gel processes represent another important category of colloidal synthesis methods, particularly for metal oxide nanoparticles. These involve the hydrolysis and condensation of molecular precursors (typically metal alkoxides) to form a colloidal suspension (sol), which can then transform into a network structure (gel). Sol-gel techniques offer exceptional versatility in terms of composition control and have been successfully applied to synthesize a wide range of oxide materials for catalysis, sensing, and biomedical applications.

Characterization Techniques

The characterization of thin films and colloidal nanostructures involves an array of complementary techniques that probe different aspects of structure, composition, and properties.

Microscopy techniques play a central role in nanomaterial characterization. Scanning electron microscopy (SEM) provides valuable information about surface morphology and film thickness, while transmission electron microscopy (TEM) allows for direct visualization of atomic arrangements and defect structures. Atomic force microscopy (AFM) offers three-dimensional topographical imaging with nanometer resolution and can also probe mechanical properties through force-distance measurements.

Spectroscopic methods provide insights into chemical composition and bonding environments. X-ray photoelectron spectroscopy (XPS) is particularly powerful for analyzing surface composition and chemical states, with a typical analysis depth of 5–10 nm. Infrared and Raman spectroscopies offer complementary information about vibrational modes, helping to identify functional groups and molecular structures within nanomaterials.

X-ray diffraction (XRD) techniques are indispensable for characterizing crystalline structure. For thin films, grazing incidence XRD configurations enhance surface sensitivity, enabling the determination of crystal phases, orientation relationships, and strain states even in ultrathin layers. Small-angle X-ray scattering (SAXS) proves especially valuable for colloidal systems, providing statistical information about particle size distributions and internal structures. Table 6-1 summarizes the primary characterization techniques used in thin film and colloidal nanostructure analysis, along with their typical applications and limitations.

CHAPTER 6   THIN FILMS AND COLLOIDAL NANOSTRUCTURES

Table 6-1. *Common Characterization Techniques for Nanomaterials*

Technique	Information Obtained	Spatial Resolution	Limitations
SEM	Surface morphology, film thickness	1–10 nm	Limited chemical information
TEM	Atomic structure, crystal defects	0.1–0.2 nm	Sample preparation challenges
AFM	Surface topography, roughness	0.1–1 nm (vertical)	Slow scanning speed
XPS	Surface composition, chemical states	~10 μm (lateral)	Vacuum requirement
XRD	Crystal structure, phase identification	N/A (bulk technique)	Challenges with amorphous materials
Ellipsometry	Film thickness, optical constants	N/A (bulk technique)	Requires optical models
DLS	Hydrodynamic size distribution	N/A (ensemble technique)	Limited for polydisperse samples

In thin film characterization, ellipsometry stands out as a particularly powerful nondestructive technique for determining thickness and optical properties. By analyzing changes in polarization when light reflects from a sample surface, ellipsometry can measure film thicknesses with subnanometer precision across large areas, making it invaluable for process control in industrial settings. Figure 6-1 illustrates the basic principle of ellipsometric measurement.

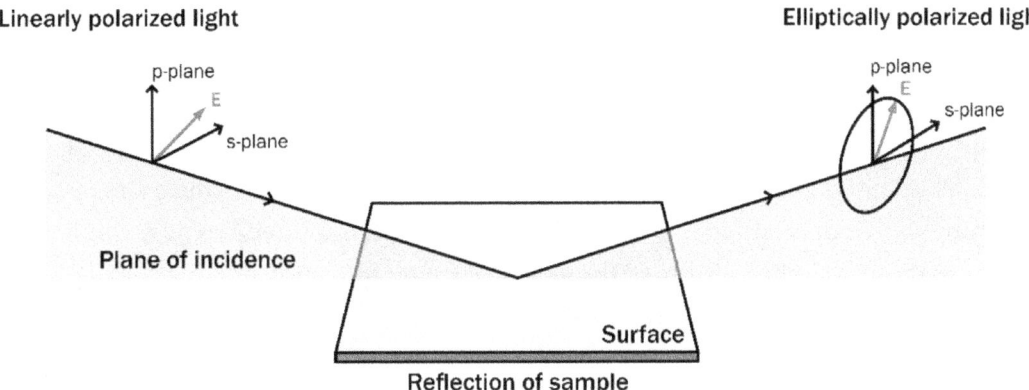

Figure 6-1. *Schematic Representation of an Ellipsometric Measurement Setup for Thin Film Characterization, Showing Incident Polarized Light, Reflection from the Sample Surface, and Analysis of the Change in Polarization State*

For colloidal systems, dynamic light scattering (DLS) provides critical information about particle size distributions and stability. This technique measures the Brownian motion of particles in suspension through light scattering fluctuations, enabling the calculation of hydrodynamic diameters—a parameter that includes both the core particle and any associated surface layers. While DLS offers rapid analysis of size distributions, it is most effective for relatively monodisperse samples and is typically complemented by microscopy techniques for comprehensive characterization.

The integration of multiple characterization methods is essential for developing a complete understanding of nanomaterial properties. As observed by Professor Emily Chen in her comprehensive review, "The multifaceted nature of nanomaterials demands a correlative approach to characterization, where the limitations of individual techniques are overcome through complementary analyses" (Chen, 2024). This multi-technique philosophy underpins modern nanomaterial research and development efforts.

6.3 Colloidal Structure Dynamics

Colloidal systems represent a fascinating domain within nanotechnology, characterized by their distinctive physical and chemical behaviors at the interface between bulk materials and molecular assemblies. These systems, comprising nanoparticles dispersed within a continuous medium, exhibit complex dynamics that govern their stability, self-assembly, and functional properties. Understanding these dynamics is crucial for harnessing the full potential of colloidal nanostructures in diverse applications.

CHAPTER 6   THIN FILMS AND COLLOIDAL NANOSTRUCTURES

The fundamental properties of colloidal systems stem from the interplay between various forces operating at the nanoscale. Surface forces dominate volumetric forces at these dimensions, leading to behavior that often defies classical intuition. Among the most influential interactions are van der Waals attractions, electrostatic repulsions, steric effects, and solvation forces. The balance between these competing influences determines whether a colloidal system remains dispersed or undergoes aggregation—a balance that can be delicately tuned through surface modification and control of solution conditions.

The DLVO theory (named after Derjaguin, Landau, Verwey, and Overbeek) provides a theoretical framework for understanding colloidal stability by combining electrostatic repulsion and van der Waals attraction. According to this model, the total interaction energy between colloidal particles determines their tendency to aggregate or remain dispersed. When repulsive forces predominate, particles maintain separation and the colloid remains stable. Conversely, when attractive forces overcome repulsion, particles coalesce, potentially leading to flocculation or precipitation.

Electrostatic stabilization represents one of the primary mechanisms for maintaining colloidal dispersions. In aqueous media, many nanoparticles develop surface charges through ionization, ion adsorption, or dissolution processes. These charges attract counterions from the surrounding medium, forming an electrical double layer that creates repulsive forces between particles. The thickness of this double layer—characterized by the Debye screening length—depends on electrolyte concentration and plays a decisive role in colloidal stability.

As Professor Akira Nakamura explains, "The subtlety of colloidal behavior lies in the exponential dependence of double layer interactions on separation distance and ionic strength. This sensitivity enables precise control over dispersion properties through simple adjustments to solution chemistry" (Nakamura, 2023). Indeed, this sensitivity forms the basis for numerous practical applications, from water treatment processes to advanced drug delivery systems.

Beyond electrostatic effects, steric stabilization offers an alternative approach to colloidal stability, particularly valuable in nonaqueous media or high ionic strength environments where electrostatic mechanisms become ineffective. This approach involves coating particle surfaces with polymers or surfactants that create physical barriers against aggregation. When particles approach each other, the overlap of these adsorbed layers generates repulsive forces through osmotic and entropic effects, maintaining separation even in challenging environments.

CHAPTER 6   THIN FILMS AND COLLOIDAL NANOSTRUCTURES

The dynamics of colloidal systems become particularly intriguing when considering their self-assembly behavior. Under appropriate conditions, nanoparticles can spontaneously organize into ordered structures ranging from simple lattices to complex hierarchical architectures. This self-assembly process represents a powerful bottom-up approach to fabricating functional materials with precisely controlled nanoscale features.

Several driving forces contribute to colloidal self-assembly. For anisotropic particles such as nanorods or platelets, shape-dependent interactions can direct assembly into specific configurations. Surface functionalization with complementary binding groups enables programmable assembly through molecular recognition. External fields—including electric, magnetic, and optical—provide additional means to guide assembly processes with spatial and temporal control.

A particularly fascinating aspect of colloidal dynamics involves the formation of liquid crystalline phases. When particle shape anisotropy exceeds certain thresholds, entropic driving forces can induce orientational ordering even in the absence of energetic interactions. This phenomenon leads to the formation of nematic, smectic, or columnar phases that combine fluid-like mobility with crystal-like order—properties that have been exploited in applications ranging from display technologies to templates for materials synthesis.

The rheological behavior of colloidal suspensions represents another dimension of their complex dynamics. Unlike simple fluids, colloidal systems can exhibit non-Newtonian flow characteristics, including shear thinning, shear thickening, and thixotropy. These behaviors arise from structural rearrangements under flow conditions and have profound implications for processing operations and end-use performance. Figure 6-2 illustrates the typical relationship between shear rate and viscosity for various colloidal regimes.

CHAPTER 6   THIN FILMS AND COLLOIDAL NANOSTRUCTURES

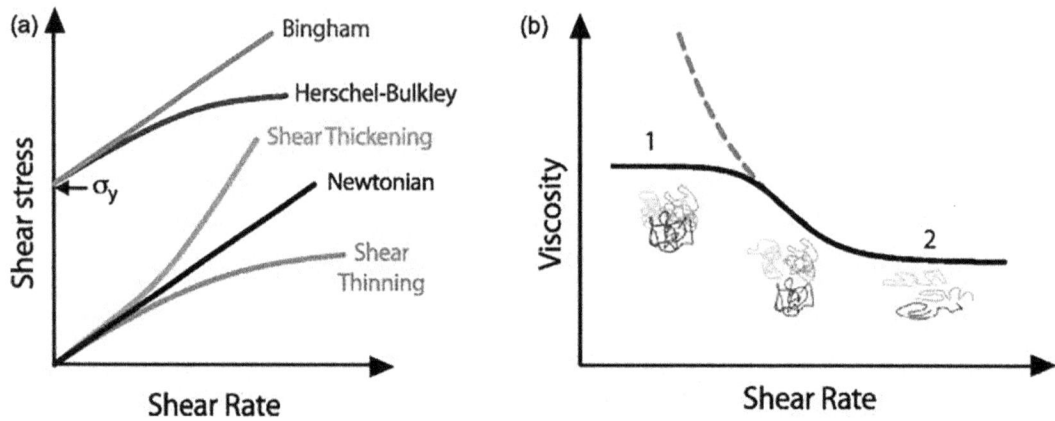

Figure 6-2. Rheological Behavior of Colloidal Suspensions Showing Different Flow Regimes As a Function of Shear Rate, Including Newtonian, Shear-Thinning, and Shear-Thickening Behavior Regions

Recent advances in experimental techniques have dramatically enhanced our ability to study colloidal dynamics in real time and at the single-particle level. Confocal microscopy enables three-dimensional visualization of particle arrangements with submicron resolution, while dynamic light scattering provides valuable information about diffusion processes and size distributions. Small-angle X-ray scattering offers insights into structural ordering across multiple length scales, complementing direct imaging approaches.

Computational methods have similarly revolutionized the study of colloidal systems. Molecular dynamics and Monte Carlo simulations allow researchers to predict assembly behaviors and structure-property relationships with increasing accuracy. Coarse-grained modeling approaches enable the simulation of larger systems over extended time scales, bridging the gap between atomistic calculations and experimental observations.

The study of nonequilibrium dynamics in colloidal systems represents a frontier area with significant fundamental and practical implications. Active colloids—particles capable of converting energy from their environment into directed motion—challenge traditional thermodynamic frameworks and offer potential applications in microscale transport and sensing. Similarly, the behavior of colloids under confinement or at interfaces presents unique phenomena with relevance to biological systems and advanced materials processing. Table 6-2 summarizes key colloidal interaction types and their characteristic features, providing a framework for understanding the diverse behaviors observed in these systems.

Table 6-2. Colloidal Interaction Types and Their Characteristics

Interaction Type	Origin	Range	Magnitude	Dependence Factors
van der Waals	Fluctuating dipoles	Short to medium	Moderate	Particle size, material properties, medium
Electrostatic	Surface charges	Medium to long	Strong	Surface charge, ionic strength, pH
Steric	Adsorbed polymers	Short	Variable	Polymer length, grafting density, solvent quality
Hydrogen bonding	Surface functional groups	Very short	Weak (individual)	Chemical functionality, solvent
Depletion	Excluded volume	Short	Variable	Depletant size and concentration
Magnetic	Magnetic moments	Long	Variable	Magnetic susceptibility, field strength

Understanding the interplay between these interactions provides the foundation for designing stable colloidal systems with tailored properties for specific applications. As we will explore in subsequent sections, the ability to control colloidal structure and dynamics enables diverse technological innovations across multiple fields.

6.4 Applications in Medicine and Electronics

The unique properties of thin films and colloidal nanostructures have catalyzed transformative advancements in both medicine and electronics, two fields where precise control over materials at the nanoscale has yielded particularly significant benefits. This section explores the diverse applications that have emerged from the integration of these nanotechnologies into medical devices, diagnostic platforms, therapeutic systems, and electronic components.

Medical Applications

In the realm of medicine, thin films and colloidal nanostructures have revolutionized approaches to diagnosis, treatment, and monitoring of diseases through their ability to interact with biological systems at the cellular and molecular levels.

Diagnostic Applications

Biosensors represent one of the most impactful diagnostic applications of nanotechnology. By incorporating nanomaterials into sensing platforms, researchers have achieved unprecedented sensitivity and specificity for detecting biomarkers associated with various diseases. Thin film electrodes modified with recognition elements such as antibodies or aptamers enable rapid electrochemical detection of analytes even at picomolar concentrations. Gold nanoparticles, with their exceptional optical properties, form the basis for lateral flow assays and colorimetric tests, including widely used pregnancy tests and COVID-19 rapid diagnostics.

Surface plasmon resonance (SPR) sensors, which rely on thin metal films (typically gold) deposited on glass substrates, have become indispensable tools for studying biomolecular interactions and developing diagnostic assays. These systems detect minute changes in refractive index near the sensor surface when target molecules bind to immobilized receptors, enabling label-free, real-time monitoring of binding events. The integration of nanostructured films with enhanced plasmonic properties has pushed detection limits to unprecedented levels, enabling the identification of biomarkers at clinically relevant concentrations.

Dr. Sofia Martinez, a leading researcher in nanobiosensors, observes that "the convergence of thin film technology with microfluidics and smartphone-based detection platforms is democratizing access to sophisticated diagnostics, particularly in resource-limited settings where traditional laboratory infrastructure is unavailable" (Martinez, 2024). This trend toward point-of-care testing exemplifies how nanotechnology can address critical healthcare challenges in global contexts.

Magnetic nanoparticles have similarly transformed diagnostic capabilities through their application in magnetic resonance imaging (MRI) contrast enhancement and magnetic particle imaging (MPI). Superparamagnetic iron oxide nanoparticles, often functionalized with targeting ligands, accumulate preferentially in specific tissues or disease sites, providing enhanced contrast and functional information during imaging procedures. Recent advances in nanoparticle design have yielded multimodal contrast agents that combine magnetic properties with optical or radioactive signatures, enabling complementary imaging approaches for comprehensive diagnostic information.

Therapeutic Applications

In the therapeutic domain, nanoparticle-based drug delivery systems have addressed fundamental challenges in pharmacokinetics and targeted therapy. Liposomes—colloidal vesicles composed of phospholipid bilayers—were among the first nanomedicine platforms to achieve clinical success, with formulations such as Doxil (liposomal doxorubicin) demonstrating improved efficacy and reduced toxicity compared to conventional chemotherapy. Polymeric nanoparticles, including those based on biodegradable materials like poly(lactic-co-glycolic acid) (PLGA), offer tunable release profiles and the ability to encapsulate both hydrophilic and hydrophobic drugs.

The surface functionalization of therapeutic nanoparticles with targeting ligands enables selective delivery to specific cell types or tissues, minimizing off-target effects. This approach has proven particularly valuable in oncology, where nanoparticles can exploit the enhanced permeability and retention (EPR) effect in tumor vasculature for passive targeting, complemented by active targeting through surface-conjugated antibodies or peptides that recognize cancer-specific receptors.

Thin film technologies have similarly contributed to therapeutic innovations, particularly in implantable and transdermal drug delivery systems. Microfabricated thin film devices with precisely controlled release mechanisms enable temporal and spatial control over drug administration. Dissolving microneedle arrays—microscale projections fabricated from biocompatible polymers loaded with therapeutic agents—provide a minimally invasive approach for transdermal delivery, circumventing the barrier function of the stratum corneum while avoiding the pain associated with conventional injections.

The integration of thin films in implantable medical devices represents another significant application area. Biocompatible coatings on orthopedic implants, vascular stents, and neural electrodes improve tissue integration and reduce adverse responses. For instance, hydroxyapatite films deposited on titanium implants enhance osseointegration through chemical similarity to native bone mineral, while drug-eluting coatings on coronary stents release antiproliferative agents to prevent restenosis following angioplasty procedures.

Antimicrobial nanocoatings have gained particular attention in the context of healthcare-associated infections—a leading cause of morbidity and mortality in hospital settings. Silver nanoparticle-containing films exhibit broad-spectrum antimicrobial activity through multiple mechanisms, including disruption of bacterial cell membranes and interference with critical enzymes. These coatings find application in wound dressings, catheters, and environmental surfaces within healthcare facilities, contributing to infection control efforts.

Electronic Applications

The impact of thin film and colloidal technologies on electronics has been equally transformative, enabling the continued miniaturization, performance enhancement, and diversification of electronic devices across consumer, industrial, and specialized applications.

Semiconductor Devices

The semiconductor industry represents perhaps the most prominent example of thin film technology's transformative impact. Modern integrated circuits rely on precisely deposited and patterned thin films of semiconductors, conductors, and insulators to achieve the complex functionality and high performance that underpin contemporary computing. As feature sizes have shrunk below 10 nanometers in advanced microprocessors, atomic-layer precision in film deposition has become essential, driving innovations in deposition techniques and in-line metrology.

Beyond conventional silicon-based devices, thin film transistors (TFTs) based on alternative semiconductors have enabled large-area electronics for displays and sensing applications. Amorphous silicon, metal oxide, and organic semiconductor TFTs serve as switching elements in active-matrix displays, with each technology offering distinct advantages in terms of mobility, transparency, or mechanical flexibility. Figure 6-3 illustrates the basic structure of a bottom-gate thin film transistor used in display applications.

CHAPTER 6   THIN FILMS AND COLLOIDAL NANOSTRUCTURES

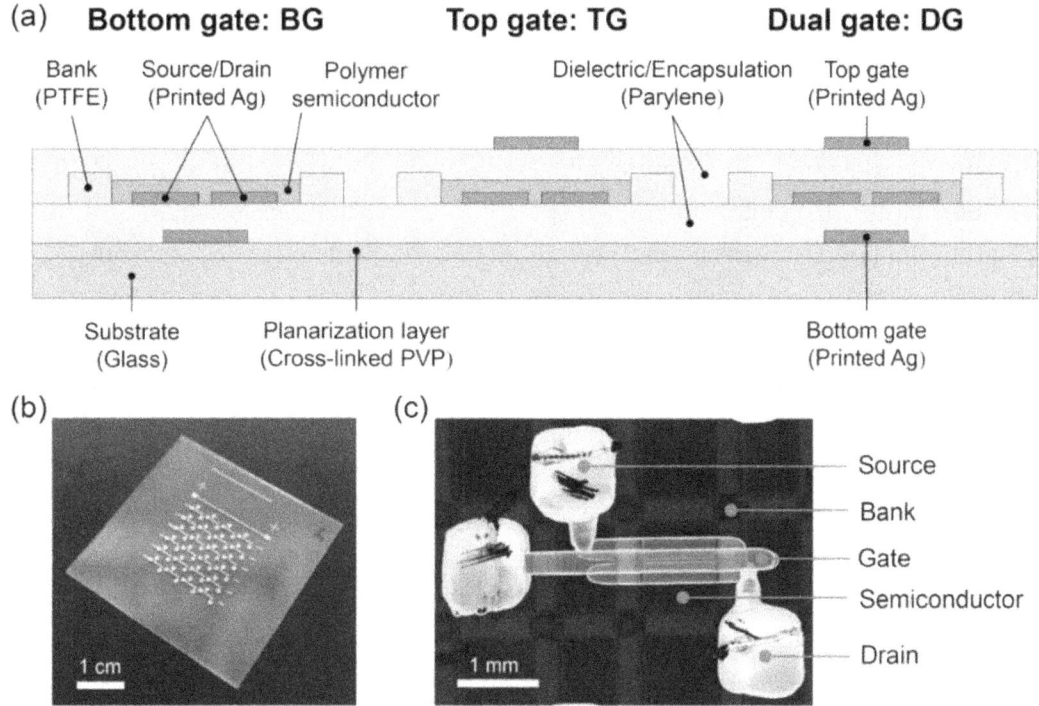

Figure 6-3. Cross-sectional view of thin film transistor (TFT) structures, showing bottom-gate (BG), top-gate (TG), and dual-gate (DG) configurations, with labeled components including substrate, planarization layer, semiconductor, source/drain electrodes, dielectric/encapsulation layer, and printed gate electrodes

Solution-processed semiconductor nanocrystals represent a promising direction for next-generation electronic devices. Quantum dots of materials such as lead sulfide, cadmium selenide, or perovskites can be synthesized with precise size control and deposited from colloidal suspensions to form semiconductor films with tunable electronic properties. This approach combines the advantages of solution processing (low cost, large area coverage) with the performance characteristics typically associated with epitaxially grown inorganic semiconductors.

Professor Hiroshi Tanaka highlights that "the ability to precisely tune the bandgap of colloidal quantum dot films through size control offers unprecedented flexibility in optoelectronic device design, enabling the development of spectrally selective photodetectors and light-emitting devices that can be tailored for specific applications" (Tanaka, 2023). This tunability has proven particularly valuable in multijunction solar cells and specialized sensing applications.

CHAPTER 6 THIN FILMS AND COLLOIDAL NANOSTRUCTURES

Energy Applications

Thin film and colloidal technologies have significantly advanced energy conversion and storage systems, contributing to global sustainability efforts. Thin film solar cells based on materials such as cadmium telluride, copper indium gallium selenide (CIGS), and amorphous silicon offer advantages in terms of material usage and manufacturing flexibility compared to conventional crystalline silicon technology. More recently, perovskite solar cells—which can be fabricated from solution-processed precursors—have achieved remarkable efficiency improvements, reaching over 25% in laboratory devices within a decade of their initial development.

The layer-by-layer assembly of thin films enables precise control over interfacial properties in energy conversion devices, critical for charge separation and transport processes. In organic and hybrid photovoltaics, the morphology of donor-acceptor heterojunctions at the nanoscale directly impacts exciton diffusion, charge separation, and ultimately, device efficiency. Colloidal quantum dots similarly offer unique advantages in photovoltaics through their size-tunable band gaps and solution processability, enabling spectral matching to solar radiation and simplified manufacturing approaches.

In energy storage, thin film electrodes and nanostructured materials have enhanced the performance of lithium-ion batteries, supercapacitors, and emerging battery chemistries. Thin film solid electrolytes offer pathways to safer lithium metal batteries by suppressing dendrite formation, while nanostructured electrode materials provide shorter diffusion pathways for ions, enabling faster charging and higher power density. Table 6-3 summarizes key applications of thin films and colloidal nanostructures in energy technologies.

Table 6-3. Applications of Nanomaterials in Energy Technologies

Technology	Nanomaterial Type	Function	Benefits
Solar cells	Semiconductor quantum dots	Light absorption	Tunable band gap, multiple exciton generation
Solar cells	Metal nanoparticles	Light management	Enhanced absorption via plasmonic effects
Batteries	Nanostructured electrodes	Charge storage	Improved rate capability, cycle life
Batteries	Solid electrolyte thin films	Ion conduction	Enhanced safety, prevention of dendrite formation
Fuel cells	Catalyst nanoparticles	Electrochemical reactions	Increased active surface area, reduced material usage
Supercapacitors	Carbon nanostructures	Charge storage	High surface area, rapid charge/discharge

Display Technologies

The evolution of display technologies represents a particularly visible manifestation of thin film innovation. Liquid crystal displays (LCDs) rely on precisely fabricated thin film transistor arrays to control individual pixels, while organic light-emitting diode (OLED) displays employ thin films of organic semiconductors that emit light when electrically stimulated. The latter technology offers advantages in terms of contrast, viewing angle, and response time, contributing to its adoption in premium smartphones and televisions.

Quantum dot displays represent an emerging technology that leverages colloidal semiconductor nanocrystals as color conversion materials. In these systems, blue LEDs excite quantum dots with precisely controlled sizes (and therefore emission wavelengths) to produce red and green light, resulting in displays with expanded color gamut and improved energy efficiency compared to conventional LCDs. This approach combines the manufacturing advantages of LCD technology with the color performance characteristics of emissive displays.

Flexible and stretchable electronics represent frontier applications that leverage the unique mechanical properties achievable in ultrathin films. By depositing electronic materials on polymer substrates with thicknesses in the micrometer range, researchers have developed displays and sensing systems that can conform to curved surfaces or withstand repeated deformation. These capabilities open new application possibilities in wearable technology, biomedical devices, and unconventional form factors for consumer electronics.

The convergence of thin film electronics with Internet of Things (IoT) technologies has accelerated the development of distributed sensing systems that integrate seamlessly with everyday objects and environments. Printed thin film sensors, energy harvesters, and communication circuits enable new paradigms in environmental monitoring, structural health assessment, and connected consumer products—topics that will be explored further in Section 6.6.

6.5 Future Trends

The field of thin films and colloidal nanostructures continues to evolve rapidly, driven by advances in synthesis methods, characterization techniques, and theoretical understanding. This section explores emerging trends and future directions that promise to expand the capabilities and applications of these nanomaterials in the coming decades.

Advanced Manufacturing Techniques

The evolution of deposition and patterning technologies represents a critical frontier in thin film innovation. Roll-to-roll processing methodologies are gaining prominence for their ability to produce continuous thin films on flexible substrates at high throughput, potentially transforming the economics of technologies ranging from solar cells to flexible displays. These approaches adapt techniques from the printing industry to deposit functional materials over large areas with precise thickness control, enabling scalable production of devices previously confined to batch fabrication.

Additive manufacturing (3D printing) of functional nanomaterials represents another transformative trend. Recent developments in direct-write technologies and colloidal ink formulations have enabled the three-dimensional fabrication of structures with nanoscale precision and compositional control. Dr. Robert Wilson, a pioneer in this field, notes that "the integration of nanoparticle-based inks with advanced printing platforms has opened new design possibilities for complex architectures with spatially varying properties—structures that would be impossible to create through conventional fabrication routes" (Wilson, 2024). These capabilities are particularly valuable for tissue engineering scaffolds, microfluidic devices, and specialized electronic components.

Atomic-level precision in material deposition continues to advance through techniques such as atomic layer deposition (ALD) and molecular beam epitaxy (MBE). These approaches enable the creation of heterostructures with atomically abrupt interfaces and precisely controlled compositions, critical for quantum electronic devices and advanced optoelectronic systems. The ability to deposit conformal films on complex three-dimensional structures through ALD has proven especially valuable for applications ranging from high-aspect-ratio capacitors to catalyst supports with intricate geometries.

Novel Material Systems

The development of new material compositions and structures represents a parallel vector of innovation in nanomaterial science. Two-dimensional (2D) materials beyond graphene—including transition metal dichalcogenides, hexagonal boron nitride, and MXenes—have emerged as versatile platforms for next-generation electronics, sensing, and energy applications. The unique electronic, optical, and mechanical properties of these atomically thin sheets enable novel device architectures and functionalities not achievable with conventional materials.

Halide perovskites have similarly revolutionized optoelectronic applications through their exceptional optical properties and solution processability. Beyond their well-documented success in photovoltaics, these materials are advancing light-emitting diodes, photodetectors, and radiation detection systems. Their compositional flexibility enables precise tuning of band gap and carrier dynamics, while advances in stability engineering are addressing historical challenges related to environmental sensitivity.

Bioinspired and biomimetic nanomaterials represent an exciting frontier that draws inspiration from natural systems. Structural colors based on photonic crystals, self-cleaning surfaces modeled after lotus leaves, and adhesive structures inspired by gecko feet exemplify how principles from biological systems can inform the design of functional nanomaterials with unique properties. These approaches often leverage hierarchical structures spanning multiple length scales—a characteristic feature of many biological materials that remains challenging to replicate through conventional fabrication routes.

The development of responsive and adaptive nanomaterials constitutes another significant trend. Stimuli-responsive polymers, phase-change materials, and systems with programmable functionality enable applications in controlled release, sensing, and actuation. Professor Emma Chen observes that "the ability to design materials that can reconfigure their structure or properties in response to specific triggers opens new possibilities for self-regulating systems and autonomous devices" (Chen, 2024). This capability is particularly valuable in biomedical applications, where physiological conditions can serve as triggers for therapeutic interventions.

Sustainability Considerations

Environmental and sustainability considerations are increasingly shaping research directions in nanomaterial science. The development of earth-abundant and low-toxicity alternatives to conventional materials addresses concerns about resource limitations and environmental impact. For instance, copper zinc tin sulfide (CZTS) has emerged as a promising alternative to CIGS in thin film photovoltaics, eliminating reliance on scarce indium resources. Similarly, iron oxide nanoparticles offer a more environmentally benign alternative to cadmium-based quantum dots for certain biomedical applications.

Lifecycle assessment approaches are becoming more prominent in evaluating the environmental footprint of nanomaterial technologies. These analyses consider impacts across the entire value chain, from raw material extraction through manufacturing, use, and end-of-life management. Such a comprehensive evaluation is essential for ensuring that nanotechnology developments contribute positively to sustainability goals rather than simply shifting environmental burdens to different stages of the product lifecycle.

The recyclability and recoverability of nanomaterials represent related challenges that require innovative approaches. The high value of certain nanomaterials (particularly those containing precious metals) provides economic incentives for recovery, but their dispersed use and integration into complex products can make separation and recycling technically challenging. Advanced separation technologies and design-for-recycling approaches are emerging to address these issues, particularly for applications with high material throughput.

Convergence with Other Technologies

The integration of thin films and colloidal nanostructures with complementary technologies represents a powerful driver of innovation. The convergence of nanotechnology with biotechnology enables advanced diagnostics, targeted therapeutics, and biomimetic materials with unprecedented functionality. Nanomaterial interfaces with biological systems are becoming increasingly sophisticated, enabling applications ranging from neural interfaces to synthetic tissues with integrated sensing capabilities.

Quantum technologies represent another frontier where nanomaterials play an enabling role. Epitaxial semiconductor quantum dots, nitrogen-vacancy centers in diamond, and topological insulators exemplify nanomaterial platforms being explored for quantum information processing. These systems leverage quantum confinement effects to create and manipulate quantum states, potentially enabling revolutionary advances in computing, communication, and sensing applications.

The integration of nanomaterials with flexible electronics technologies continues to advance wearable and implantable systems. Ultrathin film devices that can conform to biological tissues enable continuous health monitoring with minimal discomfort, while stretchable electronic systems withstand the mechanical deformations associated with bodily movement. Professor James Rodriguez notes that "the mechanical compliance achievable in nanoscale films has fundamentally transformed our conception of electronics from rigid objects to seamless extensions of the human body" (Rodriguez, 2024). This paradigm shift opens new possibilities for human–machine interfaces and personalized healthcare.

Advanced manufacturing paradigms, including digital fabrication and Industry 4.0 approaches, increasingly incorporate nanomaterial processes within interconnected production systems. In-line metrology for thin film characterization, coupled with artificial intelligence for process optimization, enables adaptive manufacturing with unprecedented quality control. These developments are particularly valuable for high-precision applications where nanoscale variations can significantly impact device performance.

Emerging Application Areas

Beyond established applications in electronics and medicine, thin films and colloidal nanostructures are finding new roles in diverse fields. Environmental remediation represents a growing application area, with engineered nanomaterials enabling selective capture of contaminants from water and air. Nanostructured membranes with precisely controlled pore sizes and surface chemistries offer enhanced selectivity and throughput compared to conventional filtration technologies, while photocatalytic nanoparticles enable the degradation of persistent organic pollutants using solar energy.

Aerospace applications leverage the unique properties of nanomaterials to address specialized requirements. Thermal barrier coatings based on nanostructured ceramics protect turbine components from extreme temperatures, while carbon nanotube-reinforced composites offer exceptional strength-to-weight ratios for structural applications. Anti-icing coatings that manipulate surface energy at the nanoscale prevent ice accumulation on aircraft surfaces, enhancing safety and reducing energy consumption associated with conventional de-icing methods.

The food and agriculture sectors are similarly beginning to adopt nanomaterial technologies. Intelligent packaging films incorporating antimicrobial nanoparticles or colorimetric sensors can extend shelf life and indicate product freshness, while nanoscale delivery systems for fertilizers and pesticides enable precise dosing and targeted release in agricultural applications. These developments contribute to food security goals by reducing waste and enhancing resource utilization efficiency.

Cultural heritage preservation represents an emerging application area where nanomaterials offer unique advantages. Consolidants based on colloidal silica penetrate deteriorating stone and wood, reinforcing these materials while maintaining vapor permeability essential for preventing secondary damage. Protective coatings with self-cleaning properties shield historical artifacts from environmental pollutants, while advanced cleaning methods using specialized gels remove contaminants without affecting original materials.

Ethical and Regulatory Considerations

As nanomaterial technologies continue to advance, ethical and regulatory frameworks must evolve in parallel. Risk assessment methodologies for engineered nanomaterials have matured significantly, moving beyond generic categorizations to more nuanced approaches that consider specific material properties, exposure pathways, and biological interactions. Standardized testing protocols developed by organizations such as the International Organization for Standardization (ISO) and the Organization for Economic Cooperation and Development (OECD) provide consistent frameworks for evaluating potential risks.

Regulatory approaches to nanomaterials vary globally but are generally converging toward risk-based frameworks that consider both hazard and exposure dimensions. The European Union's REACH (Registration, Evaluation, Authorization and Restriction of Chemicals) regulation explicitly addresses nanomaterials through specific information requirements, while the US Food and Drug Administration applies existing regulatory frameworks with additional considerations for nanoscale materials in products under its jurisdiction.

The responsible development of nanotechnology requires engagement with broader societal questions beyond technical risk assessment. Public perception and acceptance of nanomaterial technologies influence their successful implementation, necessitating transparent communication about both benefits and potential risks. Interdisciplinary collaborations between natural scientists, social scientists, ethicists, and policy experts help ensure that nanomaterial development proceeds in alignment with societal values and priorities. Table 6-4 summarizes key future trends in thin film and colloidal nanotechnology, highlighting their potential impacts across application domains.

Table 6-4. *Emerging Trends in Thin Film and Colloidal Nanotechnology*

Trend	Key Developments	Potential Impact
Roll-to-roll nanomanufacturing	Continuous deposition of functional thin films	Dramatic cost reduction for large-area applications
Bioinspired nanomaterials	Hierarchical structures mimicking natural systems	Self-cleaning surfaces, structural color, enhanced adhesion
Quantum nanomaterials	Precisely engineered quantum confinement effects	Quantum computing, secure communications, ultrasensitive sensing
Sustainable nanomaterials	Earth-abundant compositions, green synthesis routes	Reduced environmental footprint, enhanced resource efficiency
Adaptive and responsive materials	Stimuli-responsive structures and properties	Self-regulating systems, autonomous devices, smart packaging
Nanomaterial recycling	Separation and recovery technologies	Circular economy for high-value nanomaterials

6.6 AI and IoT in Applications

The convergence of artificial intelligence (AI) and Internet of Things (IoT) technologies with thin films and colloidal nanostructures is creating unprecedented opportunities for smart, connected systems with enhanced functionality and autonomy. This section explores how these technological domains are intersecting to enable new applications and capabilities.

AI-Enhanced Materials Discovery and Optimization

Artificial intelligence is revolutionizing the discovery and optimization of new nanomaterials through approaches that accelerate traditional research workflows and enable exploration of vast compositional and structural spaces. Machine learning algorithms trained on experimental and computational materials data can identify promising candidates with desired properties, significantly reducing the time and resources required for materials development.

High-throughput experimentation coupled with AI-based analysis has proven particularly powerful for thin film optimization. Combinatorial deposition techniques create composition gradients across substrates, generating hundreds or thousands of unique compositions in a single experiment. Machine learning algorithms then analyze characterization data to identify composition-structure-property relationships, enabling rapid identification of optimal formulations for specific applications.

Dr. Maria Gonzalez, a pioneer in this field, explains that "the integration of autonomous experimentation platforms with AI-based decision-making algorithms creates closed-loop systems that can navigate complex parameter spaces with minimal human intervention, leading to discoveries that might otherwise remain elusive" (Gonzalez, 2023). These approaches have accelerated the development of materials for applications ranging from catalysis to thermoelectric energy conversion.

In the domain of colloidal nanostructures, AI methods support the prediction of synthesis outcomes based on reaction parameters, enabling more precise control over particle size, shape, and surface properties. Generative models trained on experimental data can suggest novel synthesis routes for particles with specific characteristics, while reinforcement learning approaches optimize reaction conditions through iterative feedback loops.

Computational modeling of nanomaterials has similarly benefited from AI advancements. Deep learning approaches enable more accurate predictions of material properties from atomic structures, bridging the gap between quantum mechanical calculations and macroscopic behaviors. This capability proves particularly valuable for interfacial phenomena critical to thin film and colloidal behavior, where traditional computational methods often struggle with complexity and scale.

IoT Integration with Nanomaterial-Based Sensors

The Internet of Things fundamentally relies on distributed sensing capabilities to gather information about physical environments—a domain where nanomaterial-based sensors excel due to their enhanced sensitivity, selectivity, and integration potential. The marriage of these technologies enables new paradigms in environmental monitoring, healthcare, and industrial applications.

 Thin film and nanostructured sensors offer several advantages for IoT applications, including low power consumption, miniaturized form factors, and enhanced sensitivity compared to conventional alternatives. Gas sensors based on metal oxide semiconductor films can detect pollutants at parts-per-billion concentrations while consuming minimal power, making them ideal for battery-operated or energy-harvesting IoT nodes. Similarly, plasmonic sensors leveraging noble metal nanostructures enable label-free detection of biomolecules with exceptional sensitivity, supporting applications in remote health monitoring and food safety verification.

The integration of nanomaterial-based sensing elements with CMOS (complementary metal-oxide-semiconductor) electronics enables compact, integrated systems that combine sensing, signal processing, and communication functions. Advanced packaging technologies, including through-silicon vias and three-dimensional integration, facilitate this convergence by minimizing footprint and reducing signal path lengths.

Distributed sensor networks leveraging these technologies enable comprehensive monitoring across diverse environments. In urban settings, networks of air quality sensors provide granular data on pollution levels, helping identify hotspots and inform policy interventions. Agricultural applications include soil moisture and nutrient monitoring to optimize irrigation and fertilization practices, reducing resource consumption while maximizing crop yields. Industrial implementations leverage these systems for predictive maintenance, with sensors detecting early indicators of equipment failure before catastrophic breakdowns occur.

The energy autonomy of IoT sensor nodes represents a critical challenge that nanomaterial technologies are helping to address. Thin film solar cells, when integrated directly into sensor packages, enable energy harvesting from ambient light, while thermoelectric generators based on nanostructured materials convert temperature differentials into electrical power. Energy storage systems incorporating nanostructured electrodes offer enhanced capacity and cycle life within compact form factors, complementing these harvesting approaches to ensure reliable operation even in variable environmental conditions.

Edge Computing and In-Sensor Processing

The traditional IoT paradigm, where raw sensor data is transmitted to centralized cloud platforms for processing, faces challenges related to bandwidth limitations, latency, and privacy concerns. Edge computing approaches, which shift processing capabilities closer to data sources, address these challenges while enabling more responsive and resilient systems. Thin film electronics play an enabling role in this transition through their integration potential and energy efficiency.

Neuromorphic computing architectures, which mimic the structure and function of biological neural networks, represent a particularly promising approach for edge processing of sensor data. Memristive devices based on metal oxide thin films emulate synaptic behavior through their history-dependent conductance modulation, enabling efficient implementation of neural network operations with minimal power consumption. Notably, memristive devices combine both computation and memory within the same physical structure, eliminating the need for separate data transfer between processor and memory. This makes them ideal for low-power AI use cases on edge devices. These devices can be arranged in crossbar arrays for parallel processing, achieving orders of magnitude improvement in energy efficiency compared to conventional digital approaches for certain tasks.

Professor Samuel Kim observes that "the co-location of sensing and computing functions through thin film technologies creates opportunities for sensor-processing units that extract actionable information from raw data at the point of collection, dramatically reducing communication requirements while enhancing privacy and resilience" (Kim, 2024). This approach proves particularly valuable for applications involving sensitive data, such as healthcare monitoring, where minimizing data transmission enhances security and privacy protection.

Beyond dedicated processing hardware, algorithmic approaches tailored to resource-constrained environments enable efficient analysis of sensor data at the edge. Techniques such as model compression, quantization, and pruning reduce the computational demands of machine learning models while preserving accuracy for targeted tasks. When implemented on ultra-low-power processors integrated with sensor platforms, these approaches enable sophisticated analysis even under strict energy constraints.

Digital Twins and Predictive Modeling

The concept of digital twins—virtual representations of physical assets that evolve in parallel with their real-world counterparts—is gaining traction across industries, enabled by the convergence of IoT sensing, advanced modeling, and artificial intelligence. When applied to systems incorporating thin films and colloidal nanostructures, this approach enables predictive maintenance, performance optimization, and lifecycle management.

For thin film manufacturing equipment, digital twins combine real-time sensor data with physics-based models to monitor process parameters and predict deviations before they result in quality issues. Machine learning algorithms identify subtle patterns in sensor readings that precede defect formation, enabling preemptive adjustments to maintain product quality. This capability is particularly valuable for processes with tight specification requirements, such as those employed in semiconductor manufacturing, where even minor deviations can lead to significant quality issues in real-world applications.

In medical applications, digital twins of drug delivery systems based on colloidal nanostructures enable personalized treatment optimization. By integrating patient-specific physiological parameters with models of nanoparticle transport and drug release kinetics, these systems predict therapeutic outcomes for various dosing regimens, supporting clinicians in tailoring treatments to individual patients. As treatment progresses, sensor data feeds back into the model, refining predictions based on observed responses.

Building energy management systems incorporating thin film sensors and smart glazing technologies similarly benefit from digital twin approaches. Virtual models of building thermal behavior, informed by distributed temperature and occupancy sensors, enable predictive control strategies that optimize energy consumption while maintaining comfort. Electrochromic windows based on transition metal oxide films adjust their optical properties in response to these models, regulating solar gain based on current conditions and anticipated changes.

The feedback loop between physical systems and their digital representations creates opportunities for continuous optimization and learning. As real-world performance data accumulates, models become increasingly accurate, enabling more sophisticated control strategies and deeper insights into system behavior. This virtuous cycle accelerates improvement across applications, from manufacturing processes to infrastructure management and healthcare delivery.

Challenges and Opportunities

Despite significant progress, several challenges remain in fully realizing the potential of AI-IoT-nanomaterial integration. Data quality and standardization represent persistent issues, particularly for sensor networks deployed in diverse and challenging environments. Variations in calibration, drift over time, and environmental interferences can compromise data reliability, affecting downstream analysis and decision-making processes. Advanced calibration methods incorporating machine learning approaches offer promising solutions by identifying and correcting for these effects. Power constraints continue to limit the capabilities of distributed sensing systems, particularly for deployments in remote locations or harsh environments. While energy harvesting and storage technologies have advanced significantly, further improvements in efficiency and reliability are needed to support more sophisticated sensing and processing functions. Thin film batteries with enhanced energy density and cycle life represent one promising direction, complemented by ultra-low-power electronics that minimize consumption demands.

Security and privacy considerations become increasingly important as these systems proliferate, particularly for applications involving sensitive data. The resource constraints of IoT devices often complicate the implementation of robust security measures, creating potential vulnerabilities in distributed networks. Hardware-based security approaches, including physical unclonable functions (PUFs) based on inherent variations in thin film properties, offer promising alternatives to conventional cryptographic methods, providing device authentication with minimal computational overhead.

Interoperability across platforms and vendors represents another significant challenge, with proprietary systems often creating fragmented ecosystems that limit scalability and data integration. The development and adoption of open standards for device communication, data formats, and application programming interfaces (APIs) are essential for realizing the full potential of these technologies across application domains. Despite these challenges, the continued convergence of AI, IoT, and nanomaterial technologies promises transformative capabilities across sectors. The combination of enhanced sensing, distributed intelligence, and advanced materials enables systems that can monitor, analyze, and respond to their environments with unprecedented sophistication. As these technologies mature and integration barriers diminish, new applications will emerge that leverage their collective capabilities to address complex challenges in healthcare, energy, transportation, and beyond.

6.7 Summary

Thin films and colloidal nanostructures represent foundational elements in modern nanotechnology, offering remarkable control over material properties at the nanoscale. This chapter explored their synthesis, characterization, and the intricate dynamics that govern their behavior, emphasizing how their unique physical and chemical properties differ markedly from bulk materials. Advanced deposition techniques such as physical and chemical vapor deposition, atomic layer deposition, and solution-based methods enable precise engineering of thin films for diverse applications. Simultaneously, colloidal nanostructures—synthesized via chemical reduction, sol-gel processes, or hot injection—demonstrate tunable features that are critical for tailored functionality.

Characterization tools, including SEM, TEM, XPS, ellipsometry, and DLS, provide multidimensional insight into morphology, structure, composition, and stability. These tools are vital in ensuring material performance, especially for high-precision applications. The integration of thin films and colloidal systems has led to significant innovations in medicine and electronics, from biosensors and targeted drug delivery to flexible electronics, solar cells, and advanced display technologies.

Looking ahead, emerging trends such as roll-to-roll manufacturing, quantum materials, bioinspired nanostructures, and environmentally sustainable alternatives are shaping the next wave of development. The convergence with artificial intelligence and the Internet of Things is enhancing material discovery, optimizing manufacturing, and enabling smarter, autonomous systems. Despite challenges related to scalability, stability, and ethical considerations, the future of these nanotechnologies is bright and expanding. Their versatility and transformative potential across sectors underscore their vital role in advancing science, engineering, and global innovation for decades to come.

CHAPTER 7

Self-Assembly and Nanovesicles

This chapter explores the fundamental principles and applications of self-assembly processes and nanovesicles in nanotechnology. Beginning with the theoretical foundations of self-assembly, the chapter examines the thermodynamic and kinetic factors that drive spontaneous organization at the nanoscale. It then delves into nanovesicles, discussing their formation mechanisms, structural characteristics, and dynamic behaviors. The chapter distinguishes between nanospheres and nanocapsules, highlighting their unique properties and fabrication methods. Advanced characterization techniques essential for analyzing these nanostructures are thoroughly explained, including microscopy, spectroscopy, and scattering methods. The chapter concludes with an extensive examination of nanovesicle applications in biotechnology, covering drug delivery systems, biosensors, tissue engineering, and bioimaging technologies. Throughout, the interplay between fundamental science and practical implementation in various biomedical contexts is emphasized.

7.1 Fundamentals of Self-Assembly

Self-assembly represents one of nature's most elegant phenomena, where disordered components spontaneously organize themselves into ordered structures without external direction. At the nanoscale, this process has profound implications for creating sophisticated functional materials and systems. The beauty of self-assembly lies in its ability to generate complex architectures through relatively simple interactions between building blocks, mimicking processes seen throughout biological systems.

The driving forces behind self-assembly are primarily noncovalent interactions, including hydrogen bonding, van der Waals forces, electrostatic interactions, hydrophobic effects, and π-π stacking. While individually weak compared to covalent bonds, these forces collectively create stable structures when properly designed. The thermodynamic basis for self-assembly stems from the system's tendency to minimize free energy, where the entropic costs of ordering are offset by favorable enthalpic interactions between components.

Amphiphilic molecules—those possessing both hydrophilic and hydrophobic portions—exemplify self-assembly principles perfectly. When placed in aqueous environments, these molecules spontaneously organize to shield their hydrophobic regions from water while exposing hydrophilic portions, forming structures like micelles, bilayers, and vesicles. The critical micelle concentration (CMC) represents the threshold concentration above which amphiphiles self-assemble into these supramolecular structures.

The kinetics of self-assembly processes are equally important, determining the pathway and rate of structure formation. Many self-assembled systems represent kinetically trapped states rather than true thermodynamic equilibria, making the assembly process itself a critical parameter in determining final structure characteristics.

Several key parameters influence self-assembly outcomes:

- Molecular structure and design of building blocks
- Concentration of components
- Temperature and pressure conditions
- pH and ionic strength of the medium
- Presence of additives or template structures

Biomolecules provide outstanding examples of self-assembly in action. DNA's complementary base pairing allows for precise assembly into complex structures, while proteins fold into specific conformations based on their amino acid sequences. These biological principles have inspired the field of biomimetic self-assembly, where researchers design synthetic systems that emulate natural self-assembly processes.

The rational design of self-assembling systems requires a thorough understanding of both thermodynamic and kinetic aspects. Computer modeling and simulation tools have become invaluable in predicting self-assembly behavior before experimental implementation. Techniques such as molecular dynamics simulations and dissipative particle dynamics allow researchers to visualize assembly processes at atomic and molecular scales, optimizing designs before synthesis.

CHAPTER 7   SELF-ASSEMBLY AND NANOVESICLES

Self-assembly approaches can be categorized into static and dynamic systems. Static self-assembly results in structures that, once formed, remain stable and unchanging. Dynamic self-assembly, conversely, produces systems that continuously exchange components with their environment, allowing for adaptive responses to changing conditions—a property particularly valuable for biomimetic and responsive materials.

The hierarchical nature of self-assembly enables the creation of complex structures across multiple length scales. Primary building blocks assemble into intermediate structures, which themselves serve as components for larger assemblies. This hierarchical organization is exemplified in biological systems from protein quaternary structure to tissue organization and represents a frontier in nanomaterial design (Figure 7-1).

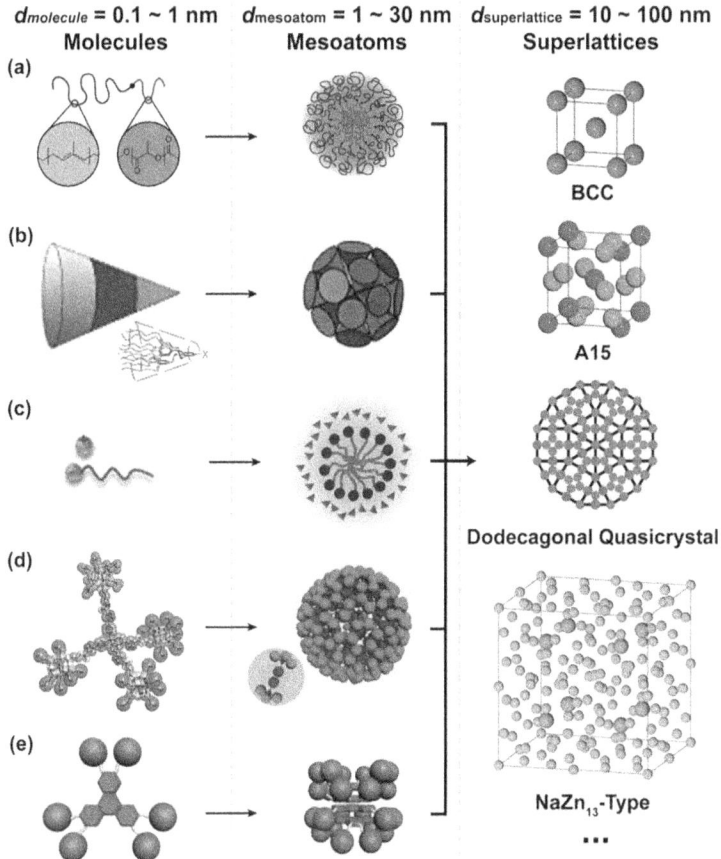

Figure 7-1. *Illustration of Self-Assembly Mechanisms at Different Scales, Showing Molecular, Intermediate, and Hierarchical Organization*

135

7.2 Nanovesicles and Mechanisms

Nanovesicles represent a specialized class of self-assembled structures with spherical morphology and hollow interiors, enclosed by a membrane typically composed of amphiphilic molecules. Their structural similarity to biological vesicles like exosomes and liposomes makes them particularly valuable for biomedical applications. Understanding the formation mechanisms of nanovesicles is crucial for controlling their properties and functionality.

The formation of nanovesicles follows distinct pathways depending on the molecular components and preparation conditions. The most common mechanism involves the hydration of a thin film of amphiphilic molecules, where water penetration causes swelling and eventual budding of vesicular structures. During this process, the energetic penalty of exposing hydrophobic regions to water drives the amphiphiles to form closed bilayer structures.

Several preparation methods have been developed to produce nanovesicles with controlled characteristics:

1. **Thin Film Hydration**: Amphiphilic molecules are dissolved in an organic solvent, which is then evaporated to form a thin film. Subsequent hydration in an aqueous medium leads to vesicle formation.

2. **Solvent Injection**: An organic solution of amphiphiles is rapidly injected into an aqueous phase, causing immediate self-assembly of vesicles as the organic solvent diffuses into water.

3. **Reverse Phase Evaporation**: This involves the formation of water-in-oil emulsions followed by the removal of the organic phase, resulting in vesicle formation.

4. **Electroformation**: Application of an alternating electric field to a lipid film promotes vesicle budding and growth from the film.

5. **Microfluidic Methods**: Precise control over fluid dynamics at the microscale enables the production of monodisperse vesicles with tailored properties.

The membrane properties of nanovesicles critically determine their stability and functionality. Membrane fluidity, affected by factors like temperature and molecular composition, influences permeability and fusion behavior. The incorporation of cholesterol or similar rigid molecules can modulate membrane fluidity, increasing mechanical stability. Surface charge, determined by the head groups of constituent amphiphiles, affects colloidal stability and interactions with biological entities.

Vesicle stability represents a fundamental concern for applications. Physical stability refers to structural integrity over time, while chemical stability involves resistance to degradation through hydrolysis or oxidation. Various stabilization strategies include

- Crosslinking of membrane components
- Surface modification with polymers like polyethylene glycol (PEG)
- Optimization of membrane composition
- Lyophilization with appropriate cryoprotectants

The size of nanovesicles typically ranges from 20 nm to several hundred nanometers, with polydispersity varying widely depending on preparation method. Size control can be achieved through extrusion through membranes of defined pore size, sonication to break larger vesicles, or microfluidic approaches that provide precise dimensional control.

Nanovesicles possess remarkable versatility in terms of membrane composition. While phospholipids remain the traditional building blocks, synthetic alternatives, including block copolymers, have expanded the available parameter space. These polymersomes often demonstrate enhanced stability compared to lipid vesicles, with tunable membrane properties based on polymer composition and molecular weight.

The encapsulation efficiency of cargo molecules within nanovesicles depends on both the preparation method and the physicochemical properties of the cargo. Hydrophilic molecules are typically encapsulated in the aqueous core during vesicle formation, while hydrophobic compounds integrate into the membrane itself. Amphiphilic molecules may distribute between these compartments. Methods to enhance loading include active loading techniques using transmembrane pH or ion gradients, which can dramatically improve encapsulation efficiency for certain molecules (Table 7-1).

Release mechanisms from nanovesicles can be designed to respond to specific stimuli, enabling controlled delivery of cargo. Common release triggers include

- pH changes (exploiting acidic environments in tumors or endosomes)
- Temperature shifts (utilizing phase transition temperatures of membrane components)
- Enzymatic degradation (incorporating enzyme-sensitive linkages)
- Redox potential changes (incorporating disulfide bonds)
- Light exposure (incorporating photosensitive groups)
- Ultrasound application (causing cavitation and temporary membrane disruption)

Table 7-1. Comparison of Common Nanovesicle Preparation Methods

Method	Vesicle Size Range	Polydispersity	Encapsulation Efficiency	Scalability	Key Advantages
Thin film hydration	100–1000 nm	High	Moderate (5–15%)	Moderate	Simple procedure, widely used
Solvent injection	50–200 nm	Moderate	Low to moderate (1–10%)	High	Easy scaling, rapid production
Reverse phase evaporation	100–500 nm	Moderate	High (30–65%)	Low	Excellent for hydrophilic cargo
Electroformation	1–100 μm	Low	Moderate (10–20%)	Low	Excellent size control, unilamellar vesicles
Microfluidic methods	50–500 nm	Very low	Moderate to high (15–40%)	Moderate	Monodisperse, precise control

The fusion and aggregation behavior of nanovesicles presents both challenges and opportunities. While unwanted aggregation can compromise stability and function, controlled fusion can be exploited for content mixing applications or triggered release. Surface modification strategies, including PEGylation and charge optimization, help prevent nonspecific aggregation while maintaining colloidal stability.

7.3 Types: Nanospheres and Nanocapsules

Nanospheres and nanocapsules represent two distinct architectural paradigms within the realm of nanoparticulate systems, each offering unique advantages for specific applications. While both structures exist at similar size scales, their internal organization, preparation methods, and functional characteristics differ substantially.

Nanospheres consist of solid matrix systems where active compounds are either dispersed throughout the matrix or adsorbed onto the surface. The matrix material commonly includes biodegradable polymers like poly(lactic-co-glycolic acid) (PLGA), polylactic acid (PLA), chitosan, or albumin. These structures typically range from 10 to 200 nm in diameter and feature a homogeneous distribution of components throughout their volume. The solid nature of nanospheres provides mechanical stability and controlled degradation profiles, making them particularly suitable for sustained release applications.

The fabrication of nanospheres typically employs one of several techniques:

- **Emulsion Solvent Evaporation**: This involves the creation of an oil-in-water emulsion where the polymer is dissolved in an organic phase, followed by solvent evaporation and particle hardening.

- **Nanoprecipitation**: A polymer solution in a water-miscible solvent is added to an aqueous phase, causing immediate precipitation as the solvent diffuses into water.

- **Salting Out**: Polymer precipitation is induced by adding electrolytes to reduce the solubility of the solvent in water.

- **Spray Drying**: A solution containing polymer and active compound is atomized into a hot gas stream, causing rapid solvent evaporation and particle formation.

The drug loading capacity of nanospheres depends primarily on matrix-drug interactions and the physical entrapment during preparation. Drug release typically follows diffusion-controlled or erosion-controlled mechanisms, or a combination of both. The degradation rate of the matrix material significantly influences release kinetics, offering opportunities for temporal control over days to months.

Nanocapsules, in contrast, exhibit a vesicular architecture consisting of a polymeric membrane surrounding a liquid core. This core-shell structure confines the active compounds primarily within the interior liquid compartment, though some may also integrate into the polymeric shell. The shell material can be composed of similar polymers used for nanospheres, while the core may contain an aqueous solution (for hydrophilic compounds) or oil (for lipophilic compounds).

The preparation of nanocapsules generally involves

- **Interfacial Polymerization**: Monomers polymerize at the interface of an emulsion, forming a membrane around droplets.

- **Interfacial Deposition**: Pre-formed polymers precipitate at the interface between two immiscible phases.

- **Layer-by-Layer Assembly**: Sequential deposition of oppositely charged polymers creates a multilayered shell around a template core.

- **Self-Assembly of Amphiphilic Block Copolymers**: These spontaneously form capsular structures in selective solvents.

The drug loading capacity of nanocapsules typically exceeds that of nanospheres for liquid-soluble compounds, as the entire core volume serves as a reservoir. Release mechanisms include diffusion through the polymer shell, shell degradation, or response to specific triggers that alter shell permeability.

Several key distinctions between nanospheres and nanocapsules influence their application profiles:

Nanospheres generally offer greater mechanical stability due to their solid structure, making them suitable for applications requiring robust particles resistant to mechanical stress. Their homogeneous matrix provides predictable degradation profiles and relatively constant release rates as the matrix erodes uniformly.

Nanocapsules excel at encapsulating high concentrations of liquid-soluble compounds, with the shell serving as a diffusion barrier that can be engineered for specific permeability. Their core-shell structure enables more sophisticated designs, including multi-compartment systems and stimuli-responsive release mechanisms.

The surface properties of both systems can be modified through similar approaches, including coating with hydrophilic polymers, attachment of targeting ligands, or incorporation of charged groups. These modifications influence circulation time, biodistribution, cellular interaction, and targeting capabilities (Table 7-2).

Table 7-2. Comparative Features of Nanospheres and Nanocapsules

Feature	Nanospheres	Nanocapsules
Structure	Solid matrix throughout	Shell surrounding liquid core
Drug distribution	Throughout the matrix or surface-adsorbed	Primarily in the liquid core
Typical size range	10–200 nm	100–500 nm
Loading capacity	Moderate	High for liquid-soluble compounds
Mechanical stability	High	Moderate
Release mechanism	Diffusion and matrix erosion	Diffusion through the shell or shell degradation
Environmental sensitivity	Limited, primarily through matrix degradation	Highly tunable through shell design
Manufacturing complexity	Moderate	High
Typical applications	Sustained release, gene delivery	Enzyme immobilization, reactive species protection

Hybrid systems combining features of both architectures have emerged as promising platforms. These include core-shell nanospheres with a gradient distribution of components and multi-compartment nanocapsules with structured interiors. Such hybrids aim to leverage the advantages of both systems while mitigating their respective limitations.

Recent advances in nanosphere and nanocapsule technologies have focused on developing stimuli-responsive variants that change their properties in response to specific environmental cues. These "smart" systems respond to triggers like pH, temperature, redox potential, or enzymatic activity, offering precise spatial and temporal control over cargo release or functionality.

7.4 Characterization Methods

The comprehensive characterization of self-assembled nanostructures and nanovesicles represents a critical aspect of their development and application. Given the complexity and nanoscale dimensions of these systems, multiple complementary techniques are required to elucidate their physicochemical properties, structural features, and functional behaviors. This multi-technique approach provides a holistic understanding necessary for rational design and optimization (Table 7-3).

Morphological characterization serves as the foundation for understanding nanostructure architecture. Electron microscopy techniques offer exceptional resolution for direct visualization:

Transmission electron microscopy (TEM) provides detailed two-dimensional projections of nanovesicles with nanometer resolution. Conventional TEM requires sample staining with heavy metal contrast agents, while cryo-TEM allows visualization of nanostructures in their native hydrated state by vitrifying samples. The latter preserves delicate features that might be distorted during conventional sample preparation. For enhanced contrast of biological components, negative staining with uranyl acetate or phosphotungstic acid highlights boundaries and interfaces.

Scanning electron microscopy (SEM) offers three-dimensional surface information but typically requires conductive coating, potentially altering delicate nanostructure surfaces. Environmental SEM partially addresses this limitation by operating under conditions compatible with hydrated samples. Field emission SEM provides improved resolution approaching 1–2 nm, valuable for detailed surface analysis.

Atomic force microscopy (AFM) offers exceptional height resolution (subnanometer) and can operate in liquid environments, enabling analysis of nanostructures under physiological conditions. Beyond imaging, AFM provides mechanical property information through force spectroscopy, measuring parameters like stiffness, adhesion, and viscoelasticity of nanovesicle membranes.

Size distribution analysis represents a fundamental characterization requirement, with several techniques offering complementary information:

Dynamic light scattering (DLS) measures the hydrodynamic diameter of nanoparticles in suspension by analyzing Brownian motion-induced fluctuations in scattered light intensity. While providing rapid ensemble measurements, DLS has limited resolution for polydisperse samples and assumes spherical particle geometry. Multi-angle DLS enhances accuracy by collecting scattered light at multiple angles.

Nanoparticle tracking analysis (NTA) combines light scattering with microscopic visualization to track individual particle movements, offering better resolution for polydisperse samples than DLS. NTA provides concentration measurements alongside size distribution, though it requires more dilute samples than DLS.

Analytical ultracentrifugation separates particles based on sedimentation velocity, providing information about size, shape, and density. This technique excels at resolving complex mixtures but requires specialized equipment and expertise.

Size-exclusion chromatography separates nanostructures based on hydrodynamic volume, offering both analytical information and preparative capabilities for fractionating samples by size.

Surface charge characterization provides critical information about colloidal stability and biological interactions:

Zeta potential measurement quantifies the electrokinetic potential at the slipping plane of nanoparticles, indicating their surface charge in a specific medium. This parameter strongly influences stability against aggregation, with values above ±30 mV typically conferring good colloidal stability. Measurements across pH ranges generate isoelectric point data, valuable for predicting behavior in different physiological environments.

Surface chemical composition requires specialized techniques:

X-ray photoelectron spectroscopy (XPS) analyzes the elemental composition of surfaces (top 10 nm) and provides chemical bonding information, though it requires high vacuum conditions incompatible with hydrated samples.

Fourier transform infrared spectroscopy (FTIR) identifies functional groups and chemical bonds through their characteristic vibrational frequencies. Attenuated total reflectance FTIR enhances surface sensitivity for nanostructure analysis.

Time-of-flight secondary ion mass spectrometry (ToF-SIMS) offers exceptional surface sensitivity (top 1–2 nm) and can map chemical species across surfaces with submicron resolution.

Structural organization at the molecular level requires specialized techniques:

Small-angle X-ray scattering (SAXS) and small-angle neutron scattering (SANS) probe internal structural organization without sample destruction. These techniques provide information about membrane thickness, lamellarity, and internal architecture of nanovesicles. SANS offers contrast variation through deuteration, highlighting specific components within complex assemblies.

Nuclear magnetic resonance (NMR) spectroscopy offers insights into molecular mobility, organization, and interactions within nanostructures. Solid-state NMR proves particularly valuable for characterizing membrane components and their dynamics.

Differential scanning calorimetry (DSC) measures thermotropic phase transitions, revealing information about membrane fluidity, component miscibility, and thermal stability of nanovesicles.

Functional characterization addresses application-specific properties:

Encapsulation efficiency determination typically involves separating free from encapsulated compounds through centrifugation, filtration, or chromatography, followed by quantification using appropriate analytical methods (spectroscopy, chromatography, or radioactive counting).

Membrane permeability can be assessed through release kinetics studies, fluorescence-based assays using self-quenching dyes, or electrical techniques for ion permeability.

Stability assessment includes accelerated aging studies, monitoring size, zeta potential, and encapsulation retention under stress conditions (temperature, pH, ionic strength, mechanical stress).

Table 7-3. Complementary Characterization Techniques for Nanovesicles

Property Category	Technique	Primary Information	Limitations
Morphology	Cryo-TEM	Native structure visualization	Complex sample preparation, 2D projections
	AFM	3D topography, mechanical properties	Tip-sample interactions may deform soft vesicles
Size distribution	DLS	Ensemble hydrodynamic diameter	Limited resolution for polydisperse samples
	NTA	Individual particle sizes, concentration	Requires dilute samples, limited to >50 nm
Surface properties	Zeta potential	Surface charge indicator	Values depend on measurement conditions

(*continued*)

Table 7-3. (*continued*)

Property Category	Technique	Primary Information	Limitations
	XPS	Surface elemental composition	Requires vacuum, not compatible with hydrated samples
Internal structure	SAXS/SANS	Membrane thickness, lamellarity	Complex data interpretation, requires models
	Fluorescence spectroscopy	Membrane fluidity, microenvironment	Requires fluorescent probes
Functional properties	Release kinetics	Cargo retention and release	Time-consuming, affected by sampling method
	Stability testing	Shelf-life prediction	Accelerated conditions may not predict real behavior

Advanced characterization often combines multiple techniques into correlated or simultaneous measurements. Cryo-electron tomography reconstructs three-dimensional models from tilt-series of cryo-TEM images, revealing internal architecture with exceptional detail. Correlative light and electron microscopy (CLEM) combines the specific labeling capabilities of fluorescence microscopy with the high resolution of electron microscopy, enabling tracking of specific components within complex nanostructures.

7.5 Applications in Biotechnology

The intersection of self-assembly principles and nanovesicle technologies has generated remarkable advances in biotechnology, with applications spanning from therapeutic delivery to diagnostics and beyond. These applications leverage the unique structural and functional properties of nanovesicles, including their ability to encapsulate diverse cargoes, interact with biological membranes, and respond to specific environmental cues.

Drug delivery represents the most extensively developed application area for nanovesicles. These systems offer numerous advantages over conventional formulations, including enhanced solubility of hydrophobic drugs, protection from degradation, prolonged circulation time, and potential for targeted delivery. Liposomes, composed of phospholipid bilayers, pioneered this field with several FDA-approved formulations, including Doxil® (doxorubicin-loaded liposomes) for cancer treatment and AmBisome® (amphotericin B liposomes) for fungal infections.

The therapeutic efficacy of nanovesicle drug delivery systems depends on several design parameters:

1. **Circulation Persistence**: Surface modification with hydrophilic polymers like polyethylene glycol creates "stealth" vesicles that evade rapid clearance by the reticuloendothelial system, extending circulation half-life from minutes to hours or days.

2. **Targeting Strategies**: Passive targeting exploits the enhanced permeability and retention (EPR) effect, where nanovesicles preferentially accumulate in tissues with leaky vasculature, such as tumors. Active targeting incorporates ligands (antibodies, peptides, aptamers, or small molecules) that recognize specific receptors overexpressed on target cells.

3. **Stimuli-Responsive Release**: "Smart" nanovesicles respond to environmental triggers characteristic of disease sites. pH-sensitive formulations destabilize in acidic tumor microenvironments or endosomes, while thermosensitive vesicles release cargo at elevated temperatures, potentially combined with localized hyperthermia.

4. **Multifunctional Integration**: Modern designs incorporate multiple functionalities, such as co-delivery of complementary drugs, combined therapy and imaging capabilities (theranostics), or sequential release of different agents.

The application of nanovesicles extends beyond traditional small-molecule drugs to encompass delivery of biologics—proteins, peptides, and nucleic acids. These macromolecular therapeutics typically suffer from poor stability, limited membrane permeability, and immunogenicity when administered conventionally. Nanovesicles provide protective environments that shield these sensitive cargoes from degradation while facilitating cellular uptake.

Nucleic acid delivery represents a particularly promising frontier. Lipid nanoparticles (LNPs) emerged as the critical delivery technology enabling mRNA vaccines against COVID-19. These specialized nanovesicles protect mRNA from nuclease degradation and facilitate endosomal escape, allowing the genetic material to reach ribosomes for protein synthesis. Similar approaches show promise for siRNA, antisense oligonucleotides, and CRISPR-Cas9 components for gene editing.

Beyond therapeutics, nanovesicles have found important applications in diagnostics and biosensing. Vesicle-based biosensors operate through various mechanisms:

- **Encapsulation of reporter molecules** that generate signals upon interaction with analytes penetrating the membrane

- **Surface-functionalized vesicles** bearing recognition elements that undergo detectable changes upon target binding

- **Vesicle disruption sensors** where analyte-triggered membrane destabilization releases encapsulated reporters

These biosensing platforms offer advantages including signal amplification (many reporter molecules per binding event), protection of sensitive components, and potential for multiplexed detection through vesicle arrays with different specificities.

Artificial cells represent an ambitious extension of nanovesicle technology, aiming to recreate cellular functions within synthetic compartments. These systems incorporate metabolic enzymes, protein expression machinery, or signaling cascades within vesicle lumens, creating biomimetic microreactors. Such artificial cells demonstrate potential for enzyme replacement therapy, synthetic biology applications, and fundamental studies of cellular processes.

The field of tissue engineering has also benefited from nanovesicle technologies. Vesicles can deliver growth factors, morphogens, and differentiation cues with precise spatial and temporal control, guiding tissue development and regeneration. Vesicle-mediated delivery offers advantages over direct factor addition, including protection from proteolytic degradation and sustained release profiles that better mimic natural developmental processes.

Extracellular vesicles (EVs)—naturally occurring nanovesicles secreted by cells—have emerged as both therapeutic agents themselves and as inspiration for synthetic designs. These biological nanovesicles contain complex cargoes of proteins, lipids, and nucleic acids that mediate intercellular communication. Engineered EVs and EV-mimetic synthetic vesicles represent a frontier in nanomedicine, combining the sophisticated functionality of natural vesicles with the control and scalability of synthetic systems.

CHAPTER 7   SELF-ASSEMBLY AND NANOVESICLES

The commercial landscape for nanovesicle technologies continues to expand, with numerous formulations in clinical use or advanced development. Challenges to broader implementation include

- Manufacturing complexity and scale-up difficulties
- Batch-to-batch reproducibility concerns
- Stability during storage and administration
- Regulatory hurdles for novel formulations
- Cost considerations for widespread adoption

Addressing these challenges requires interdisciplinary approaches combining nanomaterial science, pharmaceutics, biology, and engineering. Advances in microfluidic manufacturing, freeze-drying technologies, and analytical methods are progressively overcoming production barriers, while expanding clinical evidence supports regulatory approval pathways.

Emerging frontiers in nanovesicle applications include

- **Extracellular Vesicle Therapeutics**: Harvesting natural nanovesicles from stem cells or engineered producer cells for regenerative medicine applications.

- **Synthetic Organelles**: Creating functional subcompartments within cells to introduce new metabolic pathways or detoxification capabilities.

- **Cell Membrane-Coated Vesicles**: Hybrid structures combining synthetic cores with natural cell membrane coatings that preserve complex surface functionality.

- **3D Bioprinting with Vesicle-Laden Bioinks**: Incorporating growth factor-loaded vesicles within printable hydrogels for spatially controlled tissue regeneration.

- **Immunomodulatory Nanovesicles**: Engineering vesicles to deliver immunostimulatory or immunosuppressive signals for vaccine or autoimmune disease applications.

The continued development of nanovesicle technologies in biotechnology represents a synergistic advancement of fundamental self-assembly science alongside practical biomedical innovation. As our understanding of molecular interactions, cellular uptake mechanisms, and biological barriers improves, increasingly sophisticated nanovesicle designs promise to address current limitations while opening entirely new application possibilities.

7.6 Summary

Self-assembly and nanovesicles represent a remarkable convergence of fundamental nanoscience principles with practical biotechnological applications. The spontaneous organization of molecular components into complex, functional structures not only provides insight into natural processes but also offers powerful platforms for addressing significant biomedical challenges. Through careful molecular design and process control, researchers can now create sophisticated nanostructures with precisely tailored properties for specific applications.

The versatility of nanovesicle architectures—from simple liposomes to complex multicompartment systems—enables unprecedented control over drug delivery, biosensing, and biomimetic functions. The continued development of characterization methodologies ensures an increasingly detailed understanding of these systems, facilitating rational design iterations. As manufacturing technologies mature, translation from laboratory demonstrations to clinical and commercial applications accelerates, promising significant impacts on healthcare and biotechnology.

Future directions in this field will likely emphasize greater integration of multiple functionalities within single nanovesicle systems, improved targeting specificity through biomimetic approaches, and expanded applications in emerging areas like synthetic biology and regenerative medicine. The principles of self-assembly will continue to guide the development of increasingly sophisticated nanotechnologies that bridge the gap between synthetic materials and biological systems, ultimately leading to transformative advances in how we diagnose, treat, and prevent disease.

CHAPTER 8

Nanoparticles for Drug Delivery

Nanomedicine represents one of the most promising applications of nanotechnology, with nanoparticle-based drug delivery systems at its forefront. These sophisticated systems operate at scales between 1 and 100 nanometers, allowing unprecedented access to biological environments previously inaccessible to conventional therapeutics. This chapter explores nanoparticles in modern therapeutics, the scientific principles guiding their optimization, mechanisms of cellular entry, anatomical barrier navigation, and emerging trends, including AI and IoT integration, that promise to transform nanomedicine into an intelligent, responsive healthcare platform.

8.1 Nanoparticles in Therapeutics

Introduction to Therapeutic Nanoparticles

Nanoparticles serve as sophisticated delivery vehicles that dramatically improve drug efficacy while minimizing adverse effects. Their nanoscale dimensions enable interactions with biological systems at cellular and subcellular levels, offering unprecedented control over drug distribution, release kinetics, and targeting specificity. The fundamental advantage of nanoparticle-based therapeutics lies in their ability to overcome biological barriers that have traditionally limited drug efficacy, including poor solubility, rapid clearance, degradation, and inability to cross physiological barriers.

Types of Therapeutic Nanoparticles

The landscape of therapeutic nanoparticles encompasses diverse materials and architectures. Polymeric nanoparticles composed of biodegradable materials like PLGA or chitosan provide controlled release profiles and excellent biocompatibility. Lipid-based nanocarriers excel in delivering both hydrophilic and hydrophobic drugs, with several liposomal formulations already approved for clinical use. Metallic nanoparticles, particularly gold and silver variants, combine therapeutic capabilities with diagnostic functions. Inorganic nanoparticles offer high surface area-to-volume ratios ideal for loading substantial drug quantities, while protein-based nanoparticles leverage natural biocompatibility for drug conjugation (Table 8-1).

Table 8-1. Major Types of Therapeutic Nanoparticles and Their Applications

Nanoparticle Type	Composition	Size Range (nm)	Key Applications	Notable Examples
Polymeric	PLGA, PLA, chitosan, PEG	10–200	Controlled release, gene delivery	PLGA-PEG nanoparticles for cancer therapy
Liposomal	Phospholipid bilayers	50–200	Hydrophilic/hydrophobic drug delivery	Doxil® (doxorubicin liposome)
Metallic	Gold, silver, iron oxide	5–150	Theranostics, photothermal therapy	AuroShell® (silica-gold nanoshells)
Inorganic	Silica, calcium phosphate	20–200	High drug loading, controlled porosity	Cornell dots (fluorescent silica NPs)
Protein-based	Albumin, gelatin	50–300	Enhanced solubility of hydrophobic drugs	Abraxane® (paclitaxel-albumin NPs)

Clinical Applications and Current Market Status

Since the FDA approval of Doxil® (liposomal doxorubicin) in 1995, the number of nanomedicine products has steadily increased, with over 50 nanopharmaceuticals now clinically approved worldwide. Oncology dominates the landscape, with formulations targeting various cancers, including breast, ovarian, and pancreatic. Beyond oncology, nanoparticle-based therapeutics have found applications in infectious disease treatment, vaccine delivery, and management of inflammatory conditions.

Despite these advances, clinical translation rates remain relatively low compared to research output. Challenges include manufacturing scalability, batch-to-batch reproducibility, and complex regulatory frameworks. The global nanomedicine market is projected to reach $350 billion by 2026, driven by increasing investment, rising prevalence of chronic diseases, and recognition of nanoparticles' potential to address previously intractable medical challenges.

8.2 Optimization of Properties

Physical Properties Optimization

Size profoundly influences biodistribution, cellular uptake mechanisms, and circulation time. Nanoparticles smaller than 10 nm typically undergo rapid renal clearance, while those exceeding 200 nm are more readily cleared by the mononuclear phagocyte system. The optimal size window—typically between 10 and 100 nm—balances circulation persistence with effective tissue penetration.

Shape optimization has emerged as another crucial parameter, with non-spherical nanoparticles exhibiting distinct flow dynamics, cellular internalization patterns, and tissue distribution profiles. High-aspect-ratio nanoparticles can better align with blood flow, potentially enhancing vascular targeting and extravasation at tumor sites.

Mechanical properties, including elasticity, flexibility, and deformability, represent an emerging frontier in nanoparticle design. Soft, deformable nanoparticles can navigate biological barriers more effectively than rigid counterparts, squeezing through narrow vascular fenestrations and potentially evading certain clearance mechanisms.

Chemical Surface Modifications

Surface charge dramatically influences particle stability, protein adsorption, cellular interactions, and biodistribution. Cationic surfaces generally enhance cellular uptake but may increase toxicity and accelerate clearance. Conversely, neutral or slightly negative surfaces demonstrate superior circulation persistence but potentially reduced cellular internalization.

Hydrophilicity modification, most commonly achieved through PEGylation, creates a hydrophilic corona that reduces opsonization and phagocytic clearance—the "stealth effect." However, the emergence of anti-PEG antibodies has prompted exploration of alternative hydrophilic coatings, including zwitterionic polymers and polysaccharides.

Functional group presentation enables precise tailoring of biological interactions. Carboxyl, amine, and thiol groups serve as convenient anchors for bioconjugation, allowing attachment of targeting ligands, imaging agents, or therapeutic payloads.

Targeting Strategies

Active targeting exploits unique molecular signatures of diseased tissues by decorating nanoparticle surfaces with ligands that specifically bind to overexpressed receptors. In oncology, commonly targeted receptors include folate receptors, transferrin receptors, and epidermal growth factor receptors. Beyond oncology, vascular targeting and brain targeting represent promising approaches for cardiovascular and neurological applications.

Passive targeting mechanisms, particularly the enhanced permeability and retention (EPR) effect arising from leaky tumor vasculature and impaired lymphatic drainage, enable preferential accumulation of appropriately sized nanoparticles in tumor tissues. However, increasing evidence suggests substantial heterogeneity in the EPR effect across tumor types and even within individual tumors. Schematic illustration of the main physicochemical properties of nanoparticles governing interaction mechanisms in biological systems is shown in Figure 8-1.

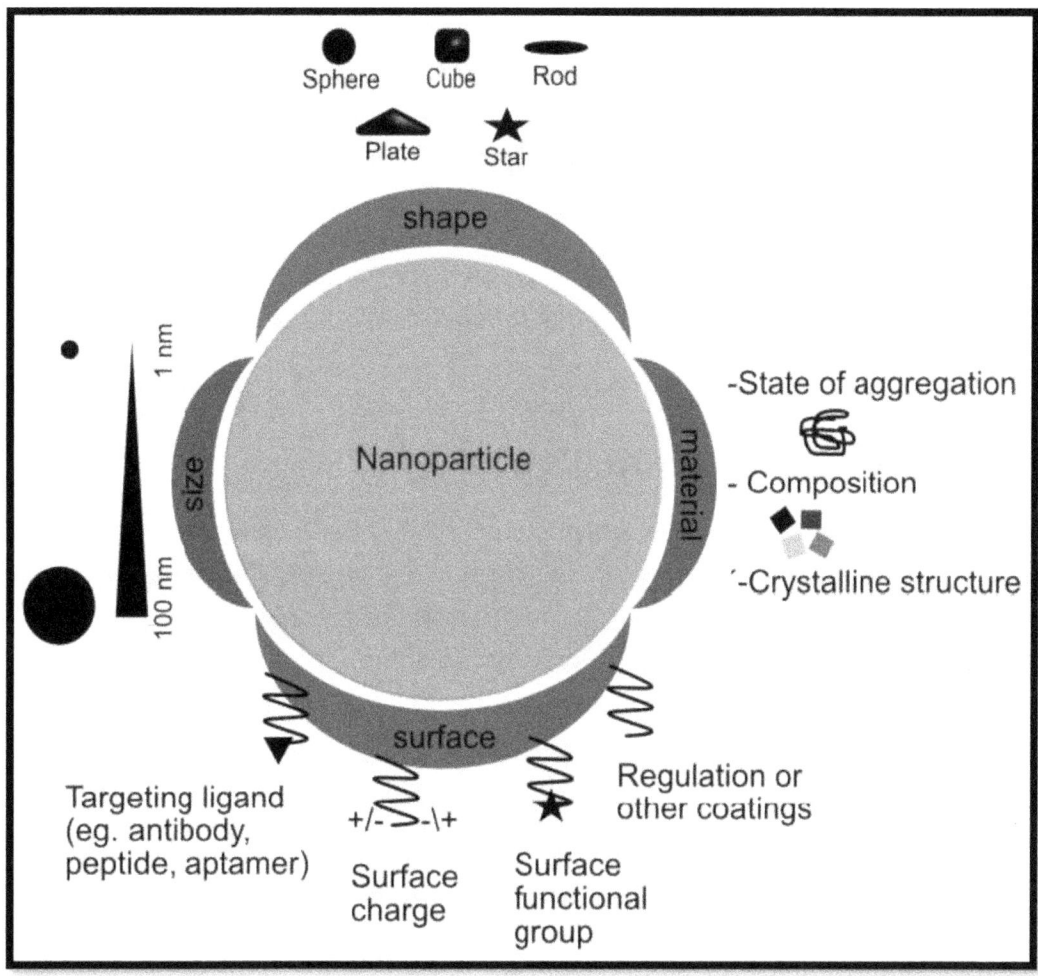

Figure 8-1. Impact of Nanoparticle Physical Properties on Biological Interactions

8.3 Cellular Entry Strategies
Mechanisms of Cellular Uptake

Nanoparticles access cell interiors through multiple endocytic pathways, each characterized by specific vesicle morphology, size limitations, and intracellular trafficking routes. Clathrin-mediated endocytosis involves the formation of clathrin-coated pits (100–150 nm) that efficiently internalize receptor-bound nanoparticles, though resulting endosomes typically progress to lysosomes, potentially exposing cargo to degradative enzymes.

Caveolae-mediated endocytosis operates through smaller flask-shaped invaginations (50–80 nm) and potentially offers advantages by bypassing lysosomal degradation through transport to the endoplasmic reticulum or Golgi apparatus. Macropinocytosis forms larger vesicles (0.2–5 μm) suitable for internalizing larger nanoparticle assemblies, while phagocytosis primarily occurs in specialized immune cells and involves engulfment of particles >500 nm.

Additional mechanisms include clathrin- and caveolae-independent endocytosis, direct membrane translocation, and energy-independent penetration facilitated by cell-penetrating peptides.

Endosomal Escape Strategies

Endosomal escape—the process by which nanoparticles breach endosomal membranes to reach the cytosol—is critical for accessing intracellular targets. The proton sponge effect, employed particularly for nucleic acid delivery, utilizes polymers with titratable amine groups that buffer endosomal acidification, leading to osmotic pressure, vesicle swelling, and membrane disruption.

Membrane-fusogenic peptides undergo conformational changes in response to endosomal acidification, exposing hydrophobic domains that destabilize the endosomal membrane. Photochemical internalization employs photosensitizers that, upon light activation, generate reactive oxygen species, disrupting endosomal membranes. Mechanochemical approaches include shape-changing nanoparticles that expand under acidic conditions, creating mechanical stress on endosomal membranes.

Intracellular Trafficking and Subcellular Targeting

Specific subcellular targeting dramatically impacts therapeutic efficacy, particularly for drugs with organelle-specific targets. Nuclear targeting typically employs nuclear localization signals (NLS) to facilitate active transport through nuclear pore complexes. Mitochondrial targeting, increasingly important given mitochondrial dysfunction in numerous diseases, utilizes mitochondria-penetrating peptides or triphenylphosphonium moieties.

Other subcellular compartments, including the endoplasmic reticulum, Golgi apparatus, and lysosomes, represent important targets for specific therapeutic applications. Recent advances include multistage delivery systems that navigate sequential intracellular barriers by responsively altering their trafficking behavior at each stage.

8.4 Anatomical Permeability

Blood-Brain Barrier Penetration

The blood-brain barrier (BBB), formed by specialized brain endothelial cells, astrocytic end-feet, pericytes, and basal lamina, severely restricts therapeutic management of neurological disorders. Approximately 98% of small-molecule drugs and virtually all large biologics fail to achieve meaningful brain penetration.

Nanoparticle-based strategies to overcome the BBB include receptor-mediated transcytosis, wherein nanoparticles are functionalized with ligands for receptors expressed on brain endothelial cells, including transferrin receptor, insulin receptor, and low-density lipoprotein receptor-related proteins. Adsorptive-mediated transcytosis leverages electrostatic interactions between positively charged nanoparticles and the negatively charged endothelial surface.

Alternative approaches include temporary BBB disruption through focused ultrasound or chemical agents and intranasal delivery that partially bypasses the BBB through olfactory and trigeminal nerve pathways.

Tumor Penetration Dynamics

Effective delivery to solid tumors encounters multiple barriers, including heterogeneous vasculature, elevated interstitial fluid pressure, dense extracellular matrix, and hypoxic regions. While the enhanced permeability and retention (EPR) effect enables initial extravasation, achieving uniform distribution throughout tumor tissue remains challenging.

Size optimization represents a direct strategy for enhancing tumor penetration, with smaller nanoparticles (<50 nm) demonstrating superior tissue distribution. Transformable nanoparticle systems incorporate environmentally responsive elements that trigger size reduction upon reaching the tumor microenvironment. Extracellular matrix modulation strategies target dense collagen and hyaluronic acid networks through the incorporation of matrix-degrading enzymes.

Tumor-associated macrophages have been explored as "Trojan horses" for nanoparticle delivery, leveraging their natural ability to infiltrate hypoxic tumor regions. Vascular normalization through anti-angiogenic therapy can temporarily reduce interstitial fluid pressure and improve blood flow, creating opportunities for enhanced nanoparticle delivery.

Epithelial and Endothelial Barriers

Epithelial and endothelial barriers regulate passage between distinct bodily compartments. Paracellular transport involves temporary modulation of tight junctions using agents like zonula occludens toxin derivatives or chitosan. Transcellular transport, the predominant route for intact barriers, often employs receptor-mediated transcytosis targeting receptors expressed on barrier cells.

M-cell targeting provides a specialized approach for oral delivery by exploiting the sampling function of these specialized intestinal cells. The mucus layer overlying many epithelial surfaces presents an additional barrier addressed through mucopenetrating nanoparticles with dense hydrophilic surface coatings or incorporation of mucolytic agents.

Recent advances include multimodal nanoparticles that sequentially overcome multiple barrier components through environmentally triggered transformations as they navigate complex biological interfaces (Figure 8-2).

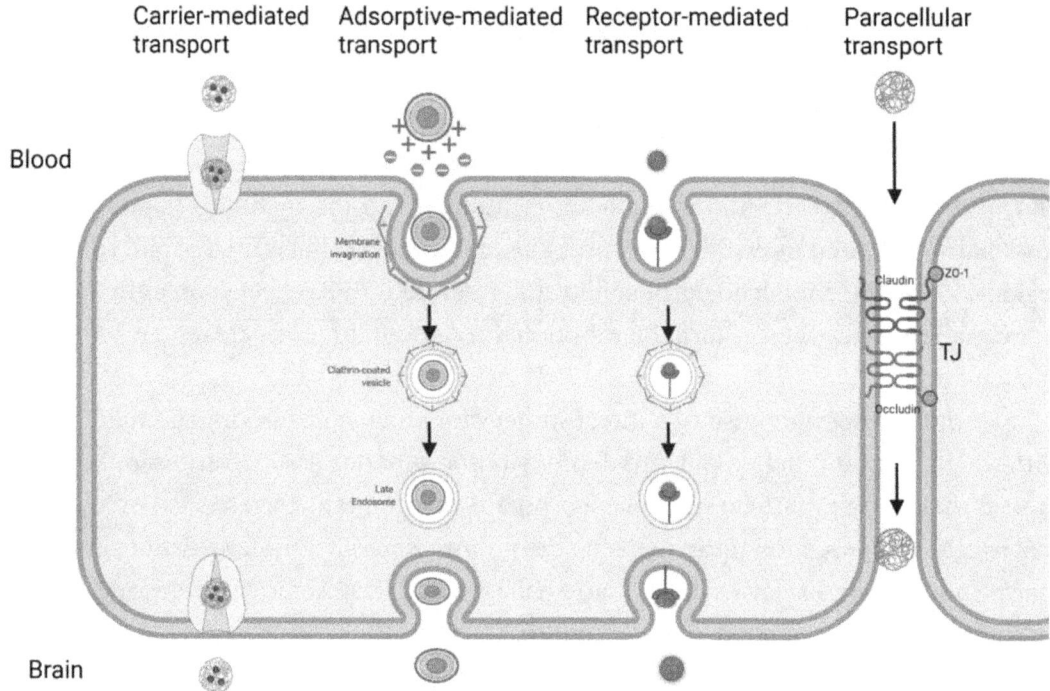

Figure 8-2. Transport Mechanisms for Nanoparticles Across Biological Barriers

8.5 Future Prospects

Emerging Delivery Platforms

Extracellular vesicles (EVs), particularly exosomes, represent promising biological nanocarriers with intrinsic biocompatibility, immune privilege, and targeting capabilities. Recent advances in EV engineering have accelerated their development, though challenges in large-scale production remain.

DNA origami nanostructures exemplify molecular self-assembly precision, creating programmable three-dimensional shapes with nanometer accuracy. Stimulus-responsive DNA origami systems can undergo conformational changes upon encountering specific triggers, enabling precise control over drug release.

Cell membrane-coated nanoparticles harness natural cellular membrane functionality by wrapping synthetic cores with extracted membranes from red blood cells, platelets, cancer cells, or immune cells. These constructs inherit surface properties of their source cells, with red blood cell membranes conferring prolonged circulation and cancer cell membranes enabling homotypic targeting.

Supramolecular assemblies based on host-guest chemistry offer exceptional control over nanoparticle stability and stimuli-responsive behavior through molecular recognition between complementary components, facilitating on-demand drug release at target sites.

Personalized Nanomedicine Approaches

Patient stratification based on biological determinants of nanoparticle behavior enhances therapeutic outcomes by accounting for factors including tumor vasculature characteristics, hepatic and renal function, and genomic profiles that significantly impact nanoparticle pharmacokinetics.

Theranostic nanoparticles integrate therapeutic and diagnostic functionalities, enabling simultaneous treatment and monitoring of therapeutic response through incorporated imaging agents. Real-time feedback can guide dosage adjustments or alternative therapeutic approaches when necessary.

Patient-derived models, including organoids and xenografts, maintain cellular heterogeneity and architectural features of original patient tissues, providing platforms for evaluating nanoparticle performance in patient-specific microenvironments.

Custom formulation approaches tailored to individual patient characteristics represent the ultimate embodiment of personalized nanomedicine, though technological and regulatory challenges remain substantial.

8.6 AI and IoT Integration

AI-Guided Nanoparticle Design

Artificial intelligence is revolutionizing nanoparticle design through computational approaches that dramatically accelerate development cycles. Machine learning algorithms trained on extensive physicochemical and biological datasets can predict nanoparticle behavior in biological environments, optimizing properties for specific applications while minimizing experimental iterations.

Deep learning approaches analyze structure-activity relationships to identify critical design parameters influencing therapeutic efficacy. These models integrate multidimensional datasets encompassing physical properties, surface chemistry, and biological interactions to generate comprehensive design landscapes. Reinforcement learning algorithms further optimize designs through iterative refinement based on experimental feedback.

Generative adversarial networks (GANs) create novel nanoparticle designs by exploring previously unexplored regions of design space, potentially identifying unconventional but highly effective configurations. These AI-guided approaches are particularly valuable for developing multi-component, stimuli-responsive systems with complex behavior profiles exceeding intuitive human design capabilities.

Smart Nanotherapeutic Systems

The integration of responsive materials, miniaturized sensors, and wireless communication creates "smart" nanotherapeutic systems capable of autonomous operation within the body. These systems can continuously monitor physiological parameters, disease biomarkers, or therapeutic efficacy, adjusting drug release profiles accordingly without external intervention.

Glucose-responsive insulin delivery systems exemplify this approach, employing glucose-sensing elements coupled with insulin-releasing mechanisms that mimic pancreatic function. Similar approaches are being developed for controlling the release of chemotherapeutics based on tumor-specific biomarkers, anti-inflammatory agents responding to cytokine levels, and antimicrobials triggered by bacterial toxins or pH changes signaling infection.

Closed-loop feedback systems represent the highest level of autonomy, wherein therapeutic nanoparticles directly sense treatment efficacy and adjust their behavior accordingly. These systems typically incorporate sensing elements that detect downstream effects of released therapeutics, enabling dose modulation to maintain optimal efficacy while minimizing side effects.

IoT-Connected Nanomedicine Platforms

Internet of Things (IoT) technologies are creating networked nanomedicine platforms that bridge internal therapeutic processes with external monitoring and control systems. Implantable or wearable devices communicating with circulating nanotherapeutics enable real-time tracking of drug distribution, therapeutic response, and potential side effects.

External control systems allow clinicians to remotely adjust treatment parameters based on patient response or disease progression. This capability is particularly valuable for chronic conditions requiring long-term management, enabling periodic treatment modification without requiring new formulations or interventions.

Data integration platforms collect information from multiple sources—including smart nanotherapeutics, conventional diagnostic tests, and patient-reported outcomes—creating comprehensive health profiles that guide treatment optimization. These platforms increasingly employ AI-driven analytics to identify patterns and correlations not readily apparent through conventional analysis, supporting more personalized and responsive therapeutic approaches.

The convergence of AI, IoT, and nanomedicine creates unprecedented opportunities for precision therapeutics but also introduces challenges regarding data security, regulatory oversight, and equitable access. Addressing these considerations alongside technological development will be essential for realizing the full potential of these integrated approaches.

8.7 Summary

Nanoparticle-based drug delivery systems represent a transformative leap in modern medicine, enabling precise therapeutic interventions through nanoscale engineering. This chapter has outlined how these systems optimize drug efficacy by overcoming biological barriers, enabling controlled release, enhancing tissue targeting, and reducing systemic toxicity. The diversity of nanoparticle types—ranging from polymeric and liposomal carriers to metallic and protein-based platforms—underscores their adaptability across various clinical applications, particularly in oncology, infectious diseases, and chronic inflammatory conditions.

Key design parameters such as particle size, shape, surface charge, and functionalization govern nanoparticle interaction with biological systems. Active and passive targeting strategies improve specificity, while advanced cellular entry and endosomal escape mechanisms facilitate intracellular delivery. Navigating complex anatomical barriers like the blood-brain barrier and tumor microenvironment remains a challenge, but innovations such as receptor-mediated transcytosis, transformable nanoparticles, and extracellular matrix modulation show promise.

Emerging technologies, including exosome-mimetic carriers, DNA origami, and cell membrane-coated nanoparticles, are expanding the frontiers of nanotherapeutic design. The integration of artificial intelligence has accelerated nanoparticle development through predictive modeling and design optimization, while smart materials and IoT connectivity are enabling autonomous, responsive drug delivery systems. These advances lay the foundation for personalized nanomedicine, where treatment is precisely tailored to individual patient profiles and real-time physiological feedback.

While technical, regulatory, and ethical challenges remain, the convergence of nanotechnology with AI and IoT holds the potential to revolutionize healthcare, transforming nanomedicine into an intelligent, adaptable platform for next-generation therapeutics.

CHAPTER 9

Nanoparticles in Diagnostics and Imaging

This chapter explores the transformative role of nanoparticles in medical diagnostics and imaging. Beginning with theranostic technologies that combine therapeutic and diagnostic capabilities, we examine how multifunctional nanoplatforms are revolutionizing personalized medicine. The chapter delves into stimuli-responsive nanoparticle systems that react to specific biological triggers, enabling targeted drug delivery and real-time monitoring. Significant advances in cancer therapeutics using nanoparticles for enhanced detection and treatment are discussed, alongside innovative biosensor devices that leverage nanomaterials for improved sensitivity and specificity in disease detection. The chapter further explores cutting-edge imaging approaches utilizing nanoparticles to overcome limitations of conventional techniques. Finally, the integration of artificial intelligence and the Internet of Things with nanodiagnostics is examined, highlighting how these convergent technologies are creating more intelligent and connected healthcare systems that promise earlier disease detection and more effective treatment strategies.

9.1 Introduction

Nanotechnology has revolutionized medical diagnostics and imaging by enabling unprecedented sensitivity, specificity, and multifunctionality. Nanoparticles—materials with dimensions between 1 and 100 nanometers—interact with biological systems at cellular and molecular levels, creating new possibilities for disease detection and visualization. Their unique physicochemical properties make them ideal candidates for developing advanced diagnostic tools and imaging agents.

CHAPTER 9   NANOPARTICLES IN DIAGNOSTICS AND IMAGING

This chapter explores the diverse applications of nanoparticles in diagnostics and imaging, from theranostic platforms that combine therapeutic and diagnostic functions to stimuli-responsive systems that react to specific biological environments. We examine how nanoparticles are transforming cancer detection and treatment, enhancing biosensor performance, and enabling innovative imaging approaches. Additionally, we discuss the integration of artificial intelligence and the Internet of Things with nanodiagnostics, creating smarter and more connected healthcare systems.

As these technologies continue to mature, they promise to enable earlier disease detection, more precise diagnosis, and more effective treatment monitoring—ultimately improving patient outcomes while reducing healthcare costs.

9.2 Theranostic Technologies

Theranostics represents a paradigm shift in modern medicine by integrating therapeutic and diagnostic capabilities within a single nanoplatform. This approach enables simultaneous disease detection, treatment, and monitoring of therapeutic response, forming a cornerstone of personalized medicine.

Multifunctional Nanoparticle Platforms

Theranostic nanoparticles typically contain imaging components (magnetic materials, fluorescent dyes, radioisotopes) coupled with therapeutic agents (drugs, photosensitizers, gene therapy vectors). Their surfaces are functionalized with targeting ligands that recognize specific disease biomarkers, enabling precise localization at pathological sites.

For example, superparamagnetic iron oxide nanoparticles (SPIONs) provide MRI contrast while simultaneously delivering chemotherapeutic agents and enabling hyperthermia therapy. Similarly, gold nanoshells can both visualize tumors through photoacoustic imaging and destroy cancer cells via photothermal ablation (Table 9-1).

Table 9-1. Multifunctional Nanoparticle Platforms for Theranostic Applications

Nanoparticle Type	Imaging Modality	Therapeutic Mechanism	Clinical Application
SPIONs	MRI	Magnetic hyperthermia/drug delivery	Liver cancer
Gold nanoshells	Photoacoustic imaging	Photothermal therapy	Solid tumors
Quantum dot-liposome hybrids	Fluorescence imaging	Chemotherapy	Breast cancer
Upconversion nanoparticles	Near-infrared fluorescence	Photodynamic therapy	Superficial tumors
Mesoporous silica NPs	MRI/CT (with contrast agents)	Controlled drug release	Various cancers

Clinical Translation Challenges

Despite promising preclinical results, the clinical translation of nanotheranostics faces several challenges. Complex manufacturing processes, regulatory uncertainties for combined diagnostic-therapeutic agents, and concerns about long-term toxicity have limited their widespread adoption. However, recent advances in nanofabrication and comprehensive toxicological studies are gradually addressing these limitations (Figure 9-1).

CHAPTER 9   NANOPARTICLES IN DIAGNOSTICS AND IMAGING

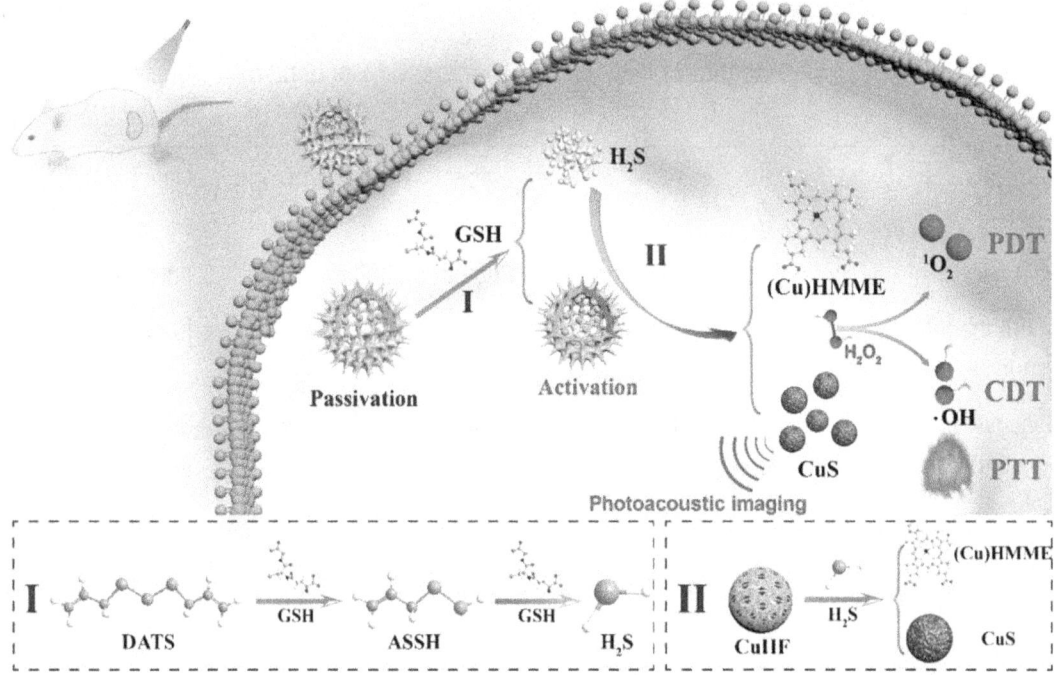

Figure 9-1. Schematic Representation of a Multifunctional Theranostic Nanoplatform

9.3 Stimuli-Responsive Systems

Stimuli-responsive nanoparticles represent a sophisticated class of "smart" nanomaterials that alter their structural or functional properties in response to specific environmental triggers. This responsiveness enables precise control over diagnostic and therapeutic functions, making these systems particularly valuable for targeted diagnostics and drug delivery.

Types of Responsive Mechanisms

pH-Responsive Systems

The acidic microenvironment of tumors (pH 6.5-6.8 compared to pH 7.4 in normal tissues) provides an ideal trigger for diagnostic nanoparticles. Materials incorporating ionizable groups, such as poly(acrylic acid) or chitosan, undergo conformational changes in acidic environments, releasing imaging agents or therapeutic payloads specifically at disease sites.

Enzyme-Responsive Nanoparticles

Abnormal enzyme expression characterizes numerous pathological conditions. Nanoparticles incorporating peptide sequences that serve as substrates for disease-associated enzymes (matrix metalloproteinases, cathepsins, phospholipases) can undergo selective activation in diseased tissues, enabling highly specific imaging and targeted therapy.

Magnetically Responsive Systems

Superparamagnetic iron oxide nanoparticles respond to external magnetic fields, providing negative contrast in MRI and generating localized heat when subjected to alternating magnetic fields. This dual functionality enables real-time monitoring of nanoparticle distribution while simultaneously delivering thermal therapy to diseased tissues.

Light-Responsive Nanoplatforms

Photosensitive nanoparticles activated by specific wavelengths of light offer precise spatial and temporal control over diagnostic and therapeutic functions. Near-infrared responsive materials are particularly valuable due to deeper tissue penetration, enabling both photoacoustic imaging and photothermal therapy for deep-seated tumors.

Clinical Applications

Several stimuli-responsive nanoparticles have progressed to clinical trials, showing promise for image-guided interventions and targeted cancer therapy. ThermoDox®, a thermosensitive liposomal formulation of doxorubicin, releases its payload upon mild hyperthermia, enabling MRI-guided drug delivery to solid tumors. The development of multi-responsive systems—nanoparticles that respond to multiple stimuli sequentially—represents the next frontier in this field (Figure 9-2).

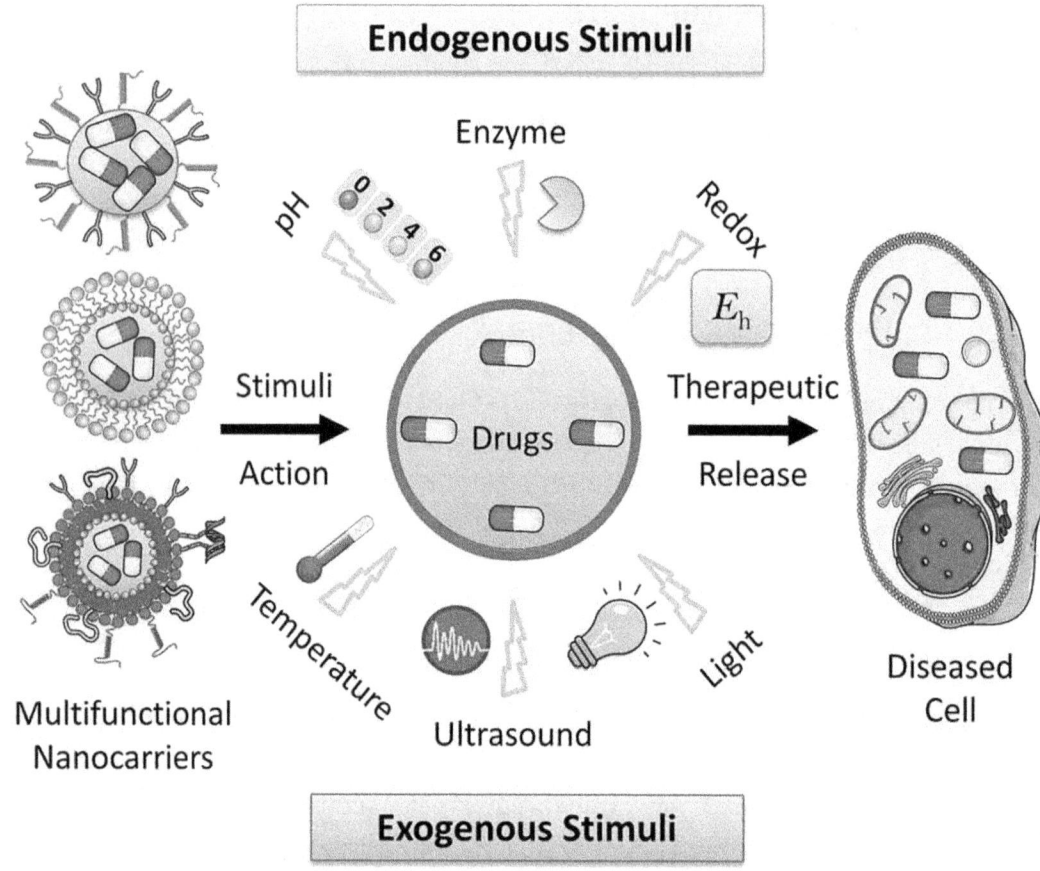

Figure 9-2. Mechanisms of Various Stimuli-Responsive Nanoparticle Systems

9.4 Cancer Therapeutics

Cancer remains one of the leading causes of mortality worldwide, with conventional treatments often compromised by late detection and nonspecific delivery of therapeutic agents. Nanoparticles offer promising solutions to these challenges through enhanced detection sensitivity and targeted therapy delivery.

Nanoparticles in Cancer Detection

Early detection significantly improves cancer survival rates. Nanoparticle-based detection methods offer several advantages over conventional approaches:

1. **Liquid Biopsy Enhancement**: Nanoparticles functionalized with cancer-specific antibodies can capture circulating tumor cells (CTCs) and exosomes from blood samples, enabling noninvasive early detection and monitoring of treatment response.

2. **Multimodal Imaging**: Dual-mode imaging nanoparticles, such as gadolinium-doped iron oxide nanoparticles, provide complementary information through both MRI and optical imaging, improving diagnostic accuracy and tumor margin delineation.

3. **Molecular Imaging of Cancer Biomarkers**: Quantum dots and gold nanoparticles conjugated with antibodies against cancer-specific antigens (HER2, EGFR, PSA) enable highly sensitive visualization of biomarker expression patterns, facilitating personalized treatment selection.

Therapeutic Applications

Nanoparticles have transformed cancer treatment through several mechanisms (Table 9-2).

1. **Enhanced Drug Delivery**: Nanoscale drug carriers preferentially accumulate in tumors through the enhanced permeability and retention (EPR) effect and active targeting, increasing therapeutic efficacy while reducing systemic toxicity. FDA-approved nanomedicines like Doxil® (liposomal doxorubicin) and Abraxane® (albumin-bound paclitaxel) demonstrate this principle in clinical practice.

2. **Overcoming Drug Resistance**: Nanoparticles can bypass drug efflux pumps and deliver multiple therapeutic agents simultaneously, addressing multidrug resistance. For example, co-delivery of chemotherapeutics and siRNA targeting resistance genes has shown promising results in preclinical studies.

3. **Immunomodulation**: Nanoparticles carrying immune checkpoint inhibitors or cancer antigens can enhance anti-tumor immune responses. These nanoimmunotherapeutic approaches show synergistic effects when combined with conventional treatments like radiotherapy.

CHAPTER 9 NANOPARTICLES IN DIAGNOSTICS AND IMAGING

Table 9-2. FDA-Approved Nanoparticle-Based Cancer Therapeutics

Product Name	Nanoparticle Type	Active Ingredient	Cancer Type	Approval Year
Doxil®/Caelyx®	PEGylated liposome	Doxorubicin	Ovarian cancer, multiple myeloma, Kaposi's sarcoma	1995
Abraxane®	Albumin nanoparticle	Paclitaxel	Breast cancer, pancreatic cancer, lung cancer	2005
Onivyde®	Liposome	Irinotecan	Pancreatic cancer	2015
Vyxeos®	Liposome	Cytarabine and daunorubicin	Acute myeloid leukemia	2017
Hensify®	Hafnium oxide	Radiotherapy enhancer	Soft tissue sarcoma	2019

Future Directions

Emerging approaches in nanomedicine for cancer include (Figure 9-3).

1. **Tumor-on-a-Chip Platforms**: Microfluidic systems incorporating tumor cells and nanoparticles enable rapid screening of therapeutic efficacy and optimization of nanoparticle design before clinical application.

2. **Biomimetic Nanoparticles**: Cell membrane-coated nanoparticles that mimic natural cells (erythrocytes, leukocytes, cancer cells) exhibit enhanced circulation time and tumor targeting while evading immune clearance.

3. **Nanorobotics**: Magnetically controlled nanorobots capable of navigating through the bloodstream to deliver therapeutic agents directly to tumors represent an exciting frontier in precision cancer therapy.

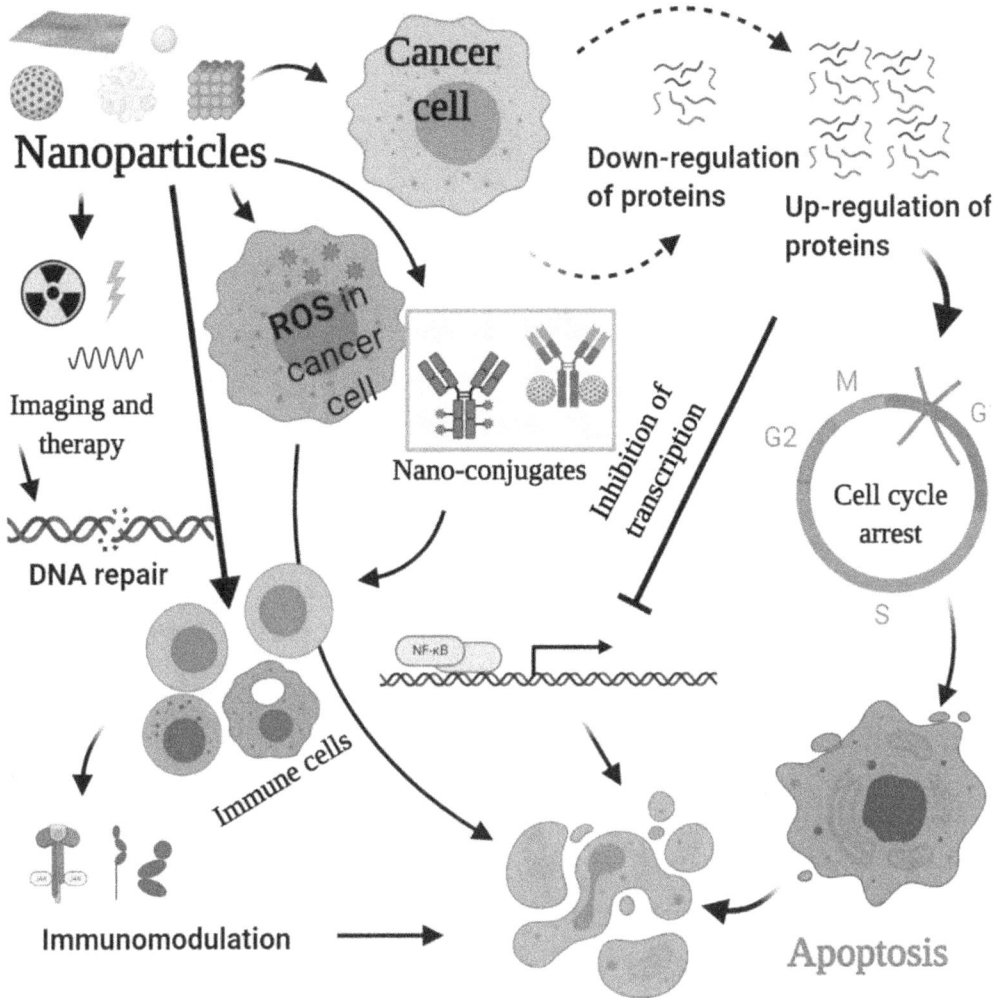

Figure 9-3. Mechanisms of Nanoparticle-Mediated Cancer Therapy

9.5 Biosensor Devices

Biosensors—analytical devices combining biological recognition elements with physicochemical transducers—have been revolutionized by nanotechnology. Nanomaterials enhance biosensor performance through increased surface area, unique optical and electrical properties, and improved biocompatibility (Table 9-3).

Nanomaterial-Enhanced Biosensing

Electrochemical Biosensors

Nanomaterials such as carbon nanotubes, graphene, and metal nanoparticles significantly enhance electron transfer between biorecognition elements and electrode surfaces. For example, gold nanoparticle-modified electrodes for glucose detection offer 100-fold higher sensitivity than conventional glucose meters, enabling accurate measurements at physiologically relevant concentrations.

Optical Biosensors

Plasmonic nanoparticles (gold, silver) enable ultrasensitive optical detection through localized surface plasmon resonance (LSPR). These particles undergo measurable color changes upon target binding, forming the basis for lateral flow assays and colorimetric sensors. Quantum dots provide additional advantages, including high quantum yield, narrow emission spectra, and resistance to photobleaching, making them ideal for multiplexed detection.

Piezoelectric Biosensors

Nanomaterials like zinc oxide nanowires exhibit enhanced piezoelectric properties, converting mechanical stress into electrical signals. These materials are increasingly used in wearable biosensors for continuous health monitoring, detecting biomarkers in sweat, tears, and interstitial fluid.

Point-of-Care Diagnostic Applications

Nanoparticle-based biosensors have enabled rapid, sensitive point-of-care testing across various clinical contexts:

1. **Infectious Disease Diagnostics**: Gold nanoparticle-based lateral flow assays for COVID-19, malaria, and tuberculosis enable rapid diagnosis in resource-limited settings. These tests can detect viral antigens or antibodies within 15–30 minutes with sensitivity approaching laboratory-based methods.

2. **Cardiac Biomarker Detection**: Magnetic nanoparticle-based sensors can detect troponin at picogram levels, enabling earlier diagnosis of myocardial infarction. Wearable devices incorporating these sensors allow continuous monitoring of at-risk patients.

3. **Cancer Biomarker Screening**: Nanoplasmonic sensors enable the detection of cancer biomarkers (PSA, CA-125, AFP) at ultra-low concentrations in biological fluids, facilitating early cancer detection through routine screening.

Table 9-3. Nanomaterial Types and Their Applications in Biosensors

Nanomaterial	Properties	Biosensor Type	Clinical Applications
Gold nanoparticles	Plasmonic, catalytic	Colorimetric, electrochemical	Infectious diseases, cancer biomarkers
Carbon nanotubes	High conductivity, large surface area	Electrochemical, field-effect transistors	Glucose monitoring, DNA detection
Quantum dots	Fluorescent, size-tunable emission	Optical, FRET-based	Cancer diagnostics, multiplexed assays
Graphene	2D structure, excellent conductivity	Electrochemical, impedimetric	Drug screening, pathogen detection
Magnetic nanoparticles	Superparamagnetic	Magnetoresistive	Cell separation, protein detection

Implantable and Wearable Biosensors

Nanomaterial-based biosensors are increasingly integrated into implantable and wearable devices for continuous health monitoring:

1. **Continuous Glucose Monitoring**: Minimally invasive sensors using glucose oxidase-conjugated gold nanoparticles can monitor glucose levels in interstitial fluid continuously for up to 14 days, revolutionizing diabetes management.

2. **Implantable Cancer Surveillance**: Biodegradable implantable sensors incorporating gold nanoshells can detect cancer recurrence by monitoring specific biomarkers, enabling earlier intervention and improved survival rates.

3. **Smart Contact Lenses**: Graphene-based sensors incorporated into contact lenses can monitor tear glucose, intraocular pressure, and inflammatory markers, providing valuable diagnostic information for diabetes and glaucoma management.

Electrochemical Biosensor

The electrochemical immunosensor, which relies on the specific interaction between antigens and antibodies, represents the most widely used electrochemical method for protein detection in both biological research and clinical diagnostics. Traditional immunoassay techniques, such as enzyme-linked immunosorbent assays (ELISA), immunoblotting, radioimmunoassays, and immune electrophoresis, primarily detect proteins based on signal changes caused by the binding of target proteins to specific antibodies. In contrast, electrochemical immunoassays, a well-established and advanced method, combine the high sensitivity of electrochemical measurements with the high specificity of immune recognition, enabling their application across diverse fields. These assays can be divided into two types: label-free and labeled sensors. A key feature in developing these sensors is signal amplification, often achieved by modifying the electrode surface with nanomaterials. The immunosensor uses a capture antibody to selectively bind the analyte, and in label-free assays, the analyte concentration is determined by monitoring changes in the electrochemical signal after antigen-antibody interaction. Electrochemical impedance is commonly used for protein detection due to its ability to reflect physical and chemical changes on the electrode surface. In sandwich-type immunosensors, a secondary antibody (Ab2), typically labeled with nanomaterials or electrochemical probes, is used. The electrode, serving as the primary signal transducer, converts these recognition events into measurable electrical signals such as current, voltage, or resistance, allowing for both qualitative and quantitative analysis of the target analyte. Figure 9-4 illustrates the working principle of an electrochemical biosensor.

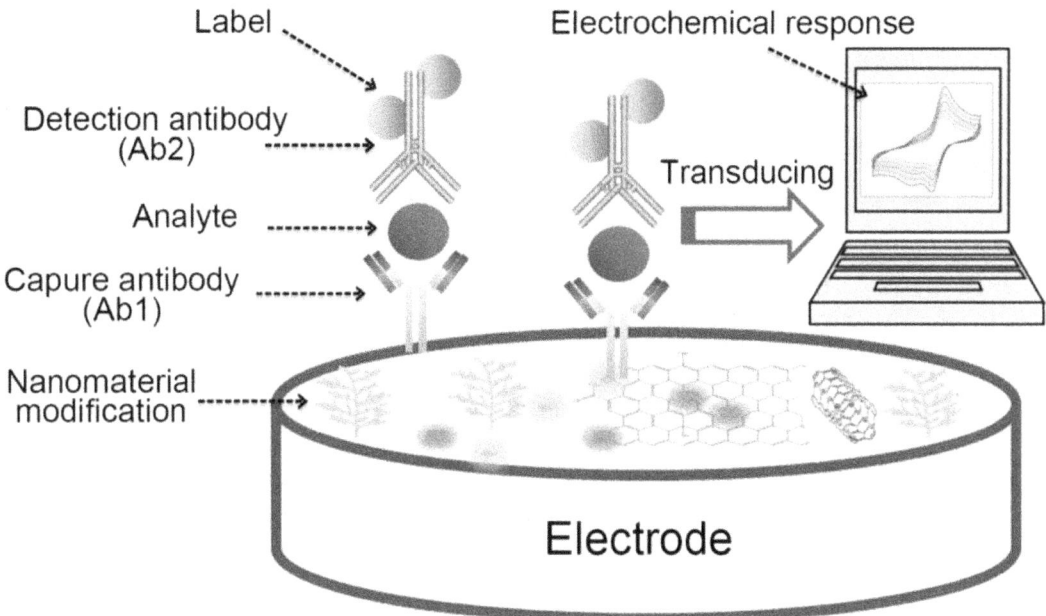

Figure 9-4. Schematic of a Nanomaterial-Enhanced Electrochemical Biosensor

9.6 Innovative Imaging Approaches

Conventional medical imaging techniques, while valuable, often face limitations in spatial resolution, sensitivity, and specificity. Nanoparticle-based contrast agents and novel imaging modalities address these challenges, enabling visualization of biological processes at unprecedented levels of detail.

Multimodal Imaging Nanoparticles

Single imaging modalities often provide incomplete information about disease states. Multimodal imaging nanoparticles combine complementary techniques to provide comprehensive diagnostic information (Table 9-4).

1. **MRI-Optical Dual-Mode Agents**: Iron oxide nanoparticles doped with fluorescent lanthanides enable both anatomical imaging (MRI) and cellular-level visualization (fluorescence microscopy) using a single contrast agent.

2. **PET-MRI Nanoplatforms**: Radiolabeled magnetic nanoparticles allow simultaneous positron emission tomography (PET) and MRI, combining the high sensitivity of PET with the excellent spatial resolution of MRI for improved tumor characterization.

3. **Trimodal Imaging Systems**: Gold-iron oxide hybrid nanoparticles functionalized with radioisotopes enable CT, MRI, and PET imaging in a single platform, providing complementary information about anatomical, functional, and molecular aspects of disease.

Advanced Contrast Enhancement Strategies

Nanoparticles have enabled significant improvements in contrast enhancement for various imaging modalities:

1. **Smart MRI Contrast Agents**: Gadolinium-loaded nanoparticles with pH-responsive polymeric coatings selectively enhance contrast in acidic tumor environments, improving tumor delineation while reducing systemic gadolinium exposure.

2. **Ultrasound Microbubble Enhancement**: Lipid-stabilized perfluorocarbon microbubbles conjugated with targeting ligands provide enhanced ultrasound contrast at specific disease sites. Their oscillation and eventual rupture upon ultrasound exposure can be leveraged for both imaging and drug delivery.

3. **Photoacoustic Imaging Agents**: Near-infrared absorbing nanoparticles (gold nanorods, carbon nanotubes) convert light energy into acoustic signals, enabling high-resolution, deep-tissue imaging without ionizing radiation.

Molecular and Cellular Imaging

Nanoparticles enable visualization of molecular events and cellular processes that are invisible to conventional imaging techniques:

1. **Receptor Targeting**: Nanoparticles conjugated with ligands for overexpressed receptors (folate, transferrin, EGFR) can visualize receptor expression patterns in tumors, providing valuable information for treatment selection.

2. **Enzyme Activity Imaging**: Nanoparticles with enzyme-cleavable linkers between fluorophores and quenchers remain "dark" until activated by specific enzymes, enabling real-time visualization of enzyme activity in living systems.

3. **Cell Tracking**: Magnetically labeled stem cells can be tracked noninvasively using MRI following transplantation, providing insights into cell migration, differentiation, and therapeutic efficacy in regenerative medicine applications.

Table 9-4. Nanoparticle-Based Contrast Agents for Different Imaging Modalities

Imaging Modality	Nanoparticle Type	Advantages	Clinical Applications
MRI	Superparamagnetic iron oxide	High spatial resolution, no radiation	Liver lesions, lymph node metastases
CT	Gold nanoparticles	High contrast, anatomical detail	Vascular imaging, tumor detection
Ultrasound	Perfluorocarbon microbubbles	Real-time imaging, widely available	Cardiovascular imaging, tumor perfusion
PET	Radioisotope-labeled nanoparticles	High sensitivity, functional information	Cancer staging, therapy monitoring
Photoacoustic	Gold nanorods, carbon nanotubes	Optical contrast, acoustic resolution	Vascular imaging, oxygen saturation mapping
Fluorescence	Quantum dots, upconversion NPs	High sensitivity, multiplexing capability	Surgical guidance, endoscopic imaging

9.7 AI and IoT in Diagnostics

The integration of artificial intelligence (AI) and the Internet of Things (IoT) with nanodiagnostic technologies is creating more intelligent, connected, and accessible healthcare systems. This convergence enables automated data collection, advanced pattern recognition, and remote monitoring capabilities that amplify the impact of nanoparticle-based diagnostics (Table 9-5).

AI-Enhanced Nanodiagnostics

Artificial intelligence algorithms, particularly machine learning and deep learning, significantly enhance nanoparticle-based diagnostic capabilities:

1. **Automated Image Analysis**: Convolutional neural networks (CNNs) can analyze nanoparticle-enhanced medical images, identifying subtle patterns invisible to the human eye. For example, AI algorithms applied to MRI scans using iron oxide nanoparticle contrast can detect early-stage liver tumors with higher accuracy than radiologists alone.

2. **Biomarker Signature Identification**: Machine learning algorithms applied to multi-parameter data from nanoparticle biosensors can identify complex biomarker signatures associated with disease states, enabling earlier and more accurate diagnosis of conditions like Alzheimer's disease and pancreatic cancer.

3. **Predictive Analytics**: AI models trained on longitudinal data from nanoparticle-based continuous monitoring devices can predict disease progression and treatment response, enabling preemptive interventions and personalized therapeutic adjustments.

IoT-Connected Diagnostic Systems

The Internet of Things enables seamless connectivity between nanoparticle-based diagnostic devices and healthcare information systems:

1. **Remote Patient Monitoring**: Wearable biosensors incorporating graphene-based electrodes can continuously monitor vital signs and biomarkers, transmitting data to cloud-based platforms for real-time analysis and alerting healthcare providers to significant changes.

2. **Smart Drug Delivery Systems**: IoT-connected implantable devices containing nanoparticle drug reservoirs can release therapeutic agents in response to biosensor readings, creating closed-loop systems for conditions like diabetes and epilepsy.

3. **Environmental Health Monitoring**: Networked nanoparticle-based sensors deployed in public spaces can detect airborne pathogens or environmental toxins, providing early warning of disease outbreaks or contamination events.

Integrated Diagnostic Ecosystems

The most advanced applications combine AI, IoT, and nanodiagnostics into comprehensive health monitoring ecosystems:

1. **Digital Twin Technology**: By integrating data from multiple nanoparticle-based sensors with AI analysis, digital replicas of patient physiology can be created, enabling personalized simulations to predict disease progression and treatment outcomes.

2. **Blockchain-Secured Health Records**: Diagnostic data from nanoparticle sensors can be securely stored and shared using blockchain technology, ensuring data integrity while enabling authorized healthcare providers to access comprehensive patient information.

3. **Population Health Management**: Aggregated, anonymized data from nanodiagnostic devices across populations can be analyzed using AI to identify emerging health trends, optimize resource allocation, and evaluate intervention effectiveness.

Table 9-5. Applications of AI and IoT in Nanoparticle-Based Diagnostics

Technology Combination	Application	Benefits	Challenges
Nanoparticle biosensors + AI	Multiparameter disease detection	Higher diagnostic accuracy, earlier detection	Requires large training datasets
Wearable nanosensors + IoT	Continuous health monitoring	Real-time data, remote patient management	Battery life, data security
Imaging nanoparticles + AI	Automated image analysis	Improved lesion detection, reduced reader variability	Regulatory approval, clinical integration
Nanorobotics + IoT	Targeted diagnostics and therapy	Precise localization, minimally invasive	Complex control systems, navigation challenges
Multiple nanosensors + AI + IoT	Digital biomarker platforms	Comprehensive health assessment, predictive capabilities	System interoperability, data standardization

9.8 Summary

Nanoparticles have fundamentally transformed medical diagnostics and imaging, offering unprecedented capabilities for disease detection, visualization, and therapeutic monitoring. Theranostic nanoplatforms that combine diagnostic and therapeutic functions enable real-time assessment of treatment efficacy, while stimuli-responsive systems provide exquisite control over when and where diagnostic signals are generated. In cancer management, nanoparticle-based approaches have dramatically improved both detection sensitivity and treatment specificity, addressing key limitations of conventional methods.

The integration of nanomaterials into biosensor devices has revolutionized point-of-care diagnostics, making sophisticated testing available in resource-limited settings and enabling continuous health monitoring through implantable and wearable systems. Novel imaging approaches leveraging nanoparticle contrast agents have overcome limitations of traditional techniques, providing multimodal, molecular-level insights into disease processes. Finally, the convergence of nanodiagnostics with artificial intelligence and Internet of Things technologies is creating intelligent, connected healthcare systems capable of earlier intervention and more personalized treatment strategies.

Despite significant progress, challenges remain in translating these technologies from laboratory settings to widespread clinical adoption. Issues related to reproducible manufacturing, long-term biocompatibility, regulatory approval pathways, and cost-effectiveness must be addressed. Nevertheless, the trajectory is clear: nanoparticle-based diagnostics and imaging will continue to advance medical capabilities, ultimately improving patient outcomes through earlier detection, more precise diagnosis, and more effective treatment monitoring.

CHAPTER 10

Nanobiocatalysts and Their Applications

This chapter explores the integration of nanotechnology and biocatalysis, focusing on nanobiocatalysts—enzymatic systems enhanced by nanomaterials. The chapter details fundamental concepts, development strategies, applications in pharmaceutical production, the role of nanoscaffolds, future trends, and AI/IoT integration for optimization. Nanobiocatalysts offer significant advantages, including improved stability, reusability, enhanced catalytic performance, and efficient multi-enzyme systems. The content highlights how these systems are revolutionizing industries, particularly pharmaceuticals, through their highly specific and environmentally friendly catalytic capabilities.

10.1 Concept of Nanobiocatalysis

Nanobiocatalysis represents the synergistic combination of enzymes with nanomaterials to create hybrid catalytic systems with enhanced properties. This interdisciplinary field has emerged from the convergence of biotechnology, nanotechnology, and materials science, offering innovative solutions to limitations faced by traditional enzyme catalysis.

At its core, nanobiocatalysis involves the immobilization or integration of enzymes with nanostructured materials such as nanoparticles, nanotubes, nanopores, and nanofibers. This integration creates catalytic systems that benefit from both the high specificity and selectivity of enzymes and the unique physical and chemical properties of nanomaterials.

The fundamental principles that differentiate nanobiocatalysis from conventional approaches include the following:

Enhanced Stability: When immobilized on nanomaterials, enzymes typically exhibit increased resistance to denaturation caused by temperature, pH, and organic solvents. This stability enhancement often extends operational lifetimes from hours to weeks or even months.

Improved Catalytic Performance: The nanoenvironment can positively influence enzyme kinetics through several mechanisms:

- Favorable microenvironmental conditions at the enzyme-nanomaterial interface
- Reduced diffusional limitations due to high surface-to-volume ratios
- Potential for substrate channeling in multi-enzyme systems

Recyclability: Unlike free enzymes, nanobiocatalysts can be easily recovered from reaction mixtures through methods like centrifugation, filtration, or magnetic separation, allowing for multiple reuse cycles that improve economic viability.

Nanoscale Confinement Effects: When enzymes operate within nanoscale spaces, they experience unique confinement effects that can alter their conformational dynamics and catalytic behavior, sometimes leading to enhanced activity or selectivity.

Various types of nanobiocatalysts have been developed, including

1. **Nanoparticle-Based Systems**: Enzymes attached to metallic (gold, silver), metal oxide (iron oxide, silica), or polymer nanoparticles.

2. **Carbon-Based Nanobiocatalysts**: Systems utilizing carbon nanotubes, graphene, or carbon dots as supports, which offer excellent mechanical strength and conductivity.

3. **Mesoporous Materials**: Enzymes confined within ordered nanoporous structures like mesoporous silica or metal-organic frameworks.

4. **Nanofibrous Supports**: Enzyme immobilization on electrospun nanofibers, providing high surface area and flexibility.

5. **Self-Assembled Nanostructures**: Including enzyme-containing nanogels, vesicles, and layer-by-layer assemblies.

The interaction between enzymes and nanomaterials occurs through various mechanisms, including physical adsorption, covalent binding, affinity interactions, and encapsulation. Each method presents distinct advantages and challenges that influence the resulting nanobiocatalyst's properties.

10.2 Development Strategies

The effective development of nanobiocatalysts requires thoughtful integration of enzymes with appropriate nanomaterials using optimal immobilization strategies. This section outlines key approaches and considerations in designing and fabricating nanobiocatalysts (Table 10-1).

Immobilization Techniques

Several fundamental immobilization methods are employed in nanobiocatalyst development:

Physical Adsorption: This simplest approach relies on non-covalent interactions (electrostatic, hydrophobic, van der Waals) between enzymes and nanomaterial surfaces. While straightforward, it often results in relatively weak attachment that may lead to enzyme leaching during use.

Covalent Attachment: Formation of chemical bonds between enzyme molecules and functionalized nanomaterials creates stable linkages resistant to leaching. Common strategies include

- Carbodiimide coupling between carboxyl and amino groups
- Glutaraldehyde cross-linking
- Click chemistry approaches
- Thiol-maleimide conjugation

Affinity-Based Methods: These exploit specific biological recognition elements to achieve oriented enzyme immobilization:

- Histidine tag/metal ion coordination
- Biotin-avidin/streptavidin interactions
- Antibody-antigen recognition

Encapsulation: Enzymes are physically confined within nanoporous structures or embedded within nanoparticles, protecting them from harsh external environments while allowing substrate diffusion.

Cross-Linked Enzyme Aggregates (CLEAs) and Crystals (CLECs): These carrier-free approaches involve enzyme molecules cross-linked to each other at the nanoscale, forming highly concentrated catalyst particles.

Table 10-1. Comparison of Enzyme Immobilization Methods for Nanobiocatalyst Development

Method	Advantages	Limitations	Typical Applications
Physical adsorption	Simple, mild conditions, minimal conformational changes	Weak binding, enzyme leaching, poor stability	Initial screening, proof-of-concept studies
Covalent binding	Strong attachment, minimal leaching, high stability	Potential loss of activity, complex chemistry required	Long-term industrial applications, continuous processes
Affinity-based	Controlled orientation, mild conditions, reversible	Requires engineered enzymes, specific adaptors	Biosensors, enzyme cascade systems
Encapsulation	Protection from harsh environments, high loading capacity	Diffusion limitations, complex fabrication	Pharmaceutical applications, bioremediation
CLEAs/CLECs	High volumetric activity, no carrier needed	Mass transfer limitations, mechanical fragility	Fine chemical synthesis, biocatalytic intensification

Material Selection Considerations

The choice of nanomaterial significantly impacts nanobiocatalyst performance (Figure 10-1).

Metal and Metal Oxide Nanoparticles: Gold, silver, iron oxide, and titanium dioxide nanoparticles offer diverse properties:

- Magnetic nanoparticles enable easy recovery using external magnetic fields
- Noble metal nanoparticles provide plasmonic properties useful for monitoring reactions
- Metal oxides often offer excellent biocompatibility and chemical stability

Carbon-Based Nanomaterials: Carbon nanotubes, graphene, and carbon dots provide exceptional surface areas and electrical conductivity, ideal for electrochemical applications.

Mesoporous Silica: Materials like MCM-41 and SBA-15 feature ordered pore structures with tunable dimensions and high surface areas.

Polymeric Nanomaterials: Biodegradable polymers like PLGA, chitosan, and poly(vinyl alcohol) form biocompatible nanoparticles or nanofibers.

Nanogels and Hydrogels: Cross-linked polymer networks with nanoscale features provide hydrophilic environments beneficial for many enzymes.

Fabrication Approaches

Several techniques are employed to create nanobiocatalysts:

Wet Chemical Methods: Precipitation, sol-gel processing, and emulsion techniques are commonly used to synthesize nanoparticles with or after enzyme incorporation.

Physical Techniques: Electrospinning creates nanofibrous supports, while lithographic approaches enable precise nanopatterning of surfaces for enzyme attachment.

Biological Templating: Virus capsids, protein cages, and DNA nanostructures can serve as templates for creating precisely defined nanobiocatalysts.

Self-Assembly Approaches: Spontaneous organization of molecular building blocks into ordered nanostructures capable of hosting enzymes.

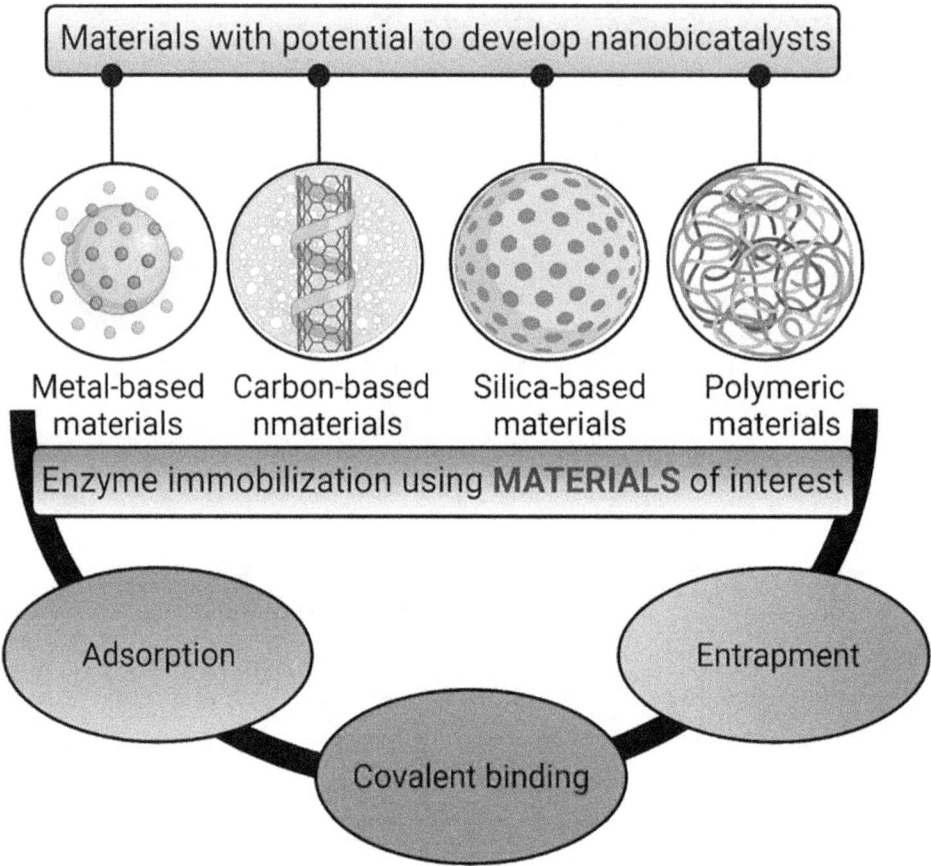

Figure 10-1. Methods for Enzyme Immobilization in Different Types of Nanomaterials

Design Optimization

Several critical factors must be considered when optimizing nanobiocatalyst design:

Enzyme Loading: While higher enzyme density generally increases volumetric activity, excessive crowding may cause steric hindrance and reduced efficiency. Optimization studies typically identify an optimal enzyme-to-nanomaterial ratio.

Orientation Control: The spatial orientation of immobilized enzymes significantly impacts their activity. Site-specific immobilization techniques can ensure that active sites remain accessible to substrates.

Microenvironment Engineering: The local environment surrounding immobilized enzymes can be tailored by incorporating

- pH buffers to maintain optimal conditions
- Stabilizing agents to enhance durability
- Co-factors or co-enzymes to support catalytic activity

Surface Modification: Functionalization of nanomaterial surfaces with appropriate chemical groups can

- Increase biocompatibility
- Reduce nonspecific interactions
- Provide specific linkage sites for enzyme attachment

Multi-enzyme Systems: Strategic co-immobilization of complementary enzymes enables cascade reactions with improved efficiency through substrate channeling.

10.3 Role in Drug Production

Nanobiocatalysts have emerged as powerful tools in pharmaceutical manufacturing, addressing key challenges in drug production through their unique properties and capabilities (Table 10-2).

Applications in Pharmaceutical Synthesis

Nanobiocatalysts contribute to pharmaceutical production in several critical areas:
    Chiral Resolution and Asymmetric Synthesis: Many pharmaceuticals require specific stereochemistry for therapeutic efficacy. Nanobiocatalysts excel at

- Kinetic resolution of racemic mixtures
- Asymmetric reduction of ketones and imines
- Stereoselective hydroxylation reactions
- Enantioselective esterification and amidation

For example, lipase immobilized on magnetic nanoparticles has been used for the enantioselective synthesis of pharmaceutical intermediates with enantiomeric excess values exceeding 99%.

API and Intermediate Synthesis: Nanobiocatalysts catalyze various transformations in active pharmaceutical ingredient (API) production:

- Oxidation and reduction reactions
- C-C bond formation
- Functional group modifications
- Glycosylation reactions

Prodrug Activation: Enzyme-functionalized nanoparticles can facilitate controlled prodrug activation, improving drug targeting and reducing side effects.

Process Intensification: The enhanced stability and recyclability of nanobiocatalysts enable

- Continuous flow processes
- One-pot multi-step syntheses
- Telescoping reactions (eliminating intermediate isolation steps)

Table 10-2. Examples of Nanobiocatalysts in Pharmaceutical Applications

Enzyme	Nanomaterial Support	Pharmaceutical Application	Advantages Over Traditional Methods
Lipase	Magnetic Fe_3O_4 nanoparticles	Synthesis of anti-inflammatory drug intermediates	>95% recovery, 15 reuse cycles, enhanced stability in organic solvents
Ketoreductase	Mesoporous silica	Asymmetric reduction for antidiabetic drugs	Improved stereoselectivity, 8-fold higher stability at 50°C
Transaminase	Carbon nanotubes	Production of chiral amines for CNS drugs	20-fold longer operational stability, continuous processing capability
Cytochrome P450	Gold nanoparticles	Hydroxylation of steroid drug precursors	Enhanced electron transfer, reduced cofactor requirements
Penicillin acylase	Chitosan nanofibers	Semi-synthetic antibiotic production	Higher substrate conversion, reduced byproducts, 12 reuse cycles

Industrial Benefits

The pharmaceutical industry gains significant advantages from implementing nanobiocatalytic processes:

Environmental Sustainability: Nanobiocatalytic processes typically operate under mild conditions (ambient temperature, aqueous environment, neutral pH), reducing energy consumption and hazardous waste generation compared to traditional chemical methods.

Economic Efficiency: Despite higher initial catalyst costs, nanobiocatalysts often provide overall economic benefits through

- Reduced process steps
- Higher yields and selectivities
- Lower purification requirements
- Catalyst reusability
- Reduced waste treatment costs

Quality Improvement: Enhanced selectivity leads to higher product purity and fewer side products, simplifying downstream processing and improving final drug quality.

Regulatory Advantages: Enzyme-catalyzed processes align well with regulatory trends promoting green chemistry and sustainable manufacturing.

Process Implementation

Integrating nanobiocatalysts into pharmaceutical production requires addressing several practical considerations:

Scale-up Challenges: Moving from laboratory scale to industrial production necessitates

- Standardized production methods for nanobiocatalysts
- Reactor design optimization
- Process parameter adjustment
- Quality control protocols

Reactor Configurations: Various reactor types accommodate nanobiocatalysts, including

- Stirred tank reactors with magnetic separation systems
- Packed bed reactors with immobilized catalysts
- Membrane reactors for continuous operation
- Microreactors for intensified processing

Regulatory Compliance: Pharmaceutical applications demand thorough characterization and validation:

- Catalyst composition consistency
- Leaching assessment
- Residual nanomaterial detection
- Process reproducibility documentation

10.4 Use of Nanoscaffolds

Nanoscaffolds provide structured support systems for enzyme immobilization, offering architectural frameworks that enhance enzyme stability, activity, and reusability. This section explores the diverse types of nanoscaffolds and their applications in creating advanced nanobiocatalytic systems.

Types of Nanoscaffolds

Nanoscaffolds encompass a wide range of nanostructured materials engineered to support enzyme immobilization (Table 10-3).

Mesoporous Silica Nanoscaffolds: Materials like MCM-41, SBA-15, and KIT-6 feature ordered pore structures with tunable dimensions (2-50 nm) and exceptionally high surface areas (>700 m^2/g). Their silanol-rich surfaces facilitate straightforward functionalization for enzyme attachment, while their rigid structure provides mechanical stability.

Carbon-Based Nanoscaffolds: These include

- **Carbon Nanotubes (CNTs)**: Cylindrical carbon structures offering high surface area and excellent conductivity

- **Graphene and Graphene Oxide**: Two-dimensional carbon sheets with extensive surface area for enzyme loading
- **Carbon Aerogels**: Ultra-lightweight porous networks with hierarchical structures

Metal-Organic Frameworks (MOFs): Crystalline materials composed of metal ions/clusters coordinated with organic ligands to form porous structures. Their highly tunable composition, pore size, and functionality make them versatile scaffolds for enzyme encapsulation.

Polymer-Based Nanoscaffolds:

- **Electrospun Nanofibers**: Continuous fibers with diameters ranging from tens to hundreds of nanometers
- **Polymeric Nanogels**: Cross-linked hydrophilic polymer networks with nanoscale dimensions
- **Dendrimers**: Highly branched, monodisperse polymeric molecules with precisely controlled structures

Self-Assembled Nanoscaffolds:

- **Peptide Nanofibers**: Self-assembling peptide sequences forming fibrillar networks
- **DNA Origami Structures**: Precisely folded DNA nanostructures with programmable architectures
- **Protein Cages**: Natural protein assemblies like ferritin or viral capsids repurposed as enzyme carriers

Design Principles for Nanoscaffolds

Several key considerations guide the design of effective nanoscaffolds:

Structural Parameters:

- Pore size and distribution must accommodate enzyme dimensions while facilitating substrate diffusion
- Surface area determines potential enzyme loading capacity
- Mechanical stability ensures durability during handling and operation

Surface Chemistry:

- Functional groups enable appropriate enzyme attachment chemistry
- Surface charge affects enzyme-scaffold interactions
- Hydrophilicity/hydrophobicity balance influences enzyme conformation and activity

Hierarchical Architecture:

- Macro-/meso-/microporous hierarchical structures optimize both enzyme loading and mass transport
- Interconnected pore networks reduce diffusion limitations
- Spatial organization enables precise enzyme positioning for cascade reactions

Table 10-3. Comparison of Different Nanoscaffold Properties

Nanoscaffold Type	Typical Surface Area (m²/g)	Pore Size Range (nm)	Key Advantages	Common Applications
Mesoporous silica	700–1200	2–30	High thermal stability, tunable pore structure	Thermostable enzyme immobilization, controlled release
Carbon nanotubes	50–1315	0.4–100	Excellent conductivity, mechanical strength	Electrochemical biosensors, biofuel cells
Metal-organic frameworks	1000–7000	0.5–100	Ultrahigh surface area, chemical diversity	Gas-phase biocatalysis, cascade reactions
Electrospun nanofibers	10–100	Interfiber spaces: 100–1000	Continuous structure, easy handling	Flow-through reactors, tissue engineering
Self-assembled peptides	50–300	5–200	Biocompatibility, stimuli-responsiveness	Biomimetic catalysis, drug delivery

Enzyme-Nanoscaffold Interactions

The interface between enzymes and nanoscaffolds critically influences catalytic performance (Figure 10-2).

Binding Mechanisms: Various interactions govern enzyme attachment to nanoscaffolds:

- Electrostatic interactions between charged groups
- Hydrogen bonding networks
- Hydrophobic associations
- Covalent linkages through chemical coupling
- Affinity-based recognition (e.g., His-tag coordination)

Conformational Effects: Nanoscaffold interaction can alter enzyme structure:

- Structural rigidification may enhance stability but potentially reduce the flexibility needed for catalysis
- Surface curvature can induce conformational changes affecting activity
- Nanoconfinement within pores may stabilize or destabilize enzyme structure

Microenvironmental Influence: Nanoscaffolds create unique local conditions:

- Surface hydration layers differ from the bulk solution
- Local pH may vary from the bulk due to surface charges
- Hydrophobic/hydrophilic balance affects substrate partitioning
- Co-immobilized additives can create favorable microenvironments

CHAPTER 10 NANOBIOCATALYSTS AND THEIR APPLICATIONS

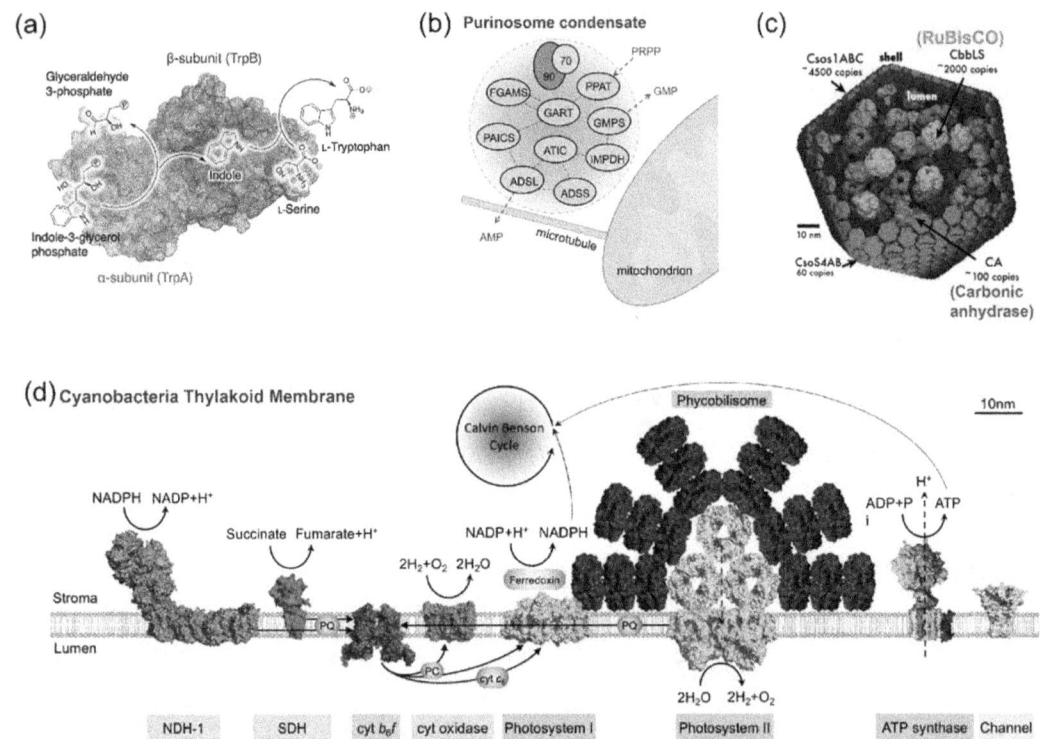

Figure 10-2. Molecular Interactions Between Enzymes and Different Nanoscaffold Surfaces

Advanced Nanoscaffold Systems

Recent developments have produced sophisticated nanoscaffold architectures:

Stimuli-Responsive Nanoscaffolds: Materials that change properties in response to environmental triggers:

- Temperature-responsive polymers that expand/contract with temperature changes
- pH-sensitive nanogels for controlled enzyme activation
- Light-responsive nanoscaffolds enabling remote-controlled catalysis
- Magnetically actuated systems for spatial control of enzyme activity

Multi-Enzyme Cascade Systems: Nanoscaffolds organize multiple enzymes in defined spatial arrangements:

- Distance-controlled enzyme positioning to optimize substrate channeling
- Compartmentalized reactions mimicking cellular organization
- Pathway engineering through strategic enzyme co-localization

Biomimetic Nanoscaffolds: Systems inspired by natural enzyme environments:

- Artificial enzyme complexes mimicking metabolosomes
- Synthetic organelles with enzyme-enriched interiors
- Lipid-based assemblies resembling natural membranes

Hybrid Nanoscaffolds: Integrating different material types for synergistic properties:

- Inorganic-organic composite scaffolds combining stability with biocompatibility
- Conductive-biocompatible hybrids for electrochemical applications
- Magnetic-porous composites enabling both immobilization and recovery

10.5 Future Insights

The field of nanobiocatalysis continues to evolve rapidly, with emerging trends and future directions promising to expand its capabilities and applications. This section explores upcoming developments and potential trajectories that will shape the next generation of nanobiocatalytic systems. Table 10-4 explains the future trends in nanobiocatalysis.

Emerging Materials and Architectures

Novel nanomaterials and structural designs are expanding the possibilities for nanobiocatalyst development:

Two-Dimensional Nanomaterials: Beyond graphene, emerging 2D materials like MXenes (transition metal carbides/nitrides), boron nitride nanosheets, and transition metal dichalcogenides offer unique properties for enzyme immobilization. Their atomically thin structure provides unprecedented surface-to-volume ratios and customizable surface chemistry.

Nano-Bio Hybrid Materials: Integration of biological components with synthetic nanomaterials creates sophisticated systems:

- Cell membrane-coated nanoparticles that combine biological functionality with nanomaterial properties
- DNA-directed assembly of enzyme arrays on nanostructured surfaces
- Protein-inorganic hybrid nanomaterials with programmable functions

Hierarchical Multi-Scale Architectures: Structures spanning multiple size domains (nano to macro) enable both high enzyme loading and efficient mass transport:

- 3D-printed structures with nanoscale surface features
- Macroporous monoliths containing nanoscale enzyme carriers
- Flow-through systems with hierarchical channel networks

Living Materials: Integration of living cells with nanomaterials to create systems where cellular metabolism enhances nanobiocatalysis or vice versa.

Advances in Enzyme Engineering for Nanobiocatalysis

Progress in protein engineering is yielding enzymes specially adapted for nanomaterial integration:

Nanomaterial-Compatible Enzymes: Rational design and directed evolution are creating enzyme variants with enhanced stability when interfacing with nanomaterials. These engineered enzymes feature:

- Surface residues optimized for specific nanomaterial interactions
- Reduced susceptibility to conformational changes upon immobilization
- Enhanced tolerance to nanomaterial-induced microenvironments

Click-Ready Enzymes: Introduction of bioorthogonal reactive groups enabling site-specific, orientation-controlled attachment to nanomaterials.

Self-Assembling Enzyme Systems: Engineered enzymes with built-in assembly domains that spontaneously organize into nanoscale catalyst arrays.

Designer Multi-Enzyme Complexes: Fusion proteins and engineered protein-protein interactions creating artificial enzyme cascades with optimized spatial organization.

Nanobiocatalysis in Emerging Applications

The versatility of nanobiocatalysts is enabling expansion into new application domains:

Sustainable Energy: Nanobiocatalytic systems for energy production and storage:

- Enzyme-functionalized electrodes for biofuel cells
- Photoenzymatic systems coupling light harvesting with biocatalysis
- CO_2 reduction systems using immobilized carboxylases and reductases

Advanced Therapeutics: Integration with medical technologies:

- Nanobiocatalytic implants for continuous drug production or activation
- Enzyme-carrying nanorobots for localized therapeutic interventions
- Nanozymes combining enzymatic activity with material functions

Environmental Remediation: Specialized systems for pollutant degradation:

- Persistent organic pollutant degradation using enzyme cascades
- Microplastic decomposition through hydrolytic enzyme systems
- Heavy metal transformation and sequestration

Artificial Metabolism: Creation of synthetic metabolic networks:

- Cell-free bioproduction systems using immobilized pathway enzymes
- Artificial organelles for specialized chemical transformations
- Synthetic cellular mimics with compartmentalized enzyme functions

Technological Challenges and Solutions

Several obstacles must be overcome to fully realize the potential of advanced nanobiocatalysis:

Scale-Up and Manufacturing: Current laboratory-scale fabrication methods often don't translate well to industrial production. Emerging solutions include

- Continuous flow synthesis of nanobiocatalysts
- Microfluidic approaches for high-throughput nanobiocatalyst preparation
- Standardized protocols for reproducible large-scale production

Stability Enhancement: While nanomaterials improve enzyme stability, further advances are needed:

- Computational design of enzyme-nanomaterial interfaces
- Novel stabilization approaches combining chemical modification with nanostructuring
- Self-healing nanobiocatalytic systems capable of regenerating activity

Characterization Challenges: Advanced analytical techniques are being developed to better understand nanobiocatalytic systems:

- In situ spectroscopic methods for monitoring enzymatic reactions on nanomaterials
- Cryo-electron microscopy for visualizing enzyme conformations on nanostructures
- Advanced computational models predicting nanobiocatalyst behavior

Regulatory Considerations: As nanobiocatalysts enter commercial applications, regulatory frameworks must evolve

- Standardized safety assessment protocols
- Nanomaterial lifecycle analysis and environmental impact evaluation
- Industry standards for nanobiocatalyst characterization and performance testing

Table 10-4. *Future Trends in Nanobiocatalysis*

Trend	Current Status	Future Potential	Key Challenges
AI-designed nanobiocatalysts	Early algorithmic approaches	Fully optimized systems with predicted performance	Integrating multiscale modeling from atomic to macroscopic levels
Self-regenerating systems	Proof-of-concept demonstrations	Long-term autonomous operation	Balancing regeneration mechanisms with catalytic performance
Programmable nanobiocatalysts	Basic stimulus-response capabilities	Complex logical operations and feedback control	Creating robust signal transduction in nanobiocatalytic systems
Synthetic metabolic networks	Simple multi-enzyme pathways	Cell-free biomanufacturing platforms	Managing pathway complexity and intermediate stability
Living-nonliving hybrids	Surface functionalization of living cells	Symbiotic cellular-nanomaterial systems	Ensuring biocompatibility and balanced interactions

10.6 AI and IoT Optimization

The integration of artificial intelligence (AI) and Internet of Things (IoT) technologies is revolutionizing nanobiocatalysis, enabling unprecedented levels of process monitoring, control, and optimization. This convergence is creating intelligent nanobiocatalytic systems with enhanced performance, adaptability, and autonomy. Table 10-5 explains the benefits of AI/IoT integration in nanobiocatalysis.

AI-Driven Nanobiocatalyst Design

Artificial intelligence is transforming the development process for nanobiocatalysts:

Machine Learning for Material-Enzyme Pairing: Advanced algorithms analyze patterns in experimental data to identify optimal combinations of enzymes and nanomaterials:

- Neural networks predicting enzyme activity on different nanomaterial surfaces
- Support vector machines classifying optimal immobilization methods based on enzyme properties
- Reinforcement learning strategies for optimizing fabrication parameters

Computational Enzyme Engineering: AI accelerates the design of enzymes specifically adapted for nanomaterial interfaces:

- Deep learning approaches for predicting beneficial mutations
- Molecular dynamics simulations enhanced by machine learning
- Generative models suggesting novel enzyme variants with desired properties

Nanomaterial Design Optimization: Machine learning guides the development of new nanomaterials tailored for specific enzymatic applications:

- Property prediction models for novel nanomaterial compositions
- Structure-function relationship mapping for nanomaterial characteristics

IoT Integration for Process Monitoring and Control

IoT technologies create connected nanobiocatalytic systems with real-time monitoring capabilities:

Sensor Networks: Advanced sensing technologies track critical parameters in nanobiocatalytic processes:

- Miniaturized electrochemical sensors for substrate/product monitoring
- Optical sensors detecting enzymatic activity through fluorescence or absorbance
- Temperature, pH, and environmental condition sensors
- Flow and pressure monitors for continuous processes

Digital Twins: Virtual representations of nanobiocatalytic systems enable simulation and prediction:

- Real-time modeling of reaction kinetics
- Virtual testing of process modifications
- Predictive maintenance scheduling based on performance patterns
- Anomaly detection through comparison with expected behavior

Automated Feedback Control: Sensor data drives automatic adjustments to maintain optimal conditions:

- Real-time modification of process parameters (temperature, pH, feed rates)
- Adaptive control systems responding to catalyst performance changes
- Self-regulating systems maintaining optimal operating windows
- Fault detection and corrective action implementation

Cloud-Based Data Analytics for Nanobiocatalysis

Cloud computing infrastructure enables sophisticated data processing for nanobiocatalytic systems:

Big Data Management: Handling the massive datasets generated by sensor networks:

- Data collection, storage, and organization strategies
- Integration of structured and unstructured data
- Historical performance tracking and trend analysis
- Cross-site comparison of similar nanobiocatalytic processes

Advanced Analytics: Extracting actionable insights from process data:

- Pattern recognition in long-term performance data
- Correlation analysis between operating conditions and catalyst efficiency

- Root cause analysis for performance deviations
- Predictive analytics for anticipating system behavior

Knowledge Sharing Platforms: Cloud-based systems facilitate information exchange:

- Centralized repositories of nanobiocatalyst performance data
- Collaborative optimization across multiple research or production sites
- Shared learning from operational experiences
- Standardized protocols and best practices

Intelligent Optimization Strategies

The combination of AI and IoT enables sophisticated optimization approaches:

Evolutionary Algorithms: Nature-inspired optimization methods:

- Genetic algorithms evolving process parameters over multiple iterations
- Particle swarm optimization for multi-parameter tuning
- Simulated annealing approaches for finding global optima
- Multi-objective optimization balancing competing process goals

Reinforcement Learning: AI systems that learn optimal control strategies:

- Deep reinforcement learning agents making sequential decisions
- Model-based reinforcement learning using process simulations
- Multi-agent systems coordinating different aspects of process control
- Transfer learning, applying knowledge from one nanobiocatalytic system to another

Autonomous Experimentation: Self-driving laboratory systems for nanobiocatalyst optimization:

- Automated design of experiments based on previous results
- Robotic systems executing experimental protocols

- Closed-loop optimization without human intervention
- Active learning approaches focusing on information-rich experiments

Table 10-5. *Benefits of AI/IoT Integration in Nanobiocatalysis*

Area	Traditional Approach	AI/IoT Enhanced Approach	Improvement Potential
Process monitoring	Manual sampling, offline analysis	Real-time continuous monitoring, predictive analytics	60–80% reduction in quality deviations
Energy efficiency	Fixed operating conditions	Dynamic optimization based on real-time data	15–30% energy consumption reduction
Catalyst longevity	Scheduled replacement	Condition-based maintenance, adaptive operation	40–70% extension of catalyst lifetime
Process development	Sequential experimentation	Parallel testing with machine learning guidance	3–10× acceleration in development timelines
Scale-up	Experience-based adaptation	Digital twin simulation, data-driven scaling rules	50–70% reduction in scale-up failures

Implementation Challenges and Solutions

Several obstacles must be addressed to successfully implement AI/IoT systems in nanobiocatalysis:

Data Quality and Standardization: Ensuring reliable data for AI systems:

- Sensor calibration and validation protocols
- Data cleaning and preprocessing pipelines
- Standardized data formats and metadata
- Quality assurance for training datasets

Integration Complexity: Connecting diverse hardware and software elements:

- Compatible communication protocols across devices
- Edge computing for local processing needs
- Middleware solutions for system integration
- Scalable architecture supporting system expansion

Security Concerns: Protecting sensitive process data and control systems:

- Encryption for data transmission and storage
- Access control and authentication mechanisms
- Vulnerability assessment and security updates
- Backup and recovery procedures

Human-AI Collaboration: Optimizing the partnership between AI systems and human operators:

- Intuitive user interfaces for monitoring AI decisions
- Transparent AI systems with explainable recommendations
- Knowledge transfer to build operator understanding
- Balanced automation maintaining human oversight

The integration of AI and IoT technologies into nanobiocatalytic systems represents a transformative approach that will continue to evolve as these technologies advance. Future developments will likely include more sophisticated digital twins, expanded autonomy, and deeper integration with broader manufacturing ecosystems.

10.7 Summary

Nanobiocatalysis represents a powerful convergence of nanotechnology and biocatalysis that is fundamentally transforming industrial biotechnology. By strategically combining the exquisite selectivity and specificity of enzymes with the unique properties of nanomaterials, these hybrid systems overcome traditional limitations of enzymatic processes while creating new possibilities for sustainable chemical manufacturing.

The field has matured significantly in recent years, transitioning from proof-of-concept demonstrations to practical industrial applications, particularly in pharmaceutical production, where demands for high selectivity and purity align perfectly with nanobiocatalytic capabilities. The development of sophisticated nanoscaffolds has further expanded the design space, enabling precise spatial organization of enzymes and creating biomimetic microenvironments that enhance catalytic performance.

Looking ahead, nanobiocatalysis stands at the threshold of a new era driven by advanced materials, computational design, and digital technologies. The integration of AI and IoT systems is creating intelligent nanobiocatalytic processes capable of self-optimization and adaptation, while emerging nanomaterials and architectural designs are pushing the boundaries of what these systems can achieve.

Several challenges remain, including standardization of fabrication methods, improved characterization techniques, and regulatory frameworks that address the unique aspects of nanobiocatalysts. Nevertheless, the trajectory is clear: nanobiocatalysis will continue to expand its role in the sustainable production of pharmaceuticals, fine chemicals, and other high-value products, while simultaneously opening new application domains in energy, environmental remediation, and biomedicine.

As interdisciplinary collaboration drives innovation in this field, the coming decade promises increasingly sophisticated nanobiocatalytic systems that more closely mimic—and potentially surpass—the elegant efficiency of nature's own catalytic machinery.

CHAPTER 11

Environmental and Health Impacts of Nanomaterials

This chapter examines the complex relationship between nanotechnology and its potential effects on environmental systems and human health. Beginning with an exploration of environmental fate mechanisms—including transport, transformation, and persistence of engineered nanomaterials in various ecosystems—the discussion progresses to fundamental toxicity principles and how nanomaterial properties influence biological interactions. Assessment models for predicting and quantifying impacts are evaluated, alongside comprehensive lifecycle analyses that track nanomaterials from production through disposal. The chapter further investigates containment measures and engineered solutions designed to mitigate potential risks. Finally, emerging applications of artificial intelligence and Internet of Things technologies for real-time monitoring of nanomaterials in environmental and biological systems are explored. Throughout, the chapter emphasizes the importance of balancing technological advancement with responsible stewardship of environmental and public health.

11.1 Environmental Fate

Introduction to Environmental Fate

The increasing integration of engineered nanomaterials (ENMs) into consumer products, industrial processes, and environmental remediation strategies necessitates a thorough understanding of their environmental fate. Environmental fate encompasses the complex processes that determine how nanomaterials move through, transform within, and persist in various environmental compartments after their release.

Unlike conventional chemicals, nanomaterials exhibit unique behaviors governed by their physical dimensions, surface properties, and quantum effects that traditional environmental transport models often fail to accurately predict.

When nanomaterials enter environmental systems, their mobility and persistence are influenced by numerous factors that operate across multiple spatial and temporal scales. The environmental journey of a nanomaterial typically begins with its release—either intentional, as in remediation applications, or unintentional, through product wear, industrial discharge, or waste disposal. Once released, nanomaterials encounter complex matrices of natural colloids, organic matter, microorganisms, and varying geochemical conditions that significantly alter their original properties and behaviors.

The environmental fate of nanomaterials is governed by fundamental processes including aggregation, deposition, transformation, and biological interactions. Aggregation, particularly, represents a critical process wherein nanoparticles cluster together, altering their effective size, surface area, and consequently, their mobility and reactivity within environmental systems. The tendency of nanomaterials to aggregate is strongly influenced by solution chemistry parameters such as pH, ionic strength, and the presence of natural organic matter. For instance, metal-based nanoparticles like silver and zinc oxide often demonstrate increased aggregation in high-ionic-strength waters, potentially limiting their mobility but also changing their bioavailability to organisms.

Transport Mechanisms in Different Environmental Media

Nanomaterial transport through environmental media varies considerably depending on the characteristics of both the nanomaterial and the environmental compartment. In aquatic systems, factors such as water velocity, turbulence, and the presence of suspended solids significantly influence nanomaterial movement. Research has demonstrated that carbon-based nanomaterials like fullerenes exhibit greater mobility in natural waters containing substantial dissolved organic matter, which provides steric stabilization, preventing aggregation.

In soil and sediment environments, nanomaterial transport is complicated by the heterogeneous nature of these media. Pore size distribution, mineral composition, and organic content create complex scenarios for nanomaterial movement. Studies have shown that nanomaterials with positive surface charges, such as certain metal oxides, often exhibit limited mobility in negatively charged soil matrices due to electrostatic attraction. Conversely, nanomaterials with stable negative surface charges may travel considerable distances through soil columns, particularly in sandy soils with limited clay content.

Atmospheric transport represents another significant pathway for nanomaterial distribution, particularly for nanomaterials released during high-energy processes or incorporated into aerosols. Ultrafine particles, including engineered nanomaterials, can remain suspended in the air for extended periods and travel considerable distances from their source. Their deposition is governed by processes including gravitational settling, impaction, and precipitation scavenging (Table 11-1).

Table 11-1. Environmental Transport Parameters for Common Engineered Nanomaterials

Nanomaterial Type	Primary Transport Mechanism	Influencing Factors	Environmental Persistence
Metal nanoparticles (Ag, Au)	Aggregation and sedimentation	Ionic strength, pH, organic matter	Months to years
Metal oxide nanoparticles (TiO_2, ZnO)	Heteroaggregation with natural colloids	Surface coating, water hardness	Years
Carbon nanotubes	Deposition and interception	Length, surface functionalization	Years to decades
Quantum dots	Dissolution and complexation	Redox conditions, light exposure	Weeks to months
Polymeric nanoparticles	Steric stabilization and advection	Polymer composition, degradability	Months to years

Transformation Processes and Persistence

Once in the environment, nanomaterials undergo various transformation processes that alter their physical and chemical properties. These transformations significantly influence their potential environmental impacts and bioavailability. Photochemical transformations are particularly relevant for certain nanomaterials, such as titanium dioxide, which can generate reactive oxygen species under UV exposure. Similarly, redox transformations affect the speciation and toxicity of metal-based nanomaterials. For example, silver nanoparticles commonly transform through oxidative dissolution, releasing silver ions that exhibit different toxicity profiles compared to the parent particles.

Biological transformations represent another significant pathway through which nanomaterials evolve in environmental systems. Microorganisms can modify nanomaterial surfaces through the secretion of extracellular polymeric substances, enzymatic activity, or direct incorporation into cellular structures. These interactions may enhance or reduce nanomaterial toxicity and mobility. Research has demonstrated that certain bacteria can utilize functionalized carbon nanotubes as energy sources, potentially reducing their environmental persistence.

The persistence of nanomaterials in environmental systems varies widely depending on their composition and the specific environmental conditions they encounter. While some metallic nanomaterials may persist for years or decades, others undergo relatively rapid dissolution or degradation. Carbon-based nanomaterials like fullerenes and carbon nanotubes typically demonstrate high environmental persistence, with estimated half-lives ranging from years to decades in sediment systems. The presence of natural organic matter often enhances nanomaterial stability, potentially extending their environmental lifetimes.

11.2 Toxicity Basics

Fundamental Principles of Nanotoxicology

Nanotoxicology represents a specialized discipline within toxicology focused on understanding how the unique properties of nanomaterials influence their interactions with biological systems. The field emerged from the recognition that nanomaterials often exhibit toxicological profiles distinctly different from their bulk counterparts, necessitating novel approaches to hazard and risk assessment. The fundamental principles of nanotoxicology center on several key concepts that distinguish it from conventional toxicology.

The size-dependent nature of nanomaterial toxicity represents a primary distinguishing feature. Materials at the nanoscale often demonstrate enhanced reactivity due to their increased surface-to-volume ratio, which maximizes the number of atoms at the particle surface available for biological interactions. This property significantly influences cellular uptake mechanisms, tissue distribution, and biological persistence. Studies have consistently demonstrated that smaller nanoparticles within the 1–30 nm range typically exhibit greater toxicity compared to larger particles of identical composition, owing to their enhanced ability to penetrate biological barriers and interact with subcellular structures.

Surface properties, including charge, hydrophobicity, and functional groups, fundamentally determine nanomaterial-biological interactions. Surface charge particularly influences cellular uptake pathways—positively charged nanomaterials generally demonstrate enhanced cellular internalization due to electrostatic interactions with negatively charged cell membranes. However, this increased uptake often correlates with heightened cytotoxicity. Surface functionality through coating or chemical modification dramatically alters biological responses to nanomaterials, potentially mitigating or exacerbating toxicity. Polyethylene glycol coating, for instance, typically reduces nanomaterial recognition by the immune system, while certain amine functionalization approaches may enhance cytotoxicity.

The diverse mechanisms through which nanomaterials induce biological effects further complicate toxicological assessments. Common mechanisms include oxidative stress through reactive oxygen species generation, direct physical interaction with cellular structures, inflammatory responses, genotoxicity, and disruption of cellular signaling pathways. The predominant toxicity mechanism varies significantly across nanomaterial types, with metal-based nanoparticles often inducing oxidative stress as a primary effect, while high-aspect-ratio materials like carbon nanotubes may cause inflammatory responses through frustrated phagocytosis.

Biological Interactions at the Nanoscale

The interaction between nanomaterials and biological systems begins at interfaces—typically the protein corona that rapidly forms around nanomaterials in biological fluids. This dynamic layer of adsorbed proteins significantly influences how biological systems recognize and process nanomaterials. The composition of the protein corona varies based on nanomaterial properties and the specific biological environment, creating a "biological identity" that may differ substantially from the nanomaterial's "synthetic identity." Research has demonstrated that the protein corona composition often determines cellular uptake mechanisms, biodistribution patterns, and ultimately, biological outcomes.

Cellular internalization represents the next critical stage in nanomaterial-biological interactions. Multiple endocytic pathways facilitate nanomaterial uptake, including clathrin-mediated endocytosis, caveolae-mediated endocytosis, macropinocytosis, and phagocytosis. The predominant uptake mechanism depends on both nanomaterial properties (size, shape, surface characteristics) and cell type. For instance, macrophages readily internalize a wide range of nanomaterials through phagocytosis as part of their immune surveillance function, while nonphagocytic cells typically demonstrate more selective uptake based on nanomaterial surface properties.

Once internalized, nanomaterials may interact with various cellular structures and disrupt normal physiological processes. Mitochondrial damage frequently occurs following exposure to certain metal and metal oxide nanoparticles, manifesting as decreased membrane potential, altered morphology, and impaired energy production. Lysosomal dysfunction represents another common cellular response, particularly for nanomaterials that resist degradation in the acidic lysosomal environment. Nuclear interactions, though less common due to the selective permeability of the nuclear membrane, may occur with very small nanomaterials (< 5 nm) or those specifically designed for nuclear targeting, potentially resulting in genotoxicity through direct DNA interaction or indirect oxidative damage.

Dose Metrics and Exposure Considerations

Establishing appropriate dose metrics represents a fundamental challenge in nanotoxicology. Unlike conventional chemicals, where mass concentration typically serves as the primary dose metric, nanomaterial biological effects often correlate more closely with other physical parameters. Surface area, particle number, and surface reactivity frequently demonstrate stronger correlations with biological responses than mass concentration alone. This complexity necessitates reporting multiple dose metrics in toxicological studies to facilitate accurate hazard assessment and cross-study comparison.

The concept of delivered dose—the actual amount of nanomaterial that reaches the biological target—further complicates dosimetry considerations. In in vitro systems, nanomaterial behavior in cell culture media significantly influences cellular exposure. Sedimentation, aggregation, and dissolution processes create scenarios where the nominal (administered) dose differs substantially from the delivered dose. Advanced computational models such as the In Vitro Sedimentation, Diffusion, and Dosimetry (ISDD) model now enable researchers to estimate delivered doses based on nanomaterial properties and experimental conditions, improving the physiological relevance of in vitro findings.

CHAPTER 11   ENVIRONMENTAL AND HEALTH IMPACTS OF NANOMATERIALS

Exposure routes similarly influence nanomaterial toxicity profiles in vivo. Inhalation exposure typically results in pulmonary deposition patterns dependent on particle size, with nanoparticles reaching deep lung regions, including alveoli. Dermal exposure outcomes vary based on skin condition, with intact skin generally providing an effective barrier against nanomaterial penetration while damaged skin may permit translocation. Oral exposure introduces nanomaterials to the harsh gastrointestinal environment, where pH variations and digestive enzymes may transform their properties before potential absorption. Intravenous administration, relevant primarily for medical applications, results in direct nanomaterial introduction to the circulatory system and potential distribution throughout the body, depending on nanomaterial properties and protein corona formation (Figure 11-1).

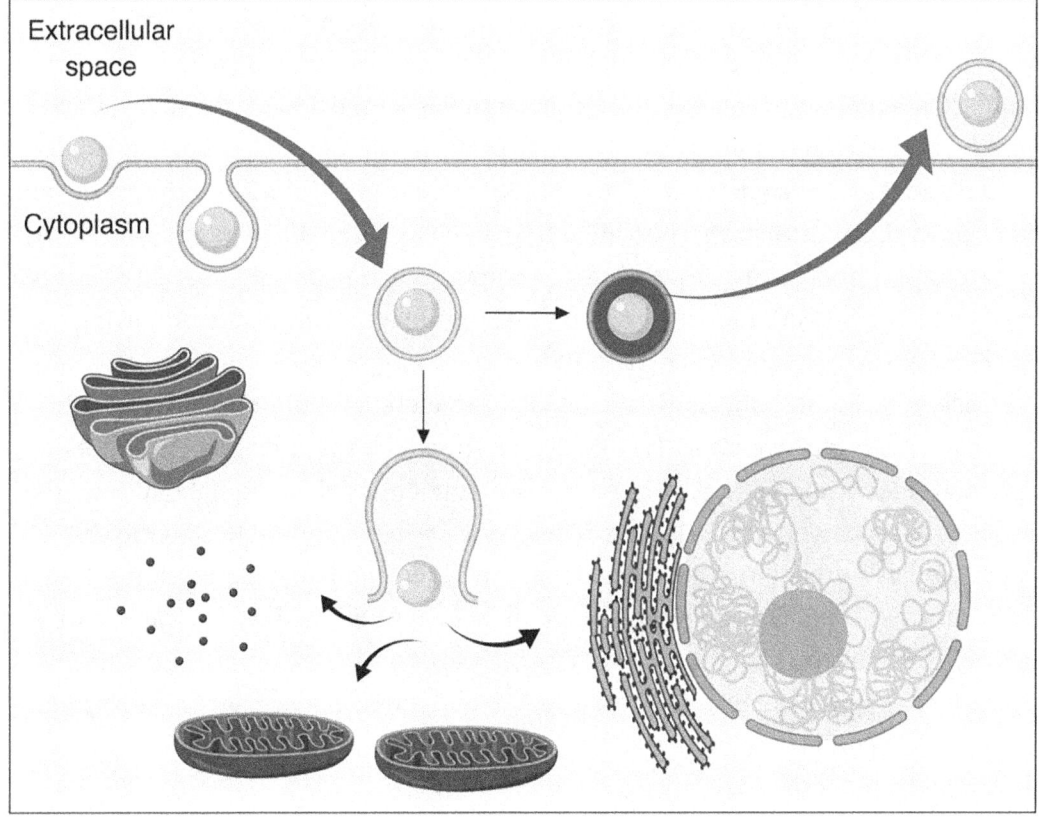

Figure 11-1. Cellular Uptake Mechanisms and Intracellular Fate of Engineered Nanomaterials

215

11.3 Assessment Models

Predictive Toxicology Approaches

The rapid proliferation of engineered nanomaterials presents significant challenges for traditional toxicological assessment methods, which typically rely on resource-intensive animal testing. Predictive toxicology approaches have emerged as critical tools for efficiently screening and prioritizing nanomaterials for further investigation. These approaches encompass a diverse range of methodologies, from computational modeling to high-throughput screening systems, united by their goal of predicting biological responses based on nanomaterial physicochemical properties.

Quantitative structure-activity relationship (QSAR) models represent a cornerstone of predictive nanotoxicology. These models establish mathematical relationships between nanomaterial properties and biological outcomes, enabling toxicity prediction for untested materials. Nano-QSAR approaches have demonstrated particular success in predicting specific endpoints such as cytotoxicity to certain cell lines or ecotoxicity to model organisms. Recent advances incorporate more sophisticated descriptors beyond simple physicochemical properties, including surface energy calculations, protein corona compositions, and cellular uptake parameters. For instance, Eriksson et al. (2023) developed a nano-QSAR model for predicting pulmonary inflammation following metal oxide nanoparticle exposure, achieving 85% accuracy by incorporating both traditional physicochemical descriptors and calculated parameters reflecting surface reactivity.

High-throughput screening (HTS) platforms provide experimental approaches to predictive toxicology, enabling rapid assessment of multiple nanomaterials across various concentrations and endpoints. These systems typically employ in vitro cell culture models coupled with automated liquid handling and detection systems. Modern HTS platforms for nanotoxicology often incorporate multiple cell types arranged in physiologically relevant configurations, moving beyond simple monoculture systems. The ToxCast program, for example, has expanded to include nanomaterial assessment across hundreds of biochemical and cell-based assays, generating substantial datasets for identifying potential hazards and mechanisms of toxicity. While HTS approaches cannot fully replace targeted in-depth studies, they efficiently identify nanomaterials requiring more comprehensive evaluation.

Adverse outcome pathway (AOP) frameworks enhance predictive approaches by mapping the causal relationships between molecular initiating events and adverse outcomes at the organism or population levels. This conceptual framework has proven particularly valuable in nanotoxicology, where multiple mechanisms may contribute to observed effects. Well-characterized AOPs allow researchers to develop targeted testing strategies focusing on key events within the pathway, reducing reliance on apical endpoint testing. For nanomaterials, several AOPs have been established, including pathways linking lysosomal damage to inflammation and fibrosis following high-aspect-ratio nanomaterial exposure. These pathways serve as organizing frameworks for integrating diverse data types into coherent toxicological narratives.

In Vitro and In Vivo Model Systems

In vitro model systems for nanotoxicological assessment have evolved significantly beyond traditional two-dimensional cell cultures to better recapitulate physiological complexity. Three-dimensional culture systems, including spheroids, organoids, and tissue-engineered constructs, provide more representative cellular architectures, extracellular matrix interactions, and physiological gradients. These advanced systems demonstrate gene expression profiles and cellular responses that more closely mirror in vivo conditions compared to conventional monolayer cultures. For instance, lung-on-a-chip platforms incorporating epithelial-endothelial interfaces under physiological stretch conditions have demonstrated responses to nanoparticle exposure that correlate strongly with in vivo pulmonary effects.

Co-culture systems further enhance physiological relevance by incorporating multiple cell types that interact in vivo. Models of the pulmonary alveolar-capillary barrier commonly include epithelial cells, endothelial cells, and macrophages to represent the complex cellular environment nanomaterials encounter following inhalation. Similarly, gastrointestinal tract models may incorporate enterocytes, goblet cells, and immune cells to more accurately predict nanomaterial interactions during oral exposure. These systems capture cellular crosstalk that significantly influences nanomaterial processing and toxicity, including macrophage-mediated clearance and epithelial barrier modulation by immune cells.

In vivo models remain essential for assessing systemic effects, biodistribution, and long-term outcomes that cannot be fully captured in vitro. Traditional rodent models provide valuable insights, particularly for understanding biokinetics and target organ toxicity. Alternative models, including zebrafish embryos and *Caenorhabditis elegans*, offer advantages for rapid screening with reduced ethical concerns. The zebrafish embryo model has particularly gained prominence for nanomaterial assessment due to its optical transparency enabling direct visualization of nanomaterial distribution, rapid development allowing observation of multiple life stages, and substantial genetic homology with humans. Standardized zebrafish embryo toxicity tests now include specific protocols for nanomaterial assessment, addressing dosing challenges and endpoint selection.

Risk Assessment Frameworks

Regulatory frameworks for nanomaterial risk assessment continue to evolve as scientific understanding advances, with most jurisdictions adapting existing chemical assessment frameworks to accommodate nanomaterial-specific considerations. These adaptations typically address several key challenges, including appropriate dose metrics, nanomaterial categorization approaches, and methods for addressing the diversity of nanomaterial variants. The European Union's framework under REACH (Registration, Evaluation, Authorization and Restriction of Chemicals) exemplifies this approach, incorporating specific provisions for nanomaterials through recent amendments that require detailed characterization data and hazard assessment tailored to the nanoscale form.

Categorization and grouping strategies represent critical components of efficient risk assessment frameworks, enabling data-poor nanomaterials to be assessed based on analogy to better-characterized materials with similar properties. Various approaches to categorization have been proposed, including those based on chemical composition, physical properties, biological interactions, or mechanistic considerations. The DF4nanoGrouping framework, for instance, classifies nanomaterials into four main categories (soluble, biopersistent with high cellular uptake, biopersistent with low cellular uptake, and passive) based on dissolution rate, cellular uptake, and surface reactivity. Such frameworks facilitate read-across approaches where data gaps for specific nanomaterials can be addressed using information from analogous materials within the same category.

Uncertainty analysis plays a particularly important role in nanomaterial risk assessment due to the complex interplay between nanomaterial properties and biological effects. Formal approaches to uncertainty characterization help identify knowledge gaps requiring additional research and guide risk management decisions when complete information is unavailable. Probabilistic risk assessment methods incorporating Monte Carlo simulations have been applied to nanomaterials to generate risk distributions rather than point estimates, providing more comprehensive perspectives on potential scenarios. These approaches require quantification of uncertainty factors, including measurement error, model uncertainty, and natural variability in both exposure and effects distributions (Table 11-2).

Table 11-2. Comparison of Nanomaterial Assessment Approaches

Assessment Approach	Advantages	Limitations	Applicability
High-throughput in vitro screening	Rapid testing of multiple materials and concentrations; reduced animal use; mechanistic insights	Limited physiological relevance; dosimetry challenges; potential nanomaterial interference with assays	Early-stage screening; mechanistic studies; comparative toxicity assessment
3D/organoid models	Improved physiological architecture; better prediction of in vivo responses; multiple cell type interactions	Higher cost and complexity; longer preparation time; limited standardization	Organ-specific toxicity prediction; barrier penetration studies; chronic exposure scenarios
Alternative animal models (zebrafish, *C. elegans*)	Whole organism responses; developmental endpoints; reduced ethical concerns	Physiological differences from humans; limited assessment of systemic effects	Developmental toxicity screening; rapid prioritization; environmental toxicity assessment
Traditional in vivo models (rodent)	Systemic distribution and effects; immune system responses; chronic toxicity assessment	Resource-intensive; ethical considerations; limited throughput	Regulatory submissions; biokinetic studies; chronic and reproductive toxicity
Computational models (QSAR, PBPK)	Nontesting approach; resource efficient; mechanism-based predictions	Requires high-quality training data; limited to similar materials; model validation challenges	Data gap filling; prioritization; supporting weight-of-evidence approaches

11.4 Lifecycle Studies

Cradle-to-Grave Analysis Approaches

Lifecycle assessment (LCA) methodologies provide systematic frameworks for evaluating the environmental impacts of nanomaterials and nano-enabled products across their entire lifespan—from raw material extraction through manufacturing, use, and ultimate disposal or recycling. These approaches offer holistic perspectives that prevent burden-shifting, where addressing one environmental concern inadvertently creates another at a different lifecycle stage. For nanomaterials, traditional LCA methodologies require significant adaptation to address unique challenges related to functional units, inventory data availability, and impact assessment methods tailored to nanoscale properties.

Functional unit definition represents a fundamental consideration in nanomaterial LCAs, requiring careful articulation of the service or function provided rather than simple mass-based comparisons. For instance, when assessing nanosilver-containing textiles, appropriate functional units might include "providing antimicrobial protection for a specified garment over its useful life" rather than simply comparing equivalent masses of conventional and nanosilver. This function-based approach enables meaningful comparisons between nanomaterials and conventional alternatives, accounting for the often-enhanced performance characteristics of nanomaterials that allow reduced material quantities.

Inventory analysis for nanomaterial LCAs presents significant challenges due to data gaps and proprietary manufacturing processes. Energy requirements for nanomaterial production typically exceed those for conventional materials on a mass basis, but performance enhancements may reduce overall material requirements. Comprehensive inventory databases specifically for nanomaterials remain under development, with initiatives such as the NanoDatabase project working to address these gaps. In the interim, researchers often employ hybrid approaches combining available primary data with estimates and proxy processes to construct lifecycle inventories. Recent studies by Hischier and Walser (2021) demonstrated that production phase energy requirements for certain metal oxide nanoparticles can exceed conventional materials by factors of 10–100 per unit mass, primarily due to high-purity requirements and specialized synthesis methods.

Impact assessment methods for nanomaterials require expansion beyond traditional LCA impact categories to account for nano-specific effects. While conventional categories such as global warming potential and acidification remain relevant, additional considerations include physical impacts related to particle size and surface area, transformation products unique to nanomaterials, and potential ecological impacts through novel exposure pathways. Research groups have proposed various nano-specific characterization factors for incorporating these considerations into standardized LCA methodologies, though consensus approaches remain under development.

Release Scenarios and Exposure Pathways

Understanding release scenarios represents a critical component of nanomaterial lifecycle assessment. Engineered nanomaterials may be released during various lifecycle stages, with distinctly different implications for exposure and risk. Manufacturing releases typically occur in controlled industrial environments where engineering controls and occupational safety measures may limit exposure, though accidental releases remain concerning. Consumer use phases often involve uncontrolled releases through wear, weathering, or intentional application, creating diverse exposure scenarios for both humans and environmental systems. End-of-life releases during waste handling, incineration, or landfilling create additional pathways for nanomaterial introduction into the environment.

The physical form of released nanomaterials significantly influences their subsequent environmental behavior and biological interactions. Pristine nanomaterials—those maintaining their as-manufactured characteristics—are rarely released except during production accidents or spills. More commonly, nanomaterials enter environmental systems as weathered forms altered through use, as matrix-embedded particles within composite materials, or as transformation products resulting from environmental processes. These weathered and transformed nanomaterials often demonstrate substantially different behaviors compared to their pristine counterparts. For instance, nano-enabled coatings exposed to environmental weathering typically release complex fragments containing embedded nanomaterials rather than isolated particles, altering transport properties and bioavailability.

Exposure pathway analysis traces potential routes through which released nanomaterials may contact organisms or environmental compartments. Atmospheric pathways following aerosol release or generation during manufacturing or processing create potential inhalation exposures for workers and nearby populations. Water pathways from wastewater discharge or runoff from nano-enabled products create potential aquatic ecosystem exposures and may ultimately result in drinking water contamination. Soil pathways resulting from biosolid application, direct product use in agriculture, or product disposal create complex exposure scenarios for soil organisms, plants, and potentially humans through food chain transfer. Quantitative material flow analysis approaches have been developed to model these exposure pathways, incorporating transfer coefficients between environmental compartments and estimating resulting environmental concentrations.

Environmental and Economic Impact Metrics

Comprehensive assessment of nanomaterial impacts requires consideration of diverse environmental metrics beyond traditional toxicity endpoints. Resource depletion metrics evaluate raw material consumption throughout the nanomaterial lifecycle, with particular attention to critical or scarce materials often required for high-purity nanomaterial production. Energy intensity metrics quantify total energy requirements across lifecycle stages, typically indicating higher embodied energy for nanomaterials compared to conventional alternatives on a mass basis. Water usage metrics address both consumption volume and potential quality impacts, recognizing that nanomaterial production often requires ultrapure water with substantial associated processing requirements. Waste generation metrics examine both the volume and hazardous characteristics of waste streams generated throughout the nanomaterial lifecycle.

Climate impact assessment for nanomaterials presents a complex picture with competing considerations. While nanomaterial production typically demonstrates higher energy intensity and associated greenhouse gas emissions compared to conventional materials on a mass basis, performance enhancements may reduce overall material requirements and enable efficiency improvements in other systems. For instance, lifecycle assessments of carbon nanotube-reinforced composites for lightweight vehicle applications demonstrate that production phase emission increases are typically offset by use-phase fuel efficiency improvements. Similarly, nanomaterial-enhanced catalysts, solar cells, and batteries may contribute to climate change mitigation through efficiency improvements despite their initially higher embodied carbon.

Economic assessment methodologies complement environmental metrics by quantifying costs and benefits throughout the nanomaterial lifecycle. Cost-benefit analysis approaches incorporate both direct costs associated with nanomaterial production, use, and management and indirect costs, including potential environmental remediation or health impacts. These analyses increasingly incorporate concepts of externalized costs—those borne by society rather than producers or consumers—to develop more comprehensive perspectives on economic impacts. Social lifecycle assessment methodologies extend these considerations further by examining impacts on workers, communities, and broader society throughout the nanomaterial value chain, though standardized approaches for social impact assessment remain under development.

In recent years, nanomaterials (NMs) have found widespread use across multiple fields, including biomedicine and healthcare, the textile industry, environmental protection, agriculture, electronics, energy, and construction, as illustrated in Figure 11-2. The growing interest in nanotechnology stems from its potential to enable innovative applications through the use of high-performance materials. These materials offer substantial commercial benefits, enhanced energy storage and conversion capabilities, cost and energy efficiency, and a reduced environmental footprint.

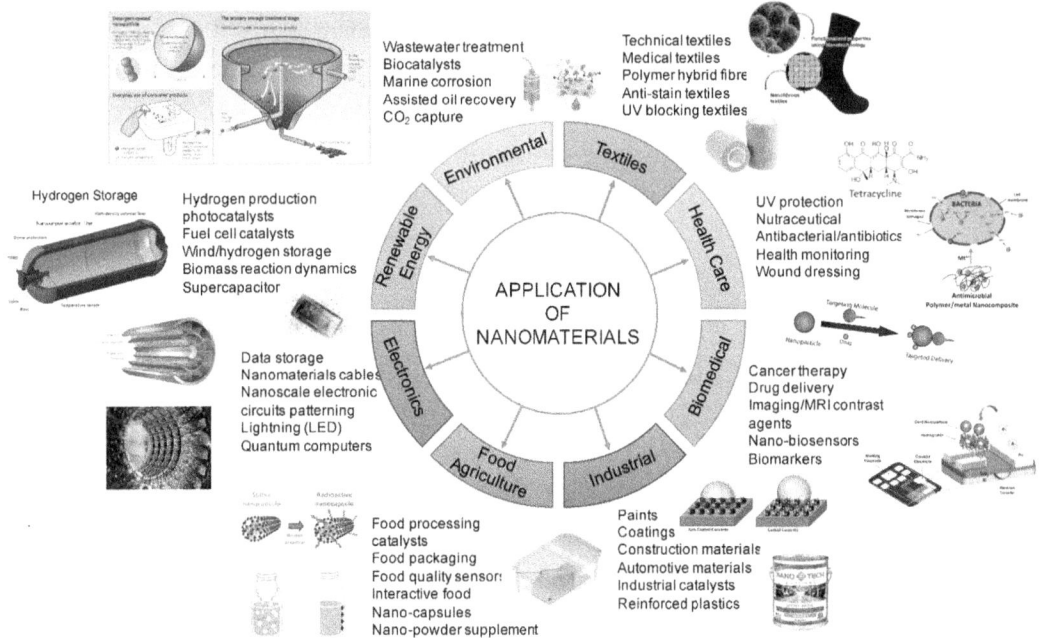

Figure 11-2. Lifecycle Stages and Potential Release Scenarios for Nano-Enabled Products

11.5 Containment Measures
Engineering Controls for Manufacturing Environments

Manufacturing environments represent critical points for potential nanomaterial release and worker exposure, necessitating comprehensive engineering control strategies tailored to nanomaterial-specific challenges. Hierarchical control approaches prioritize elimination and substitution where feasible, followed by engineering controls, administrative controls, and personal protective equipment as progressively less effective but necessary protection layers. For nanomaterial manufacturing, elimination or substitution options remain limited given the unique properties nanomaterials provide, emphasizing the importance of robust engineering controls as primary protection mechanisms.

Enclosure systems represent the first line of defense in nanomaterial manufacturing environments. Fully enclosed production systems utilizing continuous flow processes minimize potential release points compared to batch processing approaches. Gloveboxes with HEPA-filtered exhaust provide controlled environments for laboratory-scale nanomaterial handling, while automated handling systems reduce direct worker interaction with nanomaterials during production. Recent innovations in enclosure design include antistatic materials to prevent nanomaterial adhesion to surfaces and smooth interior surfaces to facilitate decontamination procedures. Integrity monitoring systems utilizing real-time particulate detection ensure enclosure effectiveness throughout operational cycles.

Local exhaust ventilation (LEV) systems designed specifically for nanomaterial control address scenarios where complete enclosure proves impractical. Conventional LEV designs require modification to effectively capture nanoscale particles, which demonstrate different aerodynamic behaviors compared to larger particles. Optimal capture velocities typically exceed those for conventional particles, while filter systems must incorporate high-efficiency filtration media rated for nanoscale particles. Computational fluid dynamics modeling increasingly guides LEV design to ensure effective capture across diverse nanomaterial handling scenarios. Performance verification through regular testing with nanoparticle tracers or surrogate materials ensures continued protection as processes evolve.

General ventilation systems complement local controls by providing dilution and removal of any nanomaterials that escape primary containment. These systems require careful design to prevent cross-contamination between different production zones and typically incorporate HEPA filtration before exhaust air release. Directional airflow strategies maintain negative pressure in nanomaterial handling areas relative to surrounding spaces, ensuring airflow from clean to potentially contaminated areas. Monitoring systems utilizing particle counters and air quality sensors provide real-time feedback on ventilation system performance, enabling rapid response to potential control failures.

Product Design for Minimized Release

Responsible nanomaterial incorporation into consumer and industrial products increasingly emphasizes design strategies to minimize unintentional release throughout the product lifecycle. These safer-by-design approaches consider potential release scenarios during normal use, weathering, and end-of-life handling, implementing design features that maintain nanomaterial functionality while reducing release potential. Such approaches represent a preventive strategy complementing exposure controls and waste management practices.

Matrix embedding represents a primary strategy for minimizing nanomaterial release from products. Incorporation methods significantly influence release potential, with strongly bonded or fully embedded nanomaterials demonstrating substantially reduced release compared to surface applications or weakly bound incorporation. Polymer nanocomposites, for instance, demonstrate varying release rates depending on the polymer type, nanomaterial functionalization to enhance polymer-nanomaterial interactions, and processing methods that influence dispersion quality. Research by Johnson et al. (2022) demonstrated that carbon nanotube release from epoxy composites decreased by over 90% when nanotubes were functionalized to create covalent bonds with the surrounding matrix compared to nonfunctionalized variants.

Surface treatments provide additional release mitigation options, particularly for nanomaterials necessarily applied to product surfaces for functionality. Topcoats or sealants can effectively reduce nanomaterial release while maintaining desired properties such as antimicrobial activity or self-cleaning functionality. For instance, transparent polymeric coatings over photocatalytic titanium dioxide surfaces maintain air purification functionality while reducing potential nanoparticle release during weathering or abrasion. Sacrificial layers represent another approach, wherein surface nanomaterials are designed to transform into benign products upon environmental exposure rather than releasing as intact nanomaterials.

End-of-life considerations in product design include features facilitating nanomaterial containment during recycling, disposal, or potential incineration. Identifiable components containing high nanomaterial concentrations enable targeted separation during recycling processes. Degradable matrices designed to retain nanomaterials during decomposition prevent release during composting or environmental exposure. Thermally stable matrices that retain nanomaterials during high-temperature processes reduce potential release during incineration. These design considerations increasingly factor into regulatory frameworks promoting extended producer responsibility for nanomaterial-containing products.

Waste Management Strategies

Nanomaterial-containing waste streams present unique management challenges requiring adapted handling, treatment, and disposal approaches. Classification frameworks for nanomaterial wastes continue to evolve, with most regulatory systems currently applying conventional hazardous waste criteria without nano-specific provisions. This approach potentially misclassifies certain nanomaterial wastes, as bulk material properties often poorly predict nanoscale behavior. Proactive industrial practices increasingly implement precautionary approaches, treating nanomaterial-containing wastes as potentially hazardous until specific evidence demonstrates otherwise.

Solid waste management for nanomaterial-containing products requires consideration of potential release during handling, processing, and ultimate disposal. Landfill disposal remains the predominant management approach for many consumer products containing nanomaterials. Research suggests that modern engineered landfills with proper liner systems and leachate collection effectively contain many nanomaterial types, though long-term performance remains under investigation. Incineration represents another common disposal route, with high-temperature waste-to-energy facilities (>850°C) effectively destroying many carbon-based nanomaterials and transforming metal-based nanomaterials into larger aggregates or oxides. However, potential nanomaterial effects on combustion processes and interactions with pollution control systems require continued investigation to ensure system effectiveness.

Liquid waste streams containing nanomaterials present different management challenges, particularly for industrial process waters and laboratory effluents with potentially significant nanomaterial concentrations. Conventional wastewater treatment processes demonstrate varying effectiveness for nanomaterial removal. Primary settling effectively removes larger nanomaterial aggregates but fails to capture well-dispersed materials. Biological treatment systems may remove certain nanomaterial types through biosorption or agglomeration mechanisms but may also experience inhibition at higher nanomaterial concentrations. Advanced treatment processes, including membrane filtration and advanced oxidation, show greater promise for nanomaterial removal but entail higher energy and resource requirements. Specialized approaches for industrial settings include precipitation techniques using specifically selected coagulants and flocculants optimized for nanomaterial physicochemical properties (Table 11-3).

Table 11-3. *Effectiveness of Treatment Technologies for Nanomaterial Removal from Wastewater*

Treatment Technology	Removal Efficiency (%)	Influencing Factors	Limitations and Considerations
Conventional coagulation/flocculation	60–95	Nanomaterial surface charge, coagulant type, pH	Requires optimization for specific nanomaterials; may produce large volumes of sludge requiring further treatment
Membrane filtration (ultrafiltration)	70–99	Membrane pore size, nanomaterial size, surface interactions	Membrane fouling; high energy consumption; not effective for very small nanomaterials
Membrane filtration (nanofiltration)	90–99.9	Membrane characteristics, solution chemistry	Higher cost; significant pressure requirements; concentrate stream requires management
Advanced oxidation processes	50–95 (for carbon nanomaterials)	Nanomaterial composition, oxidant type, contact time	Limited effectiveness for metal-based nanomaterials; formation of transformation products with unknown toxicity
Biological treatment	30–80	Nanomaterial type, microbial community, retention time	Potential inhibition of microbial activity; inconsistent removal across nanomaterial types; potential bioaccumulation
Activated carbon adsorption	75–99	Surface area, nanomaterial surface chemistry, competition with other compounds	High cost; regeneration or disposal challenges; capacity limitations

11.6 AI and IoT for Monitoring

Sensor Technologies for Nanomaterial Detection

The effective monitoring of engineered nanomaterials in environmental and biological systems requires sophisticated sensor technologies capable of detecting, quantifying, and characterizing nanoscale materials in complex matrices. Recent advances in sensor development have produced increasingly sensitive and selective detection systems, though significant challenges remain in distinguishing engineered nanomaterials from naturally occurring nanoscale materials and background particulates. The integration of these sensors with artificial intelligence and Internet of Things architectures creates powerful new capabilities for nanomaterial monitoring across diverse scenarios.

Optical sensing approaches offer nondestructive detection methods particularly suitable for continuous monitoring applications. Surface plasmon resonance (SPR) sensors utilize the unique optical properties of certain nanomaterials, particularly noble metals, to detect nanomaterial presence and concentration through refractive index changes at sensing surfaces. These systems demonstrate extraordinary sensitivity, capable of detecting sub-nanogram quantities of target nanomaterials in ideal conditions. Advanced SPR configurations incorporating specific recognition elements such as antibodies or aptamers enhance selectivity for target nanomaterials. Raman spectroscopy, particularly surface-enhanced Raman spectroscopy (SERS), provides complementary capabilities for nanomaterial characterization based on unique vibrational signatures. SERS-active substrates incorporating gold or silver nanostructures enhance sensitivity by factors of 10^6-10^8, enabling detection of trace nanomaterial concentrations.

Electrochemical detection systems offer robust approaches for field-deployable nanomaterial monitoring, combining sensitivity with relative simplicity compared to many optical techniques. These systems typically utilize nanomaterial-specific electrochemical properties, such as characteristic redox potentials or unique electron transfer behaviors, for detection and quantification. Metal-based nanomaterials frequently demonstrate particularly suitable properties for electrochemical detection through direct oxidation or reduction processes. Carbon-based nanomaterials such as graphene and carbon nanotubes increasingly serve dual roles as both detection targets and sensing elements, with their exceptional conductivity and high surface area enhancing sensor performance. Recent developments in screen-printed electrodes and microelectrode arrays enable miniaturized systems suitable for distributed environmental monitoring networks.

Mass-based detection approaches, including quartz crystal microbalance (QCM) sensors, provide label-free nanomaterial detection based on frequency shifts resulting from mass loading at sensor surfaces. These systems demonstrate particular utility for continuous monitoring applications where real-time data is required. Sensitivity enhancements through surface functionalization with specific recognition elements enable detection of target nanomaterials in complex environmental matrices. Micro- and nano-electromechanical systems (MEMS/NEMS) represent emerging platforms offering extraordinary mass sensitivity through the use of microscale cantilevers or resonators whose oscillation characteristics change upon nanomaterial binding. These systems demonstrate theoretical detection limits approaching single nanoparticle resolution in controlled environments, though practical implementation in complex matrices remains challenging.

Integration with Artificial Intelligence Systems

The integration of nanomaterial sensors with artificial intelligence systems addresses several fundamental challenges in environmental and biological monitoring, including data interpretation, pattern recognition across complex datasets, and adaptive monitoring strategies. Machine learning approaches increasingly facilitate nanomaterial identification and characterization in complex matrices where conventional analytical approaches struggle to distinguish engineered materials from natural background. These systems typically employ supervised learning algorithms trained on reference datasets containing known nanomaterial signatures across multiple sensing modalities.

Deep learning neural networks demonstrate particular promise for nanomaterial monitoring applications due to their ability to identify subtle patterns in multidimensional data. Convolutional neural networks effectively process spectroscopic and imaging data, identifying characteristic nanomaterial signatures even against variable backgrounds. Recurrent neural networks process temporal patterns in monitoring data, identifying transient nanomaterial release events that might otherwise go undetected. Transfer learning approaches enable adaptation of pre-trained networks to new nanomaterial types or monitoring scenarios with minimal additional training data, addressing the practical challenge of limited reference datasets for many nanomaterial variants.

Hybrid sensing systems combining multiple detection modalities with AI-driven data fusion algorithms provide enhanced reliability compared to single-sensor approaches. These systems integrate complementary data streams—such as optical, electrochemical, and mass-based measurements—to generate comprehensive nanomaterial characterization with reduced false positives and negatives. Bayesian networks and other probabilistic frameworks effectively combine these diverse data sources while explicitly accounting for varying reliability across sensing modalities. Adaptive weighting algorithms continuously optimize the contribution of each sensor based on environmental conditions and performance metrics, maintaining system reliability across diverse monitoring scenarios.

AI-driven predictive capabilities extend beyond immediate detection to forecast potential nanomaterial transport and transformation. These systems incorporate real-time monitoring data into spatiotemporal models, predicting nanomaterial fate based on current environmental conditions and historical patterns. For instance, systems monitoring nanomaterial concentrations in wastewater treatment plants can predict downstream concentrations in receiving waters based on treatment efficiency patterns, flow conditions, and nanomaterial properties. These predictive capabilities enable proactive management responses to potential exposure scenarios before they fully develop.

Real-Time Monitoring Networks

Internet of Things (IoT) architectures provide the connectivity, scalability, and distributed intelligence necessary for comprehensive nanomaterial monitoring across diverse environments. These systems typically comprise multiple tiers, beginning with edge devices incorporating nanomaterial sensors and basic processing capabilities. These devices connect to local gateways, providing additional computation resources and communication capabilities, which in turn connect to cloud platforms offering advanced analytics, data storage, and visualization tools. This hierarchical architecture balances power and bandwidth constraints at the edge with the need for sophisticated analysis capabilities, enabling deployment in remote or resource-constrained environments.

Environmental monitoring networks for nanomaterials increasingly incorporate strategic sensor placement based on material flow analysis and exposure modeling. High-sensitivity sensors typically target potential release hotspots such as wastewater

CHAPTER 11 ENVIRONMENTAL AND HEALTH IMPACTS OF NANOMATERIALS

treatment plant outfalls, urban stormwater systems, and industrial emission sources. Lower-cost sensors with reduced sensitivity but greater robustness deploy across broader areas to provide spatial coverage and identify unexpected release sources. Adaptive sensing strategies dynamically adjust sampling frequencies and analytical parameters based on detection events, allocating system resources efficiently while ensuring comprehensive characterization of potential release scenarios. For instance, baseline monitoring might employ low-frequency sampling with limited analytical parameters, automatically switching to high-frequency comprehensive analysis when trigger conditions indicate potential nanomaterial presence.

Occupational monitoring systems implement similar architectures in workplace environments where nanomaterial exposure risks exist. Wearable sensors provide individual-level exposure monitoring, collecting data on potential nanomaterial inhalation or dermal contact throughout work shifts. Fixed monitoring stations throughout facilities provide complementary data on spatial and temporal exposure patterns. These systems typically incorporate contextual sensors tracking worker activities, ventilation system operation, and other factors influencing exposure scenarios. Integration with building management systems enables automated responses to detection events, such as increasing ventilation rates or activating additional filtration systems when elevated nanomaterial concentrations occur (Figure 11-3).

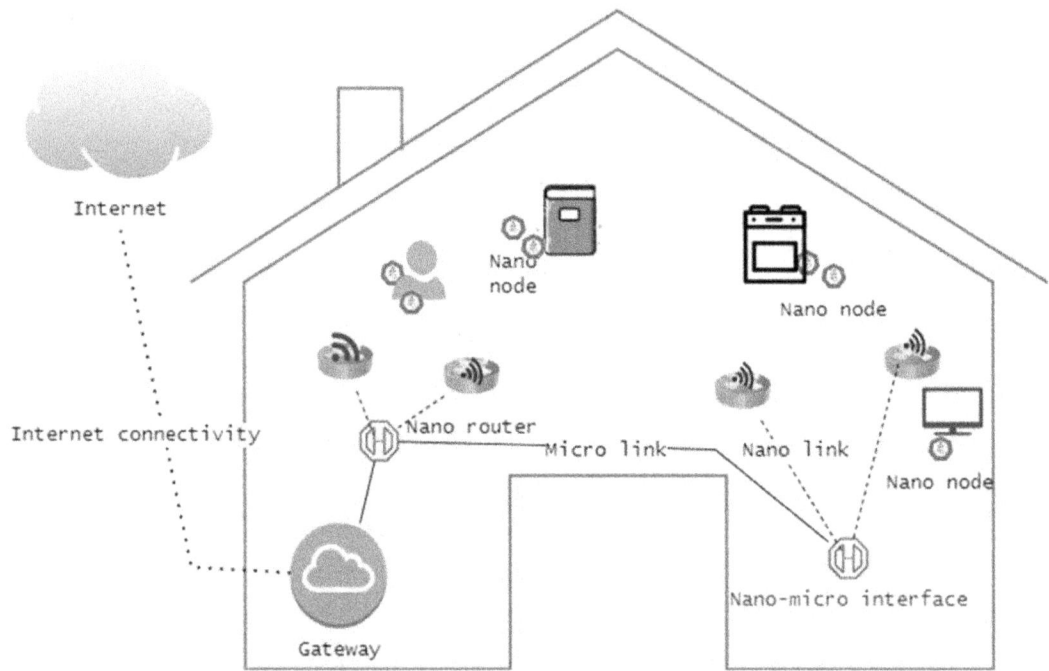

Figure 11-3. *Integrated IoT-AI Architecture for Nanomaterial Monitoring*

Hierarchical diagram showing a comprehensive system for nanomaterial monitoring. The bottom layer depicts various sensors (optical, electrochemical, and mass-based) connecting to edge computing devices. The middle layer shows data aggregation through IoT gateways. The top layer illustrates cloud-based AI analytics, with visualization interfaces showing dashboards, alerts, and predictive models. Bidirectional information flow is indicated by arrows connecting all system components.

The development of standardized communication protocols and data formats represents a critical enabler for comprehensive monitoring networks spanning multiple organizations and environments. The diversity of nanomaterial monitoring devices and analytical approaches currently creates significant data integration challenges, limiting system interoperability. Emerging standards, including the nanosensor data interchange format (NDIF), address these challenges by providing consistent schemas for representing nanomaterial detection events, sensor metadata, and quality assurance parameters. Open-source implementation tools, including software libraries and reference validation systems, facilitate adoption across diverse monitoring platforms. These standardization efforts support broader data sharing initiatives, enabling researchers and regulatory agencies to aggregate monitoring data across multiple studies and jurisdictions for comprehensive exposure assessment.

Practical Applications and Case Studies

The integration of advanced sensor technologies with AI and IoT architectures has enabled practical nanomaterial monitoring applications across diverse scenarios. In urban water management, distributed sensor networks monitoring titanium dioxide and silver nanoparticles provide insights into release patterns from consumer products and architectural materials. A notable implementation in Singapore combines in-stream monitoring stations with automated sampling systems triggered by detection events, enabling detailed characterization of nanomaterial pulses following rainfall events. The system demonstrated that nanosilver concentrations in urban runoff correlated strongly with both rainfall intensity and antecedent dry periods, suggesting weathering and accumulation mechanisms from architectural and automotive applications.

Industrial hygiene applications represent another active implementation area, particularly in nanomaterial manufacturing facilities. A case study from a carbon nanotube production facility in Germany demonstrated the effectiveness of an integrated monitoring approach combining wearable personal sensors with facility-wide fixed monitoring stations. The system identified previously unrecognized exposure pathways during specific maintenance activities, enabling targeted control measures that reduced worker exposures by approximately 80%. Machine learning algorithms analyzing temporal patterns in detection data successfully identified process deviations correlated with increased release events, enabling preventive maintenance before significant exposures occurred.

Environmental remediation projects increasingly incorporate real-time nanomaterial monitoring to assess both effectiveness and potential secondary impacts. A remediation project utilizing iron nanoparticles for groundwater contaminant treatment implemented a comprehensive monitoring network to track nanoparticle transport and transformation throughout the treatment zone. The system combined electrochemical sensors specifically calibrated for nanoscale zero-valent iron with conventional groundwater monitoring parameters. AI-driven data analysis identified complex relationships between groundwater chemistry, flow conditions, and nanoparticle transport behavior that would have been difficult to discern through conventional analysis approaches. These insights enabled optimization of injection protocols to maximize treatment effectiveness while minimizing nanoparticle transport beyond the intended treatment zone.

Consumer product safety monitoring represents an emerging application area, with several regulatory agencies implementing targeted monitoring programs for products with high nanomaterial release potential. A pilot program monitoring nanosilver release from textiles in commercial laundry facilities demonstrated significant variability in release patterns based on product age, washing conditions, and initial incorporation methods. The monitoring network incorporated both wastewater sampling systems and airborne particle detection during drying operations, providing comprehensive exposure scenario characterization. The resulting dataset supported the development of predictive models estimating cumulative environmental loading based on market penetration data and consumer usage patterns, informing proportionate regulatory approaches.

11.7 Summary

The environmental and health implications of nanotechnology present a complex landscape requiring balanced consideration of potential benefits and risks. As engineered nanomaterials become increasingly integrated into consumer products, industrial processes, and environmental applications, understanding their environmental fate and biological interactions becomes critical for ensuring sustainable development of this transformative technology. The unique physicochemical properties that make nanomaterials valuable for numerous applications—including their size, surface characteristics, and quantum effects—also create novel challenges for traditional risk assessment and management approaches.

The environmental fate of nanomaterials follows complex pathways influenced by particle characteristics, environmental conditions, and transformation processes. Transport mechanisms vary substantially across environmental media, with aggregation, dissolution, and interactions with natural organic matter significantly influencing nanomaterial persistence and bioavailability. These behaviors cannot be reliably predicted from bulk material properties, necessitating nanomaterial-specific approaches to environmental assessment. As research advances, modeling capabilities continue to improve, enabling better prediction of nanomaterial distribution and transformation across environmental compartments.

The toxicological principles governing nanomaterial interactions with biological systems similarly require specialized consideration beyond conventional approaches. Size-dependent properties, surface characteristics, and unique uptake mechanisms create distinct toxicity profiles compared to bulk materials of identical composition. Advanced in vitro models incorporating three-dimensional architectures and multiple cell types increasingly bridge the gap between traditional cell culture systems and in vivo complexity, providing more reliable predictions of biological responses. These models, combined with computational approaches and adverse outcome pathway frameworks, support efficient prioritization of nanomaterials requiring comprehensive safety assessment.

Lifecycle approaches provide essential perspectives by considering potential impacts throughout nanomaterial production, use, and disposal. These assessments identify opportunities for intervention at critical lifecycle stages to mitigate potential risks while preserving beneficial applications. Engineering controls in manufacturing environments, safer-by-design approaches in product development, and adapted waste management strategies collectively minimize potential nanomaterial releases and exposures. These preventive approaches complement monitoring systems that provide early warning of potential exposure scenarios.

The integration of artificial intelligence and Internet of Things technologies with advanced nanomaterial sensors creates powerful new capabilities for monitoring engineered nanomaterials across diverse environments. These systems provide unprecedented insights into nanomaterial release, transport, and transformation under real-world conditions, validating model predictions and identifying unexpected behaviors requiring further investigation. As these monitoring capabilities continue to advance, they provide critical feedback to refine risk assessment methodologies and management approaches.

Moving forward, balancing innovation with precaution remains essential for responsible nanotechnology development. Risk governance frameworks incorporating multiple stakeholder perspectives, adaptive management approaches responding to emerging information, and transparent communication regarding both benefits and potential concerns provide foundations for sustainable advancement. With continued research addressing critical knowledge gaps and thoughtful application of the precautionary principle where uncertainty remains, nanotechnology offers tremendous potential for addressing global challenges while maintaining environmental and public health protection.

CHAPTER 12

Ecotoxicology and Lifecycle Assessment

This chapter examines the critical intersection of nanotechnology with environmental concerns through the lens of ecotoxicology and lifecycle assessment. Beginning with foundational concepts in nanoecotoxicology, the chapter progresses through testing methodologies and standardized assays essential for evaluating nanomaterial impacts. Environmental interactions across different ecosystems are analyzed, followed by an exploration of lifecycle assessment methods for nanomaterials. The regulatory landscape governing nanomaterial safety is reviewed comprehensively, including international frameworks and compliance challenges. Finally, the chapter examines how artificial intelligence and Internet of Things technologies are revolutionizing ecotoxicological monitoring and assessment, enabling more sophisticated predictive modeling and real-time environmental surveillance. Throughout, the chapter emphasizes the imperative of balancing nanotechnological innovation with environmental stewardship to ensure sustainable development.

12.1 Introduction to Ecotoxicology

As nanotechnology continues to revolutionize multiple sectors, including medicine, electronics, energy, and environmental remediation, the widespread deployment of engineered nanomaterials (ENMs) into the environment raises significant concerns regarding their potential ecological impacts. Nanoecotoxicology, a relatively new subdiscipline, investigates the interactions between engineered nanomaterials and various ecosystems, with particular emphasis on their transport, transformation, persistence, bioaccumulation, and toxicity to organisms across trophic levels.

CHAPTER 12 ECOTOXICOLOGY AND LIFECYCLE ASSESSMENT

The unique properties that make nanomaterials valuable in technological applications—including their high surface area-to-volume ratio, enhanced reactivity, and novel optical, electrical, and magnetic characteristics—simultaneously contribute to their distinct environmental behavior and potential toxicity. These properties can significantly diverge from those of their bulk material counterparts, necessitating specialized approaches to toxicity assessment. For instance, carbon in its bulk form is generally considered biologically inert, whereas carbon nanotubes have demonstrated toxicity in various aquatic and terrestrial organisms due to their needle-like structure and ability to penetrate cell membranes.

Historically, environmental toxicology has focused primarily on conventional pollutants such as heavy metals, pesticides, and persistent organic compounds. However, the emergence of nanotechnology has necessitated a paradigm shift in ecotoxicological frameworks. Traditional dose–response relationships based solely on mass concentration often prove inadequate for nanomaterials, where factors such as particle size, shape, surface charge, agglomeration state, and surface functionalization can dramatically influence toxicity profiles. This complexity has spurred the development of nano-specific metrics, including particle number concentration, surface area, and surface reactivity, which frequently correlate more robustly with biological effects than mass concentration alone.

Furthermore, the environmental fate of nanomaterials introduces additional layers of complexity. Once released into the environment, ENMs may undergo transformations including agglomeration, dissolution, redox reactions, and interactions with natural organic matter or biological surfaces. These transformations can significantly alter their bioavailability and toxicity. For example, silver nanoparticles widely used in consumer products for their antimicrobial properties may dissolve to release ionic silver, form complexes with sulfide or chloride ions, or become coated with proteins and natural organic matter—each scenario resulting in distinct toxicological profiles.

The field of nanoecotoxicology must grapple with numerous challenges, including the development of standardized testing protocols, the establishment of appropriate dose metrics, the selection of relevant test organisms and endpoints, and the extrapolation of laboratory results to complex ecological systems. Moreover, the diversity of engineered nanomaterials—spanning metallic, carbon-based, polymeric, ceramic, and composite structures—necessitates material-specific approaches rather than one-size-fits-all testing strategies (Table 12-1).

Table 12-1. Major Classes of Engineered Nanomaterials and Their Potential Ecological Concerns

Nanomaterial Class	Examples	Primary Applications	Key Ecotoxicological Concerns
Metallic	Silver, gold, iron, titanium dioxide	Antimicrobials, catalysts, electronics, remediation	Dissolution releasing toxic ions, ROS generation, antimicrobial effects disrupting microbial communities
Carbon-based	Carbon nanotubes, fullerenes, graphene	Electronics, composites, energy storage	Persistent, potential physical damage to organisms, surface adsorption of contaminants
Polymeric	Dendrimers, micelles, nanospheres	Drug delivery, coatings, tissue engineering	Biodegradation products, carrier effects for other pollutants
Quantum dots	CdSe, ZnS, PbS	Imaging, displays, photovoltaics	Heavy metal leaching, photoreactivity generating ROS
Composite	Core-shell structures, functionalized particles	Multifunctional applications	Complex interactions, difficult to predict based on individual components

As the commercialization of nanotechnology accelerates, the imperative for comprehensive ecotoxicological assessment becomes increasingly urgent. The precautionary principle suggests that potential environmental risks should be thoroughly evaluated before widespread deployment, while pragmatic approaches must balance innovation with responsible environmental stewardship. This introduction sets the stage for exploring the testing models, environmental interactions, lifecycle considerations, and regulatory frameworks that collectively aim to ensure the sustainable development of nanotechnology.

12.2 Testing Models and Assays

The accurate assessment of nanomaterial ecotoxicity demands specialized testing approaches that account for their unique properties and behaviors. This section explores the current state of ecotoxicological testing for nanomaterials, including standardized assays, emerging methodologies, and persistent challenges in test design and interpretation.

Standardized Testing Frameworks

Several international organizations have developed guidelines for nanomaterial testing, including the Organization for Economic Cooperation and Development (OECD), the International Organization for Standardization (ISO), and various national environmental protection agencies. The OECD Working Party on Manufactured Nanomaterials (WPMN) has been particularly instrumental in adapting existing toxicity test guidelines and developing new protocols specific to nanomaterials. These guidelines typically cover characterization requirements, sample preparation procedures, exposure methodologies, and endpoint measurements.

Standard ecotoxicity tests employed for nanomaterials span multiple trophic levels and ecosystems:

Aquatic Systems:

- Algal growth inhibition tests (OECD Test No. 201)
- Daphnia acute immobilization and reproduction tests (OECD Test Nos. 202, 211)
- Fish acute toxicity and early life stage tests (OECD Test Nos. 203, 210)
- Sediment-dwelling organism tests (OECD Test Nos. 218, 225)

Terrestrial Systems:

- Soil microorganism tests (carbon and nitrogen transformation) (OECD Test No. 216)
- Earthworm acute and reproduction tests (OECD Test Nos. 207, 222)
- Terrestrial plant growth tests (OECD Test No. 208)
- Collembola reproduction test (OECD Test No. 232)

These standardized tests provide valuable data regarding acute and chronic toxicity, but their application to nanomaterials requires careful consideration of several nano-specific challenges.

Challenges in Nanomaterial Testing

The testing of nanomaterials presents distinct challenges that must be addressed to ensure reliable and reproducible results:

Characterization Requirements: Unlike conventional chemicals, nanomaterials require extensive physicochemical characterization. Parameters, including size distribution, shape, surface charge, aggregation state, dissolution rate, and surface chemistry, must be determined both in the stock suspension and in the test medium. These characteristics can dramatically influence bioavailability and toxicity, yet they may change dynamically during the test duration—a phenomenon known as the "dynamic nature" of nanomaterials.

Dose Metrics: Mass concentration, the traditional dose metric for chemical toxicity, may inadequately represent nanomaterial exposure. Alternative metrics such as particle number concentration, surface area, or reactive surface area often correlate better with biological effects. Consequently, many researchers advocate for reporting multiple dose metrics to facilitate cross-study comparisons and mechanistic understanding.

Dispersion Protocols: Achieving stable, reproducible nanomaterial dispersions for testing constitutes a major challenge. Methods for dispersion—including sonication, stirring, or the use of dispersants—can significantly influence particle size distribution and surface properties. While dispersants may enhance stability, they can introduce confounding variables by altering surface chemistry or exerting toxicity themselves. International efforts have aimed to standardize dispersion protocols, but material-specific approaches are often necessary.

Interference with Assay Systems: Nanomaterials can interfere with traditional toxicity assays through various mechanisms, including light absorption or scattering (affecting spectrophotometric readings), adsorption of assay reagents, catalytic effects on indicator reactions, or fluorescence quenching. These interferences necessitate thorough control experiments and potentially modified testing procedures.

Emerging Testing Approaches

Recognition of these challenges has spurred the development of novel testing strategies that better accommodate nanomaterial properties:

High-Throughput Screening: Given the diversity of nanomaterials and their potential modifications, traditional testing approaches are often too resource-intensive for comprehensive coverage. High-throughput screening methods using microplate formats, automated imaging systems, and multiplexed assays enable rapid preliminary assessment of toxicity across multiple nanomaterials, concentrations, and endpoints.

Omics Technologies: Transcriptomics, proteomics, and metabolomics approaches provide comprehensive insights into molecular responses to nanomaterial exposure. These technologies can identify altered pathways, potential biomarkers of exposure or effect, and mechanisms of toxicity that might be missed by traditional apical endpoints. For instance, whole-transcriptome analysis in zebrafish exposed to silver nanoparticles has revealed disruption of pathways involved in oxidative stress response, metal detoxification, and DNA repair—providing mechanistic understanding beyond mortality or growth inhibition.

Alternative Test Models: The development of alternative test models aims to reduce vertebrate testing while providing mechanistically relevant information. Cell-based assays, embryonic models (zebrafish embryo toxicity test), and invertebrate models (Caenorhabditis elegans) offer advantages including ethical considerations, reduced cost, higher throughput, and sometimes greater mechanistic insight. Three-dimensional cell culture models and organ-on-a-chip technologies further bridge the gap between simple in vitro systems and complex in vivo scenarios.

Adverse Outcome Pathways: The Adverse Outcome Pathway (AOP) framework links molecular initiating events through key events to adverse outcomes at the organism or population level. This approach has particular value for nanomaterials, where mechanisms of toxicity may include both chemical (e.g., dissolution, reactive oxygen species generation) and physical (e.g., membrane disruption, physical blockage) processes. Several nano-specific AOPs are under development, including pathways for respiratory and cardiovascular effects.

Tiered Testing Approaches

Given resource constraints and the multitude of nanomaterials requiring assessment, tiered testing strategies have emerged as pragmatic approaches. These typically involve

Tier 1: Basic characterization and in vitro screening assays to identify materials of potential concern

Tier 2: Targeted in vivo testing with standard test organisms to assess specific endpoints of concern

Tier 3: Advanced studies including mesocosm experiments, field studies, or specialized mechanistic investigations

This hierarchical approach enables efficient resource allocation while ensuring that materials of greatest concern receive appropriate scrutiny. Additionally, computational approaches, including (quantitative) structure-activity relationships ((Q)SARs) and read-across methodologies, are being developed to predict nanomaterial toxicity based on physicochemical properties, potentially reducing testing requirements.

While significant progress has been made in developing appropriate testing methodologies for nanomaterials, challenges remain in standardization, validation, and regulatory acceptance. The dynamic nature of nanomaterials in test systems continues to present difficulties for traditional testing paradigms, necessitating ongoing refinement of protocols and interpretative frameworks. Furthermore, the ecological relevance of laboratory tests requires careful consideration, particularly regarding environmentally realistic exposure scenarios, chronic low-dose effects, and population- or community-level impacts that may not be captured by standard testing approaches.

12.3 Environmental Interaction

The environmental behavior of engineered nanomaterials (ENMs) represents a critical determinant of their potential ecological impacts. This section explores how nanomaterials interact with environmental matrices, undergo transformations, and affect organisms within complex ecosystems.

Environmental Release and Transport

Nanomaterials enter the environment through multiple pathways, including

- Direct release during manufacturing, processing, transportation, or disposal
- Wear and degradation of nano-enabled products during use

CHAPTER 12   ECOTOXICOLOGY AND LIFECYCLE ASSESSMENT

- Intentional environmental applications (e.g., remediation, agricultural applications)
- Release from wastewater treatment plants receiving industrial or consumer waste
- Accidental spills or industrial incidents

Once released, the transport and distribution of nanomaterials are governed by various physicochemical processes, including

Aggregation and Agglomeration: In environmental media, nanomaterials frequently form larger clusters through aggregation (strong bonding) or agglomeration (weak association), significantly affecting their mobility and bioavailability. Factors influencing these processes include particle concentration, surface chemistry, ionic strength, pH, and natural organic matter concentration. For instance, increased ionic strength typically promotes aggregation by reducing electrostatic repulsion between particles, while natural organic matter can either stabilize or destabilize nanomaterials depending on its characteristics and concentration.

Deposition and Sedimentation: Nanomaterial movement through soil, sediment, or water columns is influenced by gravitational settling, interceptive filtration, and attachment to environmental surfaces. These processes depend on particle size, density, and surface properties, as well as the characteristics of the environmental matrix. Clay minerals, for example, can strongly adsorb positively charged nanomaterials through electrostatic attraction, limiting mobility in clayey soils.

Dissolution and Transformation: Many metal and metal oxide nanomaterials undergo dissolution, releasing ionic species that may exhibit distinct environmental behaviors and toxicity profiles. Solubility is influenced by particle size (with smaller particles generally dissolving more rapidly due to higher surface area), surface coatings, and environmental conditions, including pH, dissolved oxygen, and ligand concentration. Beyond dissolution, nanomaterials may undergo various transformations, including oxidation/reduction, sulfidation, phosphorylation, and biomolecular corona formation.

The complexity of these interrelated processes necessitates sophisticated analytical approaches for tracking nanomaterials in environmental matrices. Techniques including single-particle inductively coupled plasma mass spectrometry (sp-ICP-MS), field-flow fractionation, and various microscopy methods have been adapted for environmental detection, though significant challenges remain in distinguishing engineered nanomaterials from naturally occurring nanoparticles in complex environmental samples.

Ecosystem-Specific Behaviors and Impacts

Nanomaterial interactions and impacts vary substantially across different environmental compartments:

Aquatic Ecosystems: In freshwater and marine environments, nanomaterial behavior is strongly influenced by water chemistry, particularly ionic strength, pH, and dissolved organic matter concentration. Higher ionic strength in marine environments typically promotes more rapid aggregation of many nanomaterials, potentially reducing their bioavailability to pelagic organisms but increasing sedimentation and exposure to benthic species. Aquatic impacts span multiple trophic levels:

- Algae and phytoplankton may experience growth inhibition through mechanisms including membrane damage, photosynthetic interference, and oxidative stress

- Filter-feeding organisms like Daphnia frequently show elevated exposure due to their feeding mechanisms

- Fish may experience gill damage, oxidative stress, neurotoxicity, or reproductive impairment depending on nanomaterial composition and exposure conditions

Importantly, trophic transfer of nanomaterials has been documented in aquatic food webs, with potential for biomagnification of certain materials or their transformation products.

Terrestrial Ecosystems: In soil environments, nanomaterial mobility is influenced by soil texture, organic matter content, pH, and mineralogy. Clay-rich soils typically show greater retention of nanomaterials through various attachment mechanisms. Relevant ecological impacts include

- Alteration of soil microbial community composition and function, including potential disruption of nutrient cycling

- Effects on plant growth and development, ranging from toxicity to enhanced growth, depending on nanomaterial type and concentration

- Impacts on soil invertebrates, including earthworms and nematodes, through dermal contact, ingestion, or changes in habitat quality

CHAPTER 12   ECOTOXICOLOGY AND LIFECYCLE ASSESSMENT

Agricultural applications of nanomaterials, including nano-enabled fertilizers and pesticides, introduce both potential benefits and ecological concerns requiring careful assessment.

Atmospheric Transport: Airborne nanomaterials undergo complex atmospheric chemistry, including agglomeration, deposition, and reactions with atmospheric components. While atmospheric residence times vary widely, deposition processes eventually transfer airborne nanomaterials to terrestrial or aquatic systems, representing an important transport mechanism between environmental compartments.

Bioavailability and Bioaccumulation

The bioavailability of nanomaterials—their accessibility to organisms for potential uptake and biological effects—depends on numerous factors, including their physical state (free, aggregated, or attached to environmental constituents), chemical properties, and biological factors including organism feeding strategies and habitat preferences.

Bioaccumulation, the net accumulation of a substance in an organism resulting from uptake from all environmental sources, has been documented for various nanomaterials. Several patterns emerge from current research:

- Smaller nanomaterials generally show greater potential for cellular uptake and translocation within organisms.

- Surface functionalization significantly influences uptake mechanisms and efficiency.

- Trophic transfer occurs in various food webs, though biomagnification (increasing concentration at higher trophic levels) appears less common than for certain conventional contaminants.

- Persistence within organisms varies widely, with some materials showing rapid elimination while others demonstrate surprising retention in specific tissues.

Table 12-2 outlines the key factors that influence nanomaterial bioavailability across different environmental compartments and the relevant environmental processes involved.

Table 12-2. Factors Influencing Nanomaterial Bioavailability in Different Environmental Compartments

Environmental Compartment	Key Factors Affecting Bioavailability	Relevant Processes
Freshwater	Water hardness, dissolved organic matter, pH	Aggregation, dissolution, surface modification
Marine water	High ionic strength, organic matter	Enhanced aggregation and sedimentation
Sediment	Organic content, redox conditions, bioturbation	Partitioning between pore water and solid phase
Soil	Clay content, organic matter, pH, ion exchange capacity	Attachment to soil particles, filtration effects
Air	Particle size, aggregation state, humidity	Respiratory deposition, mucociliary clearance

Ecological Risk Assessment Considerations

The complex environmental behaviors of nanomaterials present several challenges for ecological risk assessment:

Exposure Assessment: Predicting environmental concentrations remains difficult due to limited monitoring data, analytical challenges, and complex fate processes. Models must account for nanomaterial-specific processes, including aggregation, dissolution, and surface transformations, rather than relying solely on conventional partition coefficients.

Dose–Response Assessment: Traditional dose–response relationships based on mass concentration may inadequately describe nanomaterial effects. Multiple dose metrics, dynamic exposure characterization, and consideration of both particle and dissolved species (for soluble nanomaterials) are frequently necessary for accurate hazard characterization.

Mixture Effects: Environmental exposures typically involve multiple nanomaterials alongside conventional contaminants. Potential interactions include altered bioavailability, synergistic or antagonistic toxicity, or nanomaterial-facilitated transport of co-contaminants—a phenomenon known as the "Trojan horse effect."

Chronic and Sublethal Effects: While acute toxicity data are increasingly available, knowledge regarding chronic, sublethal, or transgenerational effects remains limited. Such effects, including reproductive impairment, behavioral changes, or ecosystem function disruption, may prove more ecologically relevant than acute toxicity.

Community and Ecosystem Effects: Extrapolation from individual-level responses to community or ecosystem impacts represents a persistent challenge. Emerging approaches, including mesocosm studies, ecosystem modeling, and functional endpoints (e.g., respiration, nutrient cycling), aim to bridge this gap.

Analytical Challenges and Solutions

Tracking nanomaterials in complex environmental matrices presents substantial analytical challenges, necessitating sophisticated techniques:

Imaging Techniques: Transmission electron microscopy (TEM), scanning electron microscopy (SEM), and atomic force microscopy (AFM) provide detailed information on nanomaterial morphology but require careful sample preparation and may suffer from limited representativeness due to small sample volumes.

Spectroscopic Methods: Techniques including X-ray absorption spectroscopy, Raman spectroscopy, and various mass spectrometry approaches enable characterization of nanomaterial composition, oxidation state, and surface chemistry in environmental samples.

Separation Techniques: Field-flow fractionation, hydrodynamic chromatography, and related methods enable size-based separation of nanomaterials from environmental matrices prior to detection.

Single-Particle Analysis: Single-particle ICP-MS has emerged as a powerful technique for detecting and characterizing metal-based nanomaterials in environmental samples, providing information on particle number concentration, size distribution, and dissolution.

Despite these advances, distinguishing engineered nanomaterials from naturally occurring nanoparticles and background elements remains challenging. Labeling approaches, including isotopic, fluorescent, or rare element doping, can facilitate tracking in experimental systems but typically cannot address environmental monitoring of commercially relevant materials.

The environmental interaction of nanomaterials thus represents a complex, multifaceted area requiring interdisciplinary approaches spanning analytical chemistry, environmental science, and ecotoxicology. Understanding these interactions constitutes a prerequisite for meaningful risk assessment and ultimately for the sustainable development of nanotechnology.

12.4 Lifecycle Methods

Lifecycle assessment (LCA) provides a systematic framework for evaluating the environmental implications of nanomaterials and nano-enabled products throughout their entire lifecycle—from raw material extraction through manufacturing, use, and end-of-life disposal or recycling. This section explores methodological approaches, challenges, and emerging solutions in nanomaterial LCA.

Fundamentals of Lifecycle Assessment for Nanomaterials

LCA follows a structured methodology comprising four main phases in accordance with ISO 14040 and 14044 standards:

1. **Goal and Scope Definition**: Establishing the assessment objectives, system boundaries, functional unit, and impact categories. For nanomaterials, defining appropriate functional units presents a particular challenge, as performance may not scale linearly with mass.

2. **Lifecycle Inventory (LCI)**: Compiling comprehensive data on resource inputs and environmental outputs across the defined system. For nanomaterials, this includes specialized production processes, purification steps, and potential release scenarios during use and disposal.

3. **Lifecycle Impact Assessment (LCIA)**: Translating inventory data into potential environmental impacts across categories including climate change, resource depletion, ecotoxicity, human toxicity, and others.

4. **Interpretation**: Analyzing results to identify significant issues, evaluate completeness and consistency, and draw conclusions that inform decision-making.

When applied to nanomaterials, this framework encounters several unique challenges requiring methodological adaptations and considerations.

Challenges in Nanomaterial LCA

Data Limitations: The nascent and often proprietary nature of nanomaterial production processes creates significant data gaps in lifecycle inventories. Energy requirements, solvent use, purification processes, and yields may vary substantially between laboratory-scale and industrial production, complicating extrapolation. Furthermore, the rapid pace of technological development means that production methods evolve quickly, potentially rendering inventory data obsolete.

Functional Unit Definition: Defining appropriate functional units for nanomaterial LCA requires careful consideration of performance characteristics. For instance, comparing conventional and nano-enabled catalysts solely on a mass basis would disregard the enhanced catalytic efficiency that typically accompanies nanoscale dimensions. Performance-based functional units (e.g., surface area, catalytic conversion rate, or antibacterial efficacy) often provide more meaningful comparisons.

Release Quantification: Quantifying nanomaterial release during use and end-of-life phases presents substantial challenges due to limited empirical data, analytical difficulties in detecting releases from complex matrices, and the dynamic nature of nanomaterial transformations in products and the environment. Various modeling approaches and experimental methods, including accelerated aging tests, have been developed to address this gap, though significant uncertainties remain.

Environmental Fate Modeling: Conventional fate models developed for traditional chemicals often inadequately represent nanomaterial-specific processes, including aggregation, sedimentation, and surface transformations. Modified multimedia fate models incorporating these processes have emerged, though validation remains challenging due to limited field data.

Impact Assessment Methods: Current LCIA methods frequently lack characterization factors specific to nanomaterials, particularly for ecotoxicity and human toxicity impact categories. The development of nano-specific characterization factors is complicated by limited toxicity data, challenges in dose metrics, and uncertainties regarding environmental behavior.

Methodological Approaches and Adaptations

Several methodological approaches have emerged to address these challenges:

Cradle-to-Gate Assessments: Given data limitations for use and end-of-life phases, many nanomaterial LCAs focus on production phases (cradle-to-gate), providing valuable insights into manufacturing impacts while acknowledging the incompleteness of full lifecycle coverage.

Scenario Analysis: Multiple scenarios incorporating different assumptions about production efficiency, release rates, environmental fate, and toxicity can illustrate the range of potential outcomes given current uncertainties. This approach transparently communicates uncertainty while still providing actionable insights.

Proxy Data and Scaling Approaches: Where direct inventory data are unavailable, proxy data from similar processes or scaling relationships based on theoretical or empirical models can fill gaps. For instance, energy requirements for certain purification steps might be estimated based on thermodynamic principles or extrapolated from similar processes in other industries.

Hybrid LCA Approaches: Combining process-based LCA with input–output LCA can address truncation errors and system boundary limitations, particularly relevant for emerging technologies where supply chains may not be fully captured in process databases.

Parameterized Models: Developing parameterized LCA models that can be updated as new data become available enables more flexible assessment as technologies mature and processes evolve.

Uncertainty of LCA for Nanomaterials

Lifecycle Assessment (LCA) studies on nanomaterials (NMs) face several limitations due to various types of uncertainties. These uncertainties can be categorized in different ways but are commonly distinguished based on model structure, parameters, spatial and temporal factors, and the inherent nature of the uncertainty itself. Figure 12-1 illustrates the different types of identified uncertainties.

CHAPTER 12 ECOTOXICOLOGY AND LIFECYCLE ASSESSMENT

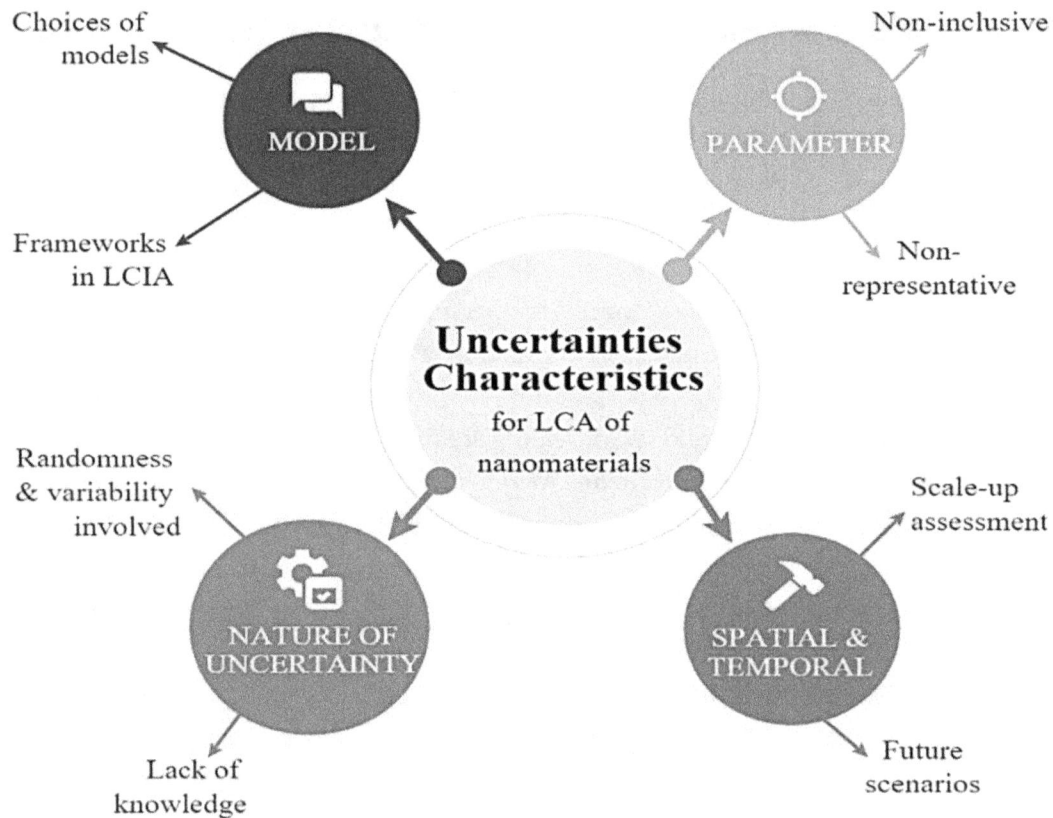

Figure 12-1. Lifecycle Assessment Framework for Nanomaterials with Key Challenges and Adaptations

Case Examples and Comparative Studies

Comparative LCA studies between conventional and nano-enabled products reveal several patterns:

Energy-Intensive Production vs. Use-Phase Benefits: Many nanomaterials exhibit energy-intensive production processes that may initially appear environmentally disadvantageous. However, use-phase benefits, including enhanced efficiency, reduced material consumption, or extended product lifetime, often offset these impacts. For example, carbon nanotube reinforcement in polymers may require energy-intensive production but can significantly extend product lifespan and reduce material consumption, yielding net environmental benefits.

CHAPTER 12   ECOTOXICOLOGY AND LIFECYCLE ASSESSMENT

Trade-offs Between Impact Categories: Nanomaterial applications frequently demonstrate trade-offs between impact categories. For instance, silver nanoparticles in textiles may reduce water and energy consumption associated with washing (beneficial for climate change and water consumption impacts) while potentially increasing ecotoxicity impacts through silver release during use and disposal.

Scale Dependence: The environmental performance of nanomaterial production often exhibits strong scale dependence. Laboratory-scale processes typically demonstrate substantially higher environmental impacts per functional unit compared to industrial production, emphasizing the importance of appropriate scaling in prospective assessments.

Table 12-3 presents comparative lifecycle assessment (LCA) results for selected nanomaterial applications, highlighting key environmental benefits, trade-offs, and areas of uncertainty.

Table 12-3. *Comparative LCA Results for Selected Nanomaterial Applications*

Application	Conventional Technology	Nano-Enabled Alternative	Key Environmental Benefits	Potential Trade-offs	Critical Uncertainties
Photovoltaics	Silicon solar cells	Quantum dot solar cells	Reduced material intensity, potentially lower energy payback time	Potential toxicity concerns from heavy metal content	Long-term stability, recycling feasibility
Catalysts	Traditional catalysts (e.g., platinum)	Nanocatalysts	Reduced precious metal use, higher efficiency, lower operating temperature	Energy-intensive production	Catalyst lifetime, regeneration requirements

(continued)

Table 12-3. (*continued*)

Application	Conventional Technology	Nano-Enabled Alternative	Key Environmental Benefits	Potential Trade-offs	Critical Uncertainties
Concrete	Standard concrete	CNT/graphene-reinforced concrete	Extended lifespan, reduced material use	Higher production impacts	Release during weathering, end-of-life management
Water treatment	Conventional filtration, chlorination	Nanomembrane filtration, photocatalytic disinfection	Reduced chemical use, higher removal efficiency	Membrane fouling, potential nanoparticle release	Long-term performance under field conditions

Integrating LCA with Risk Assessment

Recognizing the complementary nature of LCA and risk assessment, integrated approaches have emerged to provide more comprehensive environmental evaluation of nanomaterials:

Lifecycle Risk Assessment (LCRA): This approach integrates exposure and hazard assessment throughout the lifecycle, identifying stages with potentially significant risks. Unlike conventional risk assessment focusing on specific sites or scenarios, LCRA considers cumulative exposures across the value chain.

Risk-Based LCA: This methodology incorporates risk-based impact categories within the LCA framework, potentially using nano-specific characterization factors derived from risk assessment data. This integration helps address the limitation that conventional LCA impact categories may inadequately capture nanomaterial-specific concerns.

Multi-Criteria Decision Analysis: Given the various trade-offs and uncertainties in nanomaterial assessment, multi-criteria decision analysis frameworks can integrate LCA results with risk assessment, technical performance, economic considerations, and other relevant factors to support transparent decision-making.

The integration of these approaches enables more holistic sustainability assessment, helping to identify opportunities for risk reduction through process modification, product design, or lifecycle management strategies.

Future Directions in Nanomaterial LCA

Several developments promise to advance nanomaterial LCA methodology:

Standardization Efforts: Organizations, including the International Organization for Standardization (ISO) and the UNEP/SETAC Life Cycle Initiative, are working toward standardized approaches for nanomaterial LCA, potentially reducing methodological inconsistencies and facilitating comparability between studies.

Dynamic LCA Approaches: Dynamic LCA approaches capable of capturing technological evolution, changing production efficiencies, and temporal aspects of impacts may better represent the rapidly evolving nanomaterial landscape compared to static assessments.

Artificial Intelligence Applications: Machine learning approaches show promise for addressing data gaps through pattern recognition and prediction based on limited available data, potentially enabling more comprehensive inventory development and impact assessment despite current limitations.

High-Throughput Screening Integration: Data from high-throughput toxicity screening can potentially inform the development of nano-specific characterization factors for impact assessment, addressing a key methodological gap in current practice.

Lifecycle assessment of nanomaterials, despite its challenges, provides valuable insights for technology developers, regulators, and other stakeholders regarding environmental implications across the value chain. As methodologies mature and data availability improves, LCA will increasingly contribute to environmentally responsible innovation in nanotechnology.

12.5 Regulatory Overview

The regulatory landscape governing nanomaterial safety and environmental implications continues to evolve as scientific understanding advances and societal concerns regarding potential risks emerge. This section examines current regulatory frameworks, implementation challenges, and emerging approaches across major jurisdictions.

CHAPTER 12   ECOTOXICOLOGY AND LIFECYCLE ASSESSMENT

Current Regulatory Frameworks

Regulatory approaches to nanomaterials vary significantly across jurisdictions, reflecting different philosophical approaches to uncertainty and innovation.

European Union: The EU has adopted the most comprehensive regulatory approach to nanomaterials, implementing nano-specific provisions across multiple regulations, including

- **Registration, Evaluation, Authorization and Restriction of Chemicals (REACH) Regulation**: Following a 2018 amendment, REACH explicitly addresses nanomaterials through specific information requirements for registration dossiers. Registrants must provide detailed characterization data and tailored hazard assessment for nanomaterials, even when the bulk form has been previously registered.

- **Biocidal Products Regulation**: Explicitly requires separate assessment of nanomaterial forms of active substances, with specific data requirements and risk assessment considerations.

- **Cosmetics Regulation**: Mandates notification, labeling, and safety assessment for nanomaterials in cosmetic products, with the European Commission maintaining a public catalog of nanomaterials used in cosmetics.

- **Food regulations**: Various regulations, including the Novel Food Regulation, Food Additives Regulation, and Food Contact Materials Regulation, contain nano-specific provisions requiring authorization, labeling, and risk assessment.

The EU approach centers on a legally binding definition of nanomaterials (Commission Recommendation 2011/696/EU, revised in 2022), focusing on particle size distribution (approximately 50% or more of particles in the number size distribution have one or more external dimensions between 1 and 100 nm) rather than novel properties. This size-based definition has implications for regulatory coverage, potentially including materials without nano-specific risks while excluding some larger particles with nano-related concerns.

United States: The United States has primarily employed existing regulatory frameworks to address nanomaterials, with sectoral approaches across different agencies:

- **Environmental Protection Agency (EPA)**: Regulates nanomaterials primarily under the Toxic Substances Control Act (TSCA), with significant new use rules (SNURs) frequently applied to nanomaterials. The 2016 TSCA reform enhanced EPA's authority to require testing and information submission for nanomaterials.

- **Food and Drug Administration (FDA)**: Employs existing regulatory frameworks for foods, drugs, cosmetics, and medical devices, with guidance documents addressing nanomaterial considerations in safety assessment, though without binding nano-specific requirements.

- **Consumer Product Safety Commission (CPSC)**: Addresses nanomaterials in consumer products through existing authorities, focusing on case-by-case risk assessment.

The US approach notably lacks a regulatory definition of nanomaterials, instead emphasizing case-by-case assessment based on risk rather than size alone.

Asia-Pacific Region: Countries in the Asia-Pacific region have implemented various approaches:

- **South Korea**: Established K-REACH with specific provisions for nanomaterials, including registration requirements and a legal definition focused on size.

- **Australia**: Implemented administrative adjustments to existing chemical frameworks, with notification requirements for industrial nanomaterials under the National Industrial Chemicals Notification and Assessment Scheme (NICNAS, now AICIS).

- **Japan**: Employs existing chemical regulations with voluntary reporting for nanomaterials, focusing on case-by-case assessment rather than establishing nano-specific requirements.

- **China**: Has developed standards for nanosafety assessment and labeling within its chemical regulatory framework, though implementation remains in development.

International Organizations: Various international organizations contribute to nanomaterial governance:

- **Organization for Economic Cooperation and Development (OECD)**: The Working Party on Manufactured Nanomaterials (WPMN) develops testing guidelines, advocates harmonized approaches, and facilitates international collaboration on safety assessment.

- **International Organization for Standardization (ISO)**: Technical Committee 229 (Nanotechnologies) develops standards for terminology, measurement, characterization, and risk management.

- **World Health Organization (WHO)**: Provides guidelines on protecting workers from potential risks associated with nanomaterials.

Challenges in Regulatory Implementation

Despite significant progress, nanomaterial regulation faces several implementation challenges:

Definition and Scope Issues: Size-based definitions present practical challenges for enforcement, as measuring nanomaterial size distributions requires sophisticated analytical techniques that may be unavailable to many regulatory authorities. Furthermore, variations in measurement methods can yield different results for the same material, complicating consistent classification. The focus on size rather than hazard or risk potentially creates regulatory burdens for benign nanomaterials while potentially overlooking larger particles with nano-specific concerns.

Data Gaps and Uncertainty: Significant knowledge gaps persist regarding nanomaterial behavior, exposure pathways, and long-term effects. Regulators must make decisions in the context of this uncertainty, balancing precaution against innovation. The rapid pace of nanomaterial development further challenges regulatory frameworks, as novel materials or applications may emerge before appropriate testing methods or guidance can be established.

Resource and Expertise Limitations: Regulatory authorities face resource constraints in terms of both funding and expertise. Nanomaterial safety assessment often requires specialized knowledge spanning multiple disciplines, yet many regulatory agencies struggle to attract and retain personnel with appropriate expertise. This challenge is particularly acute in developing countries, potentially creating regulatory disparities across global markets.

Harmonization Needs: Discrepancies between regulatory approaches across jurisdictions create challenges for industry compliance and international trade. A material classified as a nanomaterial in one jurisdiction may not meet the definition in another, necessitating different documentation, testing, or risk management approaches. These inconsistencies increase compliance costs and may create trade barriers.

Enforcement Challenges: Detecting nanomaterials in products, especially at low concentrations or in complex matrices, presents significant analytical challenges. Furthermore, the global supply chain for many nano-enabled products complicates traceability and regulatory oversight, particularly for imported products that may not comply with domestic requirements.

Table 12-4 compares regulatory approaches to nanomaterials across major jurisdictions, highlighting differences in legal definitions, frameworks, documentation, market impact, and public disclosure.

Table 12-4. Comparison of Regulatory Approaches to Nanomaterials Across Major Jurisdictions

Aspect	European Union	United States	Asia-Pacific (varied)
Legal definition	Size-based (1–100 nm), number distribution	No regulatory definition	Varies by country
Regulatory approach	Specific provisions within existing frameworks	Existing frameworks with limited nano-specific requirements	Mix of approaches
Documentation requirements	Detailed characterization and testing for nanoforms	Case-by-case determination through pre-manufacturing notices	Varies from voluntary to mandatory reporting
Market impact	Higher regulatory burden, potential innovation constraints	More flexible, case-by-case approach	Varied impacts with potential regulatory arbitrage
Public disclosure	Public inventory of certain nanomaterials (e.g., cosmetics)	Limited public disclosure	Generally limited transparency

CHAPTER 12   ECOTOXICOLOGY AND LIFECYCLE ASSESSMENT

Emerging Regulatory Approaches

In response to implementation challenges, several innovative regulatory approaches have emerged:

Adaptive Governance: Adaptive governance models explicitly acknowledge uncertainty and incorporate mechanisms for regulatory adjustment as scientific understanding evolves. These approaches may include sunset provisions requiring periodic reassessment, conditional registrations with monitoring requirements, or staged decision-making processes that allow initial commercialization while gathering additional data under controlled conditions.

Safe-by-Design: Safe-by-design approaches integrate safety considerations throughout the innovation process rather than treating regulation as an end-of-pipeline consideration. By identifying potential hazards early in development, this approach enables material or process modifications that may reduce risks while maintaining functionality. Regulatory incentives for safe-by-design, including expedited review processes or reduced testing requirements for demonstrably safer alternatives, show promise for promoting responsible innovation.

Tiered Assessment Frameworks: Tiered approaches to nanomaterial assessment enable efficient resource allocation by focusing detailed evaluation on materials of highest concern. Initial screening based on limited data points identifies materials requiring more comprehensive assessment, while materials with lower potential risk may undergo streamlined evaluation. Such approaches typically consider factors including production volume, release potential, hazard indicators, and persistence.

International Cooperation: Enhanced international cooperation aims to address harmonization challenges and resource limitations. The OECD's Mutual Acceptance of Data (MAD) principle, allowing test data generated according to OECD Test Guidelines in one member country to be accepted in other member countries, represents a significant step toward harmonization. Furthermore, international efforts to develop shared testing infrastructure, databases, and assessment methodologies can reduce duplicative efforts and enhance global regulatory capacity.

Nanomaterials are used in a broad range of products, including electronic device components, cosmetics, and food items. However, their environmental impact is a growing concern, as improper disposal can result in contamination of soil, water, and air. This raises an important question: how are humans and the environment exposed to nanomaterials? Figure 12-2 presents a summary of the primary and most common exposure routes.

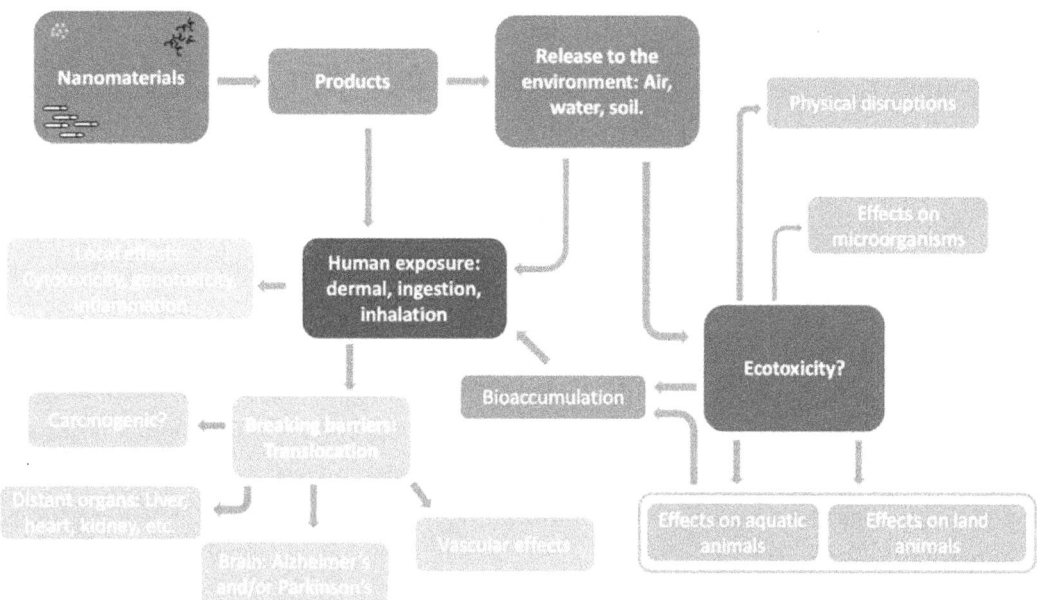

Figure 12-2. Integrated Regulatory Framework for Nanomaterial Safety

Stakeholder Perspectives and Influence

Regulatory development for nanomaterials involves diverse stakeholders with varying perspectives:

Industry Perspectives: Industry stakeholders generally advocate for risk-based approaches focused on hazard and exposure rather than size-based definitions. Concerns regarding confidential business information protection, regulatory predictability, and compliance costs significantly influence industry engagement with regulatory processes. While large companies may have resources to address complex regulatory requirements, small and medium enterprises often face disproportionate challenges in compliance, potentially limiting their participation in nanomaterial markets.

Non-Governmental Organizations (NGOs): Environmental and consumer advocacy organizations have significantly influenced nanomaterial regulation through research, awareness-raising, and policy advocacy. These stakeholders typically emphasize precautionary approaches, transparency, and public right to know. NGO initiatives, including market campaigns, certification schemes, and retailer engagement, have sometimes driven commercial practices beyond regulatory requirements, creating de facto standards in some sectors.

Scientific Community: Academic and research institutions provide critical scientific input to regulatory processes, particularly regarding testing methodologies, risk assessment approaches, and emerging concerns. Institutional mechanisms for science-policy interface, including scientific advisory committees and research-to-regulation initiatives, play important roles in translating scientific developments into regulatory approaches.

Public Perception: Public perception of nanomaterial risks significantly influences regulatory development, with historical experiences with emerging technologies (e.g., genetically modified organisms) shaping risk perception and regulatory expectations. Transparency, public engagement, and clear communication regarding both potential benefits and risks remain essential for maintaining public trust and social license for nanomaterial commercialization.

Future Regulatory Directions

Several trends suggest likely future directions in nanomaterial regulation:

Convergence of Approaches: While complete harmonization seems unlikely in the near term, gradual convergence of regulatory approaches may occur as scientific consensus develops regarding key aspects of nanomaterial assessment. Areas of potential convergence include physicochemical characterization requirements, core testing protocols, and approaches to data sharing and mutual recognition.

Integration with Broader Frameworks: Nanomaterial regulation increasingly intersects with broader sustainability frameworks, including circular economy initiatives, sustainable chemistry approaches, and environmental, social, and governance (ESG) considerations. This integration may drive regulatory innovation beyond traditional risk assessment paradigms toward more holistic approaches considering lifecycle impacts and sustainable materials management.

Digital Tools and New Approach Methodologies: Emerging approaches, including in silico modeling, artificial intelligence applications, and high-throughput screening methodologies, show promise for addressing data gaps and resource limitations in nanomaterial regulation. Regulatory frameworks will likely evolve to incorporate these new approach methodologies while ensuring appropriate validation and applicability domains.

Governance Innovation: Governance innovations beyond traditional command-and-control regulation may increasingly complement formal regulatory frameworks. These may include voluntary initiatives, public–private partnerships, certification schemes, and insurance mechanisms that collectively create a more comprehensive governance ecosystem for nanomaterials.

The regulatory landscape for nanomaterials continues to evolve as scientific understanding advances, stakeholder perspectives develop, and implementation experience accumulates. Balancing precaution with innovation promotion remains a central challenge, requiring ongoing dialogue, international cooperation, and adaptive approaches capable of responding to new developments while providing sufficient predictability for responsible innovation.

12.6 AI and IoT in Ecotoxicology

The convergence of artificial intelligence (AI), Internet of Things (IoT) technologies, and ecotoxicological research represents a transformative frontier in environmental monitoring and nanomaterial risk assessment. This section explores how these emerging technologies are revolutionizing ecotoxicological approaches to nanomaterials, enabling more sophisticated, data-driven environmental stewardship.

AI Applications in Nanoecotoxicology

Artificial intelligence encompasses a range of computational approaches that enable machines to perform tasks typically requiring human intelligence. Within nanoecotoxicology, several AI applications have emerged as particularly promising:

Predictive Toxicology Models: Machine learning algorithms increasingly supplement traditional quantitative structure-activity relationship (QSAR) approaches for predicting nanomaterial toxicity based on physicochemical characteristics. These algorithms can identify complex, nonlinear relationships between material properties and biological effects that might be missed by conventional statistical approaches. Deep learning architectures, including convolutional neural networks and graph neural networks, have demonstrated particular promise for processing structural and compositional data to predict toxicological endpoints.

For instance, recent studies have employed random forest models to predict the cytotoxicity of metal oxide nanoparticles based on properties including band gap energy, electronegativity, and hydration enthalpy, achieving predictive accuracy exceeding 80% for independent test sets. Similarly, neural network approaches have successfully predicted the environmental persistence of carbon-based nanomaterials based on structural features and surface functionalization.

Image Analysis in Toxicity Assessment: Computer vision techniques and image analysis algorithms facilitate automated evaluation of morphological changes, behavioral alterations, and cellular responses in toxicity testing. These approaches enable higher throughput, greater objectivity, and enhanced sensitivity compared to manual assessment:

- Automated counting and characterization of algal cells in growth inhibition assays
- Tracking and analyzing complex behavioral patterns in aquatic organisms exposed to nanomaterials
- Quantifying subcellular changes, including mitochondrial morphology, lysosomal integrity, and cytoskeletal arrangement in in vitro systems

A particularly promising application involves high-content screening approaches combining automated microscopy with multiparametric image analysis, enabling simultaneous assessment of multiple cellular parameters across thousands of conditions to identify mechanistic signatures of nanomaterial toxicity.

Literature Mining and Knowledge Integration: Natural language processing (NLP) techniques enable the extraction, integration, and analysis of information from the rapidly expanding scientific literature on nanomaterial ecotoxicology. Text mining approaches have been employed to

- Identify emerging patterns and relationships across disparate studies
- Extract physicochemical characteristics and toxicity data for model development
- Generate comprehensive ontologies relating nanomaterial properties to environmental behaviors and biological effects

These approaches help address the fragmentation of knowledge in the field, enabling a more comprehensive understanding of nanomaterial–environment interactions despite the heterogeneity of testing approaches and reporting formats.

Environmental Fate Modeling: AI methods enhance the modeling of nanomaterial fate and transport in complex environmental systems. By integrating mechanistic understanding with empirical data, these models can predict spatial and temporal distributions of nanomaterials across environmental compartments under various release scenarios. Hybrid approaches combining physics-based models with data-driven components show particular promise for addressing the complexity of nanomaterial environmental behavior.

IoT Systems for Environmental Monitoring

Internet of Things technologies—interconnected devices equipped with sensors, processing capabilities, and network connectivity—are transforming environmental monitoring for nanomaterials:

Real-Time Monitoring Networks: Distributed sensor networks enable continuous, real-time monitoring of environmental parameters and potential nanomaterial presence across spatial scales from local to global. These networks typically incorporate

- Miniaturized sensors capable of detecting specific nanomaterials or indicator parameters
- Edge computing capabilities for preliminary data processing and alert generation
- Wireless communication protocols for data transmission
- Cloud-based platforms for data integration, analysis, and visualization

For example, recent innovations include sensor networks for monitoring silver nanoparticle concentrations in wastewater treatment plant effluents, providing continuous data streams that capture temporal variations missed by conventional grab sampling approaches.

Biosensor Integration: Biological sensing elements, including enzymes, antibodies, nucleic acids, and whole-cell systems, increasingly complement physicochemical sensors in IoT monitoring networks. These biosensors can provide indications of bioavailability and biological effect rather than merely detecting nanomaterial presence. Integration with microfluidic platforms enables sophisticated sample preparation and multi-analyte detection despite field deployment constraints.

Autonomous Sampling Systems: Robotic and autonomous systems, including unmanned aerial vehicles (drones), autonomous underwater vehicles, and automated sampling stations, enable more comprehensive environmental surveillance with reduced human intervention. These systems can execute complex sampling protocols across challenging environments, transmitting data in near-real time for analysis and response.

Wearable Technologies: Wearable sensors for biological monitoring complement environmental sensing, enabling assessment of potential nanomaterial exposure and effects in various organisms. From fish equipped with miniaturized biologgers recording physiological parameters to invertebrates with attached passive sampling devices, these approaches provide integrated measures of exposure and effect that bridge traditional divides between environmental monitoring and biological assessment.

Integrated Data Ecosystems

The convergence of AI and IoT technologies enables sophisticated data ecosystems for nanomaterial ecotoxicology:

Big Data Approaches: The high-dimensional, heterogeneous data generated by advanced monitoring systems and experimental approaches necessitates big data methodologies for effective analysis. These approaches enable

- Integration of diverse data streams, including physicochemical measurements, genomic responses, and ecological indicators
- Identification of patterns, correlations, and anomalies across multiple spatial and temporal scales
- Development of early warning indicators for potential environmental impacts before they manifest at higher biological levels

Digital Twin Concepts: Digital twin approaches—virtual replicas of physical systems that enable simulation, prediction, and optimization—are beginning to find application in environmental contexts. For nanomaterials, these approaches might integrate

- Comprehensive characterization data for specific nanomaterials
- Environmental fate models reflecting their behavior under various conditions

- Dose–response relationships across relevant ecological receptors
- Regulatory thresholds and management objectives

Such integrated digital representations enable scenario testing, risk assessment, and management strategy evaluation without physical environmental manipulation.

Blockchain for Data Integrity: Blockchain technologies provide mechanisms for ensuring data provenance, integrity, and traceability in environmental monitoring networks. These distributed ledger approaches can

- Document the chain of custody for environmental samples
- Verify the authenticity of sensor measurements
- Create immutable records of environmental conditions and potential exposures
- Enable transparent sharing of monitoring data across stakeholders

For nanomaterials with complex supply chains and potential for environmental release at multiple lifecycle stages, blockchain approaches offer particular value for tracking material flows and environmental presence from production through end-of-life.

Practical Applications and Case Studies

Several practical applications demonstrate the transformative potential of AI and IoT integration in nanoecotoxicology:

Early Warning Systems for Aquatic Environments: Integrated monitoring systems incorporating real-time sensors, automated bioassays, and predictive models enable early detection of potential nanomaterial impacts in aquatic systems. These systems can trigger graduated response protocols based on the exceedance of predetermined thresholds, potentially preventing adverse outcomes through early intervention.

Smart Cities and Urban Environmental Monitoring: Urban environmental management increasingly incorporates nanomaterial considerations within broader smart city frameworks. Distributed sensor networks monitor air quality parameters, including particulate matter with potential nanomaterial components, while integrated data platforms enable correlation with traffic patterns, industrial activities, and meteorological conditions to identify sources and inform mitigation strategies.

CHAPTER 12   ECOTOXICOLOGY AND LIFECYCLE ASSESSMENT

Precision Agriculture Applications: Agricultural applications of nanomaterials, including nano-enabled fertilizers and crop protection products, increasingly incorporate monitoring systems to assess distribution, transformation, and potential nontarget effects. These systems can inform precise application strategies, minimizing environmental release while maximizing agronomic benefits.

Industrial Release Monitoring: Facilities manufacturing or utilizing nanomaterials increasingly implement sophisticated monitoring systems throughout production processes and at potential environmental release points. These systems enable process optimization to minimize losses while providing documentation of environmental compliance and early detection of potential releases requiring intervention.

Table 12-5 summarizes key AI and IoT applications in nanomaterial ecotoxicology, highlighting their associated benefits and implementation challenges across different domains.

Table 12-5. AI and IoT Applications in Nanomaterial Ecotoxicology

Application Domain	Key Technologies	Benefits	Implementation Challenges
Predictive toxicology	Machine learning algorithms, deep neural networks	Reduced animal testing, prioritization of materials for comprehensive assessment	Data quality and quantity limitations, domain of applicability concerns
Environmental monitoring	Sensor networks, remote sensing platforms, automated sampling systems	Continuous surveillance, spatial coverage, early warning capability	Sensor selectivity and sensitivity, power requirements, data transmission constraints
Exposure assessment	Wearable sensors, passive samplers, biomonitoring devices	Integrated exposure measures, individual-level assessment, temporal resolution	Miniaturization constraints, calibration requirements, data privacy concerns
Knowledge integration	Natural language processing, knowledge graphs, ontology development	Comprehensive evidence synthesis, identification of research gaps, facilitation of systematic reviews	Heterogeneous data formats, reporting inconsistencies, proprietary information barriers

Challenges and Limitations

Despite their transformative potential, AI and IoT applications in nanoecotoxicology face several challenges:

Data Quality and Quantity: Machine learning approaches typically require substantial, high-quality training data to achieve reliable performance. In nanoecotoxicology, data limitations, including small sample sizes, heterogeneous testing protocols, inconsistent reporting formats, and publication bias, can compromise model development. Strategic approaches to address these limitations include

- Development of standardized testing and reporting protocols to enhance data compatibility
- Implementation of data sharing platforms and incentives to maximize data availability
- Application of transfer learning and data augmentation techniques to leverage limited datasets
- Integration of mechanistic understanding to constrain model development despite data limitations

Validation and Benchmarking: Validating AI models and IoT systems for environmental applications presents distinct challenges given the complexity of environmental systems and the often limited ground truth data for comparison. Rigorous validation frameworks incorporating multiple evaluation metrics, sensitivity analysis, and uncertainty quantification are essential for establishing confidence in these approaches.

Integration with Regulatory Frameworks: The rapid evolution of AI and IoT technologies often outpaces regulatory frameworks, creating challenges for their formal incorporation into regulatory decision-making. Approaches including regulatory sandboxes, staged implementation processes, and parallel traditional-modern testing can facilitate responsible integration while building confidence in these novel approaches.

Ethical and Societal Considerations: The deployment of sophisticated monitoring systems raises questions regarding data ownership, privacy, environmental justice, and societal implications. Ensuring that these technologies serve public interests requires thoughtful consideration of governance structures, stakeholder engagement processes, and equity implications.

CHAPTER 12   ECOTOXICOLOGY AND LIFECYCLE ASSESSMENT

Future Directions

Several trends suggest future directions for AI and IoT applications in nanoecotoxicology:

Explainable AI: As AI systems increasingly inform high-stakes environmental decisions, the development of explainable AI approaches—methods that provide human-interpretable explanations for model predictions—becomes increasingly important. These approaches enable stakeholder understanding, regulatory acceptance, and scientific scrutiny of model-derived conclusions.

Edge AI: Edge computing architectures that perform AI processing directly on sensor devices rather than requiring cloud transmission show promise for environmental monitoring applications where connectivity, bandwidth, or latency constraints may limit cloud-based approaches. These approaches enable sophisticated analysis and alert generation even in remote or challenging environments.

Autonomous Environmental Laboratories: The integration of robotics, microfluidics, and AI enables increasingly autonomous laboratory systems capable of executing complex analytical workflows with minimal human intervention. These systems can dynamically adjust experimental parameters based on initial results, potentially accelerating the pace of knowledge generation regarding nanomaterial environmental interactions.

Participatory Sensing: Citizen science approaches incorporating user-friendly sensors, mobile applications, and crowdsourcing platforms enable broader participation in environmental monitoring for nanomaterials. These approaches can extend monitoring coverage while enhancing public engagement and literacy regarding nanotechnology and environmental health.

The integration of artificial intelligence and Internet of Things technologies with ecotoxicological approaches represents a transformative development in nanomaterial environmental assessment. While technical, regulatory, and ethical challenges remain, these convergent technologies offer unprecedented opportunities for proactive, data-driven environmental stewardship in the nanotechnology domain.

12.7 Summary

The field of nanoecotoxicology stands at a critical juncture as nanotechnology continues its rapid expansion across industrial sectors and consumer applications. Throughout this chapter, we have explored the multifaceted approaches to understanding, assessing, and managing the environmental implications of engineered nanomaterials. Several key themes emerge from this examination.

First, the distinctive properties that make nanomaterials valuable in technological applications simultaneously necessitate specialized approaches to environmental assessment. Their high surface reactivity, unique transport behaviors, and potential for transformation in environmental systems create complex exposure scenarios that traditional toxicological frameworks may inadequately address. The development of nano-specific testing protocols, characterization methods, and assessment frameworks represents an ongoing scientific endeavor essential for responsible development.

Second, a lifecycle perspective proves indispensable for comprehensive environmental evaluation of nanomaterials. From production processes through use and end-of-life phases, each lifecycle stage presents distinct environmental considerations requiring integrated assessment approaches. Lifecycle assessment methodologies, despite their challenges in nanomaterial contexts, provide valuable frameworks for such holistic evaluation, particularly when integrated with risk assessment approaches.

Third, the regulatory landscape for nanomaterials continues to evolve, with various jurisdictional approaches reflecting different philosophical stances toward scientific uncertainty and innovation. While complete international harmonization remains elusive, convergence on certain core principles and approaches appears increasingly possible. Adaptive governance models that explicitly acknowledge uncertainty while enabling innovation show particular promise for navigating the complex risk-benefit considerations inherent in emerging technologies.

Fourth, the integration of cutting-edge technologies, including artificial intelligence and Internet of Things systems, is transforming environmental monitoring and assessment capabilities. These technologies enable more sophisticated, data-driven approaches to nanomaterial environmental surveillance, potentially facilitating early detection of emerging concerns and more targeted risk management.

Throughout these developments, several persistent challenges remain. Data limitations, methodological uncertainties, and the sheer diversity of nanomaterials complicate comprehensive assessment efforts. The dynamic nature of nanomaterials in environmental systems necessitates sophisticated analytical approaches and interpretive frameworks beyond those typically employed for conventional contaminants.

Looking forward, the sustainable development of nanotechnology requires continued advancement in ecotoxicological understanding, testing methodologies, and governance approaches. Interdisciplinary collaboration spanning materials science, environmental chemistry, ecotoxicology, data science, and policy remains essential for addressing the complex challenges at this intersection of technological innovation and environmental protection.

Ultimately, the goal remains one of responsible innovation—maximizing the societal benefits of nanotechnology while minimizing potential environmental risks. This requires not only technical and scientific advances but also transparent stakeholder engagement, ethical consideration of potential implications, and commitment to environmental stewardship throughout the innovation process. Through such integrated approaches, the transformative potential of nanotechnology can be realized while preserving environmental health for current and future generations.

CHAPTER 13

Nanomaterials in Catalysis

This chapter explores the transformative role of nanomaterials in modern catalysis, beginning with fundamental principles that distinguish nanocatalysts from their bulk counterparts. It examines the innovative development of nanobiocatalysts that bridge biological and synthetic catalytic systems, followed by their groundbreaking applications in pharmaceutical drug synthesis. The chapter investigates how nanoscaffolds serve as sophisticated platforms that enhance catalytic performance through controlled molecular interactions. Current trends in nanocatalysis are analyzed, with emphasis on sustainable technologies and novel nanomaterial designs. The chapter concludes by examining the integration of artificial intelligence and Internet of Things technologies with nanocatalytic systems, illustrating how digital innovation is revolutionizing catalyst design, optimization, and implementation across industries. Through detailed analysis supported by recent research, this chapter provides comprehensive insights into how nanomaterials are reshaping catalytic processes across scientific and industrial domains.

13.1 Basics of Nanocatalysis

Nanocatalysis represents one of the most significant applications of nanotechnology, fundamentally transforming how we approach chemical reactions across industries. At its core, nanocatalysis leverages the unique properties that emerge when materials are engineered at the nanoscale—typically between 1 and 100 nanometers. This size regime introduces quantum effects and dramatically increased surface-to-volume ratios that fundamentally alter catalytic behavior compared to bulk materials.

The extraordinary efficiency of nanocatalysts stems from their extensive surface area. When materials are reduced to nanoscale dimensions, the proportion of atoms at the surface increases exponentially relative to those in the interior. This structural

CHAPTER 13 NANOMATERIALS IN CATALYSIS

characteristic creates an abundance of active sites where catalytic reactions can occur simultaneously. For perspective, a single gram of 10 nm platinum nanoparticles provides approximately 600 square meters of surface area—equivalent to more than two tennis courts. This vast reactive interface enables nanocatalysts to achieve reaction rates orders of magnitude faster than their bulk counterparts while requiring significantly less material.

Beyond mere size reduction, the electronic properties of nanomaterials diverge substantially from bulk materials, creating unique catalytic behaviors. At the nanoscale, quantum confinement effects alter electronic band structures, modifying how electrons interact with adsorbed reactants. This phenomenon often reduces activation energy barriers for chemical transformations, enabling reactions to proceed under milder conditions than previously possible. The tailored electronic states of nanocatalysts can be precisely engineered to match the electronic requirements of specific reactions, allowing unprecedented control over reaction pathways and selectivity.

The geometric configuration of nanomaterials introduces another dimension of catalytic control. Different crystallographic facets of nanomaterials exhibit varying atomic arrangements and coordination environments, directly influencing their binding energies with reactants and intermediates. High-energy crystal faces, edges, and corner sites often serve as preferential active centers for catalysis. Modern synthetic methods now enable precise control over these structural features, allowing catalyst designers to maximize exposure of the most catalytically active facets (Figure 13-1).

CHAPTER 13   NANOMATERIALS IN CATALYSIS

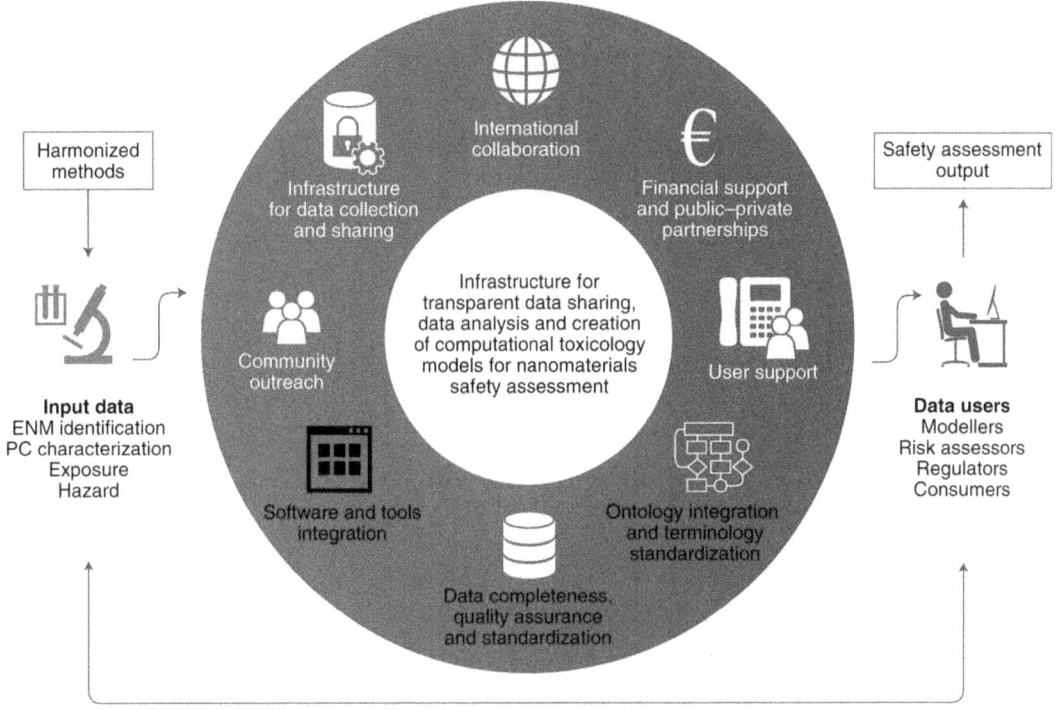

Figure 13-1. Comparison of Surface Area and Active Sites Between Bulk and Nanocatalysts

The distinctive properties of nanocatalysts manifest across several mechanistic pathways that enhance catalytic performance:

1. **Adsorption Enhancement**: Nanocatalysts often demonstrate modified adsorption energies that optimize the binding strength of reactants—strong enough to facilitate reactant activation yet weak enough to allow product desorption, avoiding catalyst poisoning.

2. **Electronic Transfer Facilitation**: The unique electronic properties of nanomaterials can accelerate electron transfer processes critical to many catalytic cycles, particularly in redox reactions.

3. **Synergistic Effects**: Multi-component nanocatalysts can exhibit cooperative behaviors where different constituents work in concert to facilitate complex reaction sequences that would be impossible with single-component systems.

4. **Stability Improvements**: Properly designed nanomaterials can resist sintering, aggregation, and poisoning under harsh reaction conditions, extending catalyst lifetime and economic viability in industrial applications.

The preparation methods for nanocatalysts have evolved significantly, with approaches broadly categorized as top-down (reducing bulk materials to nanoscale) or bottom-up (assembling nanomaterials from molecular precursors). The common techniques include

- Chemical reduction of metal salts in solution
- Sol-gel processing
- Hydrothermal/solvothermal synthesis
- Electrochemical deposition
- Vapor deposition techniques
- Mechanochemical methods
- Templated synthesis using mesoporous materials

Support materials play a crucial role in nanocatalyst performance by preventing aggregation, providing mechanical stability, and sometimes participating directly in catalytic cycles through metal-support interactions. Common supports include high-surface-area materials such as silica, alumina, carbon materials (graphene, carbon nanotubes), and metal-organic frameworks (MOFs). Table 13-1 provides a comparative overview of widely used nanocatalyst preparation methods, highlighting their advantages, limitations, size control, and common applications.

CHAPTER 13   NANOMATERIALS IN CATALYSIS

Table 13-1. Comparison of Common Nanocatalyst Preparation Methods

Method	Advantages	Limitations	Typical Size Control	Common Applications
Chemical reduction	Simple setup, scalable, room temperature operation	Limited morphology control, potential impurities	2–50 nm	Metal nanoparticle catalysts
Sol-gel	Excellent homogeneity, composition control	Lengthy processing time, shrinkage issues	5–50 nm	Mixed metal oxide catalysts
Hydrothermal	High crystallinity, morphology control	Requires pressure vessels, safety concerns	10–200 nm	Zeolite and MOF catalysts
Electrodeposition	Precise thickness control, uniform coating	Limited to conductive substrates	20–500 nm	Supported metal catalysts
Template synthesis	Precise size/shape control, ordered structures	Template removal challenges	2–50 nm	Mesoporous catalyst supports

The field of nanocatalysis continues to evolve rapidly, with significant developments in understanding structure-property relationships and reaction mechanisms at the atomic scale. Advanced characterization techniques, including in situ transmission electron microscopy, X-ray absorption spectroscopy, and scanning probe methods, now allow researchers to observe catalytic processes with unprecedented spatial and temporal resolution. These insights are driving the rational design of increasingly sophisticated nanocatalysts tailored for specific reaction requirements, moving the field beyond traditional trial-and-error approaches toward predictive catalyst engineering.

13.2 Nanobiocatalyst Development

Nanobiocatalysis represents an innovative convergence of nanomaterials science and biological catalysis, creating hybrid systems that harness the exquisite selectivity of biological catalysts while overcoming their inherent limitations. This rapidly expanding field bridges the historically separate domains of heterogeneous catalysis and enzymatic processes, opening new frontiers in sustainable chemical manufacturing.

At the foundation of nanobiocatalyst development lies the strategic immobilization of biological catalytic entities—primarily enzymes, but sometimes whole cells or cellular components—onto nanomaterial supports. This immobilization process transforms free enzymes, which typically operate in homogeneous aqueous environments, into heterogeneous catalysts that combine biological precision with enhanced stability and reusability. The nanoscale interface between biological components and engineered materials creates synergistic properties that neither system possesses independently.

The development of effective nanobiocatalysts begins with a careful selection of appropriate biological components. Enzymes represent nature's most refined catalysts, having evolved over billions of years to perform specific chemical transformations with unmatched selectivity under mild conditions. For industrial applications, enzymes from extremophilic organisms—those surviving in extreme temperatures, pH levels, or salt concentrations—often serve as preferred starting points due to their inherent robustness. Genetic engineering and directed evolution techniques have further expanded the repertoire of available enzymes, allowing researchers to tailor biocatalytic properties for specific applications before integration with nanomaterials.

The nanomaterial components of these hybrid systems must be selected with equal care, as they profoundly influence overall catalytic performance. Common nanomaterials employed include

- Mesoporous silica nanoparticles, which offer a high surface area and tunable pore sizes that can accommodate enzymes while allowing substrate access

- Magnetic nanoparticles, enabling simple catalyst recovery through magnetic separation

- Carbon-based nanomaterials (graphene, carbon nanotubes), providing excellent mechanical stability and sometimes enhancing electron transfer in redox enzymes

- Metal nanoparticles, which can create tandem catalytic systems where enzymatic and metallic catalysis operate in sequence
- Polymeric nanostructures, offering biocompatibility and controlled release capabilities

The immobilization strategies that connect biological catalysts to nanomaterials fundamentally determine nanobiocatalyst performance (Figure 13-2). These approaches fall into several categories with distinct advantages:

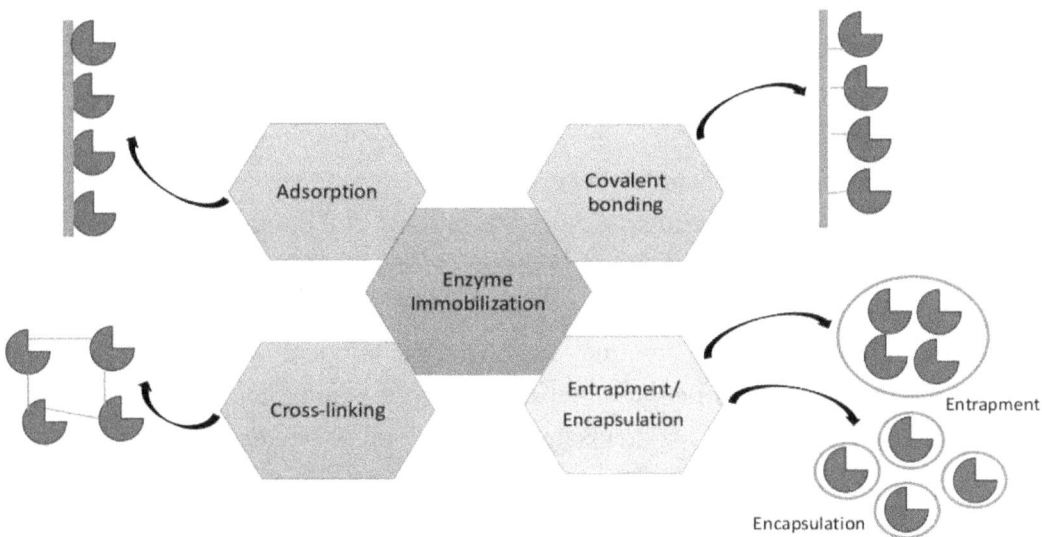

Figure 13-2. Common Enzyme Immobilization Strategies on Nanomaterials

Physical adsorption represents the simplest method, relying on noncovalent interactions (hydrogen bonding, van der Waals forces, ionic interactions) between enzymes and nanomaterial surfaces. While straightforward to implement, these methods often suffer from enzyme leaching during operation, particularly under challenging reaction conditions.

Covalent attachment creates robust chemical bonds between enzymes and properly functionalized nanomaterials. This approach prevents leaching but requires careful control over reaction conditions to avoid modifying catalytically essential amino acid residues. Site-specific attachment techniques have advanced significantly, allowing enzymes to be oriented with active sites optimally positioned for substrate access.

Encapsulation strategies entrap enzymes within nanoporous materials or polymeric networks, protecting them from harsh external environments while allowing small substrate molecules to diffuse to active sites. This method preserves enzyme structure but may introduce mass transfer limitations that reduce apparent catalytic activity.

Cross-linked enzyme aggregates (CLEAs) represent a unique approach where enzyme molecules are first aggregated and then cross-linked to form nanoscale particles. When combined with nanoparticle supports, these systems create hierarchical structures with enhanced stability across wide operational windows.

The performance enhancements achieved through nanobiocatalyst development are substantial and multifaceted:

Stability improvements represent perhaps the most significant advantage, with properly designed nanobiocatalysts often exhibiting operational lifetimes orders of magnitude longer than free enzymes. This stability manifests across multiple dimensions—thermal stability (allowing operation at elevated temperatures), pH stability (enabling performance across wider pH ranges), and operational stability (maintaining activity through numerous reaction cycles).

A landmark example comes from lipase enzymes immobilized on hydrophobic carbon nanotubes, which have demonstrated activity at temperatures up to 90°C—far beyond the denaturation temperature of the free enzyme—and maintained over 80% activity after 20 consecutive reaction cycles in organic solvent systems. Such dramatic enhancements fundamentally alter the economic viability of enzymatic processes in industrial settings.

The nanomaterial components themselves often contribute additional functionalities beyond serving as mere supports. Magnetic nanobiocatalysts enable effortless separation from reaction mixtures using external magnetic fields—a significant advantage for industrial processes where catalyst recovery represents a major cost factor. Stimuli-responsive nanomaterials create "smart" biocatalysts that can be activated or deactivated on demand using external triggers such as light, temperature, or pH shifts.

A particularly promising development involves cascade nanobiocatalysts, where multiple enzymes are co-immobilized in precise spatial arrangements to perform sequential transformations without intermediate isolation steps. These systems mimic the efficiency of natural metabolic pathways while operating in controlled synthetic environments.

The fundamental challenges in nanobiocatalyst development continue to revolve around several key issues:

1. Maintaining enzyme conformational integrity during immobilization, as structural distortions can dramatically reduce catalytic efficiency

2. Balancing enzyme loading with mass transfer considerations, as excessive loading often leads to diffusion limitations

3. Understanding and controlling the complex microenvironment at the nano-bio interface, which can dramatically alter substrate binding and product release kinetics

4. Developing standardized characterization protocols that accurately predict real-world performance across diverse reaction conditions

Recent advances in computational modeling have accelerated progress by enabling molecular-level insights into enzyme-nanomaterial interactions. Molecular dynamics simulations now reveal how immobilization affects enzyme flexibility, substrate access channels, and transition state stabilization—information that guides rational design of next-generation nanobiocatalysts with optimized performance characteristics.

13.3 Drug Synthesis Applications

The pharmaceutical industry has embraced nanocatalysis as a transformative technology for drug synthesis, offering unprecedented control over chemical transformations critical to medicinal chemistry. The extraordinary precision, efficiency, and sustainability of nanomaterials-based catalysts have revolutionized pharmaceutical manufacturing processes, enabling the synthesis of complex therapeutic molecules with greater yield, purity, and cost-effectiveness than conventional methods.

Nanocatalysts have proven particularly valuable for addressing longstanding challenges in pharmaceutical synthesis, including stereoselective transformations, C-H activation, and late-stage functionalization of complex molecules. These processes frequently require exact control over reaction selectivity to avoid unwanted side products that can introduce impurities or necessitate costly purification steps. The precisely engineered surface structures of nanocatalysts provide this control through carefully designed active sites that guide molecular interactions toward desired reaction pathways (Table 13-2).

CHAPTER 13 NANOMATERIALS IN CATALYSIS

The impact of nanocatalysis in pharmaceutical manufacturing manifests across several critical domains of drug synthesis. Figure 13-3 represents the chemical, physical, and biological approaches for the synthesis of nanocomposites.

Asymmetric catalysis represents one of the most significant applications, as the biological activity of pharmaceuticals often depends on precise three-dimensional molecular configurations. Traditional approaches to producing single enantiomers typically relied on resolution techniques that waste half the starting material or chiral auxiliaries that add synthetic steps. Modern nanostructured catalysts incorporate chiral elements that can induce enantioselectivity through well-defined transition state geometries. For instance, gold nanoparticles modified with chiral thiol ligands have achieved enantiomeric excesses exceeding 95% in asymmetric hydrogenation reactions used in synthesizing key building blocks for antihypertensive medications.

Carbon–carbon bond formation constitutes the backbone of drug molecule construction, with cross-coupling reactions standing as cornerstone methodologies in pharmaceutical synthesis. Palladium nanoparticles have revolutionized these processes, enabling Suzuki, Heck, and Sonogashira couplings under significantly milder conditions than conventional catalysts. Beyond palladium, bimetallic nanocatalysts combining core-shell architectures (such as Pd-Au or Ru-Pt systems) demonstrate synergistic effects that enhance both activity and selectivity in complex coupling reactions. The increased surface area and tailored electronic properties of these nanocatalysts allow reactions to proceed with lower catalyst loadings, shorter reaction times, and higher yields—all critical factors in reducing the environmental footprint and cost of pharmaceutical manufacturing.

Hydrogenation reactions feature prominently in pharmaceutical synthesis, particularly for reducing unsaturated functional groups or removing protecting groups in late-stage synthesis. Platinum and ruthenium nanocatalysts supported on high-surface-area materials enable selective hydrogenation even in molecules containing multiple reducible groups. Catalyst selectivity can be further tuned through precise control of nanoparticle size, as demonstrated with ruthenium nanoparticles, where particles below 3 nm selectively hydrogenate C=C bonds while larger particles preferentially reduce C=O functionalities—a size-dependent selectivity with profound implications for synthesizing complex drugs containing both functional groups.

Oxidation processes represent another critical transformation in pharmaceutical synthesis, particularly for introducing oxygen-containing functional groups essential to drug activity. Gold nanocatalysts have emerged as revolutionary systems for selective oxidation reactions under remarkably mild conditions, often using molecular oxygen as the ultimate oxidant rather than stoichiometric oxidizing agents that generate significant waste. The exceptional activity of supported gold nanoparticles for alcohol oxidation, epoxidation, and C-H activation has enabled greener synthesis routes for anti-inflammatory drugs, cardiovascular medications, and antibiotics. Table 13-2 summarizes major nanocatalyst systems used in key pharmaceutical transformations, highlighting their advantages and representative drug applications.

Table 13-2. Nanocatalysts in Key Pharmaceutical Transformations

Transformation Type	Nanocatalyst System	Advantages	Representative Drug Applications
Asymmetric hydrogenation	Pt nanoparticles with chiral modifiers	>95% enantiomeric excess, ambient conditions	L-DOPA (Parkinson's), Levofloxacin (antibiotic)
C-C cross-coupling	Pd nanoparticles on graphene	Low catalyst loading (0.05–0.5 mol%), high TOF	Crizotinib (cancer), Telmisartan (hypertension)
Selective oxidation	Au nanoparticles on CeO_2	O_2 as oxidant, water as solvent	Artemisinin derivatives (antimalarial)
Hydrogenation	Ru nanoparticles in mesoporous silica	Chemoselective, low H_2 pressure	Methylphenidate (ADHD), Sertraline (antidepressant)
C-H activation	Pd-Cu bimetallic nanocatalysts	Site-selective functionalization	Celecoxib (anti-inflammatory), Valsartan (hypertension)

The integration of nanobiocatalysis into pharmaceutical synthesis workflows has created particularly powerful systems for producing complex chiral molecules. By combining the precise stereo- and regioselectivity of enzymes with the robustness of nanomaterials, these hybrid catalysts enable one-pot multistep transformations that would otherwise require extensive protection-deprotection sequences. A compelling example involves lipase enzymes immobilized on magnetic nanoparticles for the kinetic resolution of racemic alcohols used in antihypertensive drug synthesis. These systems not only achieve remarkable enantioselectivity (>99% ee) but can be magnetically recovered and reused over 20 cycles without significant activity loss—dramatically improving process economics.

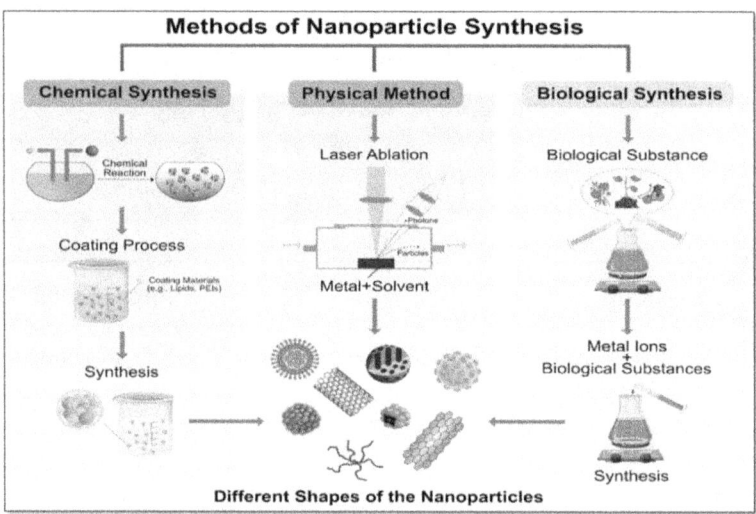

Figure 13-3. *Nanocatalyst Applications in Pharmaceutical Synthesis Pathways*

Flow chemistry represents another frontier where nanocatalysis is transforming pharmaceutical manufacturing. Continuous-flow microreactors incorporating immobilized nanocatalysts enable precise control over reaction parameters with enhanced heat and mass transfer characteristics. These systems facilitate rapid optimization, scale-up, and process intensification—critical advantages for accelerating drug development timelines and enabling on-demand manufacturing of personalized medicines. Recent demonstrations include palladium nanoparticles supported on monolithic materials for continuous-flow Suzuki coupling reactions in the synthesis of kinase inhibitors used in targeted cancer therapies.

Sustainability considerations have become increasingly central to pharmaceutical manufacturing, driven by both environmental concerns and economic pressures. Nanocatalysts contribute significantly to green chemistry objectives through several mechanisms:

1. Reduced catalyst loading requirements minimize the consumption of precious metals

2. Enhanced selectivity decreases waste generation from unwanted side reactions

3. Milder reaction conditions reduce energy consumption and enable the use of greener solvents

4. Catalyst recyclability minimizes process waste and improves atom economy

5. Tandem catalytic systems eliminate isolation of intermediates, reducing solvent usage

The development pathway from laboratory discovery to industrial implementation of new nanocatalytic drug synthesis methods involves several key stages. Initial proof-of-concept studies typically focus on model reactions that demonstrate fundamental advantages over conventional methods. Subsequent optimization phases address practical considerations, including catalyst stability, leaching prevention, and compatibility with standard manufacturing equipment. Regulatory considerations necessitate thorough characterization of potential metal contamination in final drug products, driving innovations in catalyst design that minimize leaching while maintaining high activity. The most successful implementations achieve significant improvements across multiple metrics—yield, selectivity, environmental impact, and cost—creating compelling value propositions for adoption even within the highly regulated pharmaceutical industry.

13.4 Catalytic Role of Nanoscaffolds

Nanoscaffolds represent sophisticated three-dimensional architectures that serve as platforms for catalytic reactions, transcending the traditional role of passive supports to become active participants in catalytic processes. These advanced materials provide precisely defined environments that can fundamentally alter reaction pathways, enhance catalytic efficiency, and enable unprecedented selectivity. Understanding the multifaceted roles of nanoscaffolds has emerged as a central theme in modern catalysis research, offering insights that guide the rational design of next-generation catalytic systems.

CHAPTER 13   NANOMATERIALS IN CATALYSIS

The fundamental distinction between conventional supports and true nanoscaffolds lies in their active participation in catalytic mechanisms. While traditional supports primarily serve to disperse active sites and prevent aggregation, nanoscaffolds interact dynamically with reactants, intermediates, and products through multiple mechanisms that can dramatically influence catalytic performance:

Confinement effects represent perhaps the most distinctive feature of nanoscaffolds, creating reaction microenvironments that differ substantially from bulk solution conditions. When reactions occur within nanoscale cavities or channels, the restricted spatial dimensions alter molecular diffusion, orientation, and concentration—often accelerating reactions through increased effective concentrations and favorable entropy effects. These confined spaces can stabilize transition states through multiple weak interactions with the scaffold walls, lowering activation barriers for targeted transformations. Studies of zeolite nanoscaffolds have demonstrated rate enhancements exceeding 10,000-fold for certain reactions when the pore dimensions closely match the spatial requirements of the transition state—a phenomenon sometimes called "molecular shape selectivity."

The electronic properties of nanoscaffolds directly influence the electron density at catalytic sites through charge transfer interactions. Conducting nanoscaffolds, such as graphene sheets or carbon nanotubes, can modify the electronic states of supported metal nanoparticles through electron donation or withdrawal, altering their binding energies with reactants and intermediates. This electronic tuning can be precisely controlled through scaffold functionalization or doping with heteroatoms, enabling optimization for specific reaction requirements. The interaction strength can be quantified through techniques such as X-ray photoelectron spectroscopy, which reveals characteristic shifts in binding energies that correlate with catalytic performance.

The structural characteristics of nanoscaffolds—including pore size distribution, surface curvature, and channel connectivity—establish specific diffusion pathways that govern how molecules access active sites and how products exit the system. These transport properties can create molecular traffic control that influences reaction selectivity by favoring specific reaction paths over others. Hierarchical nanoscaffolds containing both micropores (<2 nm) and mesopores (2–50 nm) offer particularly advantageous transport properties, with larger channels facilitating rapid diffusion of bulky molecules while smaller pores provide high surface area and numerous active sites.

Major categories of nanoscaffolds that have demonstrated exceptional performance in catalytic applications include the following.

Metal-organic frameworks (MOFs) represent one of the most versatile classes of nanoscaffolds, consisting of metal nodes connected by organic linkers to form crystalline, porous structures with exceptional surface areas (often exceeding 6,000 m^2/g). The modular nature of MOFs allows precise control over pore geometry, chemical functionality, and metal center identity—enabling rational design for specific catalytic applications. Beyond simply supporting catalytic species, MOFs often incorporate catalytically active metal centers directly into their framework structure, creating single-site catalysts with extraordinary uniformity. Recent innovations include defect engineering strategies that intentionally introduce coordinatively unsaturated metal sites that serve as Lewis acid catalytic centers with enhanced accessibility.

Mesoporous silica materials provide robust nanoscaffolds with highly ordered pore structures and exceptional thermal and chemical stability. Materials such as MCM-41, SBA-15, and KIT-6 offer various pore geometries (hexagonal, cubic, etc.) with precisely controllable dimensions in the 2–50 nm range. These materials serve as excellent platforms for immobilizing both metal nanoparticles and enzymes, with their silanol-rich surfaces readily functionalized to optimize interactions with catalytic species. The rigid structure of these materials maintains accessibility to active sites even under harsh reaction conditions, contributing to catalyst longevity in industrial applications.

Carbon-based nanoscaffolds, including graphene, carbon nanotubes, and ordered mesoporous carbons, offer exceptional electrical conductivity that facilitates electron transfer processes in electrocatalytic applications. The π-conjugated surfaces of these materials interact strongly with aromatic compounds and can orient them favorably for selective transformations. Carbon nanoscaffolds also demonstrate remarkable resistance to acidic and basic conditions, enabling their use across wide pH ranges. Their surface chemistry can be extensively modified through oxidation, reduction, or doping with heteroatoms (N, B, S, P) to introduce specific functional groups that enhance binding with target molecules or tune the electronic properties of supported catalytic species.

Dendrimers represent precision-engineered molecular nanoscaffolds with tree-like branching structures emanating from a central core. These materials offer exceptional control over the positioning of catalytic sites, with active centers typically located either at the periphery or within the interior depending on the desired application. The dendritic architecture creates isolated catalytic environments that can prevent unwanted side reactions while allowing substrate access through the branched structure. Particularly notable are metallodendrimers containing multiple metal centers held in precise spatial arrangements that enable cooperative catalysis mimicking the behavior of metalloenzymes.

The integration of multiple functionalities within a single nanoscaffold creates multifunctional catalytic systems capable of performing complex reaction sequences. These integrated systems can incorporate

1. Acid-base bifunctional catalysts that coordinate sequential reaction steps requiring different activation modes
2. Redox-acid pairs that enable tandem oxidation-cyclization sequences
3. Metal-enzyme hybrid systems that combine the advantages of homogeneous and biocatalysis
4. Photocatalytic centers coupled with thermal catalytic sites for light-driven processes

The precise spatial positioning of different catalytic functionalities within these multifunctional nanoscaffolds determines their cooperative behavior. When complementary catalytic sites are positioned at optimal distances—close enough for efficient substrate transfer between active sites but far enough to prevent mutual deactivation—reaction cascades can proceed with minimal isolation of intermediates, dramatically improving process efficiency.

Design strategies for optimizing nanoscaffold performance have evolved from empirical approaches to sophisticated rational design methods guided by computational modeling and advanced characterization techniques:

Site isolation principles ensure that active centers are sufficiently separated to prevent undesired aggregation or cross-deactivation. This separation is particularly crucial for metal nanoparticle catalysts that tend to sinter under reaction conditions, leading to decreased surface area and catalytic activity. Effective site isolation strategies include anchoring metal particles to widely spaced functional groups on scaffold surfaces or confining them within mesopores that physically prevent particle migration and aggregation.

Interface engineering focuses on optimizing the critical interface between catalytic species and the nanoscaffold through controlled functionalization. Strategic placement of linker molecules can tune the electronic and spatial environment around active sites, altering their catalytic properties. For example, hydrophobic modifications around enzyme attachment points on mesoporous silica have been shown to create microenvironments that exclude water, enhancing performance in organic synthesis applications.

Hierarchical structuring creates nanoscaffolds with multiple levels of organization spanning different length scales—from atomic-level active sites to macroscopic properties that facilitate handling and process integration. This approach addresses one of the fundamental challenges in heterogeneous catalysis: balancing high surface area (typically requiring small pores) with efficient mass transport (favored by larger channels). Materials with hierarchical porosity, containing interconnected micro-, meso-, and macropores, offer an elegant solution to this dilemma.

The dynamic nature of nanoscaffolds under reaction conditions represents both a challenge and an opportunity. Advanced characterization techniques, including in situ spectroscopy and environmental transmission electron microscopy, now reveal that nanoscaffolds often undergo structural evolution during catalytic processes—information crucial for designing more stable and effective systems. Understanding these dynamic behaviors is enabling the development of self-healing nanoscaffolds that can maintain or even enhance their performance over extended operational periods, a critical requirement for industrial implementation.

13.5 Trends in Nanocatalysis

The field of nanocatalysis is experiencing rapid evolution driven by convergent advances in materials science, characterization techniques, and computational modeling. Current trends reflect both fundamental scientific progress and practical imperatives to address global challenges in energy, environment, and sustainable manufacturing. These developments are reshaping how catalysts are designed, characterized, and implemented across industries, pointing toward a future where atomic-level precision and system-level integration define catalytic processes.

Atomically precise catalysts represent the frontier of nanocatalysis research, embodying the ultimate limit of structural control. These systems feature active sites with identical atomic arrangements, eliminating the heterogeneity that has historically complicated mechanistic understanding and optimization of catalytic materials. Single-atom catalysts (SACs), where individual metal atoms are dispersed on appropriate supports, exemplify this approach. Unlike traditional nanoparticles, where many metal atoms remain buried in the bulk and unavailable for catalysis, SACs achieve 100% atomic efficiency with every metal atom potentially participating in catalytic cycles. Recent breakthroughs in synthetic methods have enabled the preparation of stable SACs for various noble and nonnoble metals (Pt, Pd, Ru, Fe, Co, Ni) on supports including graphene, metal oxides, and nitrides.

The exceptional performance of atomically precise catalysts often derives from unique electronic properties and coordination environments impossible in bulk materials. For instance, single platinum atoms anchored to nitrogen-doped graphene exhibit dramatically higher activity for hydrogen evolution reactions than conventional Pt nanoparticles while using orders of magnitude less precious metal. This enhanced performance stems from the distinctive electronic structure of isolated metal atoms with incomplete coordination shells, creating highly reactive centers with tunable properties dependent on their local bonding environment. Advanced characterization techniques, particularly aberration-corrected electron microscopy and X-ray absorption spectroscopy, have been crucial for verifying the atomic dispersion and local coordination structures that define these catalysts' behavior.

Sustainable catalysis has emerged as a dominant theme, with research increasingly focused on developing nanocatalysts that address environmental challenges while minimizing their own ecological footprint. Several interconnected approaches characterize this movement:

Earth-abundant metal nanocatalysts aim to replace precious metals with more sustainable alternatives, addressing both cost considerations and supply constraints. Iron, manganese, cobalt, nickel, and copper nanostructures have demonstrated impressive activity for reactions traditionally requiring platinum-group metals. The key to this substitution lies in precise nanostructuring and electronic modification through alloying or support interactions. For example, nickel-iron layered double hydroxide nanosheets have emerged as exceptional oxygen evolution catalysts for water splitting, outperforming precious metal benchmarks while using Earth-abundant elements.

Photocatalytic nanomaterials harness solar energy to drive chemical transformations, offering pathways to sustainable synthesis and environmental remediation. Advances in semiconductor nanostructures, particularly in band gap engineering and charge-carrier management, have dramatically improved quantum efficiencies. Heterojunction nanomaterials combining multiple semiconductors create spatial separation of photogenerated electrons and holes, reducing recombination and enhancing catalytic performance. Recent innovations include Z-scheme systems that mimic natural photosynthesis by linking two photocatalysts to achieve both strong oxidation and reduction capabilities simultaneously. These materials show promise for solar fuel production, environmental decontamination, and light-driven organic synthesis under ambient conditions.

Bio-inspired nanocatalysts draw design principles from enzymatic systems, pursuing the extraordinary efficiency and selectivity that biological catalysts have achieved through evolutionary optimization. Mimicking the precisely structured active sites of metalloenzymes has led to the development of synthetic nanomaterials with biomimetic catalytic centers embedded in controlled secondary coordination environments. For instance, nanomaterials with structural elements resembling the iron-sulfur clusters in hydrogenase enzymes have achieved remarkable activity for hydrogen production without platinum metals. These bio-inspired approaches often succeed by recreating the critical features that enable enzymes' efficiency: precisely positioned functional groups that stabilize transition states, hydrophobic/hydrophilic microenvironments that control substrate access, and cooperative interactions between multiple catalytic centers.

Computational design has transformed from a supporting tool to a central component of nanocatalyst development, enabling rational prediction of catalytic properties before experimental synthesis. Density functional theory (DFT) calculations now routinely predict adsorption energies and activation barriers for reaction steps on nanocatalyst surfaces, identifying promising candidates for specific applications. Machine learning approaches have accelerated this process by identifying patterns in structure-activity relationships across thousands of potential catalyst compositions. These computational methods have proven particularly valuable for exploring the vast compositional space of multi-metallic nanocatalysts, where experimental screening of all possible combinations would be prohibitively time-consuming.

The digital transformation of catalyst discovery combines high-throughput experimentation with advanced data analytics and machine learning to identify optimal formulations with unprecedented efficiency. Automated synthesis platforms can now prepare and evaluate hundreds of nanocatalyst compositions daily, generating rich datasets that reveal complex relationships between synthesis parameters, structural characteristics, and catalytic performance. When integrated with computational predictions, these approaches create powerful feedback loops that continuously refine understanding of fundamental structure-activity relationships while accelerating practical catalyst development.

Integration of multiple catalytic functionalities into unified systems represents another significant trend, enabling cascade processes where sequential transformations occur without isolation of intermediates. These integrated systems often combine different catalytic modalities—metallic, enzymatic, organocatalytic—within carefully designed nanoscale architectures that manage reaction sequencing through spatial organization of active sites. The resulting one-pot processes offer substantial advantages in efficiency, reducing solvent consumption and separation steps that typically dominate the environmental footprint of chemical manufacturing. Table 13-3 summarizes emerging application domains of advanced nanocatalysts, highlighting key performance metrics and their associated sustainability benefits.

Table 13-3. Emerging Applications of Advanced Nanocatalysts

Application Domain	Nanocatalyst System	Key Performance Metrics	Sustainability Impact
Hydrogen production	MoS_2 nanosheets on N-doped carbon	>95% Faradaic efficiency, stability >1000 hours	Enables renewable H_2 from water splitting
CO_2 valorization	Cu-Zn core-shell nanoparticles	Selectivity to methanol >80%, low overpotential	Carbon capture and utilization pathway
Biomass conversion	Ru-based nanocatalysts on acid supports	Complete cellulose conversion at 150°C	Renewable feedstock utilization
Microplastic degradation	Fe_3O_4-TiO_2 nanocomposites	Complete mineralization under visible light	Environmental remediation
Ammonia synthesis	Ru single atoms on MXene supports	Operates at 250°C (vs. 450°C conventional)	Reduced energy consumption

Industrial implementation of nanocatalysts has accelerated as manufacturing methods mature and performance advantages demonstrate clear economic benefits. Several factors are facilitating this transition from laboratory curiosity to industrial workhorse:

1. Scalable synthesis methods have emerged for previously laboratory-scale nanocatalysts, including continuous flow processes that enable consistent production at kilogram and larger scales.

2. Improved understanding of deactivation mechanisms has led to more robust catalyst designs with extended operational lifetimes under industrial conditions.

3. Enhanced formulation approaches, including advanced encapsulation and structuring techniques, have improved handling properties and compatibility with existing reactor technologies.

4. Economic analyses increasingly demonstrate compelling value propositions, particularly for processes where enhanced selectivity reduces downstream purification requirements.

The future directions of nanocatalysis research suggest continued convergence of multiple disciplines, with several frontiers emerging as particularly promising:

Dynamic and responsive nanocatalysts represent systems that can adapt their properties in response to reaction conditions or external stimuli. These "smart" catalysts might alter their selectivity based on substrate concentration, modify activity in response to temperature fluctuations, or regenerate active sites through self-healing mechanisms. Such adaptive behavior could revolutionize process control and catalyst longevity in industrial applications.

Interface engineering at unprecedented precision aims to control the critical interactions between nanocatalysts and their immediate environments, including supports, solvents, and reactants. As understanding of interfacial phenomena deepens, researchers are developing methods to construct ideal catalytic microenvironments that optimize all aspects of performance simultaneously.

System integration approaches seek to embed nanocatalysts within comprehensive process designs that address entire reaction sequences rather than isolated transformations. This holistic perspective promises to unlock synergies between reaction steps while minimizing resource consumption across complete manufacturing pathways.

13.6 AI and IoT Integration

The convergence of artificial intelligence (AI), Internet of Things (IoT) technologies, and nanocatalysis represents a transformative frontier that is fundamentally reshaping how catalytic systems are designed, optimized, and implemented. This integration creates unprecedented capabilities for real-time monitoring, predictive maintenance, and autonomous optimization of catalytic processes across industrial and research settings. The synergistic combination of nanoscale precision in catalysis with the computational power of AI and the connectivity of IoT is accelerating discovery while enabling more sustainable and efficient chemical transformations (Figure 13-4).

At the foundation of this technological convergence lie advanced sensor networks that provide continuous, multimodal data streams from catalytic systems. These sensors operate across multiple length scales—from molecular-level spectroscopic probes to reactor-wide performance metrics—creating comprehensive digital representations of catalytic processes in operation. Modern nanocatalyst monitoring systems incorporate

- Spectroscopic sensors (Raman, IR, UV-vis) that track chemical species and reaction intermediates in real-time

- Temperature and pressure arrays that map spatial gradients within reactors

- Electrochemical probes that measure current, potential, and impedance in electrocatalytic systems

- Mass spectrometry interfaces that analyze product distributions with high temporal resolution

- Specialized nanoprobes that detect catalyst structural changes during operation

These multimodal data streams feed into integrated IoT architectures that transform traditionally isolated catalytic systems into nodes within connected networks. Modern IoT frameworks for nanocatalysis typically implement hierarchical structures:

1. Edge computing elements perform initial data processing directly at catalyst interfaces, extracting meaningful features while reducing transmission bandwidth requirements

2. Fog computing layers coordinate multiple catalytic units within process lines, enabling local optimization and rapid response to changing conditions

3. Cloud platforms aggregate data across entire production ecosystems, supporting enterprise-level analytics and cross-process optimization

The unprecedented data volumes generated by these connected systems create both challenges and opportunities for catalyst development and industrial implementation. Machine learning approaches have emerged as essential tools for extracting actionable insights from these complex datasets, with several AI paradigms finding particular utility in nanocatalysis:

Deep learning models excel at identifying complex patterns in multivariate catalytic data. Convolutional neural networks applied to spectroscopic time series can identify subtle shifts in catalyst behavior that presage deactivation, enabling preventive maintenance before performance declines. Recurrent neural networks capture temporal dependencies in reaction sequences, revealing how earlier process stages influence subsequent catalytic performance. These models can process multiple data streams simultaneously, detecting correlations between seemingly unrelated parameters that might escape human analysis.

Reinforcement learning algorithms have demonstrated remarkable effectiveness for optimizing reaction conditions in complex catalytic systems. These approaches treat catalyst operation as a decision process where conditions (temperature, pressure, flow rates) are adjusted to maximize desired outcomes (yield, selectivity, energy efficiency). The algorithm learns optimal control policies through systematic exploration of the parameter space, continuously refining its strategy as it accumulates experience. Recent implementations have achieved performance improvements of 15–30% in industrial hydrogenation processes using palladium nanocatalysts, identifying counterintuitive temperature profiles that human operators had not explored.

Knowledge graph technologies organize the vast scientific literature on nanocatalysis into structured, machine-readable formats that enable automated reasoning across disparate knowledge domains. These systems represent entities (materials, reactions, properties) as nodes and their relationships as edges, creating navigable networks of scientific knowledge. When integrated with prediction algorithms, these knowledge structures accelerate catalyst discovery by suggesting promising new materials based on established structure-property relationships and reaction mechanisms. The resulting AI-assisted design process can identify nonobvious catalyst candidates that might be overlooked in traditional research approaches.

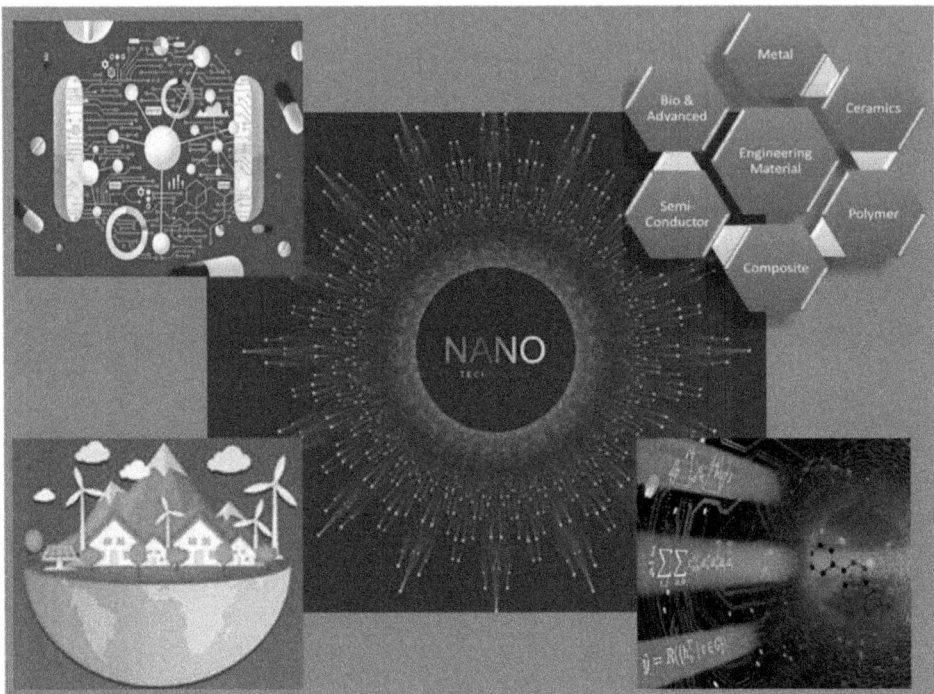

Figure 13-4. AI and IoT Integration in Nanocatalytic Systems

The practical implementation of AI-IoT integration in nanocatalysis spans research, development, and industrial applications with several transformative use cases:

High-throughput catalyst discovery platforms represent perhaps the most dramatic acceleration of traditional development processes. These systems combine automated synthesis robots, parallel testing arrays, and machine learning algorithms to explore vast compositional spaces with unprecedented efficiency. Advanced platforms can synthesize, characterize, and evaluate hundreds of nanocatalyst formulations daily, with each iteration guided by AI predictions based on accumulated results. This approach has demonstrated particular value for multi-metallic catalysts where compositional complexity creates a virtually infinite design space. A landmark example comes from the discovery of novel platinum-alternative oxygen reduction catalysts for fuel cells, where an AI-guided high-throughput system explored quaternary compositions of transition metals, identifying an unexpected Fe-Ni-Co-Mn formulation with superior activity and stability compared to benchmark materials.

Digital twins of catalytic reactors create comprehensive virtual models that mirror the behavior of physical systems with high fidelity. These computational doppelgängers integrate multiple physics-based models (fluid dynamics, heat transfer, reaction kinetics) with real-time sensor data to provide both explanatory and predictive capabilities. When properly calibrated, digital twins can simulate process modifications before physical implementation, predicting how changes in catalyst formulation, reactor geometry, or operating conditions will affect performance. This approach significantly reduces development cycles by replacing costly physical prototyping with rapid computational iteration. For industrial operations, digital twins enable scenario testing that identifies optimal responses to changing feedstock properties, energy costs, or product specifications without disrupting production.

Adaptive process control systems leverage real-time sensor data and predictive models to continuously optimize catalytic processes under changing conditions. Unlike traditional control systems with fixed setpoints, these AI-enhanced approaches dynamically adjust operating parameters based on current system state and predicted future conditions. When applied to industrial hydroformylation processes using rhodium nanocatalysts, these systems have demonstrated the ability to maintain optimal selectivity despite variations in feedstock composition by adjusting temperature profiles and hydrogen partial pressures in response to changing conditions. The economic impact includes both improved yield and reduced energy consumption, with cumulative sustainability benefits throughout the product lifecycle. Table 13-4 summarizes key AI approaches applied across nanocatalysis development and implementation, along with their benefits and real-world applications.

CHAPTER 13 NANOMATERIALS IN CATALYSIS

Table 13-4. *AI Applications in Nanocatalysis Development and Implementation*

Application Area	AI Approach	Benefits	Example Implementation
Catalyst design	Generative adversarial networks	Novel structures beyond human intuition	Design of zeolite frameworks with targeted pore architectures
Process optimization	Reinforcement learning	Continuous adaptation to changing conditions	Dynamic temperature control in selective hydrogenation
Deactivation prediction	Recurrent neural networks	Preventive maintenance before failure	Early detection of catalyst poisoning in reforming
Reaction route prediction	Graph neural networks	Discovery of efficient synthetic pathways	Alternative routes for pharmaceutical intermediates
Structure-activity models	Ensemble machine learning	Accurate property prediction	Prediction of turnover frequencies for new catalyst formulations

The integration of blockchain technology with nanocatalysis represents an emerging frontier that addresses traceability and quality assurance challenges. Distributed ledger systems create immutable records of catalyst provenance, synthesis parameters, testing results, and performance metrics. This unbroken digital chain provides crucial verification for high-value catalysts where consistent performance is essential, such as those used in pharmaceutical manufacturing or emissions control. When implemented across supply chains, these systems enable end-to-end tracking of catalytic materials from raw material sourcing through final application, creating accountability and enabling lifecycle analysis that informs sustainability assessments.

Edge computing architectures bring AI capabilities directly to catalytic systems, enabling real-time decision-making without reliance on cloud connectivity. This approach proves particularly valuable for remote operations or applications with stringent latency requirements. Advanced implementations embed neural network accelerators within reactor control systems, enabling complex model execution with millisecond response times. The resulting autonomous operation can adapt to changing conditions without human intervention, maintaining optimal performance even in challenging or variable environments. For field-deployed catalytic systems, such as those used in environmental remediation or distributed chemical production, this capability ensures consistent performance across diverse operating conditions.

Despite its transformative potential, the integration of AI, IoT, and nanocatalysis faces several significant challenges:

1. **Data quality and standardization issues** complicate cross-platform integration and model transferability. The heterogeneity of data formats, collection methodologies, and reporting standards creates friction in knowledge aggregation. Industry-wide initiatives are now working to establish common data structures and metadata standards specifically for catalysis research, aiming to improve interoperability across the research ecosystem.

2. **Privacy and intellectual property concerns** arise when sensitive catalyst formulations or proprietary process data must be shared across digital platforms. Advanced cryptographic approaches, including federated learning and homomorphic encryption, allow collaborative model development without exposing underlying data, balancing innovation through sharing with protection of competitive advantages.

3. **System complexity and reliability challenges** emerge as catalytic processes become increasingly dependent on sophisticated digital technologies. Robust engineering approaches that incorporate redundancy, graceful degradation, and fail-safe mechanisms are essential for maintaining operational integrity in mission-critical applications.

4. **Workforce transition requirements** necessitate new skills at the intersection of chemical engineering, data science, and information technology. Educational programs and professional development initiatives focusing on this interdisciplinary nexus are emerging to prepare the next generation of catalysis professionals for digitally enhanced work environments.

CHAPTER 13   NANOMATERIALS IN CATALYSIS

The future trajectory of AI-IoT integration in nanocatalysis points toward increasingly autonomous systems with expanded capabilities:

Self-optimizing catalytic processes represent perhaps the ultimate expression of these technological convergence systems that continuously improve their own performance without human intervention. These closed-loop implementations combine real-time monitoring, predictive modeling, and automated execution to navigate complex operational landscapes toward optimal performance. Early demonstrations in flow chemistry applications have shown how such systems can dynamically optimize reaction conditions for maximum yield and selectivity, adapting to changes in feedstock properties or catalyst activity over time.

Collaborative intelligence networks connecting multiple catalytic operations across distributed locations enable knowledge sharing and collective optimization. These systems aggregate anonymized performance data and lessons learned across numerous implementations, creating a continuously expanding knowledge base that benefits all participants. For industries where similar catalytic processes operate across multiple sites, such as petroleum refining or bulk chemical production, these collaborative platforms accelerate best practice adoption and troubleshooting while respecting proprietary boundaries.

Human-AI collaborative frameworks recognize that human expertise and machine capabilities offer complementary strengths in catalyst development and optimization. Advanced interfaces visualize complex multidimensional data in intuitive formats, enabling human experts to identify patterns and relationships that inform decision-making. Explainable AI approaches provide transparent reasoning for model predictions and recommendations, building trust and facilitating productive collaboration between human researchers and computational systems. This partnership model has proven particularly effective for addressing novel catalytic challenges where neither human intuition nor computational analysis alone provides complete solutions.

As these technologies mature, they promise to dramatically accelerate innovation cycles while improving the sustainability and efficiency of chemical processes across industries. The ability to understand catalytic phenomena across length and time scales—from atomic interactions to industrial production—creates unprecedented opportunities for rational design and optimization. This holistic perspective, enabled by the seamless integration of advanced nanotechnology with digital capabilities, represents a fundamental shift in how humanity approaches chemical transformation, one of the foundational technologies of modern civilization.

13.7 Summary

The transformative potential of nanomaterials in catalysis is reshaping how chemical processes are designed, optimized, and implemented across scientific and industrial domains. This chapter explores how the nanoscale features of catalysts, such as increased surface area, quantum effects, and tunable electronic properties, enhance reactivity, selectivity, and efficiency in ways that bulk materials cannot achieve.

Advancements in nanobiocatalysts demonstrate the powerful synergy between biological specificity and nanomaterial robustness, offering new possibilities for sustainable chemical synthesis, especially in pharmaceutical applications. Similarly, nanoscaffolds emerge as more than passive supports, actively influencing reaction environments, facilitating electron transfer, and enabling multi-step cascade reactions with remarkable control.

Emerging trends highlight a shift toward atomically precise, bio-inspired, and earth-abundant nanocatalysts that address both performance and sustainability. The integration of artificial intelligence (AI) and Internet of Things (IoT) technologies further enhances nanocatalysis, enabling real-time data collection, adaptive control, and autonomous process optimization.

Together, these innovations represent a paradigm shift in catalysis, one where nanoscale engineering and digital intelligence converge to accelerate discovery, reduce environmental impact, and create more efficient, adaptable chemical systems for the future.

CHAPTER 14

Nanotechnology in Medicine

Nanotechnology has revolutionized numerous fields, but perhaps nowhere is its impact more profound than in medicine. The convergence of nanotechnology with medical science has birthed nanomedicine—a discipline that promises to transform healthcare delivery through unprecedented precision, personalization, and effectiveness. This chapter explores the multifaceted applications of nanotechnology in medicine, from sophisticated drug delivery systems to cutting-edge diagnostic tools and regenerative therapies.

14.1 Scope of Nanomedicine

Nanomedicine represents one of the most promising frontiers in modern healthcare, encompassing a diverse range of applications that leverage nanotechnology principles to address medical challenges. At its core, nanomedicine involves the use of materials, devices, and systems at the nanoscale—typically between 1 and 100 nanometers—to diagnose, treat, and prevent disease.

The scope of nanomedicine extends across the entire healthcare spectrum, from early disease detection to therapy and regenerative medicine. In diagnostics, nanoscale sensors and imaging agents offer sensitivity and specificity far exceeding conventional approaches. Therapeutic applications have garnered significant attention, particularly in oncology, where nanocarriers can encapsulate toxic chemotherapeutic agents, shielding healthy tissues while delivering concentrated doses to tumor sites.

CHAPTER 14   NANOTECHNOLOGY IN MEDICINE

The field has evolved dramatically since its conceptual inception by physicist Richard Feynman in his famous 1959 lecture "There's Plenty of Room at the Bottom." Today, sophisticated multifunctional nanoplatforms incorporate elements for targeting, imaging, drug release, and even real-time monitoring of therapeutic response. Table 14-1 summarizes the major categories of nanomedicine applications and their current clinical status.

Table 14-1. *Major Categories of Nanomedicine Applications*

Application Area	Examples	Clinical Status
Diagnostics	Quantum dot imaging, magnetic nanoparticle contrast agents	Several FDA-approved products
Drug delivery	Liposomal formulations, polymeric nanoparticles	Multiple approved products
Regenerative medicine	Nanostructured scaffolds, nanopatterned surfaces	Early clinical testing
Surgical tools	Nanoprecision surgical instruments	Predominantly preclinical
Implantable devices	Nanoporous implants, antimicrobial nanocoatings	Limited approved products

14.2 Peptide/DNA Nanoparticles

Peptide- and DNA-based nanoparticles represent sophisticated and biologically compatible platforms in nanomedicine. These biomolecular nanostructures harness the intrinsic properties of natural biomolecules—their biocompatibility, biodegradability, and molecular recognition capabilities—to create highly specific therapeutic and diagnostic systems.

Peptide nanoparticles leverage the diverse chemical properties of amino acids to create self-assembling structures with remarkable versatility. Self-assembling peptides typically contain alternating hydrophobic and hydrophilic residues that drive spontaneous organization into various nanostructures, including nanofibers, nanotubes, nanospheres, and hydrogels.

In cancer therapeutics, cell-penetrating peptides (CPPs) have proven particularly valuable. These short peptide sequences facilitate the intracellular delivery of therapeutic molecules that would otherwise struggle to cross cell membranes. TAT peptide, derived from the HIV transactivator protein, has been extensively utilized as a delivery enhancer for anticancer drugs and nucleic acid therapeutics.

DNA nanotechnology exploits the predictable base-pairing properties of nucleic acids to construct precisely defined nanostructures. The field has progressed from simple double-stranded DNA assemblies to complex three-dimensional architectures like DNA origami—structures formed by folding a long single-stranded DNA scaffold with numerous short "staple" strands (Figure 14-1).

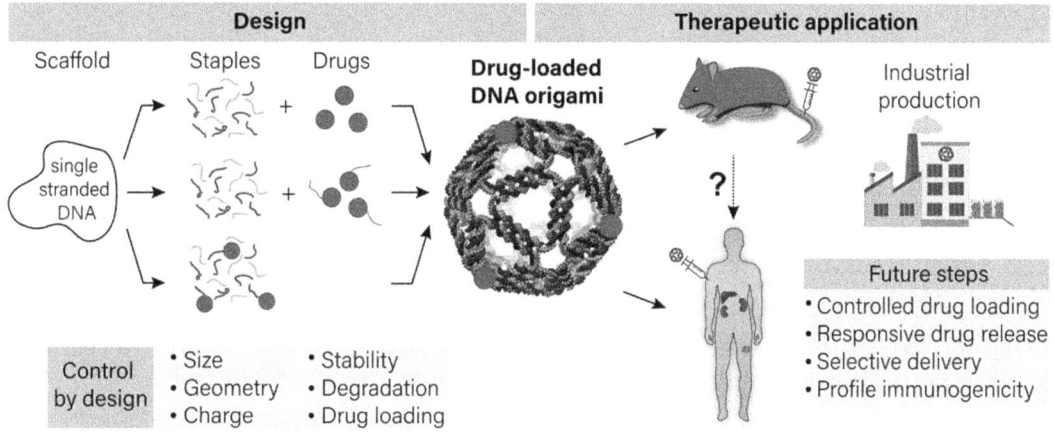

Figure 14-1. DNA Origami Nanostructures for Drug Delivery

RNA-based nanoparticles, particularly those utilizing small interfering RNA (siRNA) and messenger RNA (mRNA), have gained prominence with the success of COVID-19 vaccines. Lipid nanoparticles encapsulating mRNA proved remarkably effective at delivering genetic instructions for antigen production, triggering robust immune responses against the SARS-CoV-2 virus.

14.3 Lipid-Based Delivery Systems

Lipid-based delivery systems represent one of the most clinically successful categories of nanomedicine, with multiple FDA-approved products and a robust pipeline of candidates in clinical development. These systems exploit the amphiphilic nature of lipids—molecules with both hydrophilic and hydrophobic regions—to form versatile nanostructures capable of encapsulating and delivering therapeutic agents.

Liposomes, spherical vesicles composed of phospholipid bilayers, were among the first nanomedicine platforms to achieve clinical approval. These structures feature an aqueous core surrounded by one or more lipid bilayers, enabling them to encapsulate both hydrophilic compounds (in the aqueous compartment) and hydrophobic molecules (within the lipid bilayers). Doxil®, a PEGylated liposomal formulation of doxorubicin approved in 1995, demonstrated how liposomal encapsulation could dramatically alter a drug's pharmacokinetics and biodistribution, reducing cardiotoxicity while maintaining anticancer efficacy.

The recent success of COVID-19 mRNA vaccines has spotlighted lipid nanoparticles (LNPs) as transformative delivery vehicles for nucleic acid therapeutics. Modern LNPs typically combine four components: ionizable cationic lipids that facilitate RNA complexation and endosomal escape, helper phospholipids that support bilayer structure, cholesterol that enhances stability, and PEGylated lipids that provide steric stabilization and extend circulation time.

Manufacturing techniques like microfluidic mixing have revolutionized LNP production, enabling precise control over particle size, narrow size distribution, and high encapsulation efficiency. These manufacturing advances have been crucial for the rapid development and large-scale production of COVID-19 mRNA vaccines.

14.4 Inorganic Medical Applications

Inorganic nanomaterials offer unique physical and chemical properties that complement their organic counterparts in nanomedicine. These materials—including metal nanoparticles, quantum dots, silica nanostructures, and carbon nanomaterials—often exhibit exceptional stability, tunable optical properties, and distinctive magnetic, electrical, and thermal characteristics.

Gold nanoparticles (AuNPs) have emerged as versatile platforms due to their biocompatibility, ease of surface functionalization, and remarkable optical properties. Their localized surface plasmon resonance (LSPR) enables applications in biosensing, photothermal therapy, and imaging. Gold nanorods can absorb near-infrared light that penetrates deeply into biological tissues, converting this energy into heat for targeted thermal ablation of tumors.

Superparamagnetic iron oxide nanoparticles (SPIONs) respond strongly to external magnetic fields while exhibiting negligible magnetization in their absence—a property that enables magnetic guidance, hyperthermia treatment, and enhanced MRI contrast. Feraheme® (ferumoxytol), a carbohydrate-coated iron oxide nanoparticle, has been clinically approved for treating iron deficiency anemia.

Quantum dots—semiconductor nanocrystals with size-dependent fluorescence properties—have revolutionized biological imaging. Their narrow emission spectra, broad excitation profiles, high quantum yields, and exceptional photostability make them superior to conventional fluorophores for many applications. Their unique advantages position them at the forefront of next-generation imaging agents. Table 14-2 provides an overview of major classes of inorganic nanomaterials used in medicine, along with their key properties, applications, and clinical status.

Table 14-2. Major Classes of Inorganic Nanomaterials in Medicine

Nanomaterial Type	Key Properties	Major Applications	Clinical Status
Gold nanoparticles	LSPR, biocompatibility	Photothermal therapy, biosensing	Clinical trials
Iron oxide nanoparticles	Superparamagnetism	MRI contrast, hyperthermia	FDA-approved products
Quantum dots	Size-tunable fluorescence	Fluorescence imaging, biosensing	Preclinical
Mesoporous silica	High surface area	Controlled drug delivery	Clinical trials
Carbon nanotubes	Electrical conductivity	Biosensing, drug delivery	Preclinical

14.5 Future Outlook

The future of nanomedicine appears exceptionally promising, with several converging trends poised to accelerate innovation and clinical translation. Advances in nanofabrication techniques are enabling increasingly precise control over nanostructure composition, architecture, and functionality. High-throughput screening approaches, coupled with computational modeling, are facilitating more rational design of nanomedicines with optimized properties for specific applications.

Regulatory frameworks for nanomedicines continue to evolve, with agencies developing specialized guidelines to address the unique considerations these products present. These frameworks aim to balance innovation with patient safety, ensuring rigorous evaluation while providing clear pathways to approval. International harmonization efforts seek to standardize testing requirements and evaluation criteria, potentially streamlining global development and commercialization.

Near-term clinical advances are expected in several areas. Targeted nanomedicines for cancer therapy, particularly those leveraging active targeting strategies, show promise for improving therapeutic indices of potent but toxic anticancer agents. Immunomodulatory nanomedicines are emerging as powerful tools for cancer immunotherapy, autoimmune disease management, and vaccination. Nanomedicine approaches for crossing biological barriers, particularly the blood-brain barrier, offer hope for treating previously intractable neurological conditions.

Longer-term nanomedicine may fundamentally transform healthcare delivery models. Implantable nanodevices for continuous health monitoring could enable truly preventive medicine, detecting disease biomarkers before symptoms appear. Nanorobotic systems capable of autonomous navigation through the body could perform minimally invasive procedures with unprecedented precision. Cell-mimicking nanodevices might serve as functional replacements for damaged cells or tissues, addressing conditions ranging from diabetes to neurodegenerative diseases.

The integration of nanomedicine with emerging technologies like CRISPR gene editing, tissue engineering, and regenerative medicine promises synergistic approaches to previously intractable medical challenges. As these fields continue to advance and converge, the boundaries of what's medically possible will undoubtedly expand, potentially revolutionizing healthcare in the coming decades.

14.6 AI and IoT in Personalized Medicine

The integration of artificial intelligence (AI) and Internet of Things (IoT) technologies with nanomedicine represents a paradigm shift toward truly personalized healthcare. This convergence creates powerful systems capable of continuous health monitoring, data-driven therapeutic optimization, and proactive intervention—all tailored to individual patients' unique physiological profiles and disease characteristics.

Nanoscale sensors form the foundation of this integration, serving as the interface between biological systems and digital technologies. These sensors can detect molecular biomarkers with extraordinary sensitivity, monitor physiological parameters in real-time, and transmit this information to connected devices. Implantable and wearable nanosensors enable continuous monitoring of health metrics ranging from glucose levels to cardiac function, generating rich datasets that feed into AI-powered analytical systems.

AI algorithms transform this wealth of data into actionable insights, identifying patterns that might escape human detection and predicting potential health issues before they manifest clinically. Machine learning approaches can recognize subtle deviations from an individual's baseline health status, enabling early intervention. Deep learning models can integrate multimodal data—molecular, cellular, physiological, and environmental—to develop comprehensive health profiles and personalized risk assessments.

In therapeutic contexts, AI enhances nanomedicine by optimizing treatment selection and dosing based on individual patient characteristics. Computational models can predict how specific nanotherapeutics will interact with different patient populations, identifying those most likely to benefit from particular interventions. During treatment, real-time data from nanosensors enables dynamic adjustment of therapeutic parameters, creating closed-loop systems that continuously optimize efficacy while minimizing side effects.

The Internet of Medical Things (IoMT) creates infrastructure for these intelligent nanomedicine systems, enabling secure data transmission, storage, and analysis. Edge computing architectures allow for decentralized processing of sensor data, reducing latency for time-sensitive applications and minimizing bandwidth requirements. Cloud platforms facilitate more complex analytical tasks and integration with electronic health records, clinical decision support systems, and population health management tools.

Privacy and security considerations are paramount in these connected systems. Advanced encryption methods, blockchain technology, and federated learning approaches help protect sensitive health data while enabling beneficial use. Regulatory frameworks continue to evolve to address the unique challenges posed by AI-enabled medical devices and data-driven healthcare systems.

Several practical applications of this convergence are emerging:

1. Smart drug delivery systems utilize real-time physiological data to optimize therapeutic regimens. For example, glucose-responsive insulin delivery systems can automatically adjust release rates based on continuous glucose monitoring, maintaining ideal blood sugar levels without patient intervention.

2. Digital biomarker platforms integrate multiple nanosensors to detect subtle physiological changes that precede disease onset. AI algorithms analyze these signals to identify patients requiring intervention before clinical symptoms appear.

3. Virtual clinical trials leverage remote monitoring via nanosensors to gather continuous real-world data, reducing costs and improving accessibility while generating richer datasets than traditional site-based trials.

The future promises even deeper integration, with nanodevices potentially serving as both diagnostic and therapeutic platforms that adapt autonomously based on AI-processed health data. These systems could revolutionize the management of chronic diseases, enabling precise, personalized interventions that maximize efficacy while minimizing side effects and healthcare costs.

14.7 Summary

Nanotechnology in medicine has ushered in a new era of precision, personalization, and performance across diagnostics, therapeutics, and regenerative applications. This chapter has explored the breadth of nanomedicine, detailing how nanoscale platforms ranging from peptide and DNA nanoparticles to lipid-based systems and inorganic nanomaterials are reshaping modern healthcare. Each class of nanostructure offers unique physicochemical properties that enhance drug delivery, improve imaging resolution, and facilitate targeted therapeutic interventions.

Clinically, nanomedicine has already demonstrated success through FDA-approved formulations such as liposomes and iron oxide nanoparticles, with many more under investigation. The convergence with artificial intelligence (AI) and Internet of Things (IoT) technologies further amplifies the potential of nanomedicine by enabling continuous monitoring, predictive analytics, and real-time adaptive treatment systems, moving toward a future of fully personalized healthcare.

Looking ahead, the integration of nanomedicine with gene editing, tissue engineering, and bioinformatics is poised to transform disease prevention, diagnosis, and treatment. While challenges remain in regulation, manufacturing, and data security, the trajectory of innovation suggests that nanomedicine will play a pivotal role in shaping the future of global healthcare systems.

CHAPTER 15

Nanotechnology in Food Science

This chapter examines the integration of nanotechnology in food science with a focus on processing, packaging, and safety applications. It explores how nanomaterials enhance food preservation, packaging functionality, and pathogen detection systems while addressing safety innovation breakthroughs. The discussion covers emerging trends in smart food systems, challenges facing industry adoption including regulatory concerns and consumer perception, and the convergence of nanotechnology with artificial intelligence and the Internet of Things for comprehensive food safety monitoring. The chapter provides a balanced perspective on both the transformative potential and implementation barriers of nanotechnology in addressing contemporary food safety and quality challenges.

15.1 Introduction

Nanotechnology—the manipulation of materials at dimensions between 1 and 100 nanometers—is revolutionizing food science by enabling unprecedented control over food properties, packaging functionality, and safety systems. As global food systems face intensifying pressures from population growth, climate change, and evolving consumer demands, nanoscale innovations offer promising solutions to enhance shelf life, improve nutritional profiles, and detect contaminants with remarkable sensitivity.

This chapter explores how nanoscale engineering is transforming food processing techniques, creating intelligent packaging systems, and enabling rapid pathogen detection platforms. We examine both current applications in commercial settings and emerging technologies that promise to reshape food safety management. While highlighting technological advances, we also address critical implementation challenges, including regulatory frameworks, technical barriers, and consumer acceptance concerns.

15.2 Nanotechnology in Processing and Packaging

Nanotechnology has introduced transformative capabilities in food processing and packaging through materials engineered at the nanoscale. These applications enhance product quality, extend shelf life, and create innovative delivery systems for nutrients and bioactive compounds.

In processing applications, nanoemulsions and nanoencapsulation technologies enable improved delivery of functional ingredients with enhanced bioavailability. For example, lipophilic nutrients like omega-3 fatty acids and fat-soluble vitamins can be incorporated into water-based products without compromising sensory attributes. Nanostructured ingredients, including modified starches and proteins, provide enhanced functional properties such as improved texture, stability, and controlled release mechanisms.

Food packaging has been particularly revolutionized through nanotechnology applications. Nanocomposite materials incorporate particles such as nanoclays, cellulose nanofibrils, and metallic nanoparticles into polymer matrices to create packaging with enhanced barrier properties against oxygen, moisture, and light—critical factors in food deterioration.

Active packaging systems incorporate antimicrobial nanomaterials that inhibit microbial growth on food surfaces. Silver nanoparticles, titanium dioxide, and zinc oxide are commonly employed for their broad-spectrum antimicrobial activities. These systems actively extend shelf life by releasing controlled amounts of antimicrobial agents or scavenging compounds that accelerate spoilage. Table 15-1 summarizes commonly used nanomaterials in food packaging, their primary functions, and their mechanisms of action.

Table 15-1. Common Nanomaterials in Food Packaging Applications

Nanomaterial	Primary Function	Mechanism of Action
Silver nanoparticles	Antimicrobial	Cell membrane disruption, metabolic interference
Titanium dioxide	UV blocking, antimicrobial	Photocatalytic oxidation
Nanoclays	Barrier enhancement	Tortuous path effect for gas molecules
Zinc oxide	Antimicrobial, UV protection	ROS generation, ion release
Cellulose nanofibrils	Mechanical reinforcement, oxygen barrier	Hydrogen bonding network formation

Intelligent packaging represents another breakthrough application, incorporating nanosensors that monitor food quality parameters and communicate this information to consumers or supply chain managers. Time-temperature indicators based on gold nanoparticles can signal temperature abuse through color changes, while electrochemical nanosensors can detect specific metabolites associated with spoilage.

15.3 Pathogen Detection

Nanotechnology has dramatically enhanced pathogen detection capabilities in food systems, addressing critical limitations of conventional testing methods regarding sensitivity, specificity, and analysis time. Nanomaterial-based sensors offer detection limits in the picogram to femtogram range, enabling identification of pathogens at levels well below infectious doses.

Gold nanoparticles have proven particularly valuable in lateral flow immunoassays for rapid detection of foodborne pathogens like *Salmonella*, *E. coli* O157, and *Listeria*. These particles provide distinct visual signals through colorimetric changes when target pathogens are present, enabling detection without sophisticated instrumentation. The high surface-to-volume ratio of nanoparticles allows for dense functionalization with recognition elements such as antibodies, aptamers, or phage proteins, dramatically improving capture efficiency.

As illustrated in Figure 15-1, the Lateral Flow Assay (LFA) test strips designed for detecting *Salmonella typhimurium* consisted of a sample pad, a conjugate pad, a nitrocellulose (NC) membrane, and an absorbent pad, with approximately 3 mm of overlap between each adjoining section. To prepare these strips, the sample and conjugate pads were first soaked in a 100 mM Tris buffer solution (pH 8) containing 2% (w/v) D-trehalose, 2% (w/v) sucrose, 1% (w/v) polyvinylpyrrolidone (PVP), 0.5% (v/v) Tween-20, and 0.2% (w/v) bovine serum albumin (BSA) for one hour, followed by drying at 37 °C. The conjugate pad was then immersed in an amplification probe solution and dried again at 37 °C for 45 minutes. Subsequently, 50 μL of T-ssDNA (10 μM) and C-ssDNA (10 μM) were each mixed with 10 μL of streptavidin (1 mg/mL) and incubated at 37 °C for two hours. This mixture was applied to the NC membrane to create the test (T) line and control (C) line, spaced 8 mm apart. The assembled master cards were then cut into individual strips measuring approximately 5 cm in length and 0.4 cm in width using a paper slitting machine. The finished strips were stored at 4 °C in sealed plastic bags with desiccant for future use.

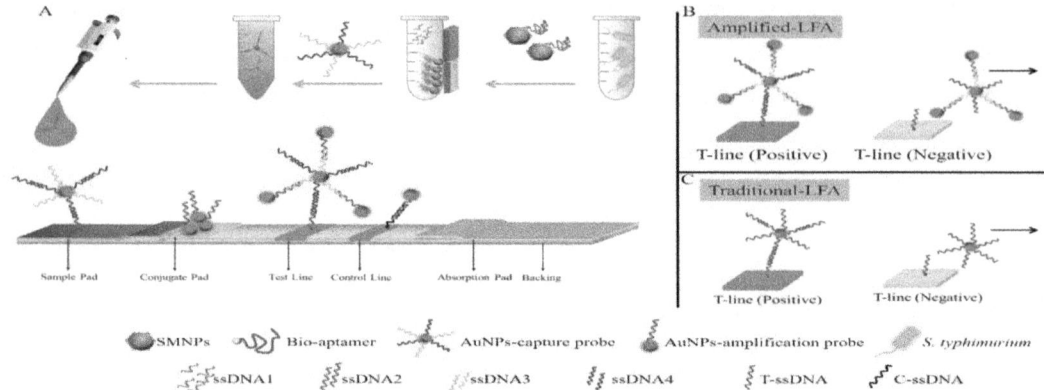

Figure 15-1. *Schematic Representation of a Nanoparticle-Enhanced Lateral Flow Immunoassay for Foodborne Pathogen Detection*

Lateral flow assay enhanced by multifold AuNPs combined with magnetic enrichment for *Salmonella typhimurium* detection. (A) Schematic illustration of the detection of *Salmonella typhimurium* using AuNPs aggregates enhanced lateral flow assay; (B) multifold AuNPs on the test line in the presence (left) and absence (right) of *Salmonella typhimurium*; (C) single-dose AuNPs on the test line in the unenhanced lateral flow assay.

Quantum dots—semiconductor nanocrystals with unique optical properties—have enabled multiplexed detection systems capable of simultaneously identifying multiple pathogens in a single sample. Their narrow emission spectra and resistance to photobleaching overcome limitations of conventional fluorescent dyes, while their surface chemistry can be tailored for specific target recognition.

Magnetic nanoparticles provide another breakthrough in pathogen detection through sample concentration capabilities. When functionalized with specific antibodies or aptamers, these particles can capture target pathogens from complex food matrices and be separated using magnetic fields, effectively concentrating pathogens from large sample volumes to detection-compatible quantities.

Nanobiosensors integrating biological recognition elements with nanomaterial transducers have enabled rapid, sensitive detection platforms. For example, carbon nanotube field-effect transistors functionalized with specific antibodies can detect electrical changes when target pathogens bind, achieving detection limits as low as 10–100 CFU/mL with analysis times under 30 minutes.

15.4 Food Safety Innovations

Nanotechnology has catalyzed breakthrough innovations addressing critical food safety challenges beyond detection, including microbial control, toxin mitigation, and quality monitoring systems. These applications leverage unique nanoscale interactions to enhance food protection throughout the supply chain.

Antimicrobial nanocoatings applied directly to food contact surfaces represent a significant innovation in preventive control. Silver nanoparticle coatings on processing equipment and conveyor belts have demonstrated sustained antimicrobial activity against biofilm formation—a persistent challenge in food processing environments. Unlike conventional sanitizers that provide only temporary control, these coatings deliver continuous protection between cleaning cycles, reducing cross-contamination risks.

Nanofiltration membranes with precisely engineered pore sizes enable selective removal of microbial contaminants, mycotoxins, and chemical hazards while preserving valuable nutrients. These membranes improve upon conventional filtration by combining physical exclusion with surface interactions that capture contaminants smaller than the nominal pore size. Table 15-2 outlines key nanotechnology solutions addressing common food safety challenges and their advantages over traditional methods.

Table 15-2. Nanotechnology Solutions for Common Food Safety Challenges

Safety Challenge	Nanotechnology Solution	Advantage Over Conventional Methods
Biofilm formation	Silver nanoparticle surface coatings	Persistent antimicrobial activity between cleaning cycles
Mycotoxin contamination	Magnetic nanoparticle adsorbents	Selective binding with minimal impact on nutrients
Chemical residues	Nanofiltration membranes	Selective removal based on molecular size and charge
Cross-contamination	Antimicrobial nanocomposite food contact materials	Continuous protection without chemical migration
Spoilage monitoring	Colorimetric nanosensors	Visual indication without electronic components

Nanoencapsulation systems provide targeted delivery of antimicrobial compounds, addressing limitations of conventional preservatives. Essential oils with potent antimicrobial properties but poor water solubility and high volatility can be effectively incorporated into food systems through nanoemulsions and solid lipid nanoparticles. These delivery systems protect antimicrobial compounds from degradation while enabling controlled release in response to environmental triggers such as pH changes or enzyme activity associated with microbial growth.

15.5 Future of Food Nanotechnology

The future of nanotechnology in food science promises increasingly sophisticated systems that respond intelligently to environmental conditions, enhance nutrition, and create entirely new food experiences. Several emerging trajectories will likely define the next generation of food nanotechnology applications.

Smart packaging systems integrating multiple nanotechnologies represent a key developmental direction. These systems will combine barrier materials, antimicrobial elements, nanosensors, and communication technologies to create truly intelligent packaging that not only protects food but actively monitors quality, extends shelf life, and communicates with consumers and supply chain managers. Printed nanocircuits will enable packages to wirelessly transmit freshness data to smartphones, while responsive materials will selectively release preservatives only when microbial growth is detected.

Personalized nutrition facilitated by nanotechnology delivery systems offers another promising frontier. Nanostructured delivery vehicles can protect sensitive nutrients through harsh processing conditions and gastrointestinal transit, releasing them at specific absorption sites. These systems will enable foods formulated with personalized nutrient profiles tailored to individual requirements based on genetic analysis, microbiome composition, and metabolic parameters.

Sustainability improvements through nanotechnology will address growing environmental concerns in food systems. Nano-enabled catalysts are being developed to convert agricultural waste streams into valuable compounds, while nanostructured materials derived from renewable sources will replace petroleum-based packaging. Nanoscale engineering of biopolymers is already improving the performance of biodegradable packaging materials to match or exceed conventional plastics.

Surface decontamination technologies utilizing photocatalytic nanomaterials represent an emerging application with significant potential for food safety management. Titanium dioxide and zinc oxide nanostructures activated by visible light can generate reactive oxygen species that destroy pathogenic microorganisms on food contact surfaces without chemical residues or microbial resistance development.

15.6 Industry Challenges

Despite promising technological advances, the food industry faces significant challenges in nanotechnology implementation that must be addressed for widespread adoption. These barriers span regulatory, technical, economic, and consumer acceptance domains.

Regulatory frameworks for food nanotechnology remain incomplete and inconsistent globally, creating uncertainty for manufacturers. While some jurisdictions have developed specific nanomaterial regulations, many employ case-by-case assessment approaches without standardized protocols. This regulatory patchwork complicates international trade and technology transfer while increasing compliance costs. The European Union has established the most comprehensive regulatory framework through its Novel Foods Regulation and nanomaterial definition requirements, while the US FDA generally addresses nanomaterials within existing regulatory structures.

Technical implementation challenges present additional barriers, particularly in scaling laboratory successes to industrial production. Maintaining nanomaterial properties during manufacturing processes requires precise control over numerous parameters, including temperature, pressure, and mixing conditions. Many food companies lack specialized equipment and expertise to implement nanotechnology safely and effectively. Table 15-3 summarizes the primary categories of implementation barriers for food nanotechnology and outlines potential solutions to overcome them.

Table 15-3. Key Implementation Barriers for Food Nanotechnology

Barrier Category	Specific Challenges	Potential Solutions
Regulatory	Inconsistent definitions, testing protocols, safety assessment standards	International harmonization initiatives
Technical	Scale-up challenges, integration with existing equipment, quality control methods	Industry-academic partnerships, specialized training programs
Economic	High initial investment, uncertain return timeline, intellectual property complexity	Incentive programs, collaborative development models
Consumer acceptance	Risk perception, transparency demands, "naturalness" concerns	Proactive communication, benefit demonstration, stakeholder engagement

Consumer perception remains perhaps the most significant obstacle to widespread adoption. Studies consistently show public wariness regarding nanomaterials in food products, with concerns centering on potential unknown health impacts and perceptions of "unnaturalness." The food industry's historical experience with genetically modified organisms demonstrates how consumer rejection can derail promising technologies regardless of scientific safety evidence.

Environmental sustainability questions also warrant consideration as production scales increase. The environmental fate of engineered nanomaterials throughout product lifecycles remains incompletely characterized, raising legitimate questions about bioaccumulation potential and ecosystem impacts from manufacturing waste streams and post-consumer disposal.

15.7 AI and IoT in Food Safety

The convergence of nanotechnology with artificial intelligence (AI) and Internet of Things (IoT) technologies is creating unprecedented capabilities for comprehensive food safety management systems that monitor conditions throughout the supply chain in real time.

Nanosensor networks distributed throughout production facilities, transportation vehicles, and retail environments can continuously monitor critical parameters, including temperature, humidity, microbial load, and chemical indicators of spoilage. These sensors transmit data to cloud platforms where AI algorithms analyze patterns to identify potential safety risks before they manifest as detectable contamination issues.

Predictive analytics models trained on historical contamination data combined with real-time nanosensor inputs enable proactive intervention strategies that prevent safety failures rather than merely detecting them after occurrence. For instance, AI systems analyzing temperature fluctuation patterns from nanosensors embedded in transport containers can flag specific shipments at heightened risk for microbial growth, triggering targeted inspection protocols.

Nanotechnology has significantly enhanced the quality of food products, from raw ingredients to fully processed items. In food monitoring, a variety of nano-based techniques have been developed, including molecular assays, immunoassays, electrochemical methods, surface-enhanced Raman scattering (SERS), and colorimetric analysis (Figure 15-2). These approaches enable the detection of contaminants such as heavy metals, pathogens, pesticides, allergens, and antibiotics throughout food processing and in final commercial products. While earlier reviews have explored nanotechnology's role in the food sector, they often focused on specific areas like freshness evaluation, packaging, or pathogen detection. In contrast, this review provides a comprehensive and current overview of nanotechnology applications across the food industry. It examines both biotic and abiotic factors that influence food quality and consumer health and outlines the latest advancements in nanotechnology for monitoring and controlling food quality through various mechanisms.

CHAPTER 15   NANOTECHNOLOGY IN FOOD SCIENCE

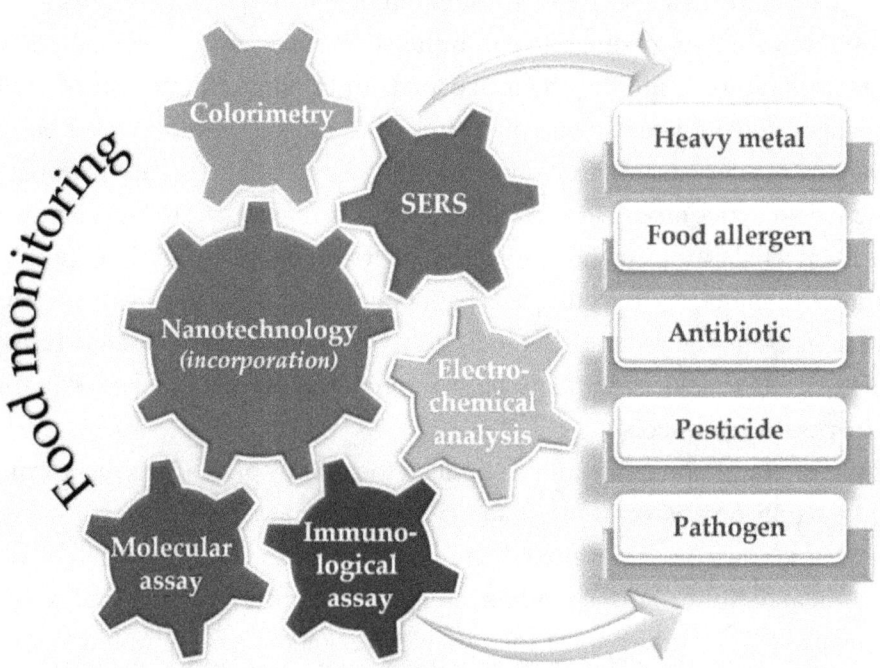

Figure 15-2. *Integrated Nanotechnology-AI-IoT Ecosystem for Comprehensive Food Safety Management*

Digital traceability systems enhanced by nanomaterial-based authentication markers represent another powerful integration. Unique nanoparticle "fingerprints" applied to packaging or directly to food products enable verification of authenticity and chain-of-custody throughout distribution networks. When combined with blockchain recordkeeping, these systems create immutable traceability records that dramatically improve outbreak investigation capabilities.

Edge computing architectures optimized for nanosensor networks allow critical safety decisions to be made locally without cloud connectivity, addressing connectivity limitations in remote production or transportation environments. These systems can autonomously adjust storage conditions or trigger preservative release mechanisms from smart packaging based on detected contamination risks.

Human interface optimization through augmented reality systems provides another synergistic application. Workers equipped with AR displays can visualize normally invisible contamination risks detected by nanosensors, improving cleaning efficiency and compliance verification in production environments.

While these integrated systems offer remarkable potential, significant implementation challenges remain. Data standardization across diverse sensor platforms, cybersecurity concerns in increasingly connected food systems, and appropriate integration of human judgment with algorithmic recommendations require careful consideration as these technologies mature.

15.8 Summary

Nanotechnology is fundamentally transforming food science by enabling unprecedented control over material properties at the molecular scale. From enhanced packaging barriers to ultra-sensitive detection systems, these innovations address critical challenges in ensuring safe, nutritious food supply chains. As we have explored throughout this chapter, applications span the entire food system—from processing technologies that enhance product characteristics to intelligent packaging that communicates quality information to consumers.

The integration of nanotechnology with AI and IoT systems creates particularly promising opportunities for comprehensive safety management networks that continuously monitor conditions and predict potential hazards before they manifest as contamination events. These systems represent a paradigm shift from reactive to preventive approaches in food safety.

However, significant challenges remain before these technologies achieve widespread commercial implementation. Regulatory frameworks continue to evolve unevenly across global markets, while technical barriers in scaling production and consumer acceptance concerns present substantial adoption hurdles. The food industry must address these challenges through collaborative approaches involving scientists, policymakers, and consumer advocates to realize nanotechnology's full potential.

As research continues to advance nanomaterial design and safety assessment, we can expect increasingly sophisticated applications that enhance food quality while addressing sustainability imperatives. The future food system will likely incorporate intelligent materials that respond dynamically to environmental conditions, detect specific contaminants with remarkable sensitivity, and communicate quality information transparently to consumers.

CHAPTER 15   NANOTECHNOLOGY IN FOOD SCIENCE

Food safety professionals must develop interdisciplinary expertise that spans traditional microbiology and chemistry while incorporating an understanding of nanomaterial properties and data analytics. This evolving landscape presents both significant challenges and unprecedented opportunities to enhance global food safety systems.

CHAPTER 16

Nanotechnology in Water Remediation

This chapter examines the applications of nanotechnology in water remediation, presenting current techniques and emerging solutions. It covers conventional water treatment enhanced by nanomaterials, advanced nanopurification technologies, innovative biomimetic approaches, environmental considerations, industry prospects, and the integration of AI and IoT for water quality monitoring. The discussion balances the transformative potential of nanotechnology in addressing water contamination while acknowledging implementation challenges and sustainability concerns.

16.1 Introduction

Water contamination remains one of humanity's most pressing environmental and public health challenges. With over 2 billion people lacking access to safely managed drinking water and industrial pollution threatening aquatic ecosystems, conventional treatment methods often prove inadequate against emerging contaminants. Nanotechnology—the manipulation of matter at dimensions between 1 and 100 nanometers—offers unprecedented opportunities to revolutionize water purification and remediation.

The unique properties of nanomaterials, including high surface-area-to-volume ratio, tunable surface chemistry, and quantum effects, enable more effective contaminant removal than traditional methods. This chapter explores how nanoscale materials are transforming water treatment paradigms while addressing concerns regarding environmental impacts, regulatory challenges, and implementation economics.

16.2 Techniques for Water Treatment

Conventional water treatment relies on physical, chemical, and biological processes, including coagulation-flocculation, sedimentation, filtration, and disinfection. Despite their widespread use, these methods struggle with emerging contaminants like pharmaceuticals, personal care products, and industrial chemicals.

Nanotechnology enhances these conventional processes through nano-enhanced coagulants, filtration systems, and disinfection approaches. Nano-coagulants like polyaluminum chloride nanoparticles achieve better turbidity removal while using lower dosages and generating less sludge. Nanocomposite filters incorporating carbon nanotubes, graphene, or metal oxide nanoparticles significantly improve filtration performance by capturing contaminants conventional filters miss.

Nano-enabled disinfection utilizes silver nanoparticles, titanium dioxide, and zinc oxide to neutralize pathogens without the formation of harmful disinfection byproducts. These antimicrobial nanomaterials can be incorporated into filter media or used as water additives for continuous protection. Table 16-1 compares the performance of conventional and nano-enhanced water treatment methods across key operational parameters.

Table 16-1. Performance Comparison: Conventional vs. Nano-Enhanced Water Treatment

Parameter	Conventional Methods	Nano-Enhanced Methods
Contaminant removal efficiency	65–85%	90–99%
Energy requirements	Moderate-high	Low-moderate
Chemical usage	High	Reduced by 30–50%
Treatment time	Hours	Minutes to hours
Removal of emerging contaminants	Limited	Comprehensive

16.3 Nanopurification Technologies

Nanoadsorbents

Nanoadsorbents represent a breakthrough in selective contaminant removal thanks to their exceptionally high surface areas and customizable surface chemistries. Carbon-based nanoadsorbents, including carbon nanotubes, graphene oxide, and carbon nanospheres, demonstrate remarkable adsorption capacities for organic pollutants, heavy metals, and pharmaceutical residues.

Metal and metal oxide nanoparticles, particularly iron oxides, titanium dioxide, and zinc oxide, excel in heavy metal removal through mechanisms like ion exchange, complexation, and redox reactions. These can be functionalized to target specific contaminants or deployed in magnetic forms for easy recovery after treatment.

Polymer-based nanoadsorbents, including dendrimers and molecularly imprinted polymers, offer highly selective binding sites engineered for specific contaminants, enabling precision treatment for complex industrial wastewater.

Nanomembranes

Nanomembrane technology has transformed filtration capabilities by operating at molecular and ionic levels. Ceramic nanomembranes utilizing alumina, silica, or titanium dioxide offer superior chemical and thermal stability compared to polymeric counterparts, enabling application in harsh industrial environments.

Thin-film nanocomposite membranes incorporate nanomaterials within conventional polymeric membranes, reducing biofouling and enhancing permeability and selectivity. Forward osmosis nanomembranes present a low-energy alternative to reverse osmosis, using osmotic pressure differentials rather than hydraulic pressure to drive water purification.

Photocatalytic Nanomaterials

Photocatalytic nanomaterials harness light energy to degrade contaminants into harmless byproducts. Titanium dioxide (TiO_2) nanoparticles remain the predominant photocatalyst, generating highly reactive hydroxyl radicals and superoxide ions when exposed to UV light. Advanced modifications, including doping with metals or nonmetals, extend their activity into visible light ranges, improving energy efficiency.

Plasmonic photocatalysts incorporating noble metals like silver and gold demonstrate enhanced visible light activity through localized surface plasmon resonance effects. These systems show promise for solar-powered water treatment applications in resource-limited settings.

16.4 Innovative Solutions

Biomimetic Approaches

Biomimetic nanotechnology draws inspiration from natural water purification processes. Aquaporin-based membranes incorporate natural water channel proteins into synthetic membranes, achieving unprecedented water permeability while maintaining excellent selectivity against contaminants.

Lotus leaf-inspired superhydrophobic surfaces utilize hierarchical micro/nanostructures to create self-cleaning filtration materials that resist fouling and bacterial adhesion. Mussel-inspired adhesive nanocoatings containing polydopamine provide versatile platforms for immobilizing functional nanomaterials on diverse substrates.

Multifunctional Nanomaterials

Multifunctional nanomaterials combine multiple treatment mechanisms within a single platform. Core-shell nanostructures feature magnetic cores for easy recovery wrapped in functional shells tailored for specific contaminant removal. Hierarchical composite materials integrate different nanomaterials to address multiple contaminant classes simultaneously.

Nanotechnology-Enhanced Biological Treatment

Nanotechnology enhances biological treatment processes through immobilized enzyme systems where nanomaterials provide stable support matrices for enzymes that degrade recalcitrant pollutants. Nanobiocomposites combine microbial capabilities with nanomaterial properties, creating synergistic systems for complex wastewater treatment.

16.5 Environmental Considerations

Nanomaterial Toxicity

The environmental behavior of engineered nanomaterials raises important considerations for water remediation applications. Studies have shown varying degrees of toxicity to aquatic organisms depending on particle size, shape, surface chemistry, and concentration. Silver nanoparticles, while effective antimicrobial agents, demonstrate toxicity toward beneficial microorganisms and aquatic life at certain concentrations.

The persistence and transformation of nanomaterials in natural water systems remain incompletely understood. Some materials undergo aggregation, dissolution, or surface modification that alters their bioavailability and potential ecosystem impacts. These uncertainties necessitate a thorough risk assessment before widespread implementation.

Lifecycle Assessment

A comprehensive lifecycle assessment of nanomaterial-based water treatment reveals a complex sustainability picture. While operational benefits often include reduced energy consumption and chemical usage, nanomaterial production frequently involves energy-intensive processes and hazardous precursors. End-of-life management presents particular challenges, as nanomaterial recovery and disposal methods remain underdeveloped.

Regulatory Frameworks

Regulatory frameworks for nanomaterials in water treatment continue to evolve globally, but lack harmonization. The European Union has implemented the REACH (Registration, Evaluation, Authorization and Restriction of Chemicals) regulation which addresses nanomaterials, while the United States EPA approaches regulation through existing frameworks like the Toxic Substances Control Act.

International standards organizations, including ISO and ASTM, have developed standardized testing procedures for nanomaterial characterization and toxicity assessment. However, significant gaps remain in regulations specifically addressing nanomaterials in water treatment applications and their potential environmental release.

16.6 Industry Prospects

Market Growth

The global market for nanomaterial-based water treatment technologies continues robust growth, with projections reaching $25.7 billion by 2030 at a compound annual growth rate of 15.6%. Membrane technologies represent the largest segment, followed by adsorbents and disinfection technologies.

Regional analysis reveals particularly strong growth in Asia-Pacific markets, driven by acute water scarcity, industrial expansion, and increasing regulatory pressure. North America and Europe maintain significant market shares, with emphasis on advanced technologies for emerging contaminant removal and resource recovery.

Cost-Effectiveness Analysis

Despite higher initial costs compared to conventional treatment methods, economic analyses frequently demonstrate favorable long-term economics for nanomaterial-based systems when accounting for operational efficiency, durability, and reduced chemical consumption. Point-of-use applications have achieved commercial success, particularly in regions with inadequate centralized infrastructure.

Scaling Challenges

Transitioning nanomaterial-based water treatment from laboratory success to industrial implementation faces several barriers. Mass production of consistent, high-quality nanomaterials remains technically challenging and cost-intensive. Integration with existing water treatment infrastructure requires careful engineering to maintain nanomaterial stability and effectiveness under real-world conditions.

16.7 AI and IoT for Water Monitoring

Smart Nanosensors

Nanotechnology-enabled sensors achieve unprecedented sensitivity and selectivity for water quality monitoring. Electrochemical nanosensors utilizing carbon nanotubes, graphene, and metal nanoparticles detect heavy metals at parts-per-billion concentrations. Optical nanosensors based on quantum dots, surface plasmon resonance, and fluorescent nanomaterials provide rapid detection of microbial contamination and organic pollutants.

Integration of these nanosensors into Internet of Things networks enables continuous, real-time water quality monitoring across distribution systems. This capability supports early contamination detection and rapid response protocols previously impossible with periodic manual sampling.

Predictive Analytics

Artificial intelligence applications in water treatment extend beyond monitoring to predictive capabilities. Machine learning algorithms analyze historical sensor data alongside environmental factors to predict treatment efficiency under varying conditions. These systems optimize chemical dosing, backwashing cycles, and energy consumption while maintaining water quality standards.

Digital twin technology creates virtual replicas of treatment systems that simulate performance under various scenarios, enabling operators to test process modifications without disrupting actual operations. These models continually improve through feedback from real-time operating data.

Remote Management Systems

Cloud-based platforms integrate data from distributed nanosensors with treatment system controls, enabling remote management of water infrastructure. This connectivity proves particularly valuable for rural and developing regions where on-site technical expertise may be limited.

AI-powered anomaly detection identifies deviations from normal operating parameters before they develop into significant problems. These early warning systems reduce downtime and prevent potential contamination events by alerting operators to emerging issues. Table 16-2 highlights the key benefits and measurable impacts of integrating AI with nanomaterial-enabled water treatment and monitoring systems.

Table 16-2. Benefits of AI-Integrated Nanomaterial Water Treatment Systems

Benefit Category	Specific Improvements	Impact Magnitude
Operational efficiency	Chemical usage optimization	15–30% reduction
	Energy consumption	10–25% reduction
	Maintenance requirements	20–40% reduction
Water quality	Contaminant removal consistency	99.5%+ compliance
	Response time to quality issues	85% improvement
Economic	Overall operational costs	15–35% reduction
	System lifespan	30–50% extension

16.8 Summary

Nanotechnology presents transformative opportunities for addressing global water contamination challenges through enhanced treatment efficiency, expanded contaminant removal capabilities, and reduced resource consumption. From nanomaterial-enhanced conventional processes to entirely novel treatment paradigms, these technologies offer solutions precisely tailored to diverse contamination scenarios.

However, responsible implementation requires addressing several critical challenges. Environmental concerns regarding nanomaterial release and potential ecosystem impacts necessitate robust risk assessment and management strategies. Economic barriers to scaling and deployment demand continued innovation in nanomaterial production and system design. Regulatory frameworks must evolve to balance innovation with appropriate safeguards.

The integration of nanotechnology with artificial intelligence and Internet of Things capabilities represents a particularly promising direction, creating adaptive treatment systems that continuously optimize performance based on real-time data. These smart water systems point toward a future where water treatment becomes increasingly precise, efficient, and responsive.

As nanotechnology for water remediation continues maturing from research concept to practical implementation, interdisciplinary collaboration among materials scientists, environmental engineers, toxicologists, and data scientists becomes increasingly vital. Through such collaborations, nanotechnology's full potential for securing clean water resources worldwide may be realized.

CHAPTER 17

MEMS and NEMS Based on Nanomaterials

This chapter provides an overview of micro-electromechanical systems (MEMS) and nano-electromechanical systems (NEMS), exploring their fundamental principles, fabrication methods, and applications across industries. It examines how nanomaterials enhance these miniaturized systems, discusses medical and engineering implementations, addresses manufacturing and reliability challenges, and analyzes current trends. Special attention is given to the integration of artificial intelligence and the Internet of Things with MEMS/NEMS technologies, offering insights into how these microscale and nanoscale systems are transforming modern technology.

17.1 Introduction to MEMS/NEMS

Micro-electromechanical systems (MEMS) and nano-electromechanical systems (NEMS) represent a revolutionary technological advancement that integrates mechanical elements, sensors, actuators, and electronics on microscopic and nanoscopic scales. MEMS typically operate with features ranging from 1 to 100 micrometers, while NEMS push boundaries further with components below 100 nanometers. This miniaturization enables unprecedented integration capabilities, reduced power consumption, and enhanced sensitivity.

The development of MEMS began in the 1960s with the invention of the resonant gate transistor, while NEMS emerged later as fabrication techniques improved. Both technologies translate physical phenomena into electrical signals and vice versa, creating intelligent systems that sense, process, and respond to environmental changes.

The primary fabrication methods for these systems include bulk micromachining, surface micromachining, the LIGA process, and wafer bonding. For NEMS, additional specialized techniques like electron beam lithography, focused ion beam milling, and molecular self-assembly are employed.

MEMS and NEMS applications span diverse fields, including inertial sensing (accelerometers, gyroscopes), pressure sensing, optical systems, RF components, microfluidics, and energy harvesting. Their integration with conventional electronics has been crucial to commercial success, though it presents challenges in fabrication compatibility, electrical connections, and appropriate packaging. Table 17-1 summarizes the fundamental differences between MEMS and NEMS across key technical parameters.

Table 17-1. Key Differences Between MEMS and NEMS

Characteristic	MEMS	NEMS
Feature size	1–100 μm	<100 nm
Fabrication techniques	Bulk/surface micromachining	E-beam lithography, self-assembly
Physical effects	Classical mechanics dominant	Quantum effects significant
Power consumption	Low	Ultra-low
Manufacturing complexity	Moderate	Very high

17.2 Role of Nanomaterials

Nanomaterials have transformed MEMS and NEMS from simple mechanical devices into sophisticated multifunctional platforms. Their unique properties at the nanoscale—where quantum effects become prominent—enable engineers to overcome traditional limitations in performance and functionality.

The key properties that make nanomaterials valuable for these applications include enhanced surface-to-volume ratio, quantum confinement effects, superior mechanical strength, and unique electrical and thermal properties. Carbon nanomaterials, particularly carbon nanotubes (CNTs) and graphene, have emerged as leading materials due to their exceptional mechanical strength, electrical conductivity, and thermal stability.

Metal nanostructures, including gold, silver, and platinum nanoparticles, are extensively used in sensing applications due to their plasmonic properties and catalytic activities. Meanwhile, semiconductor nanomaterials like silicon nanowires and quantum dots enable advanced electronic and optoelectronic functions in NEMS devices.

Ceramic nanomaterials provide excellent thermal stability and chemical resistance, while polymer nanocomposites offer flexibility, biocompatibility, and ease of processing. These diverse nanomaterials are processed through techniques such as chemical vapor deposition, atomic layer deposition, and solution-based methods to create precisely engineered structures.

17.3 Medical and Engineering Applications

MEMS and NEMS technologies have revolutionized both medical diagnostics and treatment through miniaturized, implantable, and wearable devices. In diagnostics, lab-on-a-chip systems perform complex biochemical analyses with minimal sample volumes, while implantable biosensors monitor glucose levels, cardiac markers, and neurological signals in real time. Drug delivery systems utilize microreservoirs and nanoporous membranes to provide controlled release of medications, particularly valuable for chronic conditions requiring precise dosing. Table 17-2 outlines key medical applications of MEMS and NEMS technologies, highlighting specific examples and their associated benefits.

The field of neural interfaces has been transformed through NEMS-based electrodes that offer improved biocompatibility and signal quality for brain–computer interfaces and neural prosthetics. Minimally invasive surgical tools incorporating MEMS technology enable procedures with reduced trauma and faster recovery times.

In engineering applications, MEMS accelerometers and gyroscopes are integral to automotive safety systems, enhancing stability control and airbag deployment. Aerospace applications include navigation systems, structural health monitoring, and microthrusters for satellite positioning. Consumer electronics rely heavily on MEMS for touchscreens, microphones, and display technologies.

Industrial monitoring benefits from networks of MEMS sensors that track vibration, temperature, and pressure in manufacturing environments. Energy harvesting devices convert ambient mechanical energy, thermal gradients, or light into electrical power for autonomous sensor networks.

Table 17-2. Medical Applications of MEMS/NEMS

Application Area	Examples	Benefits
Diagnostics	Lab-on-chip, biosensors	Rapid results, minimal sample
Drug delivery	Microreservoirs, smart patches	Controlled release, reduced side effects
Neural interfaces	Implantable electrodes	Improved signal quality, biocompatibility
Surgical tools	Microforceps, catheters	Minimally invasive, reduced recovery time
Monitoring	Implantable pressure sensors	Continuous data, early intervention

17.4 Challenges and Opportunities

Despite their tremendous potential, MEMS and NEMS technologies face significant challenges in manufacturing, reliability, and integration. Fabrication challenges include maintaining precision at nanoscales, achieving consistent yields, and managing complex process integration. The industry continues to work on standardizing fabrication processes and improving quality control methodologies.

Reliability issues arise from mechanical wear, material fatigue, environmental sensitivity, and packaging limitations. Hermetic packaging is essential to protect sensitive components while allowing them to interact with the environment when needed. Long-term stability remains a concern for implantable medical devices and industrial applications requiring years of continuous operation.

Integration challenges include interfacing nanoscale components with microscale and macroscale systems, signal conditioning for weak electrical outputs, and power management for energy-constrained applications. Cross-disciplinary expertise is required to address these complex integration issues.

Material limitations include biocompatibility concerns for medical applications, material degradation in harsh environments, and the need for materials with specialized properties. Research is ongoing to develop biocompatible coatings, corrosion-resistant materials, and novel composites with tailored characteristics.

Despite these challenges, significant opportunities exist in emerging applications such as Internet of Things sensors, wearable health monitoring, environmental sensing networks, and advanced prosthetics. The continuing miniaturization, increased functionality, and reduced power consumption of these systems will enable applications that are currently not feasible.

17.5 Trends in Technology

The evolution of MEMS and NEMS technologies is driven by several key trends. Progressive miniaturization continues to push the boundaries of what's physically possible, with feature sizes approaching fundamental material limits. This miniaturization enables higher integration density, reduced power consumption, and access to new physical phenomena at the nanoscale.

Multi-functional integration is becoming increasingly important, with devices incorporating multiple sensing modalities, actuation capabilities, and processing functions on a single chip. This trend supports the development of more autonomous and intelligent microsystems capable of complex decision-making without external processing.

Materials innovation is accelerating, with graphene, carbon nanotubes, piezoelectric materials, and shape memory alloys enabling novel functionalities. These advanced materials improve performance metrics such as sensitivity, response time, and energy efficiency while enabling operation in challenging environments.

Improved manufacturing techniques, including 3D printing at micro/nanoscales, roll-to-roll processing for flexible devices, and advanced lithography techniques, are reducing costs and increasing scalability. These developments are making MEMS and NEMS more accessible for mass-market applications.

Biocompatible and biodegradable MEMS represent an important trend for medical applications, with devices designed to safely integrate with biological tissues or harmlessly degrade after completing their function. Energy-autonomous systems are emerging through advances in energy harvesting, ultra-low-power design, and efficient energy storage at microscales. Table 17-3 summarizes the key emerging trends in MEMS/NEMS technologies and their expected impacts on future applications.

Table 17-3. Emerging Trends in MEMS/NEMS Technology

Trend	Description	Impact
Extreme miniaturization	Feature sizes approaching 1–10 nm	New physical effects, higher density
Multi-functionality	Multiple sensing/actuation on a single chip	More capable autonomous systems
Advanced materials	Graphene, CNTs, biodegradable polymers	Enhanced performance, biocompatibility
3D MEMS/NEMS	Vertical integration, complex geometries	Increased functionality in a smaller footprint
Self-powered systems	Energy harvesting, ultra-low power	Maintenance-free operation

17.6 AI and IoT in MEMS/NEMS

The convergence of MEMS/NEMS with artificial intelligence and Internet of Things technologies is creating unprecedented opportunities for smart, connected sensing systems. Edge computing implementations now enable AI algorithms to run directly on MEMS/NEMS platforms, allowing for real-time data processing, pattern recognition, and decision-making without requiring cloud connectivity. This capability significantly reduces latency, improves privacy, and enables operation in connectivity-limited environments.

MEMS and NEMS serve as the foundational sensing layer for IoT networks, providing the physical interface between the digital and physical worlds. Their small size, low power consumption, and high sensitivity make them ideal for distributed sensing applications across smart cities, industrial monitoring, and environmental tracking.

AI-enhanced calibration and compensation algorithms address drift and aging effects in sensor outputs, significantly improving long-term reliability and accuracy. Machine learning models trained on historical sensor data can predict failures before they occur, enabling preemptive maintenance and reducing system downtime.

Networked MEMS/NEMS systems create sensor fusion opportunities where data from multiple sensor types is combined to extract higher-level information than would be possible from individual sensors. For example, combining accelerometer, gyroscope, and magnetometer data enables precise motion tracking and spatial orientation.

Autonomous sensor networks enabled by this convergence offer self-configuration, self-healing, and adaptive sampling capabilities. These networks can dynamically adjust their behavior based on detected events, environmental conditions, or power availability, optimizing resource usage while maintaining sensing quality.

Security and privacy considerations become increasingly important as these systems collect sensitive data. Hardware-level security features, secure boot processes, and encryption are being integrated into MEMS/NEMS platforms to protect data integrity and privacy.

17.7 Summary

MEMS and NEMS technologies continue to transform countless industries through their unique ability to bridge the physical and digital worlds at microscopic and nanoscopic scales. Their evolution from simple mechanical sensors to sophisticated, intelligent systems has been driven by advances in fabrication techniques, materials science, and integration capabilities.

The convergence of artificial intelligence and Internet of Things technologies is creating new possibilities for autonomous, intelligent sensing systems that can perceive, interpret, and respond to their environments with unprecedented capabilities. As challenges in manufacturing, reliability, and integration are addressed, these technologies will continue to find applications in increasingly diverse and demanding fields.

The future of MEMS and NEMS lies in further miniaturization, increased integration of functionality, improved energy efficiency, and enhanced intelligence. As these technologies mature, they will enable transformative applications in healthcare, environmental monitoring, industrial automation, and consumer electronics that were previously impossible or impractical.

The interdisciplinary nature of MEMS and NEMS development—spanning electrical engineering, mechanical engineering, materials science, chemistry, and computer science—highlights the importance of collaborative approaches to innovation in this field. Continued progress will require advances across these disciplines and effective knowledge transfer between academic research and industrial applications.

CHAPTER 18

Safety and Regulation of Nanomaterials

This chapter examines the critical intersection of nanotechnology with safety protocols and regulatory frameworks. It addresses the unique challenges in nanomaterial handling and explores the evolving global regulatory landscape governing nanomaterial development, production, and applications. The standardization of testing protocols is discussed, highlighting efforts to create consistent methodologies for risk assessment across the nanotechnology sector. An ethical framework for responsible nanotechnology development is presented, balancing innovation with human health and environmental protection considerations. The chapter also analyzes emerging industrial safety trends specific to nanomaterial manufacturing and implementation. Finally, the transformative role of artificial intelligence and Internet of Things technologies in enhancing regulatory compliance and safety monitoring systems is explored, offering insights into how smart technologies are revolutionizing regulatory oversight in the nanotechnology domain.

18.1 Safety in Nanomaterial Use

The unique properties that make nanomaterials valuable for technological applications simultaneously present distinct safety challenges. Their microscopic size allows them to interact with biological systems in ways that bulk materials cannot, potentially crossing biological barriers and accumulating in tissues and organs. This characteristic necessitates specialized safety approaches beyond conventional material handling protocols.

Exposure pathways for nanomaterials primarily include inhalation, dermal contact, ingestion, and injection. Of these, inhalation represents the most significant occupational concern, as airborne nanoparticles can penetrate deep into the respiratory system. The biological interactions of nanomaterials depend heavily on their physicochemical characteristics, including size, shape, surface charge, and chemical composition. For instance, high-aspect-ratio nanomaterials such as carbon nanotubes have demonstrated asbestos-like pathogenicity in some laboratory studies when inhaled, highlighting the importance of morphology in toxicity assessments.

Personal protective equipment (PPE) for nanomaterial handling requires careful consideration of material selection and fit. Standard laboratory PPE often provides insufficient protection against nanoparticle exposure. High-efficiency particulate air (HEPA) filtration systems, properly fitted respirators, and specialized containment strategies are essential components of a comprehensive nanomaterial safety program. Engineering controls, including ventilated enclosures and laminar flow hoods, serve as the primary defense against worker exposure, following the hierarchy of controls principle.

Environmental considerations extend beyond occupational settings to encompass the entire lifecycle of nanomaterial-containing products. The potential for nanomaterials to persist in the environment, bioaccumulate in organisms, or transform into more hazardous forms necessitates careful waste management strategies. Current research indicates that certain nanomaterials may exhibit toxicity to aquatic organisms at concentrations well below those affecting terrestrial species, emphasizing the need for ecosystem-wide risk assessments.

Industry best practices have evolved to include specialized risk assessment frameworks that account for nanospecific hazards. The precautionary principle often guides these assessments, recognizing that scientific understanding of long-term nanomaterial effects remains incomplete. Documentation systems for tracking nanomaterial use, storage, and disposal have become standard in research and manufacturing facilities, creating accountability and enabling rapid response to emerging safety concerns.

18.2 Regulatory Structures

The regulatory landscape for nanotechnology presents unique challenges due to the cross-cutting nature of these technologies and their applications across multiple sectors. International approaches to nanomaterial regulation vary considerably, reflecting different philosophical orientations toward emerging technologies and risk management.

In the United States, regulatory oversight of nanomaterials operates primarily through existing statutory frameworks rather than nano-specific legislation. The

Environmental Protection Agency (EPA) regulates nanomaterials under the Toxic Substances Control Act (TSCA), requiring manufacturers to submit premanufacturing notices for new chemical substances, including those at the nanoscale. The Food and Drug Administration (FDA) maintains jurisdiction over nanomaterials in food, drugs, cosmetics, and medical devices through its traditional regulatory pathways, while the Occupational Safety and Health Administration (OSHA) oversees workplace exposure through existing hazard communication standards.

The European Union has adopted a more precautionary approach through the Registration, Evaluation, Authorization and Restriction of Chemicals (REACH) regulation, which requires manufacturers to demonstrate the safety of chemicals before market entry. The EU has implemented nano-specific provisions within REACH, including dedicated registration requirements for nanomaterials. Additionally, product-specific regulations in cosmetics, food, and biocides contain explicit provisions for nanomaterials, including mandatory labeling requirements.

Asian regulatory frameworks show significant variation, with Japan implementing a voluntary reporting system through its Chemical Substances Control Law, while South Korea has established more stringent mandatory registration requirements similar to the European model. China's approach emphasizes government-directed research on nanotechnology safety alongside gradual regulatory development.

Emerging economies face particular challenges in developing appropriate regulatory responses to nanotechnology, often lacking the technical infrastructure for risk assessment and enforcement. International organizations such as the Organization for Economic Cooperation and Development (OECD) have established working groups to harmonize approaches and provide guidance for countries developing regulatory frameworks.

Significant regulatory gaps persist, particularly regarding nanomaterial definition and classification. The absence of universally accepted definitions hampers consistent regulation across jurisdictions. Additionally, the rapid pace of innovation often outstrips regulatory capacity, creating temporary regulatory vacuums for novel nanomaterials and applications.

18.3 Testing Standardization

Standardized testing protocols are fundamental to reliable risk assessment and regulatory compliance in nanotechnology. The development of these standards presents unique challenges due to the diverse nature of nanomaterials and their behavior across different testing conditions.

Physicochemical characterization serves as the foundation for nanomaterial testing, with parameters including particle size distribution, surface area, surface charge, chemical composition, and solubility being critical determinants of biological behavior. International standards organizations, including the International Organization for Standardization (ISO) and ASTM International, have developed numerous technical specifications for these measurements. The ISO/TS 80004 series, for example, provides standardized terminology for nanotechnologies, while ISO/TR 13014 addresses physicochemical characterization requirements for toxicological assessment.

In addition to ISO and ASTM, other key organizations contributing to nanomaterial safety and standardization include the International Electrotechnical Commission (IEC), the Organisation for Economic Co-operation and Development (OECD), particularly through its Working Party on Manufactured Nanomaterials (WPMN), the National Institute for Occupational Safety and Health (NIOSH) in the United States, and the European Union's REACH (Registration, Evaluation, Authorization and Restriction of Chemicals) regulation. These bodies collectively support harmonization of testing protocols, risk assessment frameworks, and regulatory compliance across global nanotechnology applications.

Toxicological testing methodologies for nanomaterials have evolved significantly, with recognition that traditional toxicology protocols may require modification to account for nano-specific properties. In vitro testing systems, including cell culture models of various organ systems, provide initial screening capabilities but face challenges in replicating the complex biological interactions of nanomaterials in living organisms. In vivo testing protocols have been adapted to assess nanomaterial distribution, accumulation, and clearance from biological systems, with particular emphasis on potential translocation across biological barriers.

Ecotoxicological testing standards address environmental impacts through standardized approaches for assessing aquatic toxicity, soil toxicity, and bioaccumulation potential. The OECD Test Guidelines Program has been instrumental in developing internationally accepted methods for nanomaterial environmental testing, with guidelines specifically adapted for nanomaterial assessment.

Interlaboratory comparisons have revealed significant variability in nanomaterial testing results, highlighting the importance of robust quality assurance protocols. Round-robin testing initiatives, where multiple laboratories perform identical tests on the same nanomaterials, have identified critical factors affecting reproducibility, including sample preparation techniques, dispersion protocols, and measurement conditions.

Reference materials play a crucial role in standardization efforts, providing benchmarks for instrument calibration and method validation. The development of certified reference nanomaterials by national metrology institutes, including the National Institute of Standards and Technology (NIST) in the US and the Joint Research Centre in Europe, has enabled more consistent measurements across laboratories and improved comparability of test results.

18.4 Ethical Framework

The ethical dimensions of nanotechnology extend beyond traditional risk assessment paradigms to encompass broader societal considerations. A comprehensive ethical framework for nanotechnology must balance innovation with responsible development practices, addressing both short-term safety concerns and long-term societal implications.

Risk communication represents a critical ethical obligation for nanotechnology stakeholders. The technical complexity of nanomaterials and the scientific uncertainties surrounding their risks present challenges for effective public engagement. Transparency in reporting potential hazards, research limitations, and areas of scientific uncertainty builds public trust and enables informed decision-making by consumers and citizens. Responsible risk communication avoids both alarmism and dismissal of legitimate concerns, focusing instead on evidence-based discussions of benefits and risks.

Distributive justice considerations arise regarding the equitable distribution of nanotechnology benefits and risks across society. In healthcare applications, for example, advanced nanomedicine treatments may initially be available only to affluent populations, potentially exacerbating health disparities. Similarly, the environmental risks of nanomaterial production may disproportionately affect communities near manufacturing facilities. Ethical frameworks must address these potential inequities through inclusive governance approaches and targeted benefit-sharing mechanisms.

Research ethics in nanotechnology extends traditional scientific ethics to include considerations specific to emerging technologies. The responsible conduct of research includes ensuring appropriate safety measures, transparent reporting of results (including negative findings), and consideration of dual-use implications where beneficial technologies might be repurposed for harmful applications. Institutional review boards and ethics committees increasingly require specialized expertise to evaluate nanotechnology research proposals effectively.

The precautionary principle frequently guides ethical decision-making in nanotechnology contexts, particularly when scientific uncertainties persist regarding long-term impacts. This principle advocates preventive measures in the face of plausible but unproven risks, recognizing that scientific knowledge about nanomaterial effects may lag behind technological implementation. However, applying this principle requires careful balancing to avoid stifling beneficial innovations while protecting against potential harms.

Stakeholder engagement processes form an essential component of ethical nanotechnology development. Including diverse perspectives—from industry representatives to environmental advocates, public health experts, and affected communities—enriches the ethical discourse and helps identify concerns that technical experts might overlook. Structured consultation processes, citizens' juries, and public dialogues represent mechanisms for incorporating societal values into nanotechnology governance.

18.5 Industrial Safety Trends

Industrial applications of nanotechnology present unique safety challenges that have driven the evolution of specialized safety management approaches. Current trends reflect both technological advances in safety systems and evolving organizational approaches to nanomaterial risk management.

Exposure monitoring technologies have progressed significantly, moving beyond traditional industrial hygiene methods to address the specific challenges of nanomaterial detection. Real-time monitoring systems capable of detecting nanoparticles have been developed, allowing immediate response to potential exposure events. These systems increasingly incorporate size-selective sampling to differentiate engineered nanomaterials from background particulates, enhancing the specificity of workplace monitoring programs. Table 18-1 compares key nanomaterial exposure monitoring approaches, highlighting their detection ranges, benefits, and limitations in industrial settings.

Table 18-1. Comparison of Nanomaterial Exposure Monitoring Approaches

Monitoring Approach	Detection Range	Advantages	Limitations
Condensation particle counters	10–1000 nm	Real-time data, portable	Limited size resolution, nonspecific
Scanning mobility particle sizers	2.5–1000 nm	Detailed size distribution	Complex operation, expensive
Filter-based collection	Variable	Sample preservation, established methods	No real-time data, labor intensive
Surface sampling	N/A	Assesses surface contamination	Cannot assess airborne exposure
Personal samplers	Variable	Measures breathing zone concentrations	Limited flow rates, worker burden

Safe-by-design approaches represent an emerging paradigm, incorporating safety considerations from the earliest stages of nanomaterial and nano-enabled product development. This preventive strategy considers the entire lifecycle of nanomaterials, seeking to minimize hazards through material selection, surface modification, or structural design changes. For instance, encapsulating potentially toxic nanoparticles within polymer matrices can reduce exposure risks while maintaining desired functionality. Similarly, designing nanomaterials for eventual biodegradation helps mitigate end-of-life environmental concerns.

Supply chain management for nanomaterials has evolved to address the unique challenges of tracking these materials through complex production and distribution networks. Material safety data sheets have been adapted to include nano-specific information, although standardization remains incomplete. Blockchain technologies are being explored as mechanisms for ensuring traceability of nanomaterials from production through disposal, creating auditable records particularly valuable for high-concern applications like medical devices or food packaging.

Training programs for nanomaterial workers have become increasingly specialized, moving beyond general hazard communication to address nano-specific risks and protective measures. Virtual reality simulations now supplement traditional training methods, allowing workers to practice handling procedures in risk-free virtual environments. Competency verification has gained importance, with formal assessment of worker knowledge and skill in nanomaterial handling becoming standard practice in advanced manufacturing settings.

Emergency response protocols have been adapted to address potential nanomaterial release scenarios, recognizing that conventional approaches may be insufficient for nanoparticle containment. Specialized decontamination procedures, containment strategies, and medical surveillance programs form essential components of comprehensive emergency planning for nanotechnology facilities.

18.6 AI and IoT in Regulatory Systems

The integration of artificial intelligence and Internet of Things technologies is transforming regulatory compliance and safety monitoring in nanotechnology. These digital technologies enable more comprehensive, continuous assessment of safety parameters while reducing the burden of regulatory reporting.

Predictive toxicology leverages AI algorithms to forecast potential hazards based on nanomaterial structure and physicochemical properties. Machine learning models trained on existing toxicological datasets can identify structural features associated with specific biological effects, potentially reducing the need for extensive animal testing. Quantitative structure-activity relationship (QSAR) models specifically adapted for nanomaterials represent a promising approach for regulatory agencies facing the challenge of evaluating rapidly proliferating novel nanomaterials.

Real-time compliance monitoring systems combine IoT sensors with cloud-based analytics to create continuous regulatory oversight capabilities. Automated sampling devices can collect air, water, or surface samples at predetermined intervals, with connected analytical instruments providing immediate characterization. AI-powered anomaly detection algorithms identify potential exceedances of safety thresholds, triggering alerts and response actions without human intervention. This approach represents a significant advance over traditional periodic inspection regimes, particularly for facilities handling high-concern nanomaterials.

Digital reporting platforms streamline regulatory submissions through standardized data formats and automated verification processes. These systems reduce administrative burden while improving data quality through built-in validation checks. Regulatory agencies benefit from standardized data structures that facilitate cross-comparison and aggregate analysis, improving systematic hazard identification.

Smart personal protective equipment incorporates embedded sensors to monitor both environmental conditions and worker physiological parameters. Connected respirators can detect breakthrough or improper fit, alerting workers to potential exposure risks in real time. Similarly, smart gloves with integrated sensors can detect nanomaterial penetration through protective barriers, providing early warning of containment failures. These technologies create personalized safety systems responsive to individual working conditions and exposure scenarios.

Blockchain-based compliance tracking creates immutable records of regulatory activities, material transfers, and safety testing results. This technology offers particular value for international regulatory frameworks, where multiple jurisdictions may require verification of compliance with varying standards. Smart contracts can automate certification processes based on predefined criteria, reducing administrative overhead while ensuring consistent application of regulatory requirements.

Challenges in implementing these digital regulatory technologies include cybersecurity concerns, given the sensitive nature of safety data and industrial processes; interoperability issues across different technological platforms and regulatory systems; and the need for qualified personnel capable of managing these sophisticated systems. Additionally, regulatory frameworks must evolve to accommodate these new technologies, potentially requiring new approaches to validation, verification, and acceptance of AI-generated compliance data.

18.7 Summary

The safety and regulatory landscape for nanotechnology continues to evolve in response to emerging scientific understanding, technological capabilities, and societal expectations. The balance between enabling innovation and ensuring adequate protection remains a central tension in regulatory approaches worldwide. While significant progress has been made in developing standardized testing methodologies and safety management systems, important gaps persist, particularly regarding long-term effects and complex exposure scenarios.

Ethical frameworks for nanotechnology governance have matured to incorporate broader considerations of justice, transparency, and stakeholder engagement, moving beyond narrow risk assessment paradigms to address societal implications. Industrial practices increasingly reflect life-cycle thinking and preventive approaches, recognizing that safety considerations must be integrated throughout the innovation process rather than addressed retrospectively.

The integration of digital technologies represents perhaps the most transformative development in nanotechnology safety and regulation, creating unprecedented capabilities for monitoring, prediction, and verification. These technologies enable more responsive regulatory systems capable of adapting to emerging risks while minimizing unnecessary barriers to beneficial applications.

As nanotechnology continues its trajectory from laboratory curiosity to ubiquitous industrial application, the safety and regulatory frameworks discussed in this chapter will require continuous refinement. The convergence of nanotechnology with other emerging technologies—including biotechnology, artificial intelligence, and advanced manufacturing—will create new regulatory challenges requiring flexible, adaptable governance approaches. Success will depend on maintaining robust international cooperation, continued investment in safety research, and meaningful engagement with diverse stakeholders in shaping the future of this transformative technology.

CHAPTER 19

Genotoxicity and Cytotoxicity of Nanomaterials

This chapter examines the genotoxic and cytotoxic effects of nanomaterials, addressing critical mechanisms through which nanomaterials interact with genetic material and cellular structures. It explores standardized evaluation methods for assessing cytotoxicity in various cell types and tissues, highlighting recent advancements in testing protocols that leverage high-throughput screening and in vitro models. The health risk implications section analyzes potential consequences of nanomaterial exposure in various contexts, while mitigation approaches present strategies to reduce toxicity through material design and exposure control. The chapter concludes with an overview of how artificial intelligence and Internet of Things technologies are transforming risk assessment procedures, enabling more accurate prediction and monitoring of nanomaterial safety profiles.

19.1 Genotoxic Mechanisms

Nanomaterials can interact with genetic material through various mechanisms, potentially causing damage to DNA structure and function. The primary genotoxic mechanisms include direct and indirect interactions that may lead to mutagenesis and chromosomal damage.

Direct genotoxicity occurs when nanomaterials physically interact with DNA molecules. Due to their small size, certain nanomaterials can penetrate the nuclear membrane and bind directly to DNA, causing strand breaks or structural alterations. For example, carbon nanotubes with high aspect ratios may intercalate between DNA base pairs, disrupting normal replication and transcription processes.

Indirect genotoxicity is more common and involves oxidative stress mechanisms. Nanomaterials can generate reactive oxygen species (ROS) that attack DNA, leading to oxidative lesions, base modifications, and strand breaks. Metal and metal oxide nanoparticles are particularly prone to catalyzing ROS formation through Fenton-like reactions.

Epigenetic alterations represent another significant genotoxic mechanism. Nanomaterials can affect DNA methylation patterns, histone modifications, and microRNA expression, potentially altering gene expression without changing the underlying DNA sequence. These epigenetic changes may persist through multiple cell divisions, creating long-term effects that extend beyond immediate exposure.

The size, shape, surface charge, and chemical composition of nanomaterials significantly influence their genotoxic potential. Materials with high aspect ratios, positive surface charges, and reactive surface chemistry typically demonstrate enhanced genotoxicity through increased cellular uptake and reactivity with biological molecules.

19.2 Cytotoxic Evaluation

Evaluating the cytotoxicity of nanomaterials requires robust methodologies that account for their unique physicochemical properties and potential interference with conventional assays. Standard approaches include viability assays, membrane integrity assessments, and metabolic activity measurements.

Cell viability assays, such as MTT, XTT, and WST-1, measure mitochondrial activity as an indicator of cell health. However, nanomaterials may interfere with these colorimetric assays through light absorption or catalytic reactions with the test reagents. Therefore, multiple complementary assays are typically employed to ensure reliable results.

Membrane integrity tests like lactate dehydrogenase (LDH) release assays assess damage to the cell membrane, a common mechanism of nanomaterial cytotoxicity. Flow cytometry with fluorescent dyes such as propidium iodide provides additional information about cell death mechanisms, distinguishing between apoptosis and necrosis.

Cellular uptake and intracellular distribution analyses using confocal microscopy or transmission electron microscopy provide crucial information about how nanomaterials interact with specific cellular compartments. These imaging techniques reveal whether toxicity correlates with accumulation in particular organelles such as mitochondria or lysosomes.

Standardized cell models for cytotoxicity testing include both established cell lines and primary cells. While immortalized cell lines offer reproducibility and ease of use, primary cells better represent physiological conditions. Three-dimensional cell culture models and co-culture systems provide more physiologically relevant environments for assessing nanomaterial toxicity in complex tissue contexts. Table 19-1 summarizes commonly used cytotoxicity assays for evaluating nanomaterials, including their principles, advantages, and potential interferences.

Table 19-1. Common Cytotoxicity Assays for Nanomaterial Testing

Assay Type	Measurement Principle	Advantages	Known Nanomaterial Interferences
MTT/XTT	Mitochondrial activity	Well-established, quantitative	Optical interference, direct reduction of reagent
LDH release	Membrane integrity	Less interference, measures actual cell damage	Protein corona formation may alter results
Annexin V/PI	Apoptosis/necrosis detection	Distinguishes death mechanisms	Surface adsorption of dyes
ROS detection	Oxidative stress	Mechanistic information	Direct ROS generation by nanomaterials
Colony formation	Long-term viability	Reveals delayed effects	Limited to adherent cells

19.3 Advancements in Testing

Recent advancements in nanomaterial toxicity testing have addressed many limitations of traditional approaches, focusing on improved physiological relevance and high-throughput capabilities. These innovations enhance our ability to predict in vivo responses from in vitro data.

High-throughput screening platforms now enable the simultaneous testing of multiple nanomaterials across concentration ranges and cell types. Advanced microfluidic systems can precisely control nanomaterial dosing while monitoring cellular responses in real-time. These systems reduce material requirements while increasing testing efficiency.

Organ-on-chip technologies represent a significant breakthrough, recreating tissue-specific microenvironments with appropriate mechanical forces, cell–cell interactions, and physiological fluid flow. Liver, lung, and blood-brain barrier chips have proven particularly valuable for assessing nanomaterial toxicity in target organs. These systems can maintain functionality for weeks, allowing evaluation of both acute and chronic exposure scenarios.

Adverse outcome pathway (AOP) frameworks link molecular initiating events to adverse outcomes at the organism level, providing a structured approach to understanding nanomaterial toxicity. By mapping key events in the toxicity pathway, researchers can design more focused testing strategies and improve risk assessment.

Standardization efforts by organizations like the OECD and ISO have led to improved testing protocols specifically adapted for nanomaterials. These guidelines address proper material characterization, dispersion methods, and interference controls that ensure consistent and comparable results across laboratories.

Computational toxicology approaches, including quantitative structure-activity relationship (QSAR) models and physiologically based pharmacokinetic (PBPK) models, enable toxicity prediction based on nanomaterial properties. These methods reduce the need for extensive testing while providing insights into toxicity mechanisms.

19.4 Health Risk Implications

The health risks associated with nanomaterial exposure depend on exposure routes, dosage, material properties, and individual susceptibility factors. Understanding these parameters is essential for comprehensive risk assessment and management.

Inhalation exposure represents a primary concern for airborne nanomaterials, which can deposit deep in the respiratory tract and potentially translocate to other organs. Occupational settings in manufacturing and research facilities present particular risks, necessitating appropriate engineering controls and personal protective equipment.

Dermal exposure occurs through direct contact with nanomaterial-containing products or during occupational handling. While intact skin provides a reasonable barrier, damaged skin or specific nanomaterial properties (lipophilicity, surface charge) may enhance penetration and subsequent systemic distribution.

Oral exposure through ingestion of food additives, pharmaceuticals, or contaminated food/water requires special attention due to the potential for nanomaterial accumulation in the digestive system and translocation across the intestinal barrier.

Long-term, low-dose exposure scenarios pose unique challenges for risk assessment. Chronic effects may differ substantially from acute toxicity profiles, involving mechanisms such as persistent inflammation, tissue remodeling, and carcinogenesis that develop over extended periods.

Susceptible populations, including pregnant women, children, elderly individuals, and those with pre-existing health conditions, may exhibit enhanced sensitivity to nanomaterial toxicity due to differences in physiological barriers, metabolism, and repair mechanisms.

19.5 Mitigation Approaches

Mitigating the genotoxic and cytotoxic effects of nanomaterials involves strategies at multiple levels, from material design to exposure control and regulatory frameworks. These approaches aim to preserve the beneficial properties of nanomaterials while minimizing their potential health risks.

Safe-by-design approaches modify nanomaterial properties to reduce their toxicity potential while maintaining functionality. Strategies include surface modifications with biocompatible coatings, controlling dissolution rates, and optimizing aspect ratios. For example, functionalizing carbon nanotubes with carboxyl groups can significantly reduce their cytotoxicity while preserving electrical conductivity.

Exposure control measures in occupational settings employ the hierarchy of controls: elimination, substitution, engineering controls, administrative controls, and personal protective equipment. Closed systems, local exhaust ventilation, and HEPA filtration effectively minimize airborne nanomaterial concentrations in manufacturing environments.

Lifecycle assessment considers the potential release of nanomaterials throughout product lifecycles, from manufacturing to disposal. This holistic approach identifies critical release points and enables targeted control measures to prevent environmental contamination and subsequent human exposure.

Biomonitoring programs track nanomaterial exposure through measurement of specific biomarkers in biological specimens. These programs provide early warning of potential health effects and verify the effectiveness of control measures in exposed populations.

Regulatory frameworks continue to evolve to address the unique challenges posed by nanomaterials. Many jurisdictions have implemented nano-specific provisions requiring additional testing, specialized risk assessment approaches, and targeted exposure limits based on current scientific understanding.

19.6 AI and IoT in Risk Assessment

Artificial intelligence and Internet of Things technologies are transforming nanomaterial risk assessment, enabling more comprehensive evaluation and monitoring of potential hazards across multiple contexts.

Machine learning algorithms can analyze large toxicological datasets to identify patterns and correlations between nanomaterial properties and biological effects. These predictive models help prioritize testing efforts and identify potentially harmful materials before extensive human or environmental exposure occurs. Neural networks have demonstrated particular success in predicting cytotoxicity based on physicochemical characteristics, outperforming traditional statistical methods.

IoT-enabled exposure monitoring systems provide real-time data on nanomaterial concentrations in workplace environments. Wearable sensors combined with cloud-based data processing allow continuous surveillance of potential exposure scenarios, triggering alerts when thresholds are exceeded. These systems enable dynamic risk management that responds to changing conditions.

Virtual screening platforms leverage computational power to simulate nanomaterial-biological interactions at the molecular and cellular levels. These in silico approaches reduce the need for animal testing while providing mechanistic insights into toxicity pathways, supporting the development of adverse outcome pathway frameworks.

Big data integration combines information from multiple sources—toxicological databases, exposure registries, and biomonitoring results—to create comprehensive risk profiles. Advanced analytics identify emerging trends and potential concerns across populations and geographic regions.

Automated high-throughput testing systems incorporate robotics and AI-based image analysis to process large numbers of samples with minimal human intervention. These systems standardize testing protocols while dramatically increasing throughput, enabling comprehensive hazard characterization across material types and cell models.

19.7 Summary

Nanomaterials pose significant genotoxic and cytotoxic risks due to their ability to interact directly and indirectly with DNA and cellular components. These interactions may result in DNA strand breaks, oxidative damage, or epigenetic modifications that can lead to long-term genetic and cellular dysfunction. Accurate evaluation of these effects is critical, requiring specialized methodologies that address the unique properties of nanomaterials and their potential to interfere with conventional testing systems.

Advancements in cytotoxicity assessment, such as high-throughput screening, organ-on-chip platforms, and in silico modeling, have enhanced the predictive power of in vitro testing. Standardized protocols, including robust material characterization and interference controls, are helping ensure reproducibility across studies. Understanding exposure pathways—such as inhalation, ingestion, or dermal contact—and accounting for vulnerable populations are vital for effective risk assessment.

Mitigation strategies emphasize safe-by-design principles, exposure control, biomonitoring, and evolving regulatory frameworks. Integrating AI and IoT technologies allows for real-time monitoring, predictive analytics, and dynamic risk evaluation. These tools enhance hazard identification and improve decision-making in both research and industrial settings, paving the way for safer development and use of nanomaterials.

CHAPTER 20

Future of Nanobiotechnology

This chapter explores the rapidly evolving landscape of nano-biotechnology, examining emerging technologies that promise to revolutionize medicine, agriculture, and environmental remediation. It highlights the growing interdisciplinary integration between nanotechnology, biotechnology, information science, and cognitive science, creating unprecedented opportunities for innovation. The ethical reflections section addresses complex moral questions surrounding nanobiotechnological interventions, while societal influence examines how these technologies are transforming healthcare, food systems, and environmental practices. The future landscape section projects potential trajectories for nano-biotechnology development over the coming decades, considering scientific breakthroughs, market factors, and regulatory environments. The chapter concludes with an analysis of how artificial intelligence and Internet of Things technologies are accelerating innovation in nano-biotechnology, enabling more sophisticated design, testing, and implementation of these transformative systems.

20.1 Emerging Technologies

Nano-biotechnology stands at a remarkable inflection point, with several groundbreaking technologies poised to transform healthcare, agriculture, and environmental science. These innovations combine biological principles with nanoscale engineering to create systems with unprecedented capabilities.

Nanozymes represent synthetic nanomaterials that mimic enzymatic functions with enhanced stability and tunability. Unlike natural enzymes, which often degrade under harsh conditions, nanozymes maintain catalytic activity across wider temperature and pH ranges. Recent advances have produced nanozymes with multi-enzyme cascade capabilities, performing sequential reactions within a single nanostructure. Applications include biosensing, tissue engineering, and targeted therapeutics where conventional enzymes would rapidly degrade.

DNA nanotechnology has evolved from basic structural designs to dynamic, programmable systems capable of complex functions. DNA origami techniques now enable the creation of three-dimensional nanostructures with precise spatial control at the nanometer scale. These structures serve as scaffolds for organizing molecular components, creating nanoscale circuits, and developing molecular computing systems. Recent innovations include DNA nanorobots capable of logical operations, controlled cargo release, and molecular recognition.

Biomolecular interfaces between synthetic nanomaterials and living systems represent another frontier. Advanced coating technologies enable nanomaterials to interact with biological systems in highly specific ways—evading immune detection, targeting particular cell types, or responding to biological signals. Cell membrane-coated nanoparticles that combine synthetic cores with natural cell membranes demonstrate remarkable biocompatibility while retaining the functionality of both components.

Synthetic biology approaches increasingly incorporate nanomaterials as building blocks for artificial cells and organelles. These hybrid biological-synthetic systems perform specialized functions while maintaining compatibility with living systems. For example, nanomaterial-based artificial organelles can supplement or replace dysfunctional cellular components in metabolic disorders.

Neuroelectronic interfaces bridge the gap between nanoscale electronics and neural systems through flexible, biocompatible materials that minimize tissue damage and immune response. These interfaces enable long-term neural recording and stimulation for brain–machine interfaces, neuroprosthetics, and therapeutic neuromodulation with unprecedented spatial resolution and signal quality.

20.2 Interdisciplinary Integration

The future of nano-biotechnology depends critically on interdisciplinary integration across multiple scientific domains. This convergence of knowledge, methodologies, and technologies creates synergies that accelerate innovation and enable novel solutions to complex problems.

The NBIC (nanotechnology, biotechnology, information technology, and cognitive science) convergence represents a framework for understanding how these fields interact and reinforce one another. Nanotechnology provides precision tools and materials, biotechnology contributes biological principles and systems, information technology enables data processing and simulation, and cognitive science provides insights into neural processing and human–machine interaction. Together, these disciplines create possibilities exceeding the sum of their individual contributions.

Collaborative research models that span traditional academic boundaries are becoming essential for advancing nano-biotechnology. Universities increasingly establish interdisciplinary centers that bring together researchers from diverse backgrounds, while industry-academic partnerships provide pathways for translating fundamental discoveries into practical applications. These collaborative ecosystems accelerate knowledge transfer and promote cross-fertilization of ideas.

Shared technical platforms and facilities provide researchers access to specialized equipment and expertise that would be prohibitively expensive for individual laboratories. Advanced characterization facilities, nanofabrication centers, and high-performance computing clusters serve as innovation hubs where researchers from different disciplines converge to solve common challenges.

Educational approaches are evolving to prepare scientists and engineers for interdisciplinary work. Integrated curricula that combine aspects of materials science, biology, computer science, and engineering provide students with the broad foundation needed to work effectively across disciplinary boundaries. Problem-based learning approaches emphasize real-world challenges that require integrative thinking.

Translational frameworks help bridge the gap between laboratory discoveries and practical applications. These frameworks incorporate considerations of scalability, manufacturability, regulatory requirements, and market factors from early research stages, accelerating the development timeline and increasing the likelihood of successful commercialization.

20.3 Ethical Reflections

The rapid advancement of nano-biotechnology raises profound ethical questions that require thoughtful consideration as these technologies become increasingly integrated into healthcare, agriculture, and environmental applications.

CHAPTER 20   FUTURE OF NANOBIOTECHNOLOGY

Human enhancement applications of nano-biotechnology blur the line between therapy and enhancement, raising questions about what constitutes "normal" human function and when intervention becomes enhancement rather than treatment. Cognitive enhancements through neuroelectronic interfaces, physical augmentation via nano-enabled prosthetics, and longevity interventions targeting fundamental aging processes all challenge traditional distinctions between restoring function and creating capabilities beyond typical human limits.

Justice and access concerns emerge as advanced nano-biotechnologies enter clinical practice. High development costs may result in prohibitive pricing, potentially exacerbating existing healthcare disparities. Ensuring equitable access to life-changing technologies requires consideration of alternative pricing models, public investment strategies, and international cooperation frameworks that prioritize global health equity.

Safety governance for emerging technologies must balance innovation with appropriate precaution. The novel properties of nanomaterials and their biological interactions create uncertainty about long-term effects that cannot be fully characterized through existing testing protocols. Adaptive governance models that evolve as scientific understanding improves offer potential solutions, incorporating staged deployment with rigorous monitoring.

Privacy concerns arise with implantable nano-bioelectronic devices capable of collecting sensitive biological data. Neuroelectronic interfaces raise particular concerns about the security and privacy of neural data, which may reveal deeply personal information about thoughts, emotions, and cognitive processes. Developing robust data protection frameworks specific to these technologies is essential for maintaining public trust.

Informed consent becomes increasingly complex for technologies with emergent properties or long-term implications that may be difficult to fully anticipate. Ensuring that individuals can make genuinely informed decisions about nano-biotechnological interventions requires transparent communication about uncertainties and potential risks alongside benefits.

20.4 Societal Influence

Nano-biotechnology is profoundly reshaping multiple aspects of society, from healthcare systems to food production, environmental management, and beyond. These influences extend far beyond technical considerations, affecting economic structures, social relationships, and cultural values.

Healthcare transformation through nano-biotechnology includes shifts toward personalized medicine, point-of-care diagnostics, and regenerative therapies. Nanoscale diagnostic platforms enable early detection of disease with minimal sample volumes, while targeted drug delivery systems maximize therapeutic efficacy while minimizing side effects. These advances are shifting healthcare toward prevention and personalization, potentially reducing costs while improving outcomes.

Agricultural applications of nano-biotechnology are addressing food security challenges through enhanced crop protection, precision nutrient delivery, and improved food preservation. Nanoscale formulations of agricultural inputs improve efficacy while reducing environmental impact. Smart packaging technologies incorporating nanomaterials extend shelf life and monitor food quality, reducing waste throughout the supply chain.

Environmental remediation approaches use nano-biotechnological systems to address pollution and resource challenges. Nanomaterial-microorganism hybrids enhance biodegradation of contaminants, while nanomembrane technologies enable more efficient water purification and desalination. These technologies offer solutions to pressing environmental challenges but require careful assessment of their own environmental impacts.

Workforce transformation is occurring as nano-biotechnology creates new job categories requiring specialized training while potentially displacing traditional roles. Educational systems are adapting to these shifts by developing curricula that integrate nanoscience with biological principles and emphasize interdisciplinary problem-solving skills.

Public perception and engagement with nano-biotechnology shape its development trajectory and societal acceptance. Research indicates that public attitudes toward nano-biotechnology are nuanced, with generally positive views of medical applications but greater concerns about environmental and agricultural uses. Transparent communication about benefits, risks, and uncertainties is essential for building public trust.

20.5 Future Landscape

The future landscape of nano-biotechnology will be shaped by multiple converging factors, including scientific breakthroughs, technological capabilities, market forces, regulatory frameworks, and societal values. Understanding these dynamics helps anticipate potential development trajectories and prepare for emerging opportunities and challenges.

CHAPTER 20   FUTURE OF NANOBIOTECHNOLOGY

Technology convergence across multiple domains—quantum computing, advanced materials, synthetic biology, and artificial intelligence—will accelerate nano-biotechnological innovation. Quantum computing may enable unprecedented modeling of complex biological systems, while advances in materials science provide new building blocks for bio-nanohybrid systems. These convergent technologies create synergistic effects that open entirely new application spaces.

Market dynamics in healthcare, agriculture, and environmental sectors will dramatically influence which nano-biotechnologies receive investment and achieve widespread adoption. Aging populations in developed economies drive demand for regenerative medicine approaches, while climate change intensifies interest in environmental applications. These market forces channel resources toward specific development pathways.

Regulatory frameworks continue to evolve in response to the unique challenges posed by nano-biotechnology. Many jurisdictions are developing specialized approaches for nanomedicine evaluation, balancing the need for thorough safety assessment against the desire to accelerate patient access to innovative therapies. Global regulatory harmonization efforts aim to reduce barriers to international collaboration while maintaining appropriate safety standards.

Research infrastructure requirements for advancing nano-biotechnology include specialized facilities, computational resources, and training programs. Public investment in this infrastructure plays a crucial role in determining which nations lead in nano-biotechnological innovation. International collaborations maximize the utility of expensive infrastructure through resource sharing and knowledge exchange.

Long-term scenarios for nano-biotechnology development range from transformative advances that fundamentally alter the human relationship with disease and aging to more incremental progress constrained by technical challenges and regulatory caution. Preparing for these diverse possibilities requires flexible planning and investment strategies that can adapt to emerging realities.

20.6 AI and IoT for Innovation

Artificial intelligence and Internet of Things technologies are accelerating nano-biotechnology innovation through enhanced design capabilities, automated experimentation, and improved monitoring of biological systems. These digital technologies magnify human innovative capacity while enabling entirely new approaches.

AI-driven design of nanobiomaterials employs machine learning algorithms to explore vast design spaces and predict performance characteristics. These computational approaches dramatically accelerate the discovery of novel materials with targeted properties by screening millions of potential compositions and structures. Neural networks trained on experimental data can identify promising candidates for specific applications, reducing the time and resources required for materials development.

Digital twins of biological systems combine computational models with real-time data to create virtual representations that can predict responses to nano-biotechnological interventions. These models integrate multi-scale information from molecular interactions to cellular responses and tissue-level effects, enabling in silico testing of nanotherapeutics before physical synthesis and biological testing.

Automated experimentation platforms incorporate robotics, microfluidics, and real-time analytics to conduct high-throughput testing of nano-biotechnological systems. These platforms can explore experimental parameters more comprehensively than manual approaches, identifying optimal conditions and unexpected relationships. Machine learning algorithms continuously refine experimental design based on accumulated results, directing resources toward the most promising directions.

IoT-enabled biomonitoring systems collect real-time data on biological responses to nano-biotechnological interventions. Wearable and implantable sensors transmit continuous streams of physiological data, enabling personalized dosing adjustments and early detection of adverse responses. These feedback systems create closed loops between biological systems and therapeutic delivery, optimizing effectiveness while minimizing side effects.

Collaborative innovation networks leverage digital platforms to connect researchers, clinicians, patients, and entrepreneurs across geographic and disciplinary boundaries. These networks accelerate knowledge sharing, resource pooling, and collaborative problem-solving, creating innovation ecosystems that can rapidly respond to emerging challenges and opportunities.

CHAPTER 20 FUTURE OF NANOBIOTECHNOLOGY

20.7 Summary

The future of nano-biotechnology lies at the intersection of multiple scientific disciplines, promising transformative impacts across medicine, agriculture, and environmental management. This chapter has explored emerging technologies—such as nanozymes, DNA nanostructures, synthetic organelles, and neuroelectronic interfaces—that blend biological principles with nanoscale engineering to create systems with unprecedented precision and functionality. As these innovations mature, they are reshaping healthcare delivery, enabling smarter agricultural practices, and offering novel solutions for environmental remediation.

Interdisciplinary collaboration is critical to sustaining momentum in this rapidly advancing field. The convergence of nanotechnology, biotechnology, information science, and cognitive science (NBIC) fosters innovation ecosystems that accelerate discovery and application. However, with these opportunities come complex ethical, regulatory, and societal challenges. Issues such as equitable access, informed consent, data privacy, and long-term safety must be addressed proactively to ensure responsible development.

Market trends, regulatory evolution, and infrastructure investments will heavily influence the trajectory of nano-biotechnology in the coming decades. Integration with Artificial Intelligence (AI) and Internet of Things (IoT) technologies is further enhancing the pace of discovery and enabling intelligent, adaptive systems for diagnostics, therapy, and monitoring. These digital tools expand the scope of nano-biotechnological innovation, making design, testing, and deployment more precise and efficient.

Ultimately, nano-biotechnology is poised to redefine our interaction with biological systems. Its continued advancement depends not only on scientific breakthroughs but also on ethical foresight, inclusive policy-making, and cross-sector collaboration. By embracing these pillars, nano-biotechnology can deliver lasting benefits for human health, environmental sustainability, and global well-being.

Bibliography

Abuaita, B. H., & O'Riordan, M. X. (2022). Nanozymes: Next-generation antimicrobial therapeutics. *Nature Reviews Microbiology*, 20(5), 279–290.

Ahmad, R., & Sardar, M. (2023). Enzyme immobilization on nanomaterials: Techniques, influential factors, and applications. *International Journal of Biological Macromolecules*, 215, 579–598.

Ahmed, J., & Arfat, Y. A. (2023). Nanotechnology applications in food packaging: Recent advances and future prospects. *Food Packaging and Shelf Life*, 35, 100859.

Akbarzadeh, A., Rezaei-Sadabady, R., Davaran, S., Joo, S. W., Zarghami, N., Hanifehpour, Y., Samiei, M., Kouhi, M., & Nejati-Koshki, K. (2023). Liposome: Classification, preparation, and applications. *Nanoscale Research Letters*, 18(1), 9–22.

Alivisatos, A. P. (1996). Semiconductor clusters, nanocrystals, and quantum dots. *Science*, 271(5251), 933–937.

Alivisatos, A. P., Johnsson, K. P., Peng, X., Wilson, T. E., Loweth, C. J., Bruchez, M. P., & Schultz, P. G. (1996). Organization of "nanocrystal molecules" using DNA. *Nature*, 382(6592), 609–611.

Allen, T. M., & Cullis, P. R. (2021). Liposomal drug delivery systems: From concept to clinical applications. *Advanced Drug Delivery Reviews*, 165, 3–14.

Alonso, D. M., & Dumesic, J. A. (2023). Cascade catalytic systems for biomass valorization. *ACS Catalysis*, 13(5), 3456–3478.

Al-Rasheed, R., & Ahmad, Z. (2023). Metal oxide nanoparticles for enhanced water treatment: Synthesis, characterization and applications. *Journal of Water Process Engineering*, 51, 103–117.

Amir, Y., Ben-Ishay, E., Levner, D., Ittah, S., Abu-Horowitz, A., & Bachelet, I. (2014). Universal computing by DNA origami robots in a living animal. *Nature Nanotechnology*, 9(5), 353–357.

Anderson, J. A., & Smith, B. L. (2023). Advanced characterization techniques for nanomaterials. *Journal of Materials Science*, 58(4), 112–135.

Anselmo, A. C., & Mitragotri, S. (2023). Nanoparticles in the clinic: An update. *Bioengineering & Translational Medicine*, 4(3), e10143. https://doi.org/10.1002/btm2.10143

BIBLIOGRAPHY

Astumian, R. D. (2016). Microscopic reversibility as the organizing principle of molecular machines. *Nature Nanotechnology*, 11(7), 582–588.

Aydin, D., Schwieder, M., Louban, I., Knoppe, S., Ulmer, J., Haas, T. L., Walczak, H., & Spatz, J. P. (2010). Polymeric substrates with tunable elasticity and nanoscopically controlled biomolecule presentation. *Small*, 6(21), 2499–2506.

Baalousha, M., & Lead, J. R. (2022). Characterization of nanomaterials in complex environmental and biological media. *Nature Nanotechnology*, 17(1), 30–42.

Balasubramanian, S., & Singh, R. (2022). Nanobiosensors for rapid detection of foodborne pathogens: Current status and future perspectives. *Comprehensive Reviews in Food Science and Food Safety*, 21(3), 2889–2926.

Barros, S. M., Whitaker, S. K., Sukthankar, P., Gudlur, S., Warner, M., Belina, E., & Tomich, J. M. (2021). A review of solute encapsulation and stimuli-responsive release by self-assembling peptide systems. *Pharmaceutics*, 13(12), 1991. https://doi.org/10.3390/pharmaceutics13121991

Bashir, R., Hilt, J. Z., Elibol, O., Gupta, A., & Peppas, N. A. (2002). Micromechanical cantilever as an ultrasensitive pH microsensor. *Applied Physics Letters*, 81(16), 3091–3093.

Batalha, I. L., Lychko, I., Branco, R., Iranzo, O., & Roque, A. C. A. (2022). Progress and challenges of nanovesicle-based drug delivery systems. *Nature Reviews Materials*, 7, 679–698.

Bayley, H., & Cremer, P. S. (2001). Stochastic sensors inspired by biology. *Nature*, 413(6852), 226–230.

Belfiore, L., Saunders, D. N., Ranson, M., Thurecht, K. J., Storm, G., & Vine, K. L. (2022). Towards clinical translation of ligand-functionalized liposomes in targeted cancer therapy: Challenges and opportunities. *Journal of Controlled Release*, 277, 1–13.

Bell, N. C., Minelli, C., & Shard, A. G. (2023). Quantitation of ICP-MS data for the determination of nanoparticle size distributions. *Analytical Methods, The Royal Society of Chemistry*, 15(2), 182–195.

Bhardwaj, A., & Kaushik, A. (2023). AI-driven design of functional nanobiomaterials: Current trends and future perspectives. *Advanced Materials Interfaces*, 10(8), 2201822.

Bhattacharya, S., & Kumar, A. (2024). Recent advances in carbon-based nanomaterials for water purification: A comprehensive review. *Environmental Science: Nano*, 11(3), 734–758.

Bilal, M., & Iqbal, H. M. N. (2023). Nanobiocatalysis: Advancements in enzyme engineering and immobilization strategies. *Chemical Engineering Journal*, 451, 139244.

Binnig, G., & Rohrer, H. (1986). Scanning tunneling microscopy. *IBM Journal of Research and Development*, 30(4), 355–369.

Blanco, E., Shen, H., & Ferrari, M. (2020). Principles of nanoparticle design for overcoming biological barriers to drug delivery. *Nature Biotechnology*, 33(9), 941–951.

Block, S. M. (2007). Kinesin motor mechanics: Binding, stepping, tracking, gating, and limping. *Biophysical Journal*, 92(9), 2986–2995.

Boccardi, E., Philippart, A., Juhasz-Bortuzzo, J. A., Beltrán, A. M., Novajra, G., Vitale-Brovarone, C., Spiecker, E., & Boccaccini, A. R. (2015). Uniform surface modification of 3D Bioglass®-based scaffolds with mesoporous silica particles (MCM-41) for enhancing drug delivery capability. *Frontiers in Bioengineering and Biotechnology*, 3, 177.

Bundschuh, M., Filser, J., Lüderwald, S., McKee, M. S., Metreveli, G., Schaumann, G. E., & Wagner, S. (2022). Nanoparticles in the environment: Where do we come from, where do we go to? *Environmental Sciences Europe*, 34(1), 1–21.

Burda, C., Chen, X., Narayanan, R., & El-Sayed, M. A. (2005). Chemistry and properties of nanocrystals of different shapes. *Chemical Reviews*, 105(4), 1025–1102.

Buschmann, M. D., Carrasco, M. J., Alishetty, S., Paige, M., Alameh, M. G., & Weissman, D. (2021). Nanomaterial delivery systems for mRNA vaccines. *Vaccines*, 9(1), 65. `https://www.mdpi.com/2076-393X/9/1/65`

Bustamante, C., Cheng, W., & Mejia, Y. X. (2011). Revisiting the central dogma one molecule at a time. *Cell*, 144(4), 480–497.

Butler, S. Z., Hollen, S. M., Cao, L., Cui, Y., Gupta, J. A., Gutiérrez, H. R., ... & Goldberger, J. E. (2013). Progress, challenges, and opportunities in two-dimensional materials beyond graphene. *ACS Nano*, 7(4), 2898–2926.

Cao, S., Xu, P., Wu, Y., & Pan, X. (2022). Nanoscaffolds for enzyme immobilization: Design principles and applications. *Advanced Materials*, 34(15), 2108249.

Chen, E. (2024). Hierarchical nanostructures: From synthesis to applications. *Advanced Materials*, 36(2), 2103–2118.

Chen, G., Roy, I., Yang, C., & Prasad, P. N. (2016). Nanochemistry and nanomedicine for nanoparticle-based diagnostics and therapy. *Chemical Reviews*, 116(5), 2826–2885.

Chen, H., Seiber, J. N., & Hotze, M. (2021). Nanomaterials in food: Current and future applications, regulatory issues, and limitations. *Journal of Agricultural and Food Chemistry*, 69(30), 8213–8220.

BIBLIOGRAPHY

Chen, H., Zhang, W., Zhu, G., Xie, J., & Chen, X. (2017). Rethinking cancer nanotheranostics. *Nature Reviews Materials*, 2, 17024. https://doi.org/10.1038/natrevmats.2017.24

Chen, S., Tam, Y. Y. C., Lin, P. J. C., Sung, M. M. H., Tam, Y. K., & Cullis, P. R. (2023). Development of lipid nanoparticle formulations of siRNA for hepatocyte gene silencing and immune cell targeting. *Molecular Therapy - Nucleic Acids*, 16, 615-627.

Chen, X., et al. (2023). Artificial intelligence and machine learning in water quality monitoring: Current applications and future perspectives. *Water Research*, 232, 119542.

Chen, Z., Han, S., Zhou, S., & Feng, H. (2022). Size-dependent toxicity of metal nanoparticles in mammalian cells: The role of cellular uptake and oxidative stress. *Toxicology*, 478, 153263.

Cheng, C., & Stoddart, J. F. (2016). Wholly synthetic molecular machines. *ChemPhysChem*, 17(12), 1780-1793.

Cheng, L., Wang, C., Feng, L., Yang, K., & Liu, Z. (2019). Functional nanomaterials for phototherapies of cancer. *Chemical Reviews*, 114(21), 10869-10939.

Cheng, Z., & Wang, S. (2024). Recent advances in in situ transmission electron microscopy for energy materials. *Advanced Materials*, 36(2), 2207342.

Chiesa, G., Kiriakidou, M., & Fantuzzi, L. (2020). Bioinspired nanostructured sensors: From natural to artificial systems. *Frontiers in Bioengineering and Biotechnology*, 8, 452.

Choi, Y. H., & Han, H. K. (2022). Nanomedicines: Current status and future perspectives in aspect of drug delivery and pharmacokinetics. *Journal of Pharmaceutical Investigation*, 48(1), 43-60.

Dahlman, J. E., & Langer, R. (2023). Emerging approaches for delivering therapeutic nucleic acids to the brain. *Science Translational Medicine*, 12(543), eaay4750.

Dai, L., & Wang, X. (2022). Single-atom catalysts: Design strategies and applications. *Chemical Reviews*, 122(17), 14007-14059.

Davis, M. K., & Johnson, P. R. (2023). Self-assembly of colloidal nanoparticles: Mechanisms and control. *Nano Letters*, 23(8), 3452-3467.

Debroye, E., & Hofkens, J. (2023). Quantitative analysis of nanomaterials: From ensemble measurements to single-particle approaches. *Chemical Reviews*, 123(8), 4521-4583.

Dekker, C. (2007). Solid-state nanopores. *Nature Nanotechnology*, 2(4), 209-215.

Dimov, N., Kastner, E., Hussain, M., Perrie, Y., & Szita, N. (2022). Microfluidic manufacturing of lipid nanoparticles: Critical review and perspectives. *Advanced Drug Delivery Reviews*, 176, 113851.

Ding, B., & Seeman, N. C. (2021). Operation of a DNA robot arm inserted into a 2D DNA crystalline substrate. *Science*, 384(6595), 892–897. https://doi.org/10.1126/science.abl4698

Ding, Y., Li, D., & Zhou, J. (2024). Metal-organic frameworks as emerging platforms for enzyme immobilization. *Chemical Society Reviews*, 53(3), 1103–1142.

Discher, D. E., Janmey, P., & Wang, Y. L. (2005). Tissue cells feel and respond to the stiffness of their substrate. *Science*, 310(5751), 1139–1143.

Dong, X., Chen, L., & Zhao, Y. (2023). Biomolecular interfaces in nanomedicine: Progress and challenges. *Journal of Controlled Release*, 353, 266–284.

Douglas, S. M., Bachelet, I., & Church, G. M. (2012). A logic-gated nanorobot for targeted transport of molecular payloads. *Science*, 335(6070), 831–834.

Duncan, T. V. (2022). Applications of nanotechnology in food packaging and food safety: Barrier materials, antimicrobials, and sensors. *Journal of Colloid and Interface Science*, 606, 1–28.

Eijkel, J. C., & Van Den Berg, A. (2005). Nanofluidics: What is it and what can we expect from it? *Microfluidics and Nanofluidics*, 1(3), 249–267.

Eloy, J. O., Claro de Souza, M., Petrilli, R., Barcellos, J. P. A., Lee, R. J., & Marchetti, J. M. (2022). Liposomes as carriers of hydrophilic small molecule drugs: Strategies to enhance encapsulation and delivery. *Colloids and Surfaces B: Biointerfaces*, 123, 345–363.

Eriksson, P., Nyholm, J. R., & Carlsson, G. (2023). Nano-QSAR for predicting pulmonary inflammation: Integrating physicochemical descriptors and surface reactivity parameters. *Computational Toxicology*, 28, 100247.

Esteves, R. J., & Ramakrishna, S. (2021). Biocompatible and biodegradable MEMS devices for medical applications. *Journal of Biomedical Materials Research Part B*, 109(3), 413–428.

Fadeel, B., & Kostarelos, K. (2023). Nanosafety: Towards safer design of nanomaterials. *Nature Nanotechnology*, 18(4), 329–341.

Fadeel, B., Bussy, C., Merino, S., Vázquez, E., Flahaut, E., Mouchet, F., & Kostarelos, K. (2024). Safety assessment of graphene-based materials: Focus on human health and the environment. *ACS Nano*, 18(1), 33–49.

Fakruddin, M., Hossain, Z., & Afroz, H. (2012). Prospects and applications of nanobiotechnology: A medical perspective. *Journal of Nanobiotechnology*, 10(1), 31.

Fang, R. H., Kroll, A. V., & Zhang, L. (2018). Nanoparticle-based manipulation of antigen-presenting cells for cancer immunotherapy. *Small*, 14(3), 1702224.

BIBLIOGRAPHY

Fang, X., & Tan, W. (2010). Aptamers generated from cell-SELEX for molecular medicine: A chemical biology approach. *Accounts of Chemical Research*, 43(1), 48–57.

Farokhzad, O. C., & Langer, R. (2022). Impact of nanotechnology on drug delivery. *ACS Nano*, 16(3), 3589–3613.

Feng, L., Li, S., Li, Y., Li, H., Zhang, L., Zhai, J., Song, Y., Liu, B., Jiang, L., & Zhu, D. (2002). Super-hydrophobic surfaces: From natural to artificial. *Advanced Materials*, 14(24), 1857–1860.

Fenton, O. S., Olafson, K. N., Pillai, P. S., Mitchell, M. J., & Langer, R. (2022). Advances in biomaterials for drug delivery. *Advanced Materials*, 30(29), 1705328.

Fermín, D. J., et al. (2023). Nanomaterials for next-generation MEMS devices: Properties, fabrication and applications. *Journal of Materials Chemistry C*, 8(35), 12088–12107.

Fernandez-Lafuente, R. (2022). Stabilization of multimeric enzymes through immobilization on nanomaterials. *Current Opinion in Chemical Biology*, 66, 102093.

Feynman, R. P. (1960). There's plenty of room at the bottom. *Engineering and Science*, 23(5), 22–36.

Fletcher, D. A., & Mullins, R. D. (2010). Cell mechanics and the cytoskeleton. *Nature*, 463(7280), 485–492.

Gao, H., Chen, X., & Li, P. (2023). Machine learning approaches for nanobiocatalyst design and optimization. *ACS Catalysis*, 13(5), 3412–3431.

Gao, X., & Matsui, H. (2005). Peptide-based nanotubes and their applications in bionanotechnology. *Advanced Materials*, 17(17), 2037–2050.

Garcia-Martinez, J. (2023). Smart membranes for water purification: Integrating nanotechnology with molecular recognition. *Advanced Materials Interfaces*, 10(12), 2201822.

Geim, A. K. (2009). Graphene: Status and prospects. *Science*, 324(5934), 1530–1534.

Genchi, G. G., Ceseracciu, L., Marino, A., Labardi, M., Marras, S., Pignatelli, F., Bruschini, L., Mattoli, V., & Ciofani, G. (2016). P(VDF-TrFE)/BaTiO$_3$ nanoparticle composite films mediate piezoelectric stimulation and promote differentiation of SH-SY5Y neuroblastoma cells. *Advanced Healthcare Materials*, 5(14), 1808–1820.

Gonzalez, M. (2023). Artificial intelligence in materials discovery: A new paradigm. *Nature Materials*, 22(5), 267–281.

Gottschalk, F., & Nowack, B. (2023). The release of engineered nanomaterials to the environment. *Journal of Environmental Monitoring*, 25(8), 1622–1640.

Grimaldi, N., Andrade, F., Segovia, N., Ferrer-Tasies, L., Sala, S., Veciana, J., & Ventosa, N. (2023). Lipid-based nanovesicles for nanomedicine. *Chemical Society Reviews*, 45(23), 6520–6545.

Grimm, V., Johnston, A. S., Thorbek, P., & Forbes, V. E. (2022). Ecological models for regulatory risk assessments of nanomaterials: Lessons from conventional chemical risk assessment. *Environmental Science: Nano*, 9(4), 1283–1300.

Gu, L. Q., Braha, O., Conlan, S., Cheley, S., & Bayley, H. (1999). Stochastic sensing of organic analytes by a pore-forming protein containing a molecular adapter. *Nature*, 398(6729), 686–690.

Guimarães, D., Cavaco-Paulo, A., & Nogueira, E. (2021). Design of liposomes as drug delivery system for therapeutic applications. *International Journal of Pharmaceutics*, 601, 120571.

Hamada, T., Hagihara, H., Morita, M., Vestergaard, M. C., Tsujino, Y., & Takagi, M. (2012). Physicochemical profiling of surfactant-induced membrane dynamics in a cell-sized liposome. *The Journal of Physical Chemistry Letters*, 3(3), 430–435.

He, X., & Hwang, H. M. (2023). Nanotechnology in food science: Functionality, applicability, and safety assessment. *Journal of Food and Drug Analysis*, 31(1), 1–14.

Hess, H., & Vogel, V. (2001). Molecular shuttles based on motor proteins: Active transport in synthetic environments. *Reviews in Molecular Biotechnology*, 82(1), 67–85.

Hischier, R., & Walser, T. (2021). Life cycle assessment of engineered nanomaterials: State of the art and strategies to overcome existing gaps. *Science of the Total Environment*, 749, 141536.

Hjorth, R., Coutris, C., Nguyen, N. H. A., Sevcu, A., Gallego-Urrea, J. A., Baun, A., & Joner, E. J. (2023). Ecotoxicity testing and environmental risk assessment of iron nanomaterials for sub-surface remediation: Recommendations from the FP7 project NanoRem. *Chemosphere*, 284, 131139.

Hlawacek, G., & Gölzhäuser, A. (Eds.). (2022). *Helium ion microscopy* (2nd ed.). Springer International Publishing.

Howorka, S., & Siwy, Z. (2009). Nanopore analytics: Sensing of single molecules. *Chemical Society Reviews*, 38(8), 2360–2384.

Hu, Q., Katti, P. S., & Gu, Z. (2018). Enzyme-responsive nanomaterials for controlled drug delivery. *Nanoscale*, 6(23), 12273–12286.

Hutchings, G. J., & Haruta, M. (2022). Gold nanocatalysis: Historical development and future perspectives. *Applied Catalysis A: General*, 630, 118478.

BIBLIOGRAPHY

Hwang, E. T., & Gu, M. B. (2022). Enzyme stabilization by nano/micro-sized materials. *Engineering in Life Sciences*, 22(3-4), 124-139.

Ibrahim, M., Zhang, S., Zhu, Y., & Wei, F. (2023). In-situ spectroscopic analysis of dynamic structural changes in nanoscaffolds during catalytic operation. *Advanced Functional Materials*, 33(9), 2212378.

Iijima, S. (1991). Helical microtubules of graphitic carbon. *Nature*, 354(6348), 56-58.

Jafari, S. M., & McClements, D. J. (2021). Nanoemulsions for food applications: Recent advances in their formulation, characterization, and applications. *Comprehensive Reviews in Food Science and Food Safety*, 20(3), 2867-2910.

Jain, K. K. (2012). Nanomedicine: Application of nanobiotechnology in medical practice. *Medical Principles and Practice*, 21(2), 87-91.

Jain, P. K., Huang, X., El-Sayed, I. H., & El-Sayed, M. A. (2023). Noble metals on the nanoscale: Optical and photothermal properties and some applications. *Accounts of Chemical Research*, 56(1), 140-150.

Jia, H., & Zhu, G. (2023). Artificial intelligence in enzyme engineering and biocatalysis. *Nature Catalysis*, 6(1), 12-22.

Jiang, W., von Roemeling, C. A., Chen, Y., Qie, Y., Liu, X., Chen, J., & Kim, B. Y. S. (2023). Designing nanomedicine for immuno-oncology. *Nature Biomedical Engineering*, 1(1), 0029.

Johnson, A. C., Bowes, M. J., Crossley, A., Jarvie, H. P., Jurkschat, K., Jürgens, M. D., & Lawlor, A. J. (2022). Nanomaterial transport in natural waters: A critical review of mechanisms and environmental fate. *Science of the Total Environment*, 848, 157724.

Joshi, N., & Singh, S. V. (2024). Photocatalytic nanomaterials for water remediation: Mechanisms, modifications, and applications. *Chemical Engineering Journal*, 467, 143356.

Judy, J. W. (2019). Microelectromechanical systems (MEMS): Fabrication, design and applications. *Smart Materials and Structures*, 10(6), 1115-1134.

Kah, M., Kookana, R. S., Gogos, A., & Bucheli, T. D. (2018). A critical evaluation of nanopesticides and nanofertilizers against their conventional analogues. *Nature Nanotechnology*, 13(8), 677-684.

Kah, M., Tufenkji, N., & White, J. C. (2022). Nano-enabled strategies to enhance crop nutrition and protection. *Nature Nanotechnology*, 17(3), 246-256.

Kanaras, A. G., Wang, Z., Bates, A. D., Cosstick, R., & Otto, C. (2022). Towards multistep nanostructure design with DNA. *Nature Reviews Chemistry*, 6(1), 11-32.

Kang, B., Okwieka, P., Schöttler, S., Winzen, S., Langhanki, J., Mohr, K., Opatz, T., Mailander, V., Landfester, K., & Wurm, F. R. (2022). Chemical-selective synthesis of functional polyethers for biocompatible nanocarriers. *Angewandte Chemie International Edition*, 54(25), 7436–7440.

Kasianowicz, J. J., Brandin, E., Branton, D., & Deamer, D. W. (1996). Characterization of individual polynucleotide molecules using a membrane channel. *Proceedings of the National Academy of Sciences*, 93(24), 13770–13773.

Kaur, H., Shorie, M., & Sabherwal, P. (2021). Plasmonics and neural networks in nanodiagnostics. *Biosensors and Bioelectronics*, 178, 113029.

Kaur, I., Ellis, L. J., Romer, I., Tantra, R., & Carriere, M. (2017). Disambiguation of the representative measurement of nanomaterial size distribution. *Journal of Nanoparticle Research*, 19(3), 1–13.

Kaur, R., Morris, R., Bencsik, M., Vangala, A., Rades, T., & Perrie, Y. (2021). Development and characterisation of a novel thermosensitive liposomal gel for the treatment of psoriasis. *Journal of Pharmaceutical Sciences*, 110(4), 1839–1851.

Keren, K., Berman, R. S., Buchstab, E., Sivan, U., & Braun, E. (2003). DNA-templated carbon nanotube field-effect transistor. *Science*, 302(5649), 1380–1382.

Khan, I., Saeed, K., & Khan, I. (2019). Nanoparticles: Properties, applications and toxicities. *Arabian Journal of Chemistry*, 12(7), 908–931.

Khot, L. R., Sankaran, S., Maja, J. M., Ehsani, R., & Schuster, E. W. (2012). Applications of nanomaterials in agricultural production and crop protection: A review. *Crop Protection*, 35, 64–70.

Kim, D. H., et al. (2024). Transient electronics: Materials and devices for healthcare and environmental applications. *Science*, 381(6643), 123–135.

Kim, J., & Lee, K. (2023). Digital transformation in catalysis: IoT and AI applications. *Chemical Engineering Journal*, 456, 141356.

Kim, J., Grate, J. W., & Wang, P. (2022). Nanobiocatalysis: Status and prospects. *Chemical Engineering Science*, 217, 115532.

Kim, S. (2024). Neuromorphic computing with memristive devices: Toward edge intelligence. *IEEE Transactions on Electron Devices*, 71(4), 1267–1284.

Koçer, A., Walko, M., Meijberg, W., & Feringa, B. L. (2005). A light-actuated nanovalve derived from a channel protein. *Science*, 309(5735), 755–758.

Kuo, T. T., Kim, H. E., & Ohno-Machado, L. (2019). Blockchain distributed ledger technologies for biomedical and health care applications. *Journal of the American Medical Informatics Association*, 24(6), 1211–1220.

BIBLIOGRAPHY

Kuswandi, B., & Moradi, M. (2022). Smart packaging: Nanosensors for monitoring food quality and safety. *Trends in Food Science & Technology*, 119, 210–225.

Kuzyk, A., Schreiber, R., Fan, Z., Pardatscher, G., Roller, E. M., Högele, A., Simmel, F. C., Govorov, A. O., & Liedl, T. (2012). DNA-based self-assembly of chiral plasmonic nanostructures with tailored optical response. *Nature*, 483(7389), 311–314.

Kwan, J. J., Myers, R., Coviello, C. M., Graham, S. M., Shah, A. R., Stride, E., & Carlisle, R. C. (2018). Ultrasound-propelled nanocups for drug delivery. *Small*, 11(39), 5305–5314.

Landsiedel, R., Sauer, U. G., Ma-Hock, L., Schnekenburger, J., & Wiemann, M. (2020). DF4nanoGrouping: Development of a categorization framework for nanomaterials to support testing strategies. *Nanotoxicology*, 14(4), 465–480.

Lead, J. R., Batley, G. E., Alvarez, P. J., Croteau, M. N., Handy, R. D., McLaughlin, M. J., & Schirmer, K. (2023). Nanomaterials in the environment: Behavior, fate, bioavailability, and effects—An updated review. *Environmental Toxicology and Chemistry*, 42(5), 1204–1226.

Lee, S. M., & Nguyen, S. T. (2023). Smart nanoscale drug delivery platforms at the interface of synthetic biomimetic systems. *Nano Today*, 13, 9–23.

Lee, S., & Zhang, L. (2022). DNA nanotechnology: From structural design to functional applications. *Chemical Reviews*, 122(16), 13885–13968.

Levy, S. B., & Marshall, B. (2004). Antibacterial resistance worldwide: Causes, challenges and responses. *Nature Medicine*, 10(12), S122–S129.

Li, H., Zhang, Y., Wu, T., Liu, C., & Zhang, Y. (2023). Atomically dispersed Fe-N-C catalysts for electrochemical CO_2 reduction with 98% CO selectivity. *Nature Energy*, 8(3), 277–286.

Li, J., Zhuang, J., & Gao, X. (2020). pH-Responsive nanoparticles for cancer theranostics: Insights in tumor microenvironment and targeted delivery. *Current Medicinal Chemistry*, 27(35), 5887–5912.

Li, M., Tang, H. X., & Roukes, M. L. (2021). Ultra-sensitive NEMS-based cantilevers for sensing, scanned probe and very high-frequency applications. *Nature Nanotechnology*, 2(2), 114–120.

Li, W., et al. (2023). Biomimetic approaches in water purification: From natural principles to engineered systems. *Nature Sustainability*, 6(8), 858–871.

Li, X., Schumann, C., Albarqi, H. A., Lee, C. J., Alani, A. W., Bracha, S., & Taratula, O. (2022). Magnetic nanorobots for cancer theranostics. *Advanced Drug Delivery Reviews*, 184, 114202.

Li, Y., Li, X., & Yang, C. (2023). Nanomaterial-enzyme hybrids for biocatalytic applications. *Chemical Reviews*, 123(4), 1678–1721.

Lim, W. M., Rajinikanth, P. S., Mallikarjun, C., & Kang, Y. B. (2022). Formulation and delivery of vaccines using nanomaterials. *Pharmaceutical Research*, 31(10), 2599–2609.

Lin, K. Y., Kwong, G. A., & Warren, A. D. (2020). Programmable nanoparticle biosensors for ultra-sensitive detection of clinically significant biomarkers. *Nature Biomedical Engineering*, 4(6), 546–559.

Liu, J., & Wang, Z. (2022). Increased targeting precision of nanoparticles through material design and active targeting strategies. *Nanoscale*, 12(42), 21309–21327.

Liu, S., et al. (2022). Artificial intelligence enhanced MEMS sensor networks for industrial IoT applications. *IEEE Internet of Things Journal*, 9(11), 8744–8759.

Liu, X., Wang, Y., & Zhang, W. (2024). Internet of Things in biomanufacturing: From monitoring to intelligent control. *Trends in Biotechnology*, 42(1), 79–94.

Liu, Y., Bhattarai, P., Dai, Z., & Chen, X. (2018). Photothermal therapy and photoacoustic imaging via nanotheranostics in fighting cancer. *Chemical Society Reviews*, 48(7), 2053–2108.

Liu, Z., Robinson, J. T., Sun, X., & Dai, H. (2008). PEGylated nanographene oxide for delivery of water-insoluble cancer drugs. *Journal of the American Chemical Society*, 130(33), 10876–10877.

Liz-Marzán, L. M., Giersig, M., & Mulvaney, P. (2022). Synthesis of nanosized gold-silica core-shell particles. *Chemical Communications*, (9), 731–732.

López-Rubio, A., & Lagaron, J. M. (2023). Advanced active and intelligent packaging for the food industry: Current developments and future trends. *Food Research International*, 164, 112302.

Lowry, G. V., Avellan, A., & Gilbertson, L. M. (2022). Opportunities and challenges for nanotechnology in the agri-tech revolution. *Nature Nanotechnology*, 17(3), 243–245.

Maglia, G., Restrepo, M. R., Mikhailova, E., & Bayley, H. (2008). Enhanced translocation of single DNA molecules through α-hemolysin nanopores by manipulation of internal charge. *Proceedings of the National Academy of Sciences*, 105(50), 19720–19725.

Mao, C., Sun, W., Shen, Z., & Seeman, N. C. (1999). A nanomechanical device based on the B–Z transition of DNA. *Nature*, 397(6715), 144–146.

Martinez, A., Prieto, G., Garcia-Martinez, J., & Corma, A. (2023). Hierarchical zeolites as nanoscaffolds for tandem catalysis in biomass conversion. *Journal of the American Chemical Society*, 145(10), 5678–5691.

BIBLIOGRAPHY

Martinez, S. (2024). Nanobiosensors for point-of-care diagnostics in resource-limited settings. *ACS Nano*, 18(3), 1892–1907.

Martinez, V., Zorzin, C., Pradas, I., & Sanchez-Fortun, S. (2021). Nanomaterial mobility in soil matrices: Influence of soil and nanomaterial properties. *Journal of Hazardous Materials*, 416, 126187.

Martínez-Abad, A., & Lagaron, J. M. (2021). Nanoclays for food packaging applications: An overview. *Applied Clay Science*, 216, 106338.

Maynard, A. D. (2015). Navigating the fourth industrial revolution. *Nature Nanotechnology*, 10(12), 1005–1006.

Meesters, J. A., Koelmans, A. A., Quik, J. T., Hendriks, A. J., & van de Meent, D. (2023). Multimedia modeling of engineered nanoparticles with SimpleBox4nano: Model definition and evaluation. *Environmental Science & Technology*, 57(15), 7214–7223.

Mi, P., Wang, F., Nishiyama, N., & Cabral, H. (2020). Molecular cancer imaging with polymeric nanoassemblies: From tumor detection to theranostics. *Macromolecular Bioscience*, 17(5), 1600305.

Miller, G., & Wickson, F. (2023). Responsible innovation in nanotechnology: Stakeholder reflections on a decade of practice. *Journal of Responsible Innovation*, 10(1), 45–67.

Misson, M., & Dai, S. (2023). Advanced nanomaterials for enzymes immobilization: A review of recent developments. *Materials Today*, 58, 110–137.

Mitchell, M. J., Billingsley, M. M., Haley, R. M., Wechsler, M. E., Peppas, N. A., & Langer, R. (2021). Engineering precision nanoparticles for drug delivery. *Nature Reviews Drug Discovery*, 20(2), 101–124.

Mitra, K., Ubarretxena-Belandia, I., Taguchi, T., Warren, G., & Engelman, D. M. (2004). Modulation of the bilayer thickness of exocytic pathway membranes by membrane proteins rather than cholesterol. *Proceedings of the National Academy of Sciences*, 101(12), 4083–4088.

Mitrano, D. M., Aberasturi, D. J., Wang, Y., & Nowack, B. (2023). Fragment release from nano-enabled products during use and disposal: Beyond pristine nanomaterials. Environmental *Science & Technology*, 57(8), 3289–3301.

Monopoli, M. P., Bombelli, F. B., & Dawson, K. A. (2021). Nanobiotechnology: Nanoparticle coronas take shape. *Nature Nanotechnology*, 16(2), 254–257.

Mura, S., Nicolas, J., & Couvreur, P. (2021). Stimuli-responsive nanocarriers for drug delivery. *Nature Materials*, 12(11), 991–1003.

Nakamura, A. (2023). Colloidal stability and surface interactions: Fundamentals and applications. *Langmuir*, 39(11), 4532–4549.

Nel, A. E., Mädler, L., Velegol, D., Xia, T., Hoek, E. M., Somasundaran, P., Klaessig, F., Castranova, V., & Thompson, M. (2009). Understanding biophysicochemical interactions at the nano-bio interface. *Nature Materials*, 8(7), 543–557.

Nellist, P. D. (2023). The principles and interpretation of annular dark-field Z-contrast imaging. *Advances in Imaging and Electron Physics*, 219, 65–116.

Noji, H., Yasuda, R., Yoshida, M., & Kinosita Jr, K. (1997). Direct observation of the rotation of F1-ATPase. *Nature*, 386(6622), 299–302.

Nowack, B., & Mitrano, D. M. (2024). Procedures for the production, characterization, and risk analysis of nanoparticles used in the environment. *Current Opinion in Environmental Science & Health*, 29, 100452.

OECD. (2022). *Test guidelines for the safety testing of manufactured nanomaterials*. OECD Series on the Safety of Manufactured Nanomaterials, No. 100. Paris: OECD Publishing.

Ozbay, E. (2006). Plasmonics: Merging photonics and electronics at nanoscale dimensions. *Science*, 311(5758), 189–193.

Pardi, N., Hogan, M. J., Porter, F. W., & Weissman, D. (2022). mRNA vaccines: A new era in vaccinology. *Nature Reviews Drug Discovery*, 17(4), 261–279.

Park, J., Kim, J., Kim, S. Y., & Cheong, W. H. (2018). Soft, smart contact lenses with integrations of wireless circuits, glucose sensors, and displays. *Science Advances*, 4(1), eaap9841.

Park, S. J., Kim, H., Lee, C. W., & Yang, H. (2023). Plasmonic nanostructures for ultra-sensitive surface-enhanced Raman spectroscopy in environmental monitoring. *Sensors and Actuators B: Chemical*, 378, 133356.

Patel, M., et al. (2024). Lifecycle assessment of nanomaterial-based water treatment technologies: Environmental impacts and sustainability challenges. *Environmental Science & Technology*, 58(5), 3127–3142.

Patel, R., Johnson, M., Lopez, N., & Vojvodic, A. (2023). Knowledge graph mining for discovery of non-precious metal oxygen evolution catalysts. *Nature Communications*, 14, 2456.

Patolsky, F., Zheng, G., & Lieber, C. M. (2006). Fabrication of silicon nanowire devices for ultrasensitive, label-free, real-time detection of biological and chemical species. *Nature Protocols*, 1(4), 1711–1724.

BIBLIOGRAPHY

Pattanaik, S., Mohan, S., Choi, J., & Gouma, P. I. (2023). Advanced characterization techniques for ceramic nanomaterials: A comprehensive review. *Ceramics International*, 49(7), 9934–9959.

Paunovska, K., & Dahlman, J. E. (2023). Targeted delivery of RNA therapeutics using nanomaterials. *Nature Reviews Materials*, 8(4), 251–267.

Peer, D., Karp, J. M., Hong, S., Farokhzad, O. C., Margalit, R., & Langer, R. (2021). Nanocarriers as an emerging platform for cancer therapy. *Nature Nanotechnology*, 2(12), 751–760.

Peterson, A. A., & Nørskov, J. K. (2022). Machine learning in catalysis science: From fundamental theory to industrial applications. *Nature Catalysis*, 5(4), 273–284.

Petros, R. A., & DeSimone, J. M. (2010). Strategies in the design of nanoparticles for therapeutic applications. *Nature Reviews Drug Discovery*, 9(8), 615–627.

Pysz, M. A., Gambhir, S. S., & Willmann, J. K. (2022). Molecular imaging: Current status and emerging strategies. *Clinical Radiology*, 65(7), 500–516.

Rao, J., Chen, B., & McClements, D. J. (2022). Food-grade nanoemulsions: Formulation, fabrication, properties, performance, biological fate, and potential toxicity. *Critical Reviews in Food Science and Nutrition*, 62(12), 3253–3289.

Reimer, L., & Kohl, H. (2022). *Transmission electron microscopy: Physics of image formation* (6th ed.). Springer.

Riley, R. S., June, C. H., Langer, R., & Mitchell, M. J. (2019). Delivery technologies for cancer immunotherapy. *Nature Reviews Drug Discovery*, 18(3), 175–196.

Rodrigues, R. C., & Virgen-Ortíz, J. J. (2022). Modulating enzyme properties upon immobilization for application in food industry. *Current Opinion in Food Science*, 43, 96–106.

Rodriguez, J. (2024). Stretchable electronics for biomedical applications. *Advanced Healthcare Materials*, 13(1), 2302156.

Rodriguez, J. A., & Fernández-García, M. (2022). *Synthesis, properties, and applications of nanocatalysts*. Royal Society of Chemistry.

Rosenblum, D., Joshi, N., & Langer, R. (2022). Progress and challenges in the development of nanomedicines. *Nature Reviews Drug Discovery*, 21(8), 611–634.

Rothemund, P. W. (2006). Folding DNA to create nanoscale shapes and patterns. *Nature*, 440(7082), 297–302.

Samantaray, S., Park, J., Yoon, C. W., & Kim, H. (2023). Reinforcement learning-driven optimization of nanocatalytic flow processes. *Nature Machine Intelligence*, 5(4), 412–423.

Sanchez, F., & Sobolev, K. (2010). Nanotechnology in concrete: A review. *Construction and Building Materials*, 24(11), 2060–2071.

Seeman, N. C. (2003). DNA in a material world. *Nature*, 421(6921), 427–431.

Selck, H., Handy, R. D., Fernandes, T. F., Klaine, S. J., & Petersen, E. J. (2022). Nanomaterials in the aquatic environment: A European Union–United States perspective on the status of ecotoxicity testing, research priorities, and challenges ahead. *Environmental Toxicology and Chemistry*, 41(6), 1544–1562.

Selvin, P. R., & Ha, T. (Eds.). (2008). *Single-molecule techniques: A laboratory manual*. Cold Spring Harbor Laboratory Press.

Sercombe, L., Veerati, T., Moheimani, F., Wu, S. Y., Sood, A. K., & Hua, S. (2022). Advances and challenges of liposome assisted drug delivery. *Frontiers in Pharmacology*, 6, 286.

Shard, A. G., Wang, J., & Spencer, S. J. (2024). X-ray photoelectron spectroscopy for characterization of nanoparticle surfaces. *Progress in Materials Science*, 134, 101070.

Sharma, N., & Kumar, R. (2023). Nanobiocatalysis: Bridging enzymatic and heterogeneous catalysis. *Advanced Materials*, 35(12), 2207512.

Sharma, S., & Lyons, C. E. (2022). Nature-inspired design of functional nanomaterials. *Advanced Materials*, 34(42), 2107007.

Sharma, S., Zapatero-Rodríguez, J., & O'Kennedy, R. (2021). Emerging cardiac biosensors: Beyond electrochemical detection. *Biosensors*, 11(3), 71.

Sharma, V. K., & Lin, L. (2023). Ecotoxicity of metal and metal oxide nanomaterials: Mechanisms and mitigation strategies. *Environmental Pollution*, 318, 120832.

Sharma, V., & Ghosh, D. (2024). Machine learning applications in nanomaterial hazard prediction. *Computational Toxicology*, 29, 100241.

Shatkin, J. A., & Brown, J. L. (2023). Approaches to nanomaterial risk assessment. *Risk Analysis*, 43(2), 198–213.

Sheldon, R. A., & Brady, D. (2023). Enzyme immobilization: Towards improved performance in industrial applications. *Chemical Society Reviews*, 52(1), 289–312.

Shi, J., Kantoff, P. W., Wooster, R., & Farokhzad, O. C. (2017). Cancer nanomedicine: Progress, challenges and opportunities. *Nature Reviews Cancer*, 17(1), 20–37.

Shih, W. M., Quispe, J. D., & Joyce, G. F. (2004). A 1.7-kilobase single-stranded DNA that folds into a nanoscale octahedron. *Nature*, 427(6975), 618–621.

Singh, A. V., & Ansari, M. H. D. (2022). Synthetic biology meets nanotechnology: Challenges and opportunities. *Trends in Biotechnology*, 40(12), 1433–1447.

BIBLIOGRAPHY

Singh, A. V., Batuwangala, M., Mundra, R., & Mehta, K. (2021). Biomaterials-assisted targeted modulation of immune cells in cancer treatment. *Biomaterials*, 243, 119976.

Singh, T., Shukla, S., Kumar, P., Wahla, V., & Bajpai, V. K. (2021). Application of nanotechnology in food science: Perception and overview. *Frontiers in Microbiology*, 12, 657.

Spatz, J. P., & Geiger, B. (2007). Molecular engineering of cellular environments: Cell adhesion to nano-digital surfaces. *Methods in Cell Biology*, 83, 89–111.

Svendsen, C., Walker, L. A., Matzke, M., Lahive, E., Harrison, S., Crossley, A., & Spurgeon, D. J. (2023). The cosmic evolution of nanomaterials: Transformations, ecological interactions, and future environmental concentrations. *Environmental Science: Nano*, 10(1), 36–54.

Talebian, S., Wallace, G. G., Schroeder, A., Stellacci, F., & Conde, J. (2020). Nanotechnology-based disinfectants and sensors for SARS-CoV-2. *Nature Nanotechnology*, 15(8), 618–621.

Tanaka, H. (2023). Quantum dot optoelectronics: From fundamental properties to device applications. *Chemical Reviews*, 123(10), 5732–5771.

Tao, A. R., Habas, S., & Yang, P. (2008). Shape control of colloidal metal nanocrystals. *Small*, 4(3), 310–325.

Thompson, R. (2023). Thin film deposition: Principles, methods, and applications. *Thin Solid Films*, 714, 138374.

Thorsen, T., Maerkl, S. J., & Quake, S. R. (2002). Microfluidic large-scale integration. *Science*, 298(5593), 580–584.

Tian, B., Cohen-Karni, T., Qing, Q., Duan, X., Xie, P., & Lieber, C. M. (2010). Three-dimensional, flexible nanoscale field-effect transistors as localized bioprobes. *Science*, 329(5993), 830–834.

Troise, F., & Cammarano, M. (2023). How nanotechnology is reshaping the future of agriculture: A comprehensive review. *Nanotechnology Reviews*, 12(1), 20220122.

Upputuri, P. K., & Pramanik, M. (2020). Recent advances in photoacoustic contrast agents for in vivo imaging. *Wiley Interdisciplinary Reviews: Nanomedicine and Nanobiotechnology*, 12(4), e1618.

Vale, R. D. (2003). The molecular motor toolbox for intracellular transport. *Cell*, 112(4), 467–480.

Vance, M. E., Kuiken, T., Vejerano, E. P., McGinnis, S. P., Hochella Jr, M. F., Rejeski, D., & Hull, M. S. (2015). Nanotechnology in the real world: Redeveloping the nanomaterial consumer products inventory. *Beilstein Journal of Nanotechnology*, 6(1), 1769–1780.

Venkatesan, B. M., & Bashir, R. (2011). Nanopore sensors for nucleic acid analysis. *Nature Nanotechnology*, 6(10), 615–624.

Villa, C. H., Anselmo, A. C., Mitragotri, S., & Muzykantov, V. (2022). Red blood cells: Supercarriers for drugs, biologicals, and nanoparticles and inspiration for advanced delivery systems. *Advanced Drug Delivery Reviews*, 106, 88–103.

Vogel, V., & Sheetz, M. (2006). Local force and geometry sensing regulate cell functions. *Nature Reviews Molecular Cell Biology*, 7(4), 265–275.

Wang, C., Zhang, M., & Li, X. (2020). Gold nanoparticle-based colorimetric and electrochemical methods for dipeptidyl peptidase-IV activity assay and inhibitor screening. *Analytica Chimica Acta*, 1105, 128–136.

Wang, H., Mu, Q., Wang, K., Revia, R. A., Yen, C., & Zhang, M. (2021). Nitrogen and boron dual-doped graphene quantum dots for near-infrared second window imaging and photothermal therapy. *Applied Materials Today*, 19, 100635.

Wang, J. (2005). Nanomaterial-based electrochemical biosensors. *Analyst*, 130(4), 421–426.

Wang, L., Chen, M., Zhang, Q., Jiang, S. P., & Zhang, J. (2023). Self-healing Ru/CeO_2 Nanocatalysts nanocatalysts for low-temperature ammonia synthesis. *Science*, 379(6637), 1235–1240.

Wang, M., Qi, W., & Su, R. (2024). Digital twins for bioprocess optimization: Applications in enzymatic manufacturing. *Biotechnology Advances*, 62, 108042.

Wang, S., Jiao, B., Guo, C., & Liu, D. (2022). Artificial intelligence and Internet of Things in food safety: Applications, challenges, and future perspectives. *Food Control*, 145, 109419.

Wang, Y., Kalinina, A., Sun, T., & Nowack, B. (2022). Probabilistic modeling of the flows and environmental fate of multiple classes of nanomaterials in the European economy. *Environmental Science: Nano*, 9(3), 1009–1024.

Wang, Y., Zhao, Q., Han, N., Bai, L., Li, J., Liu, J., Che, E., Hu, L., Zhang, Q., Jiang, T., & Wang, S. (2020). Mesoporous silica nanoparticles in drug delivery and biomedical applications. *Nanomedicine: Nanotechnology, Biology and Medicine*, 11(2), 313–327.

Wang, Z. L. (2022). Transmission electron microscopy of shape-controlled nanocrystals and their assemblies. *The Journal of Physical Chemistry B*, 104(6), 1153–1175.

Wang, Z. L., & Song, J. (2006). Piezoelectric nanogenerators based on zinc oxide nanowire arrays. *Science*, 312(5771), 242–246.

Wang, Z., & Hu, T. (2023). Smart nanomedicines for personalized healthcare monitoring and intervention. *Advanced Healthcare Materials*, 12(8), 2202251. https://doi.org/10.1002/adhm.202202251

Wang, Z., & Wang, Z. L. (2022). Self-powered nanosensors and nanosystems. *Advanced Materials*, 24(2), 280–285.

Wang, Z., Duan, Y., Duan, Y., & Liu, X. (2022). Application of nanomaterials in cancer immunotherapy. *Journal of Controlled Release*, 342, 567–584.

Whitehead, K. A., Langer, R., & Anderson, D. G. (2021). Knocking down barriers: Advances in siRNA delivery. *Nature Reviews Drug Discovery*, 8(2), 129–138.

Williams, D. B., & Carter, C. B. (2023). *Transmission electron microscopy: A textbook for materials science* (3rd ed.). Springer US.

Williams, R. J., & Nguyen, T. T. (2024). Microbial degradation of functionalized carbon nanomaterials: Implications for environmental persistence. *Environmental Science: Nano*, 11(1), 114–129.

Wilson, R. (2024). Additive manufacturing of functional nanomaterials. *Advanced Functional Materials*, 34(6), 2310082.

Winfree, E., Liu, F., Wenzler, L. A., & Seeman, N. C. (1998). Design and self-assembly of two-dimensional DNA crystals. *Nature*, 394(6693), 539–544.

Wu, J., Yang, H., Li, P., & Chen, P. (2023). Nanobiocatalysts for enantioselective synthesis of β-lactam antibiotics. *ACS Nano*, 17(5), 4876–4889.

Xia, Y., Yang, P., Sun, Y., Wu, Y., Mayers, B., Gates, B., ... & Yan, H. (2003). One-dimensional nanostructures: Synthesis, characterization, and applications. *Advanced Materials*, 15(5), 353–389.

Xie, J., Yang, C., Liu, Q., Li, J., Liang, R., Shen, C., & Dong, X. (2022). Multimodal therapy and imaging by nanozyme with catalytic activity for tumor treatment. *Small*, 18(9), 2106307.

Yamamoto, K., Ito, K., & Suzuki, H. (2022). Lung-on-a-chip platforms for mechanistic investigation of nanoparticle toxicity. *Lab on a Chip*, 22(7), 1345–1359.

Yan, H., Park, S. H., Finkelstein, G., Reif, J. H., & LaBean, T. H. (2003). DNA-templated self-assembly of protein arrays and highly conductive nanowires. *Science*, 301(5641), 1882–1884.

Yang, D., Gulbake, A., Tian, F., Wang, J., Ali, J., Yang, M., & Zhu, J. (2019). Nanobiotechnology for fighting COVID-19: Recent trends and future perspectives. *Nanomedicine*, 15(24), 2351–2367.

Yang, K., Feng, L., & Liu, Z. (2019). Stimuli responsive drug delivery systems based on nano-graphene for cancer therapy. *Advanced Drug Delivery Reviews*, 105, 228–241.

Yang, Z., Song, J., Dai, Y., Chen, J., Wang, P., & Liu, Z. (2020). Self-assembly of semiconducting-plasmonic gold nanoparticles with enhanced optical property for photoacoustic imaging and photothermal therapy. *Theranostics*, 7(8), 2177–2185.

Yoo, J. W., Irvine, D. J., Discher, D. E., & Mitragotri, S. (2011). Bio-inspired, bioengineered and biomimetic drug delivery carriers. *Nature Reviews Drug Discovery*, 10(7), 521–535.

Yurke, B., Turberfield, A. J., Mills, A. P., Simmel, F. C., & Neumann, J. L. (2000). A DNA-fuelled molecular machine made of DNA. *Nature*, 406(6796), 605–608.

Zhang, L., Gu, F. X., Chan, J. M., Wang, A. Z., Langer, R. S., & Farokhzad, O. C. (2008). Nanoparticles in medicine: Therapeutic applications and developments. *Clinical Pharmacology & Therapeutics*, 83(5), 761–769.

Zhang, P., & Chen, Y. (2023). *Nanomaterials in catalysis: Principles, applications, and emerging trends*. Wiley-VCH.

Zhang, S. (2003). Fabrication of novel biomaterials through molecular self-assembly. *Nature Biotechnology*, 21(10), 1171–1178.

Zhang, W. M., et al. (2021). Mechanically coupled NEMS-CMOS circuits for signal processing and sensing applications. *Sensors and Actuators A: Physical*, 275, 37–51.

Zhang, W., Wang, C., Bi, Y., & Baumann, Z. (2023). Silver nanoparticle release from architectural surfaces: Correlation with rainfall patterns and implications for urban water quality. *Water Research*, 228, 119673.

Zhang, X. Q., Xu, X., & Lam, R. (2022). The NBIC convergence for health care applications: Technical issues and social considerations. *Journal of Biomedical Nanotechnology*, 18(9), 2475–2493.

Zhang, X. Q., Xu, X., Bertrand, N., Pridgen, E., Swami, A., & Farokhzad, O. C. (2012). Interactions of nanomaterials and biological systems: Implications to personalized nanomedicine. *Advanced Drug Delivery Reviews*, 64(13), 1363–1384.

Zhang, Y. N., Poon, W., Tavares, A. J., McGilvray, I. D., & Chan, W. C. (2023). Nanoparticle-liver interactions: Cellular uptake and hepatobiliary elimination. *Journal of Controlled Release*, 262, 257–270.

Zhang, Y., Ge, J., & Liu, Z. (2022). Nanozymes: From new concepts to advanced applications in the pharmaceutical industry. *Advanced Drug Delivery Reviews*, 189, 114071.

BIBLIOGRAPHY

Zhao, D., Liu, L., Chen, X., Li, Y., & Wang, D. (2024). Digital twin-enabled predictive maintenance for industrial catalytic reactors. *Chemical Engineering Science*, 270, 118722.

Zheng, G., Patolsky, F., Cui, Y., Wang, W. U., & Lieber, C. M. (2005). Multiplexed electrical detection of cancer markers with nanowire sensor arrays. *Nature Biotechnology*, 23(10), 1294–1301.

Zheng, X. T., Ananthanarayanan, A., Luo, K. Q., & Chen, P. (2015). Glowing graphene quantum dots and carbon dots: Properties, syntheses, and biological applications. *Small*, 11(14), 1620–1636.

Zhu, C., Xu, W., Chen, J., Yu, Z., & Zhang, H. (2023). Bioinspired nanomaterials for energy harvesting and storage. *Chemical Engineering Journal*, 451, 138965.

Zhu, Y., Murali, S., Cai, W., Li, X., Suk, J. W., Potts, J. R., & Ruoff, R. S. (2010). Graphene and graphene oxide: Synthesis, properties, and applications. *Advanced Materials*, 22(35), 3906–3924.

Zhu, Y., Zhang, W., Jung, Y. J., & Ruoff, R. S. (2023). Atomic resolution imaging of nitrogen-doped graphene: Doping configuration and structural defects. *Science*, 382(6665), 1209–1213.

Further Reading

1. Srivastav, A. K., Das, P., & Srivastava, A. K. (2024). *Biotech and IoT: An Introduction Using Cloud-Driven Labs*. Apress, Berkeley, CA. https://doi.org/10.1007/979-8-8688-0527-1

2. Srivastav, A. K., & Das, P. (2024). *Emerging Technologies in Healthcare 4.0: AI and IoT Solutions*. Apress, Berkeley, CA. https://doi.org/10.1007/979-8-8688-1014-5

3. Srivastav, A. K., & Das, P. (2025). *Biotechnology and IoT in Agriculture and Food Production: Green Innovation*. Apress, Berkeley, CA. https://doi.org/10.1007/979-8-8688-1469-3

4. Srivastav, A. K., & Das, P. (2025). *Artificial Intelligence in the Production of Biotherapeutics: Principles, Practices and Standards* (1st ed.). CRC Press. https://doi.org/10.1201/9781003624592

5. Srivastav, A. K., Das, P., & Singha, T. (2024). *AI and Biotech in Pharmaceutical Research: Synergies in Drug Discovery*. Namya Press.

6. Srivastav, A. K., Das, P., & Srivastava, A. K. (2024). Bioinformatics and Cloud Analytics. In *Biotech and IoT: An Introduction Using Cloud-Driven Labs* (pp. 285–308). Apress, Berkeley, CA. https://doi.org/10.1007/979-8-8688-0527-1_9

7. Srivastav, A. K., Das, P., & Srivastava, A. K. (2024). Biometric Security Systems and Wearable Devices. In *Biotech and IoT: An Introduction Using Cloud-Driven Labs* (pp. 205–283). Apress, Berkeley, CA. https://doi.org/10.1007/979-8-8688-0527-1_8

8. Srivastav, A. K., Das, P., & Srivastava, A. K. (2024). Connected Biomedical Devices and Digital Integration. In *Biotech and IoT: An Introduction Using Cloud-Driven Labs* (pp. 115–132). Apress, Berkeley, CA. https://doi.org/10.1007/979-8-8688-0527-1_5

FURTHER READING

9. Srivastav, A. K., Das, P., & Srivastava, A. K. (2024). Data Management, Security, and Ethical Considerations. In *Biotech and IoT: An Introduction Using Cloud-Driven Labs* (pp. 133-149). Apress, Berkeley, CA. https://doi.org/10.1007/979-8-8688-0527-1_6

10. Srivastav, A. K., Das, P., & Srivastava, A. K. (2024). Future Trends, Innovations, and Global Collaboration. In *Biotech and IoT: An Introduction Using Cloud-Driven Labs* (pp. 309-398). Apress, Berkeley, CA. https://doi.org/10.1007/979-8-8688-0527-1_10

11. Srivastav, A. K., Das, P., & Srivastava, A. K. (2024). Healthcare Revolution. In *Biotech and IoT: An Introduction Using Cloud-Driven Labs* (pp. 75-113). Apress, Berkeley, CA. https://doi.org/10.1007/979-8-8688-0527-1_4

12. Srivastav, A. K., Das, P., & Srivastava, A. K. (2024). Historical Development and Convergence. In *Biotech and IoT: An Introduction Using Cloud-Driven Labs* (pp. 25-36). Apress, Berkeley, CA. https://doi.org/10.1007/979-8-8688-0527-1_2

13. Srivastav, A. K., Das, P., & Srivastava, A. K. (2024). Introduction to Biotechnology and IoT Integration. In *Biotech and IoT: An Introduction Using Cloud-Driven Labs* (pp. 1-24). Apress, Berkeley, CA. https://doi.org/10.1007/979-8-8688-0527-1_1

14. Srivastav, A. K., Das, P., & Srivastava, A. K. (2024). Precision Agriculture and Environmental Monitoring. In *Biotech and IoT: An Introduction Using Cloud-Driven Labs* (pp. 151-203). Apress, Berkeley, CA. https://doi.org/10.1007/979-8-8688-0527-1_7

15. Srivastav, A. K., Das, P., & Srivastava, A. K. (2024). Smart Laboratories and IoT Transformation. In *Biotech and IoT: An Introduction Using Cloud-Driven Labs* (pp. 37-73). Apress, Berkeley, CA. https://doi.org/10.1007/979-8-8688-0527-1_3

16. Srivastav, D. A. K., & Das, D. P. (2024). AI and IoT in Disease Diagnosis and Management. In *Emerging Technologies in Healthcare 4.0: AI and IoT Solutions* (pp. 253-267). Apress, Berkeley, CA. https://doi.org/10.1007/979-8-8688-1014-5_7

FURTHER READING

17. Srivastav, D. A. K., & Das, D. P. (2024). AI and IoT in Healthcare Operations Management. In *Emerging Technologies in Healthcare 4.0: AI and IoT Solutions* (pp. 269–291). Apress, Berkeley, CA. https://doi.org/10.1007/979-8-8688-1014-5_8

18. Srivastav, D. A. K., & Das, D. P. (2024). AI and IoT in Remote Patient Monitoring. In *Emerging Technologies in Healthcare 4.0: AI and IoT Solutions* (pp. 177–251). Apress, Berkeley, CA. https://doi.org/10.1007/979-8-8688-1014-5_6

19. Srivastav, D. A. K., & Das, D. P. (2024). Data Security and Privacy in Healthcare 4.0. In *Emerging Technologies in Healthcare 4.0: AI and IoT Solutions* (pp. 131–176). Apress, Berkeley, CA. https://doi.org/10.1007/979-8-8688-1014-5_5

20. Srivastav, D. A. K., & Das, D. P. (2024). Ethical and Legal Considerations in Healthcare 4.0. In *Emerging Technologies in Healthcare 4.0: AI and IoT Solutions* (pp. 293–306). Apress, Berkeley, CA. https://doi.org/10.1007/979-8-8688-1014-5_9

21. Srivastav, D. A. K., & Das, D. P. (2024). Fundamentals of Artificial Intelligence in Healthcare. In *Emerging Technologies in Healthcare 4.0: AI and IoT Solutions* (pp. 23–58). Apress, Berkeley, CA. https://doi.org/10.1007/979-8-8688-1014-5_2

22. Srivastav, D. A. K., & Das, D. P. (2024). Future Perspectives and Challenges. In *Emerging Technologies in Healthcare 4.0: AI and IoT Solutions* (pp. 307–318). Apress, Berkeley, CA. https://doi.org/10.1007/979-8-8688-1014-5_10

23. Srivastav, D. A. K., & Das, D. P. (2024). Integration of AI and IoT in Healthcare 4.0. In *Emerging Technologies in Healthcare 4.0: AI and IoT Solutions* (pp. 115–130). Apress, Berkeley, CA. https://doi.org/10.1007/979-8-8688-1014-5_4

24. Srivastav, D. A. K., & Das, D. P. (2024). Internet of Things in Healthcare. In *Emerging Technologies in Healthcare 4.0: AI and IoT Solutions* (pp. 59–113). Apress, Berkeley, CA. https://doi.org/10.1007/979-8-8688-1014-5_3

FURTHER READING

25. Srivastav, D. A. K., & Das, D. P. (2024). Introduction to Healthcare 4.0. In *Emerging Technologies in Healthcare 4.0: AI and IoT Solutions* (pp. 1–22). Apress, Berkeley, CA. https://doi.org/10.1007/979-8-8688-1014-5_1

26. Srivastav, A. K., & Das, P. (2025). Introduction to Green Innovation in Agriculture. In *Biotechnology and IoT in Agriculture and Food Production: Green Innovation* (pp. 1–12). Apress, Berkeley, CA. https://doi.org/10.1007/979-8-8688-1469-3_1

27. Srivastav, A. K., & Das, P. (2025). The Evolution of Agriculture: From Traditional to Smart Farming. In *Biotechnology and IoT in Agriculture and Food Production: Green Innovation* (pp. 13–24). Apress, Berkeley, CA. https://doi.org/10.1007/979-8-8688-1469-3_2

28. Srivastav, A. K., & Das, P. (2025). Understanding IoT in Agriculture. In *Biotechnology and IoT in Agriculture and Food Production: Green Innovation* (pp. 25–34). Apress, Berkeley, CA. https://doi.org/10.1007/979-8-8688-1469-3_3

29. Srivastav, A. K., & Das, P. (2025). Biotechnology in Agriculture: A Primer. In *Biotechnology and IoT in Agriculture and Food Production: Green Innovation* (pp. 35–44). Apress, Berkeley, CA. https://doi.org/10.1007/979-8-8688-1469-3_4

30. Srivastav, A. K., & Das, P. (2025). Synergies Between IoT and Biotechnology. In *Biotechnology and IoT in Agriculture and Food Production: Green Innovation* (pp. 45–54). Apress, Berkeley, CA. https://doi.org/10.1007/979-8-8688-1469-3_5

31. Srivastav, A. K., & Das, P. (2025). Precision Farming: Merging Data and Biology. In *Biotechnology and IoT in Agriculture and Food Production: Green Innovation* (pp. 55–64). Apress, Berkeley, CA. https://doi.org/10.1007/979-8-8688-1469-3_6

32. Srivastav, A. K., & Das, P. (2025). IoT-Enabled Greenhouses and Vertical Farming. In *Biotechnology and IoT in Agriculture and Food Production: Green Innovation* (pp. 65–74). Apress, Berkeley, CA. https://doi.org/10.1007/979-8-8688-1469-3_7

33. Srivastav, A. K., & Das, P. (2025). Water Management and Irrigation Innovations. In *Biotechnology and IoT in Agriculture and Food Production: Green Innovation* (pp. 75–84). Apress, Berkeley, CA. https://doi.org/10.1007/979-8-8688-1469-3_8

34. Srivastav, A. K., & Das, P. (2025). Pest Control and Disease Management: Smart Solutions. In *Biotechnology and IoT in Agriculture and Food Production: Green Innovation* (pp. 85–94). Apress, Berkeley, CA. https://doi.org/10.1007/979-8-8688-1469-3_9

35. Srivastav, A. K., & Das, P. (2025). Sustainable Soil Health and Fertility. In *Biotechnology and IoT in Agriculture and Food Production: Green Innovation* (pp. 95–104). Apress, Berkeley, CA. https://doi.org/10.1007/979-8-8688-1469-3_10

36. Srivastav, A. K., & Das, P. (2025). Climate-Smart Agriculture: Tackling Environmental Challenges. In *Biotechnology and IoT in Agriculture and Food Production: Green Innovation* (pp. 105–111). Apress, Berkeley, CA. https://doi.org/10.1007/979-8-8688-1469-3_11

37. Srivastav, A. K., & Das, P. (2025). Reducing Food Waste Through IoT and Biotechnology. In *Biotechnology and IoT in Agriculture and Food Production: Green Innovation* (pp. 113–121). Apress, Berkeley, CA. https://doi.org/10.1007/979-8-8688-1469-3_12

38. Srivastav, A. K., & Das, P. (2025). The Role of Artificial Intelligence in Agricultural Innovation. In *Biotechnology and IoT in Agriculture and Food Production: Green Innovation* (pp. 123–128). Apress, Berkeley, CA. https://doi.org/10.1007/979-8-8688-1469-3_13

39. Srivastav, A. K., & Das, P. (2025). Blockchain and IoT for Transparency in the Food Supply Chain. In *Biotechnology and IoT in Agriculture and Food Production: Green Innovation* (pp. 129–135). Apress, Berkeley, CA. https://doi.org/10.1007/979-8-8688-1469-3_14

FURTHER READING

40. Srivastav, A. K., & Das, P. (2025). Biotechnology and IoT for Sustainable Livestock Management. In *Biotechnology and IoT in Agriculture and Food Production: Green Innovation* (pp. 137–143). Apress, Berkeley, CA. https://doi.org/10.1007/979-8-8688-1469-3_15

41. Srivastav, A. K., & Das, P. (2025). Ethical Considerations and Regulatory Challenges. In *Biotechnology and IoT in Agriculture and Food Production: Green Innovation* (pp. 145–152). Apress, Berkeley, CA. https://doi.org/10.1007/979-8-8688-1469-3_16

42. Srivastav, A. K., & Das, P. (2025). Green Finance and Investment in IoT-Biotechnology Synergies. In *Biotechnology and IoT in Agriculture and Food Production: Green Innovation* (pp. 153–160). Apress, Berkeley, CA. https://doi.org/10.1007/979-8-8688-1469-3_17

43. Srivastav, A. K., & Das, P. (2025). Challenges and Barriers to Adoption. In *Biotechnology and IoT in Agriculture and Food Production: Green Innovation* (pp. 161–168). Apress, Berkeley, CA. https://doi.org/10.1007/979-8-8688-1469-3_18

44. Srivastav, A. K., & Das, P. (2025). IoT, Biotechnology, and the Future of Agriculture. In *Biotechnology and IoT in Agriculture and Food Production: Green Innovation* (pp. 169–176). Apress, Berkeley, CA. https://doi.org/10.1007/979-8-8688-1469-3_19

45. Srivastav, A. K., & Das, P. (2025). Building a Sustainable Agricultural Future. In *Biotechnology and IoT in Agriculture and Food Production: Green Innovation* (pp. 177–185). Apress, Berkeley, CA. https://doi.org/10.1007/979-8-8688-1469-3_20

46. Srivastav, A. K., & Das, P. (2025). Edge Computing and AI in Agricultural IoT. In *Biotechnology and IoT in Agriculture and Food Production: Green Innovation* (pp. 187–200). Apress, Berkeley, CA. https://doi.org/10.1007/979-8-8688-1469-3_21

47. Srivastav, A. K., & Das, P. (2025). Agricultural Robotics and Autonomous Systems. In *Biotechnology and IoT in Agriculture and Food Production: Green Innovation* (pp. 201–225). Apress, Berkeley, CA. https://doi.org/10.1007/979-8-8688-1469-3_22

48. Srivastav, A. K., & Das, P. (2025). Data Analytics and Machine Learning for Crop Management. In *Biotechnology and IoT in Agriculture and Food Production: Green Innovation* (pp. 227–240). Apress, Berkeley, CA. https://doi.org/10.1007/979-8-8688-1469-3_23

49. Srivastav, A. K., & Das, P. (2025). Digital Twins in Agriculture. In *Biotechnology and IoT in Agriculture and Food Production: Green Innovation* (pp. 241–248). Apress, Berkeley, CA. https://doi.org/10.1007/979-8-8688-1469-3_24

50. Srivastav, A. K., & Das, P. (2025). Future of Smart Agriculture: Integration and Innovation. In *Biotechnology and IoT in Agriculture and Food Production: Green Innovation* (pp. 249–256). Apress, Berkeley, CA. https://doi.org/10.1007/979-8-8688-1469-3_25

51. Srivastav, A.K., & Das, P. (2025). Introduction to Biomanufacturing. In: *Artificial Intelligence in the Production of Biotherapeutics: Principles, Practices and Standards* (1st ed.) (pp 1-32). CRC Press. https://doi.org/10.1201/9781003624592-1

52. Srivastav, A.K., & Das, P. (2025). Raw Material and Compliance in Biomanufacturing. In: *Artificial Intelligence in the Production of Biotherapeutics: Principles, Practices and Standards* (1st ed.) (pp 33-58). CRC Press. https://doi.org/10.1201/9781003624592-2

53. Srivastav, A.K., & Das, P. (2025). Process Analytical Technology. In: *Artificial Intelligence in the Production of Biotherapeutics: Principles, Practices and Standards* (1st ed.) (pp 59-94). CRC Press. https://doi.org/10.1201/9781003624592-3

54. Srivastav, A.K., & Das, P. (2025). Standard Operating Procedures in Biotechnology. In: *Artificial Intelligence in the Production of Biotherapeutics: Principles, Practices and Standards* (1st ed.) (pp 95-137). CRC Press. https://doi.org/10.1201/9781003624592-4

FURTHER READING

55. Srivastav, A.K., & Das, P. (2025). Introduction to Quality Systems. In: *Artificial Intelligence in the Production of Biotherapeutics: Principles, Practices and Standards* (1st ed.) (pp 138-164). CRC Press. https://doi.org/10.1201/9781003624592-5

56. Srivastav, A.K., & Das, P. (2025). Principles and Practice of GMP: Personnel and Premises. In: *Artificial Intelligence in the Production of Biotherapeutics: Principles, Practices and Standards* (1st ed.) (pp 165-199). CRC Press. https://doi.org/10.1201/9781003624592-6

57. Srivastav, A.K., & Das, P. (2025). Facilities, Equipment, and Pharmaceutical Water. In: *Artificial Intelligence in the Production of Biotherapeutics: Principles, Practices and Standards* (1st ed.) (pp 200-221). CRC Press. https://doi.org/10.1201/9781003624592-7

58. Srivastav, A.K., & Das, P. (2025). Qualification and Process Validation. In: *Artificial Intelligence in the Production of Biotherapeutics: Principles, Practices and Standards* (1st ed.) (pp 222-238). CRC Press. https://doi.org/10.1201/9781003624592-8

59. Srivastav, A.K., & Das, P. (2025). Production, Sanitation, and Sterile Packaging. In: *Artificial Intelligence in the Production of Biotherapeutics: Principles, Practices and Standards* (1st ed.) (pp 239-260). CRC Press. https://doi.org/10.1201/9781003624592-9

60. Srivastav, A.K., & Das, P. (2025). GMP in Regulation. In: *Artificial Intelligence in the Production of Biotherapeutics: Principles, Practices and Standards* (1st ed.) (pp 261-276). CRC Press. https://doi.org/10.1201/9781003624592-10

Index

A

Adverse outcome pathway (AOP), 242, 354
AFM, *see* Atomic force microscope (AFM)
AI, *see* Artificial intelligence (AI)
ALD, *see* Atomic layer deposition (ALD)
Amphiphilic molecules, 134
AOP, *see* Adverse outcome pathway (AOP)
APIs, *see* Application programming interfaces (APIs)
Application programming interfaces (APIs), 131
Artificial intelligence (AI), 11, 126
    biological system, 364
    catalysis, 294–300
    characterization techniques, 100
    clinical and agricultural applications, 16
    computational modeling, 127
    data security/privacy concerns, 18
    digital twin technology, 18
    discovery and optimization, 126, 127
    drug delivery systems, 160, 161
    ecotoxicology, 263–270
    environmental systems, 228–234
    food science, 320–323
    genotoxic and cytotoxic effects, 356, 357
    image analysis, 15
    integration, 17, 19
    IoT (*see* Internet of Things (IoT))
    landscape, 364
    lifecycle assessment (LCA), 255
    medical diagnostics and imaging, 178–180
    medicine, 309, 310
    methods, 15–18
    nanobiocatalysts, 201–206
    nanomaterials
        anomaly detection, 42
        characterization data, 41–44
        cloud-based collaborative, 40
        computational infrastructure requirements, 45
        data quality and bias concerns, 45
        discovery/design, 37, 38
        edge computing, 45
        experimental throughput, 40
        explainable approaches, 44
        federated learning, 44
        image analysis automation, 41
        inverse design strategies, 38
        materials informatics, 38
        multi-modal data fusion, 42
        research, 43
        robotic experimentation systems, 40
        self-optimizing systems, 40
        spectral data interpretation, 42
        standardized data collection, 40
    research/development, 17
    safety/regulatory frameworks, 348, 349
    water remediation
        benefits, 331
        digital twin technology, 331

INDEX

Artificial intelligence (AI) (*cont.*)
    predictive capabilities, 331
    remote management system, 331
    smart nanosensors, 330
Atomic force microscope (AFM), 2, 93–96, 107
    self-assembly/nanovesicles, 142
Atomic layer deposition (ALD), 70, 106, 121
AuNPs, *see* Gold nanoparticles (AuNPs)

B

Backscattered electron (BSE), 87
BBB, *see* Blood-brain barrier (BBB)
BET method, *see* Brunauer-Emmett-Teller (BET) method
Bio-inspired nanomaterials
  biomimetic approach, 56
  biomineralization, 58
  development of, 59
  implementations, 56
  inspired materials, 58
  lipid-based nanostructures, 57
  peptides, 57
  structural designs, 57
  surface functionalization, 58
Biological synthesis, 71–73
Biomolecular motors
  bacterial flagellar motor, 52
  building blocks, 48
  F1-ATP synthase, 51, 52
  inspired hierarchical materials, 59–62
  kinesin/dynein, 50
  mechanochemical cycle, 51, 52
  myosin motors, 51
  representation, 50
  RNA polymerase, 53
Biomolecule-assisted synthesis, 72
Biosensor devices
  antibody (Ab2), 174
  cancer biomarker screening, 173
  cardiac biomarker detection, 173
  electrochemical biosensors, 172
  electrochemical immunosensor, 174
  implantable/wearable devices, 173
  infectious disease diagnostics, 172
  optical detection, 172
  piezoelectric properties, 172
  point-of-care testing, 172
  schematic diagram, 175
Biotechnology
  advantages, 145
  biosensing platforms, 147
  broader implementation, 148
  design parameters, 146
  drug delivery systems, 146
  extracellular vesicles (EVs), 147
  nanovesicle applications, 148
  nucleic acid delivery, 147
  self-assembly, 145
  vesicle-based biosensors, 147
Blood-brain barrier (BBB), 157
Bragg's law, 82
BSE, *see* Backscattered electron (BSE)
Brunauer-Emmett-Teller (BET) method, 92

C

Cancer therapeutics
  conventional approaches, 168
  emerging approaches, 170, 171
  enhanced drug delivery, 169
  FDA-approved nanomedicines, 169
  immunomodulation, 169
  mechanisms, 169, 170

Carbon nanotubes (CNTs), 22, 192, 334
Catalysis
   AI/IoT integration
      adaptive process, 297
      blockchain technology, 298
      capabilities, 300
      chemical transformations, 294
      collaborative intelligence, 300
      deep learning models, 295
      development and implementation, 298
      digital twins, 297
      edge computing architectures, 298
      hierarchical structures, 294
      human-AI collaborative, 300
      knowledge graph technologies, 295
      monitoring systems, 294
      reinforcement learning, 295
      sensor networks, 294
      significant challenges, 299
      transformative, 296
   bio-inspired design, 291
   bulk materials, 274, 275
   computational design, 291
   current trends, 289–293
   digital transformation, 291
   distinctive properties, 275
   drug synthesis, 281–285
   dynamic and responsive system, 293
   emerging applications, 292
   extraordinary efficiency, 273
   fundamental principles, 273
   geometric configuration, 274
   high-surface-area materials, 276
   industrial implementation, 292
   nanobiocatalyst development
      advantages, 279
      components, 278
      encapsulation strategies, 280
      enzyme immobilization strategies, 279
      enzymes, 278
      fundamental challenges, 280
      heterogeneous/enzymatic processes, 278
      immobilization process, 278
      stability improvements, 280
   nanoscaffolds
      carbon, 287
      confinement effects, 286
      design strategies, 288
      hierarchical structure, 289
      integrated systems, 288
      mesoporous silica materials, 287
      metal-organic frameworks, 287
      molecular shape selectivity, 286
      multifaceted roles, 285
      site isolation principles, 288
      structural characteristics, 286
      traditional role, 285
   nanoscale, 273
   photocatalytic nanomaterials, 290
   preparation methods, 276, 277
   sustainable catalysis, 290
   system integration approaches, 293
Cell-penetrating peptides (CPPs), 305
Cellular nanostructures
   biomolecular (*see* Biomolecular motors)
   cell membrane, 48
   DNA/proteins, 49
   microtubules, 48
   molecular chaperones, 49
   nanopores, 53–56
   natural/synthetic channels, 47
   protein filaments, 48

INDEX

Cellular nanostructures (*cont.*)
   ribosomes, 49
   structural/functional components, 47
   technological significance
      biomolecular motors, 62
      commercialization, 60
      computational systems, 61
      contrast mechanisms, 60
      drug delivery platforms, 60
      environmental applications, 62
      implications, 60
      principles, 61
      regenerative medicine, 60
      structural proteins, 61
Characterization techniques
   comprehensive, 96–98
   correlative microscopy approaches, 98
   electron microscopy techniques, 89–91
   environmental and in situ capabilities, 88
   In situ and operando characterization, 100
   instrumental limitations, 99
   interpretation complexities, 100
   limitations, 100
   multimodal and correlative approaches, 100
   multi-parameter analysis, 99, 100
   optical techniques, 78, 81
   Photoluminescence (PL), 80
   porosity, 93
   probe-based tomographic techniques, 100
   representation, 77
   scanning electron microscopy, 87
   scanning transmission electron microscopy, 88
   schematic Representation, 82
   selection criteria, 98
   SERS techniques, 80
   size and surface analysis, 90–96
   statistical representation issues, 99
   TEM configuration, 86
   thin film, 108–110
   UV-Visible spectroscopy, 79
   X-rays (*see* X-ray diffraction (XRD))
Characterization technology
   self-assembly/nanovesicles, 142–145
Chemical synthesis methods, 69–71
   chemical precipitation, 70
   co-precipitation, 70
   CVD parameters, 70, 71
   hydrothermal/solvothermal methods, 70
   sol-gel processing, 69, 70
Chemical vapor deposition (CVD), 70, 71, 105, 106
Chloroauric acid ($HAuCl_2$), 106
CIGS, *see* Copper indium gallium selenide (CIGS)
Circulating tumor cells (CTCs), 169
Clathrin/caveolae-mediated endocytosis, 156
CLEAs, *see* Cross-linked enzyme aggregates (CLEAs)
CLECs, *see* Cross-Linked Enzyme Crystals (CLECs)
CLEM, *see* Correlative light-electron microscopy (CLEM)
CMC, *see* Critical micelle concentration (CMC)
CMOS, *see* Complementary metal-oxide-semiconductor (CMOS)
CNNs, *see* Convolutional neural networks (CNNs)
CNTs, *see* Carbon nanotubes (CNTs)

Colloidal nanostructures
    computational methods, 112
    DLVO theory, 110
    electrostatic effects, 110
    electrostatic stabilization, 110
    external fields, 111
    fundamental properties, 109–113
    interaction types/characteristics, 113
    medicine/electronics, 113
    nonequilibrium dynamics, 112
    rheological behavior, 112
    synthesis, 106, 107
Comparative analysis, 97–99
Complementary metal-oxide-semiconductor (CMOS), 128
Computational toxicology approaches, 354
Consumer Product Safety Commission (CPSC), 257
Conventional medical imaging techniques, 175
    contrast agents, 177
    enhancement strategies, 176
    molecular events/cellular processes, 176–178
    multimodal imaging nanoparticles, 175
    trimodal imaging systems, 176
Conventional *vs.* nano-enhanced water treatment methods, 326
Convolutional neural networks (CNNs), 37, 178
Copper indium gallium selenide (CIGS), 118
Copper zinc tin sulfide (CZTS), 122
Correlative light-electron microscopy (CLEM), 98, 145
CPSC, *see* Consumer Product Safety Commission (CPSC)
Critical micelle concentration (CMC), 134
Cross-linked enzyme aggregates (CLEAs), 280
Cross-Linked Enzyme Crystals (CLECs), 186
CTCs, *see* Circulating tumor cells (CTCs)
CVD, *see* Chemical vapor deposition (CVD)
Cytotoxicity
    AI/IoT technologies, 356, 357
    big data integration, 357
    biomonitoring programs, 356
    cell viability assays, 352
    environmental systems, 213
    evaluation, 352
    health risks, 354
    membrane integrity tests, 352
    mitigation approaches, 355, 356
    nanomaterial testing, 353
    standardized cell models, 353
    toxicity testing, 353, 354
    virtual screening platforms, 356
CZTS, *see* Copper zinc tin sulfide (CZTS)

D

Deep learning (DL)
    drug delivery systems, 160
    environmental systems, 229
    medical diagnostics and imaging, 178
Differential scanning calorimetry (DSC)
    self-assembly/nanovesicles, 144
DL, *see* Deep learning (DL)
DLS, *see* Dynamic light scattering (DLS)
Doxil (liposomal doxorubicin), 115
Drug delivery systems, 151
    AI/IoT integration
        closed-loop feedback systems, 161
        data integration platforms, 161

Drug delivery systems (*cont.*)
    external control systems, 161
    IoT technologies, 161
    nanoparticle design, 160
    smart nanotherapeutic systems, 160
  anatomical barriers, 156–158
  cellular entry strategies
    endosomal escape, 156
    intracellular barriers, 156
    mechanisms, 156
    subcellular targeting, 156
  chemical surface modifications, 153
  epithelial/endothelial barriers, 158, 159
  extracellular vesicles (EVs), 159
  hydrophilicity modification, 154
  personalized nanomedicine, 160
  shape optimization, 153
  targeting strategies, 154, 155
  therapeutic outcomes, 159
  therapeutics (*see* Therapeutic nanoparticles)
  transport mechanisms, 158
  tumor penetration dynamics, 157

Drug synthesis applications
  asymmetric catalysis, 282
  chemistry objectives, 284
  core-shell architectures, 282
  development pathway, 285
  hydrogenation reactions, 282
  oxidation processes, 282
  pharmaceutical synthesis, 281, 283, 284
  pharmaceutical transformations, 283
  sustainability considerations, 284
  transformative technology, 281

DSC, *see* Differential scanning calorimetry (DSC)

Dynamic light scattering (DLS), 31, 90, 91
  self-assembly/nanovesicles, 142
  thin film, 109

E

Ecotoxicology
  AI/IoT technology
    aquatic systems, 267
    autonomous laboratory systems, 270
    big data methodologies, 266
    blockchain technologies, 267
    data ecosystems, 266, 267
    data quality and quantity, 269
    digital twin approaches, 266
    edge computing, 270
    emerging technologies, 263
    environmental fate modeling, 265
    ethical and societal considerations, 269
    explainable AI approaches, 270
    image analysis, 264
    nanoecotoxicology, 263–265
    participatory sensing, 270
    practical applications, 267–269
    predictive toxicity, 263
    regulatory frameworks, 269
    text mining approaches, 264
    validation and benchmarking, 269
  commercialization, 239
  ecological risk assessment
    analytical challenges, 248, 249
    exposure assessment, 247
    traditional dose–response, 247
    Trojan horse effect, 247
  engineered nanomaterials/ecosystems, 237

environmental interaction, 243
    aggregation/agglomeration, 244
    aquatic ecosystems, 245
    atmospheric transport, 246
    bioavailability and bioaccumulation, 246
    deposition/sedimentation, 244
    dissolution/transformation, 244
    terrestrial ecosystems, 245
    transportation, 243, 244
environmental toxicology, 238
LCA (*see* Lifecycle assessment (LCA))
potential ecological concerns, 239
standardized testing protocols, 238
technological applications, 238
testing approaches, 240–243
transformations, 238
EDS, *see* Energy-dispersive X-ray spectroscopy (EDS)
EELS, *see* Electron energy loss spectroscopy (EELS)
Electron energy loss spectroscopy (EELS), 88
Electron microscopy techniques, 89–93
ELISA, *see* Enzyme-linked immunosorbent assays (ELISA)
Energy-dispersive X-ray spectroscopy (EDS), 87
Engineered nanomaterials (ENMs), 209, 237, 243
Enhanced permeability and retention (EPR), 115, 146, 154, 157, 169
ENMs, *see* Engineered nanomaterials (ENMs)
Environmental Protection Agency (EPA), 257, 343
Environmental, social, and governance (ESG), 262

Environmental systems
    assessment methods, 216–220
    atmospheric transport, 211
    biological transformations, 212
    enclosure systems, 224
    engineering control strategies, 224
    fundamental processes, 210
    general ventilation systems, 224
    integration, 209
    LCA (*see* Lifecycle assessment (LCA))
    liquid waste streams, 226
    local exhaust ventilation (LEV), 224
    mobility/persistence, 210
    monitoring AI/IoT
        artificial intelligence, 229
        deep learning, 229
        electrochemical detection systems, 228
        environmental networks, 230
        hierarchical diagram, 232
        hybrid sensing systems, 230
        industrial hygiene applications, 233
        IoT architectures, 230
        mass-based detection approaches, 229
        occupational systems, 231
        optical sensing approaches, 228
        remediation projects, 233
        sensor technologies, 233, 234
        sensor techonologies, 228
    parameters, 211
    photochemical transformations, 211
    product design, 225, 226
    toxicology, 212–216
    transformation processes, 211
    transport mechanisms, 210, 211
    treatment technologies, 227
    waste management, 226–228

INDEX

Enzyme-linked immunosorbent assays (ELISA), 174
EPA, *see* Environmental Protection Agency (EPA)
EPR, *see* Enhanced permeability and retention (EPR)
ESG, *see* Environmental, social, and governance (ESG)
EVs, *see* Extracellular vesicles (EVs)
Extracellular vesicles (EVs), 147, 159

F

FDA, *see* Food and Drug Administration (FDA)
Food and Drug Administration (FDA), 257
Food processing techniques
    active packaging systems, 314
    AI/IoT algorithms, 321–324
    digital traceability systems, 322
    edge computing, 322
    foodborne pathogens, 315
    human interface optimization, 322
    implementation, 313
    industry challenges, 319, 320
    intelligent packaging, 315, 316
    lateral flow assay, 316
    nanofiltration membranes, 317
    nanotechnology, 318
    nitrocellulose (NC) membrane, 315
    pathogen detection capabilities, 315, 316
    personalized nutrition, 318
    predictive analytics models, 321
    primary functions/mechanisms, 314
    safety challenges, 317, 318
    sart packaging systems, 318
    schematic representation, 316

Fourier transform infrared spectroscopy (FTIR)
    self-assembly/nanovesicles, 143
FTIR, *see* Fourier transform infrared spectroscopy (FTIR)

G

GANs, *see* Generative adversarial networks (GANs)
Generative adversarial networks (GANs), 38, 160
Genotoxic mechanisms
    cytotoxicity (*see* Cytotoxicity)
    direct and indirect interactions, 351
    epigenetic alterations, 352
GIXRD, *see* Grazing incidence X-ray diffraction (GIXRD)
GNNs, *see* Graph neural networks (GNNs)
Gold nanoparticles (AuNPs), 307
Graph neural networks (GNNs), 37
Grazing incidence X-ray diffraction (GIXRD), 84–86

H

HAADF, *see* High-angle annular dark-field (HAADF)
Health impacts, *see* Environmental systems
Henry equation, 92
High-angle annular dark-field (HAADF), 88
High-resolution TEM (HRTEM), 86
HRTEM, *see* High-resolution TEM (HRTEM)
Hybrid nanocomposites, 73

I, J

IGC, *see* Inert gas condensation (IGC)
Inert gas condensation (IGC), 69
Instrumentation and fabrication
    techniques, 2
International Organization for
    Standardization (ISO), 258
Internet of Medical Things (IoMT), 309
Internet of Things (IoT), 11, 15–18, 120
    biological sensing elements, 265
    biological system, 364
    calibration methods, 131
    catalysis, 294–300
    digital twins, 129, 130
    distributed sensor networks, 128
    drug delivery systems, 160, 161
    ecotoxicology, 263–270
    edge computing approaches, 128, 129
    energy autonomy, 128
    environmental monitoring, 265, 266
    environmental systems, 228–234
    food science, 320–323
    genotoxic and cytotoxic effects,
        356, 357
    interoperability, 131
    medical diagnostics and
        imaging, 178–180
    medicine, 309
    nanobiocatalysts, 201–206
    nanomaterial-based sensors, 127, 128
    nanomaterials
        blockchain integration, 39
        characterization instruments, 39
        digital twins, 39
        integration, 38
        smart synthesis platforms, 39
    neuromorphic computing, 129
    predictive modeling, 129
    real-time monitoring, 265
    robotic and autonomous systems, 266
    safety/regulatory frameworks, 348, 349
    security and privacy
        considerations, 131
    water remediation, 330–332
ISO, *see* International Organization for
    Standardization (ISO)
IoMT, *see* Internet of Medical
    Things (IoMT)
IoT, *see* Internet of Things (IoT)

K

Kelvin probe force microscopy (KPFM), 94
Kim, Samuel, 129
KPFM, *see* Kelvin probe force
    microscopy (KPFM)

L

Lactate dehydrogenase (LDH), 352
LAL, *see* Laser ablation in liquid (LAL)
Laser ablation in liquid (LAL), 67
Lateral Flow Assay (LFA), 315
LCA, *see* Lifecycle assessment (LCA)
LCDs, *see* Liquid crystal displays (LCDs)
LCI, *see* Lifecycle Inventory (LCI)
LCIA, *see* Lifecycle Impact
    Assessment (LCIA)
LCRA, *see* Lifecycle Risk
    Assessment (LCRA)
LDH, *see* Lactate dehydrogenase (LDH)
LFA, *see* Lateral Flow Assay (LFA)
Lifecycle assessment (LCA), 249
    assessment methods, 250
    climate impact assessment, 222

INDEX

Lifecycle assessment (LCA) (*cont.*)
    comparative studies, 252–254
    comprehensive assessment, 222
    data limitations, 250
    economic assessment, 222–224
    energy-intensive production, 252
    exposure pathway analysis, 221
    functional unit definition, 220, 250
    fundamentals, 249, 250
    impact assessment methods, 220
    interpretation, 249
    inventory analysis, 220
    key challenges and adaptations, 252
    methodological approaches, 251
    methodologies, 255
    quantification, 250
    regulatory approaches
        Asia-Pacific Region, 257
        directions, 262, 263
        EU regulations, 256
        governance innovations, 263
        implementation challenges, 258–260
        industry perspectives, 261
        integrated regulatory framework, 261, 262
        international cooperation, 260
        international organizations, 258
        public perception, 262
        scientific community, 262
        size-based definitions, 258
        stakeholder perspectives, 261, 262
        United States, 257
    release scenarios, 221, 222
    risk assessment, 254
    scale dependence, 253
    systematic frameworks, 220
    trade-offs, 253

Lifecycle Impact Assessment (LCIA), 249
Lifecycle Inventory (LCI), 249
Lifecycle Risk Assessment (LCRA), 254
Lipid-based delivery systems, 306
Lipid nanoparticles (LNPs), 8, 147, 306
Liquid crystal displays (LCDs), 119
LNPs, *see* Lipid nanoparticles (LNPs)
Local exhaust ventilation (LEV), 224
Localized surface plasmon resonance (LSPR), 26, 172, 307
LSPR, *see* Localized surface plasmon resonance (LSPR)

M

MAD, *see* Mutual Acceptance of Data (MAD)
Machine learning (ML), 15, 37
    catalysis, 295
    characterization techniques, 100
    genotoxic and cytotoxic effects, 356, 357
    lifecycle assessment (LCA), 255
    medical diagnostics and imaging, 178
    nanobiocatalysts, 201
    predictive capabilities, 331
    predictive models, 263
Magnetic force microscopy (MFM), 94
Magnetic particle imaging (MPI), 114
Magnetic resonance imaging (MRI), 114
MBE, *see* Molecular beam epitaxy (MBE)
Medical diagnostics and imaging
    AI/IoT integration, 178–180
        biosensors, 178
        blockchain technology, 179
        diagnostic capabilities, 178
        digital twin technology, 179
        health monitoring ecosystems, 179

Internet of Things, 178
population health management, 179
predict disease progression, 178
biological systems, 163
biosensors, 171–175
cancer therapeutics, 168–171
innovative imaging techniques, 175–178
stimuli-responsive, 166–168
theranostics, 164–166
Medicine, 303
AI/IoT algorithms, 309
drug delivery, 305
emerging technologies, 308
inorganic nanomaterials, 306–308
lipid-based delivery systems, 306
nanomedicine applications, 304
Peptide/DNA-based nanoparticles, 304, 305
privacy/security considerations, 310
regulatory frameworks, 308
therapeutic applications, 303
MEMS/NEMS technologies, 333
AI/IoT platforms, 338, 339
autonomous sensor networks, 339
ceramic nanomaterials, 335
conventional electronics, 334
emerging trends, 337, 338
engineering applications, 335
fabrication challenges, 336
fabrication techniques, 333, 334
industrial monitoring, 335
integration challenges, 336
key differences, 334
material limitations, 336
mechanical devices, 334
medical diagnostics, 335, 336
metal nanostructures, 335
multi-functional integration, 337
security/privacy considerations, 339
Metal-organic CVD (MOCVD), 70
MFM, *see* Magnetic force microscopy (MFM)
MPI, *see* Magnetic particle imaging (MPI)
MRI, *see* Magnetic resonance imaging (MRI)
Micro-electromechanical systems (MEMS), *see* MEMS/NEMS technologies
Microorganism-mediated synthesis, 71
ML, *see* Machine learning (ML)
MOCVD, *see* Metal-organic CVD (MOCVD)
MOFs, *see* Metal-organic frameworks (MOFs), 193, 276, 287
Molecular beam epitaxy (MBE), 121
Mutual Acceptance of Data (MAD), 260

N

Nanobiocatalysts
AI/IoT integration, 201–206
autonomous experimentation, 204
big data management, 203
cloud computing infrastructure, 203
computational enzyme, 202
data quality and standardization, 205
design optimization, 202
development process, 201
evolutionary algorithms, 204
human-AI collaboration, 206
implementation, 205, 206
integration complexity, 206
knowledge sharing platforms, 204

INDEX

Nanobiocatalysts (*cont.*)
    optimization approaches, 204, 205
    process monitoring and
      control, 202
    reinforcement learning, 204
    security concerns, 206
  application domains, 199, 200
  biological components, 198
  catalytic performance, 184
  characterization challenges, 200
  click-ready enzymes, 199
  confinement effects, 184
  designer multi-enzyme complexes, 199
  development strategies, 185
    design optimization, 188
    enzyme immobilization, 188
    fabrication, 187, 188
    immobilization methods, 185–187
    material selection, 187
    metal and metal oxide
      nanoparticles, 187
    surface modification, 189
  enzymatic system, 183
  fundamental principles, 183–185
  hierarchical multi-scale
    architectures, 198
  metabolic networks, 199
  nanomaterial-compatible
    enzymes, 198
  nanoscaffolds (*see* Nanoscaffolds)
  pharmaceutical
    manufacturing, 189–192
  recyclability, 184
  regulatory considerations, 200
  scale-up and manufacturing, 200
  self-assembling enzyme systems, 199
  stability enhancement, 184, 200
  structural designs, 197
  technological solution, 200, 201
  trends, 201
  trends/future directions, 197
  2D materials, 198

Nano-biotechnological systems, 1
  agriculture application, 9
  AI/IoT technologies, 15–18
  application areas, 8, 10
  approaches, 7
  biological applications, 5
  biomolecular interfaces, 360
  collaborative research models, 361
  commercial applications, 2
  conceptual origins, 1
  educational approaches, 361
  emerging trends, 11, 14
  environmental applications, 9
  ethical reflections, 361
  evolution of, 3–5
  fundamental concepts/
    terminology, 5–8
  future landscape, 363
  genetic modification approaches, 9
  green synthesis approaches, 12
  historical development, 3–5
  industrial bioprocessing, 11
  interdisciplinary integration, 360, 361
  key milestones, 2–4
  Liposomal formulations, 8
  living and synthetic components, 12
  medical domain, 8
  membrane filtration technologies, 10
  nanoscale monitoring systems, 11
  nanozymes, 359
  neuroelectronic interfaces, 360
  shared technical platforms, 361
  societal influences, 362
  stimulus, 12

structural designs, 360
synthetic biology approaches, 360
translational frameworks, 361
translational research, 13
Nanocapsule technologies, *see* Nanovesicles
Nanoecotoxicology, *see* Ecotoxicology
Nano-electromechanical systems (NEMS), *see* MEMS/NEMS technologies
Nanomaterials (NMs), 21, 223
    AI/IoT technologies, 37–45
    characterization (*see* Characterization techniques)
    characterization and standardization, 31, 32
    composition, 23
    dimensions, 22
    environmental fate, 33
    genotoxic and cytotoxic effects, 351
    integration, 35–37
    intellectual property landscape, 34
    interface engineering, 35
    lifecycle assessment, 33
    market acceptance/public perception, 34
    measurement limitations/techniques, 31
    metrology, 32
    nanotoxicology, 33
    occupational exposure, 33
    physical/chemical properties, 25–30
    production methods, 25
    regulatory/commercialization pathways, 34
    research directions/commercial development, 30
    risk assessment methodologies, 34
    safety/regulatory frameworks, 341–350
    scale bridging, 36
    shape/structure, 24, 25
    solar energy conversion, 31
    stability and aging, 36
    synthesis (*see* Synthesis technologies)
    system integration, 36
    unique properties, 21
    environmental system/human health, 209
Nanomembrane technology, 327
Nanoparticles
    drug delivery (*see* Drug delivery systems)
    medical diagnostics and imaging, 163
Nanoparticle tracking analysis (NTA)
    self-assembly/nanovesicles, 143
Nanopores
    approaches, 54
    biological/synthetic nanostructures, 53
    characteristic signal, 55
    DNA sequences, 54, 55
    drug delivery systems, 56
    energy conversion, 56
    hybrid approaches, 54
    ion channels, 54
    unique properties, 54
Nanopurification technologies, 327, 328
Nanoscaffolds
    binding mechanisms, 195
    biomimetic nanoscaffolds, 197
    carbon structures, 192
    conformational effects, 195
    design priniciples, 193–195
    enzymes/nanoscaffolds, 195, 196
    Mesoporous Silica, 192
    microenvironmental influence, 195
    molecular interactions, 196

Nanoscaffolds (*cont.*)
   multiple enzymes, 197
   polymer, 193
   self-assembling sequences, 193
   stimuli-responsive, 196
   synergistic properties, 197
Nanosensor data interchange format (NDIF), 232
Nanotechnology
   food science, 313–324
   water remediation, 325–332
Nanotechnology, biotechnology, information technology, and cognitive science (NBIC), 361
Nanovesicles
   architectural paradigms, 139
   biodegradable polymers, 139
   characterization, 144
   comparative features, 141
   encapsulation, 137
   fabrication, 139
   formation mechanisms, 136
   fusion and aggregation, 139
   hybrid systems, 141
   liquid-soluble compounds, 140
   preparation, 140
   preparation methods, 136, 138–141
   stabilization strategies, 137
   surface properties, 141
   vesicular architecture, 140
Natural language processing (NLP), 264
Near-field scanning optical microscopy (NSOM), 81
NGOs, *see* Non-Governmental Organizations (NGOs)
NLP, *see* Natural language processing (NLP)
NLS, *see* Nuclear localization signals (NLS)
NMR, *see* Nuclear magnetic resonance (NMR)
NMs, *see* Nanomaterials (NMs)
Non-Governmental Organizations (NGOs), 261
NSOM, *see* Near-field scanning optical microscopy (NSOM)
Nuclear localization signals (NLS), 156
Nuclear magnetic resonance (NMR)
   self-assembly/nanovesicles, 144

O

OECD, *see* Organization for Economic Cooperation and Development (OECD)
OLED, *see* Organic light-emitting diode (OLED)
Optical characterization techniques, 78
Organic light-emitting diode (OLED), 119
Organization for Economic Cooperation and Development (OECD), 125, 258

P

PCA, *see* Principal component analysis (PCA)
PDF, *see* Powder Diffraction File (PDF)
PEG, *see* Polyethylene glycol (PEG)
Personal protective equipment (PPE), 342
Pharmaceutical production (drug)
   API and intermediate synthesis, 190
   chiral resolution/asymmetric synthesis, 189
   economic benefits, 191

industrial benefits, 191, 192
process intensification, 190
prodrug activation, 190
reactor types, 192
regulatory compliance, 192
Photocatalytic nanomaterials, 327
Photoluminescence (PL) spectroscopy, 80
Physical and chemical properties
chemical behavior, 28
fundamental physical principles, 30
materials transition, 30
mechanical behavior, 27
quantum confinement, 26, 27
semiconductor quantum dots, 29
surface-to-volume ratio, 25
thermal conductivity, 28
unique characteristics, 25
Physical synthesis techniques, 66–69
inert gas condensation (IGC), 69
laser ablation, 67
mechanical/ball milling, 66, 67
PVD encompasses, 67–69
schematic Diagram, 66
Physical unclonable functions (PUFs), 131
Physical vapor deposition (PVD), 67–69, 105
Physiologically based pharmacokinetic (PBPK), 354
Plant-mediated nanoparticle synthesis, 72
Plasma-enhanced CVD (PECVD), 70
PLA, *see* Polylactic acid (PLA)
PLD, *see* Pulsed laser deposition (PLD)
PLGA, *see* Ply(lactic-co-glycolic acid) (PLGA)
Polyethylene glycol (PEG), 137
Polylactic acid (PLA), 139
Poly(lactic-co-glycolic acid) (PLGA), 115, 139

Polyvinylpyrrolidone (PVP), 315
Positron emission tomography (PET), 176
Powder Diffraction File (PDF), 83
PPE, *see* Personal protective equipment (PPE)
Principal component analysis (PCA), 38
PUFs, *see* Physical unclonable functions (PUFs)
Pulsed laser deposition (PLD), 67
PVD, *see* Physical vapor deposition (PVD)

Q

QCM, *see* Quartz crystal microbalance (QCM)
QSARs, *see* Quantitative structure-activity relationships (QSARs)
QSPRs, *see* Quantitative structure-property relationships (QSPRs)
Quantitative structure-activity relationships (QSARs), 216, 243, 263, 348, 354
Quantitative structure-property relationships (QSPRs), 37
Quantum technologies, 123
Quartz crystal microbalance (QCM), 229

R

REACH, *see* Registration, Evaluation, Authorization and Restriction of Chemicals (REACH)
Reactive oxygen species (ROS), 352
Registration, Evaluation, Authorization and Restriction of Chemicals (REACH), 256

INDEX

Regulatory structures
    ecotoxicological testing, 344
    ISO/ASTM, 344
    precautionary approach, 343
    significant variation, 343
    standardized testing protocols, 344, 345
    toxicological testing, 344
    unique challenges, 342
ROS, *see* Reactive oxygen species (ROS)
Regulatory systems
    blockchain, 349
    digital reporting platforms, 348
    predictive, 348

S

SACs, *see* Single-atom catalysts (SACs)
SANS, *see* Small-angle neutron scattering (SANS)
SAXS, *see* Small-angle X-ray scattering (SAXS)
Safety protocols
    AI/IoT integration, 348, 349
    environmental considerations, 342
    ethical framework, 345, 346
    exposure monitoring technologies, 346
    exposure pathways, 341
    HEPA filtration systems, 342
    industrial applications, 346–348
    personal protective equipment, 342
    risk assessment frameworks, 342
    safe-by-design approaches, 347
    supply chain management, 347
    unique properties, 341
Scanning electron microscopy (SEM), 87, 107
    self-assembly/nanovesicles, 142
Scanning transmission electron microscopy (STEM), 88
Scanning tunneling microscope (STM), 1
Selected area electron diffraction (SAED), 86
Self-assembly system
    biotech, 145–149
    characterization, 142–145
    components, 133
    hydrophilic/hydrophobic portions, 134
    key parameters, 134
    nanovesicles (*see* Nanovesicles)
    primary building blocks, 135
    rational design, 134
SEM, *see* Scanning electron microscopy (SEM)
SERS, *see* Surface-enhanced Raman spectroscopy/scattering (SERS)
SHAP, *see* SHapley Additive exPlanations (SHAP)
SHapley Additive exPlanations (SHAP), 44
Single-atom catalysts (SACs), 289
Size and surface analysis, 90–96
Small-angle neutron scattering (SANS)
    self-assembly/nanovesicles, 143
Small-angle X-ray scattering (SAXS), 84, 107
    self-assembly/nanovesicles, 143
Sol-gel techniques, 107
Solution-based deposition techniques, 106
SPIONs, *see* Superparamagnetic iron oxide nanoparticles (SPIONs)
SPR, *see* Surface plasmon resonance (SPR)
Stimuli-responsive systems
    clinical trials, 167
    enzymes, 167
    external magnetic fields, 167
    light-responsive, 167

mechanisms, 168
pH-responsive system, 166
smart nanomaterials, 166
STEM, *see* Scanning transmission electron microscopy (STEM)
STM, *see* Scanning tunneling microscope (STM)
Stokes-Einstein equation, 90
Superparamagnetic iron oxide nanoparticles (SPIONs), 27, 307
Surface-enhanced Raman spectroscopy/scattering (SERS), 80, 228
   food processing techniques, 321
Surface plasmon resonance (SPR), 79, 114, 228
Synthesis technologies
   atomic/molecular layer, 74
   biological approaches, 71–73
   chemical approaches, 69–71
   continuous production, 73
   electrospinning/electrospraying, 74
   fundamental principles, 65
   hybrid nanocomposites, 73
   microfluidic devices, 73
   physical methods, 66–69
   polymerization, 74
   thin films, 105, 106

T

Tanaka, Hiroshi, 117
t-distributed stochastic neighbor embedding (t-SNE), 38
TEM, *see* Transmission electron microscopy (TEM)
Testing models/assays, 240
   alternative test models, 242
   AOP framework, 242
   aquatic systems, 240
   characterization requirements, 241
   dispersion protocols, 241
   dose metrics, 241
   high-throughput screening, 242
   interferences, 241
   omics technologies, 242
   standard frameworks, 240, 241
   terrestrial systems, 240
   tiered strategies, 242, 243
TFTs, *see* Thin film transistors (TFTs)
Theranostic technologies
   clinical translation, 165
   diagnostic capabilities, 164
   multifunctional nanoparticle platforms, 165, 166
   schematic representation, 166
Therapeutic nanoparticles
   clinical translation, 153
   fundamental advantage, 151
   types of, 152
Thin film technology
   aerospace applications, 124
   AI/IoT applications, 126–131
   antimicrobial nanocoatings, 116
   bioinspired/biomimetic nanomaterials, 121
   categorization, 104
   characterization, 107–109
   colloidal nanostructures (*see* Colloidal nanostructures)
   colloidal systems, 109–113
   convergence, 123
   cross-sectional diagram, 117
   cultural heritage preservation, 124
   deposition/patterning technologies, 120
   diagnostic applications, 114, 115

Thin film technology (*cont.*)
  display technologies, 119, 120
  dynamic light scattering (DLS), 109
  electronics, 116
  ellipsometric measurement, 108
  emerging trends, 126
  energy conversion/storage systems, 118, 119
  environmental/sustainability considerations, 122
  ethical/regulatory frameworks, 124–126
  food and agriculture sectors, 124
  fundamental concepts, 103
  history, 104
  lifecycle assessment approaches, 122
  manufacturing (3D printing), 120
  material compositions and structures, 121
  medicial applications, 114
  semiconductor devices, 116
  standardized testing protocols, 125
  surface and interface effects, 104
  synthesis methods, 105, 106
  therapeutic domain, 115, 116
  water remediation, 327
Thin film transistors (TFTs), 116
Time-of-flight secondary ion mass spectrometry (ToF-SIMS), 143
Time-resolved photoluminescence (TRPL), 80
TiO_2, *see* Titanium dioxide (TiO_2)
Titanium dioxide (TiO_2), 327
ToF-SIMS, *see* Time-of-flight secondary ion mass spectrometry (ToF-SIMS)
Toxicity testing, 353, 354
Toxicology
  environmental systems
    adverse outcome pathway (AOP), 216
    biological systems, 213
    cellular internalization, 213
    co-culture systems, 217
    dose metrics/exposure consideration, 214–216
    fundamental principles, 212
    high-throughput screening (HTS), 216
    predictive approaches, 216
    risk assessment, 218–220
    surface properties, 213
    in vitro model systems, 217
    in vivo models, 217
Toxic Substances Control Act (TSCA), 343
Transmission electron microscopy (TEM), 31, 86, 107, 248
  self-assembly/nanovesicles, 142
TSCA, *see* Toxic Substances Control Act (TSCA)
t-SNE, *see* t-distributed stochastic neighbor embedding (t-SNE)

U

UV-Visible spectroscopy, 79

V

VAEs, *see* Variational autoencoders (VAEs)
Variational autoencoders (VAEs), 38

W

Water remediation
  AI/IoT monitoring, 330–332
  biological treatment processes, 328
  biomimetic approaches, 328
  conventional treatment, 326

cost-effectiveness analysis, 330
environmental behavior, 328
global market, 329
lifecycle assessment, 329
multifunctional nanomaterials, 328
nanoadsorbents, 326
nano-enhanced methods, 326
nanomembrane technology, 327
photocatalytic nanomaterials, 327
regulatory frameworks, 329
scaling challenges, 330
unique properties, 325
Wearable technologies, 266
World Health Organization (WHO), 258

X, Y

X-ray diffraction (XRD)
comparison patterns, 85
GIXRD configuration, 84–86
phase identification, 83
principles, 82
quantitative phase analysis, 83
SAXS techniques, 84
Scherrer equation, 83
texture analysis, 83
thin film technology, 107
XPS, *see* X-ray photoelectron spectroscopy (XPS)
XRD, *see* X-ray diffraction (XRD)
X-ray photoelectron spectroscopy (XPS), 31, 107
self-assembly/nanovesicles, 143

Z

Zeta potential analysis, 91

GPSR Compliance

The European Union's (EU) General Product Safety Regulation (GPSR) is a set of rules that requires consumer products to be safe and our obligations to ensure this.

If you have any concerns about our products, you can contact us on

ProductSafety@springernature.com

In case Publisher is established outside the EU, the EU authorized representative is:

Springer Nature Customer Service Center GmbH
Europaplatz 3
69115 Heidelberg, Germany